A Complexity Theory for Public Policy

Routledge Research in Public Administration and Public Policy

1 **A Complexity Theory
for Public Policy**
Göktuğ Morçöl

A Complexity Theory
for Public Policy

Göktuğ Morçöl

Routledge
Taylor & Francis Group
NEW YORK   LONDON

First published 2012
by Routledge
711 Third Avenue, New York, NY 10017

Simultaneously published in the UK
by Routledge
2 Park Square, Milton Park, Abingdon, Oxon OX14 4RN

*Routledge is an imprint of the Taylor & Francis Group,
an informa business*

Library of Congress Cataloging-in-Publication Data

Morçöl, Göktuğ.
  A complexity theory for public policy / Göktuğ Morçöl.
    p. cm. — (Routledge research in public administration and public
policy ; 1)
  Includes bibliographical references and index.
  1. Policy sciences. 2. Policy sciences—Mathematical models.
  3. Political planning. I. Title.
  H97.M673 2012
  320.601—dc23
  2011052508

ISBN13: 978-0-415-51827-7 (hbk)
ISBN13: 978-0-203-11269-4 (ebk)

Typeset in Sabon by IBT Global.

Printed and bound in the United States of America on sustainably sourced
paper by IBT Global.

I dedicate this book to all those who dedicated their lives to understanding the complexities of our world and those who deal with the complexities of life every day.

Contents

PART III
Methodology

Figures and Tables

FIGURES

TABLES

Preface

As with any other book, there is a personal and intellectual history behind this book. It was almost two years of intensive writing and revising that led to the final product, but the thinking process behind this book began when I finished my earlier book *A New Mind for Policy Analysis* (Greenwood, 2002). In *A New Mind* I argued that policy scholars should pay attention to the implications of quantum mechanics, the sciences of complexity, and cognitive science. Soon I realized that the most relevant and important of these three areas of advances in sciences was the sciences of complexity, or *complexity theory* as it is more properly called, and the name I use in this book.

I published papers and chapters on complexity theory and public policy/administration in between the two books. I have used some of the material published in those papers and chapters in this book. In the meantime it occurred to me that there was no commonly agreed upon conceptual framework among those researchers who applied the concepts of complexity theory in public policy/administration or in any other area of study. Complexity theory is not a complete framework, yet. It is quite possible that it will never be a complete framework. I discuss the reasons for this possibility in the following chapters. There are good epistemological reasons for this: It may not be possible to develop a framework to know the incessantly dynamic complex systems in their entirety. Yet, we need to develop a more-or-less commonly agreed upon framework for complexity theory so that we can call it a theory and apply its concepts in a more-or-less coherent fashion. This need was the motivation behind writing this book.

My first goal in writing this book was to articulate a complexity theory for public policy. This is *a* theoretical framework, obviously, not the final word. I hope others will critique it and build on it. I aimed to develop a theoretical framework for understanding particularly public policy processes. The aim of the book is limited in that sense. The reader will notice, however, that the topics I cover in the book span a wide range, from phase transitions in water molecules to the problems in phenomenology, hermeneutics, and post-structuralism. These are not typical topics covered in public policy texts. This is why some of the reviewers of earlier versions of this book commented that I should change the title of the book to one that will represent its wide contents more accurately. I did not take that route because despite the wide range of the topics I covered in the book, I centered the discussions on the issues in public policy processes. This is a book about public policy, although some of the discussions may sound like distracting detours. I hope the reader will be patient with me when we take these detours together.

There are good reasons for centering the discussion on a particular area, like public policy, when developing a framework for complexity theory. First, for reasons that will become apparent in the following chapters, it may not be possible at all to develop an overarching framework for complexity theory—a framework that would encompass all realms of human experience, natural and social. One has to focus on the problems of a particular area to be able to conceptualize their complexity in a coherent fashion. I chose public policy processes for that. Second, there is a potential hazard in trying to develop an all-encompassing complexity theory. As the discussions in the chapters of this book will illustrate, there are several complexity theory concepts that are transferred from one area of study to another rather casually. These concept transfers are necessary and potentially useful, but much more work needs to be done to clarify them in the areas to which they have been transferred. That takes focused attention to a particular area of study.

When I began thinking of this book project, I had a second goal in mind. It was to compare the implications of complexity theory with those of other theories of policy processes, particularly with well-established theories like the institutional analysis and development framework and advocacy coalition framework. I highlight these two because they are the ones that place the problems of micro–macro relations, or agency–structure relations, at the center of their conceptualizations of policy processes. I argue in this book that this micro–macro problem is the core problem of applying complexity theory to public policy. Each framework in its own way has made significant contributions to our understanding of policy processes. Elinor Ostrom, the main architect of the institutional analysis and development framework, won a Nobel Prize in Economics in 2009 for a good reason. If complexity theory is going to be a serious alternative, complexity theorists must deal with and interact with these theories, either to show why theirs is better or acknowledge the compatibilities and differences between theirs and these theories. Ostrom acknowledges some of the implications of complexity theory and incorporates them into her own work.[1]

I was unable to accomplish my second goal for this book, because it turned out to be a much bigger task than what I had naively anticipated. Instead, I ended up making a few references to the institutional analysis and development framework in the book. A comprehensive discussion of the institutional analysis and development framework and the advocacy coalition framework remains to the task of a future work.

Certainly whatever I have accomplished in articulating a complexity theory for public policy in this book stands on what several other colleagues had accomplished before. I cite their articles and books extensively. In a way, this book is a reframed résumé of the accomplishments of these colleagues. I will not list their names here because the reader will read about them extensively in the following chapters.

I do want to acknowledge the contributions of four colleagues who read the earlier versions of the manuscript and gave me immensely good and helpful feedback. These colleagues are listed in alphabetic order by last name: Lasse Gerrits of Erasmus University, Erik Johnston of Arizona State University, Christopher Koliba of the University of Vermont, and Asim Zia of the University of Vermont. I also want to acknowledge the equally valuable feedback and advice the two anonymous reviewers of the last draft of the book gave me. Thanks to the comments and contributions of all these colleagues; this is a better book. I did not agree with all of their advice, however, so all the errors are mine.

There is one stylistic issue a couple of the reviewers raised, but I disagree with them. They suggested that I should refrain from using the first person in my discussions. I am aware of the long-running controversy among scholars on whether or not to use the first person. I prefer to use "I" for two reasons. First, in many occasions, the usage of the first person makes the statements and intentions behind them clearer. I follow the advice of the *Publication Manual of the American Psychological Association* (2010, p. 69) on this and try to avoid the use of the third person, the editorial we, and passive voice for more clarity in my expressions. Second, I believe that the author should take direct responsibility for what he/she argues for and his/her findings. I think using the first person and active voice helps the reader locate the responsibility for thoughts and research findings better. There are numerous references to other authors' thoughts and other researchers' findings in this book. If I did not use the first person, I would run the risk of not clarifying where the responsibility lies in many of those occasions.

I want thank my colleagues Aaron Wachhaus, Triparna Vasavada, and Sohee Kim who allowed me to use the ideas in parts of the products of our collaborative works in this book.

This may be unusual, but I also want to thank the creators, managers, and workers of Google, Wikipedia, and the *New York Times*. These three were the most valuable sources of information for me during the writing of this book.

I also owe thanks to Pennsylvania State University for allowing me to take time off for my sabbatical leave. I really needed that time to be able to focus on writing my manuscript without distractions.

Last, but not least, I want to thank the Routledge editorial and production staff, particularly acquisitions editor Natalja Mortensen and editorial assistants Mary Altman and Darcy Bullock, for handling the review, editorial, and production processes efficiently and professionally.

Copyright Acknowledgments

The author and publisher gratefully acknowledge permissions granted to use selected material in the following publications in this book by the publishers or editors of them.

Seven figures from and summaries of the descriptions in Bin, H., and Zhang, D. (2006). Cellular-automata based qualitative simulation for nonprofit group behavior. *Journal of Artificial Societies and Social Simulation, 10*(1), (http://jasss.soc.surrey.ac.uk/10/1/1.html); accessed on February 17, 2012).

Two figures from Fiddaman, T. (2007). Dynamics of climate policy. *System Dynamics Review, 23*(1), 21–34.

Selected material from Morçöl, G. (2001). What is complexity science: Post-modernist or postpositivist? *Emergence: A Journal of Complexity Issues in Organizations and Management 3*(1), 104–119.

Selected material from Morçöl, G. (2002). *A new mind for policy analysis: Toward a post-Newtonian and postpositivist epistemology and methodology.* Westport, CT: Praeger.

Selected material from Morçöl, G. (2005). A new systems thinking: Implications of the sciences of complexity for public policy and administration. *Public Administration Quarterly, 29*(3), 297–320.

Selected material from Morçöl, G. (2008). A complexity theory for policy analysis: an outline and proposals. In L. F. Dennard, K. A. Richardson, and G. Morçöl (Eds.), Complexity and policy analysis: Tools and concepts for designing robust policies in a complex world (pp. 23–35). Goodyear, AZ: ISCE Publishing.

Selected material in Morçöl, G. (2010). Reconceptualizing public policy from the perspective of complexity theory. *Emergence: A Journal of Complexity Issues in Organizations and Management, 12*(1), 52–60.

Introduction

WHAT THIS BOOK IS ABOUT

Public policy processes are complex. Nobody would dispute this. Then why do we need a complexity theory for public policy? What would it add to our intuitive understanding that it is a complex world out there? In this book I make the case, hopefully a convincing one, that complexity is not just a negative designation (that "the world is too complex to comprehend") but a positive one. Complexity theory is a broad framework of positively describing the complexity of the world.

It is not a fully articulated theory, however, at least not yet. A series of concepts have been formulated by different theorists and considered as components of complexity theory (nonlinearity, emergence, self-organization, coevolution, dissipative structures, power laws, and the like). These concepts do connect with each other intuitively; it is meaningful to talk about a "complexity theory" in this sense. Complexity theorists have not specifically synthesized them into a coherent whole, however.

My goal in writing this book was to take on this problem, particularly in the context of public policy. I define public policy as a complex system in Chapter 1 and elaborate on the characteristics of complex systems in that chapter and the following chapters. Articulating a complexity theory for public policy in the absence of a general coherent framework is a challenge. This is partly because the concepts of complexity theory originated in evolutionary biology, chemistry, physics, and information sciences, and they need to be translated to the language of public policy and re-interpreted. This is not merely a problem of translation and re-interpretation, however. As one translates the concepts, gaps and holes appear in the body of the theory. To fill those gaps and holes, other concepts should be borrowed from the existing theories of social life. For example, I borrow concepts and conceptualizations from Anthony Giddens' theory of structuration.

Articulating a complexity theory for public policy is a challenge also because, as the reader will notice in the following chapters, complexity theorists and researchers interpret the key concepts of the theory somewhat differently and disagree among themselves over their meanings and significance (e.g., see the issues with the concept of emergence in Chapter 3). One has to choose between these different interpretations. I did make choices when writing the following chapters, but I also aimed to present the different interpretations and the disagreements among the theorists as fairly and comprehensively as I could. When there were unresolved conceptual issues, I presented the issues without taking sides or reaching any conclusions. This is why the theory I present in this book is neither completely articulate, nor is it complete. Instead, I chose to articulate a general framework and left further developments to future studies.

COMPLEXITY THEORY: A BACKGROUND

In one of the most comprehensive books that have been written on the concepts and history of complexity theory to this date, Melanie Mitchell (2009) states that there is no unified complexity theory, but still we can talk about a complexity theory in the sense that there are some conceptual tools commonly used in different conceptualizations (pp. 14, 95). In her own words

> There is no single theory of complexity or complexity science. There are multiple conceptualizations that share some concepts and tools. Despite this disparate nature of the research and conceptualization, complex systems research has made a significant contribution to our understanding of science. It challenges some long-held views of science [reductionism, linearity] and offers a new set of concepts to understand complex problems. (pp. 300–301)

In her historical account of complexity science, Mitchell cites a few strains of philosophical thought and scientific theory as its predecessors and/or components: from dynamical systems theory, to chaos theory, theories of information and computation, theories of biological evolution and genetics, cybernetics, game theory, and the science of networks. As she notes, there is no universal agreement on the boundaries of the complexity theory that is constituted by these components. In this book, I discuss the philosophies and theories Mitchell mentions and the more specific models and methodologies that have been developed within these theoretical frameworks (e.g., agent-based simulations and social network analyses). I also include in my discussions the general system theory of Ludwig von Bertalanffy (1968) and the theory of autopoiesis (Maturana and Varela, 1980). General system theory is important, because the roots of today's conceptualizations of complex systems can be found in it (see Chapter 2). Autopoiesis theory has serious and intriguing implications for understanding complex social systems, as I discuss in Chapters 4, 5, and 6.

Sawyer (2005, chap. 2) points out that complexity theory is a descendent of systems theories. He cites the general systems theory, chaos theory, and autopoiesis theory as the "second wave of systems theories" and separates them from what he calls the "third wave of systems theories," which is the theory of emergence (see Chapter 3 of this book). He notes that the term "complexity theory" refers to both the second and third waves. I use the term complexity theory in this comprehensive meaning.

The histories of the multiple strains of complexity theory, or the "science(s) of complexity," have been narrated by Prigogine and Stengers (1984), Gleick (1987), Waldrop (1992), Michaels (1995) and M. Mitchell (2009). In each book the author(s)' particular conceptualization of complexity theory is presented. I do not cite these historical accounts extensively in this book; I only make brief references to them.

When the concepts of a theory have disparate sources, as is the case for complexity theory, a common vocabulary is necessary for the advancement of that theory, as M. Mitchell (2009, p. 301) points out. I would add to Mitchell's point that a common conceptual framework in which the terms of such a vocabulary would take on specific meanings is also necessary. This book is an attempt to develop such a framework. In the first part of the book, I describe and elaborate on the basic terms of this vocabulary: nonlinearity, systems, complexity, emergence, self-organization, system dynamics, coevolution, and the like. In the second part, I discuss the epistemological underpinnings and implications of these concepts. The third part of this book is about the methods with which these concepts are operationalized and applied in empirical studies.

HUMAN PROPENSITY TO SIMPLIFY AND COMPLEXITY THEORY

As M. Mitchell (2009) notes, the concepts and methods of complexity theory are "moving into mainstream science" (p. 301), which in itself is a significant development. But, I think, complexity theory has broader implications. Even in the absence of a coherent framework for it, complexity theory offers a perspective that helps us appreciate the complexity of all aspects of life. In doing so, the theory runs against a basic human propensity: the propensity to simplify. One can find examples of this human propensity in all aspects of life. I want to cite a few examples here.

Conspiracy theories are the most extreme examples of the human propensity to simplify. In these theories complex realities of social life and politics are reduced to simple explanations. The most common theme in conspiracy theories is that there is an omnipotent outside force/entity/actor that meddles in the affairs of our team, tribe, party, nation, etc., to harm us. The complexity of all the events one experiences are reduced to a simple explanation: One omnipotent actor designs and executes a conspiracy to achieve his/her/its own goals and, in doing so, controls all the other actors and forces. If something goes wrong in one's life, if things change in an undesirable direction, it/they must be caused by this omnipotent actor and his/her/its ill intentions. In the mindset conspiracy theories are hatched, there is a simple explanation for everything; there are no accidents, no uncertainty, nothing unknown, or unknowable. Stories different conspiracy theorists tell may have different actors and different settings, and the stories may have different variants and some imaginative elements in them, but there still is one core storyline: one omnipotent actor designing and executing a conspiracy. No complexity is allowed into conspiracy theorists' pictures of the world.

Zaitchik (2010) compiled a list of the most popular conspiracy theories in the US in the early 21st century. Most of these theories were constructed by the members of various right-wing political groups, the so-called "Patriot" groups, but some by those on the left. Zaitchik notes that conspiracy theories have a long history in American politics. At different points in US history, conspiracy theorists warned against imaginary "malicious intentions" of and the "threats" posed by Catholics, Mormons, Jews, American Communists, Freemasons, bankers, and the US government or its officials and agencies. As these stories went, all these supposedly powerful actors conspired against "the American people" and tried to manipulate, control, or even subdue them, one way or the other.

He notes that recently most conspiracy theories merged into one grand narrative: The omnipotent forces of the "New World Order" trying to take over the US with the ultimate goal of creating one big world government. This is the common theme in various conspiracy stories. In the "chemtrail" stories, air and water vapor contrails that form in the wake of high-altitude aircraft are in fact "clouds of toxic soup being deliberately sprayed by secret government planes executing the designs of the New World Order" (Chemtrails section, para. 2). In the "Federal Emergency Management Agency (FEMA) concentration camps" stories, the federal government is in cahoots with the United Nations (UN), and possibly with some foreign countries, to send urban gangs and foreign troops into the US. These gangs and troops will sweep in from the coasts, confiscate the guns of the people, and round them up to send them to internment camps run by FEMA (FEMA Concentration Camps section, para.1). In the "population control" conspiracy stories, the US will be depopulated by the government in compliance with the "United Nations' plan to create a 'biosphere' out of most of the United States" (Population Control section, para. 4). The reason the UN wants to do this is because it wants to eliminate those humans who put pressure on the environment. These and other conspiracies are all parts of the grand plan to create the New World Order. The conspiracy theorist may disagree on who the omnipotent actors in these stories are, but they agree that there are individual or collective actors with malicious intentions and enough power to control all the other actors to reach their goals.

Conspiracy theories are extreme examples of simplification, but they are not the only ones. The US war on Iraq, which was started by President Bush in the March 2003 and "officially ended" by President Obama in August 2010, illustrates that major policies, even a deadly and massive war, can be started and executed with simplified views of how the world works and the roles major actors play in it.[1] In their book *Complexity and Public Policy* (2010), Geyer and Rihani demonstrate that the Iraq War was a product of such a simplified view of the world and the role US plays in it. Many critics of this war argued that the case to go to the war was built not only a simplified view of the world, but a series of intentional falsehoods, deceptions, and pretenses (e.g., that Iraq under the regime of Saddam Hussein had developed weapons of mass destruction and that the Iraqi regime had had connections with, even harbored, Al Qaeda). Whether they were intentional falsehoods or not, the stories that were told to justify going to the war were simplistic. Geyer and Rihani's description and analysis aptly illustrates this.

The authors demonstrate that a linear and mechanistic thinking was behind the justification for the war and the overall war strategy. This thinking was actually a reflection of the long traditions of the US foreign policy. The most fundamental belief in the US foreign policy is that with good intentions and application of military force, "it is possible to redesign whole nations in a matter of a few years to bring them into line with European and American norms that took centuries to evolve" (p. 147). In this belief system the complexities of the histories of human societies are ignored, and it is assumed that linear cause–effect relations exist between the application of military force and desired goals. Geyer and Rihani also make the observation that even when it became clear during the process of the war that the fundamental assumptions made in the beginning were wrong, the decision makers did not change their simplistic ways of reasoning; they were stuck in it.

Brown, Potoski, and van Slyke's (2008) discussion of the contracting out practices in public service delivery is another illustration of the human tendency to simplify. The authors note that in recent decades the federal and state governments in the US have increasingly obtained products and services they needed from outside vendors and contracted out some of the services they were expected to deliver to the public. These practices increased the complexity of public administration. Despite that, public administration thinking and practice remained stuck in the simplified abstractions and rules it is accustomed to. According to the authors, these abstract rules miss the point that some goods and services public agencies acquire are simple, while others are complex, and that same rules cannot apply to all of them. For instance, copy machines and papers are simple products, and an agency can describe its needs and monitor its acquisitions easily. The health, police, and social services public agencies provide are complex, and it is harder to codify and monitor their acquisitions and delivery. Simple rules of contracting out cannot apply to these services. In the conclusion of their article the authors admit that their conceptual framework of "simple versus complex goods/services" is a simplification too.

To these examples from conspiracy theories, waging war, and contracting out public services, I can add that even scientific theories simplify. The guiding principle of the Newtonian/positivist science has been to simplify and reduce phenomena to explain them, as I discussed elsewhere (Morçöl, 2002). The Newtonian universe is a clockwork mechanism, and the Newtonian/positivist science is reductionist. It is assumed that scientists can gain certain and complete knowledge of this universe by breaking down the clockwork to its most basic elements. This scientific view is encapsulated best in the principle of "Occam's razor": that the simplest scientific explanation is the best one. Scientists aim to find ways to reduce the information about complex realities into simple formulas. Einstein's formula of $E = mc^2$ is an iconic example of this. It describes the relations between energy (E), mass (m), and speed of light (c) in a simple manner.

Taylor (2001, p. 137) points out that reducing complexity to simplicity is one of the humankind's ancient dreams. The efforts to explain the world in terms of simple laws by reducing phenomena to simple equations are products of this dream. This dream has been expressed in the theology of monotheistic religions, he notes. These religions aspire to achieve simplicity by explaining the world as a creation of a single god and his commandments.

Then why do human beings—conspiracy theorists, politicians, public administration theorists, scientists, theologians, and others—simplify? Ornstein and Ehrlich (2000) argue that the human tendency to simplify has its roots in the biological evolution of our species. Many thousands of years ago, our ancestors lived in relatively stable environments, and they faced short-term challenges. Their challenge was to survive immediate threats. They needed to develop the skills to simplify the perceptions of the entities, organisms, and events in their environments. For example, they needed skills to recognize immediately and sharply the image of a predator that is behind a bush and separate it from all the other details in the environment. It would be irrelevant, even dangerous, to perceive the colors of the berries on the bush, the smell of the flowers around, and the shapes of the clouds in the sky at the same time when a predator was approaching. In order to meet the need to simplify, our nervous system evolved to select only small extracts of reality and ignore the rest. This is why we tend to perceive sharp images and sudden changes in our environments and ignore the background information. According to Ornstein and Ehrlich, this tendency to perceive reality as simplified pictures turned into the "mental defaults" of human beings: We apply the methods of simplification automatically when perceiving realities around us.

These defaults are both useful and constricting. They enable us to perceive and act on immediate threats. They also limit our ability to detect broader, dynamic, and interconnected aspects of reality. This limitation is important particularly in today's world, Ornstein and Ehrlich point out, because our species have contributed to the creation of a complex world in which simple routines and caricatures are counterproductive for the survival of our species. They give examples of eye-catching images, such as murders, taking of hostages, and sharp changes in stock prices and point out that while most people's minds are fixed on these images, far more important changes that are taking place—global warming, proliferation of nuclear arms, exponential increases in population, and lack of education for millions—are hardly noticed.

Because they are products of the biological evolution, the simplifying mechanisms of the human mind are encoded in our genes, according to Ornstein and Ehrlich. Although these mechanisms are deeply ingrained in our minds, their effects can be partly remedied through cultural evolution, particularly education. The authors call for developing a "new mind" through cultural evolution, particularly education. The conceptual tools of complexity theory can contribute to developing this new mind, as I argued elsewhere (Morçöl, 2002).

Complexity theory, as incomplete as it is, makes us appreciate the complex nature of realities and the uncertainties in knowledge processes this complexity generates. Thus it challenges the human tendency to simplify. Complexity theory is not a negation of the notion that there is orderliness in the universe; it does not suggest that all events are random and completely incomprehensible. As I demonstrate in the following chapters, complexity theorists attempt to understand the coexistence of order and disorder and the constant dynamic transformations from one to the other.

Complexity theory simplifies too. It has to, because it is a product of the simplifying human mind. Like any other theory, it uses conceptual tools (see Part I of this book) and methodological tools (see Part III of this book). Many of these tools are borrowed from other theories and conceptual frameworks, and they are tools of simplification. Complexity theorists also try to understand complexities. As I show in the following chapters, complexity theorists and researchers aim to understand complex natural and social systems as wholes, not as aggregations of their parts, and they appreciate the contextuality of the knowledge of complex systems (see particularly Chapter 6).

COMPLEXITY OF PUBLIC POLICY

Public policy processes are complex. Nobody would dispute this, in principle. However, not everybody would agree on what "complexity" means. Nor would everybody agree on whether or not, or to what extent, policy analysts should include the complexity of policy processes in their analyses. The question is, should complexity be simplified, or should it be recognized and built into the conceptualizations and models of policy processes? A brief overview of some of the seminal works in the literature here will help clarify the points I will make later in the chapter about the nature of complexity and its implications for public policy.

The most common textbook definition of public policy is "whatever governments do or not to do" (Dye, 1992, p. 2) or "what governments *ought or ought not do*, and *does* or *does not do*" [emphasis in original] (C. Simon, 2007, p. 1). In both definitions there is a singular collective actor (government) that decides and acts, or should act, in a certain manner. The view that a policy is an intentional act of a singular actor is a simplification. All definitions simplify, by definition, particularly the definitions in introductory text books, like Dye's and Simon's.

This tendency to simplify is not limited to definitions; it can also be seen in the practice and theorization of public policy. As Sharkansky (2002) puts it, policymaking is a search for simplicity. Analysts and policy makers ignore complexities, take shortcuts, and use simple routines. Sharkansky observes that using simple methods to deal with complexities may lead to further complications. The simplifying acts of policymaking—from setting up bureaucratic rules to privatization and outsourcing—will only shift responsibilities of dealing with complexities from one set of actors to others but will not diminish complexities. Nevertheless, simplification is a long tradition in policy analysis. In their classic introductory text to policy analysis, for example, Stokey and Zeckhauser (1978, p. 5–6) recommend that complexities be simplified or marginalized in analytical processes.

There are those who attempt to break away from this tendency to simplify in policy analysis. Social constructionists are primary examples. In the social constructionist view, the methods that were developed for the natural sciences, which are sometimes casually called "positivistic methods," cannot be used in understanding the social world. These methods are not good for understanding social phenomena, because their ultimate goal is to simplify and capture the laws of nature in simple formulas like $E = mc^2$. This may be feasible in the natural sciences, but not in the social sciences, because the subject matter of the latter is far more complex. That is because human beings are not atoms or molecules, but meaning-making entities whose existence and behaviors depend largely on the structured relationships with other human beings (cultures, norms, laws, etc.). This is why social constructionists are critical of the "rational model of decision making" and its derivatives, such as cost-benefit analysis and decision trees, which are modeled after the simplifying positivistic methods of the natural sciences. The assumption that undergirds these methods is that problem solving is a purposeful activity by a rational, singular collective decisions maker.

Roe's (1994, 1998, 2007), Schneider and Ingram's (1997), and Stone's (2002), works represent the social constructionist way of thinking in policy theory. Schneider and Ingram acknowledge that policies are purposeful acts, but they dispute the premise that these are acts of unified and central actors. They view policies as dynamic, context-dependent, and socially constructed processes that "revealed through texts, practices, symbols, and discourses that define and deliver values, including goods and services as well as regulations, income, status, and other positively and negatively valued attributes" (p. 2). According to Stone, policies are collective actions in which actors cooperate and compete and pursue power not only out of self-interest but also out of passion and loyalty to other actors and ambiguous and incomplete ideas. Although neither Schneider and Ingram nor Stone use the term complexity specifically, with their descriptions, they acknowledge the complexity of policy processes implicitly. Roe acknowledges the complexity of policy processes explicitly and points to the contradictory roles "policy narratives" play in them. On the one hand, policy narratives are the primary tools policy actors utilize in their attempts to simplify and stabilize decision making. On the other hand, when they do so within their respective socially constructed worlds, the actors generate multiple and usually conflicting narratives, which in turn contributes to the uncertainties and complexities in policy processes.

Sabatier (2007b, pp. 3–4) and Dunn (2008, pp. 75–76) acknowledge the role socially constructed values and perceptions of policy actors play in making policy processes complex. They also point out that the interactions among multiple policy areas and the dynamism of policy problems contribute to this complexity. Policy actors use the information about events subjectively and selectively. It may be convenient to conceptually separate policy problems in healthcare, the economy, and the natural environment, but actually the programs in these areas interact with each other constantly. Policy actions and their effects take place in long time periods, and in the meantime the nature and configurations of policy problems change: a solution in a particular time period may not be relevant in another time frame.

Sabatier's and Dunn's descriptions of the complexity of policy processes and problems bring us close to complexity theory's understanding of the complexity of public policy: multiple actors with multiple definitions of problems, policy processes that have interacting components, and dynamism of policy problems. I will elaborate on these issues in the remainder of this chapter and the following chapters. I begin with a complexity theory definition of public policy.

A DEFINITION OF PUBLIC POLICY FROM A COMPLEXITY THEORY PERSPECTIVE

I propose the following definition of public policy from a complexity theory perspective: *Public policy is an emergent, self-organizational, and dynamic complex system. The relations among the actors of this complex system are nonlinear and its relations with its elements and with other systems are coevolutionary.* I will unpack this definition in the rest of the book. I will define and discuss the terms in it: complexity, nonlinearity, system, emergence, self-organization, and coevolution. These definitions and discussions will not proceed in a linear fashion in the coming chapters, however;

that is because of the twists and turns in the histories of the concepts and the controversies among the authors who use them.

I will first elaborate on my definition as a whole. A key notion in this definition is that public policy should not be viewed as an intentional act by a government. Public policy may, and usually does, involve some governmental action, but as a whole it is an emergent, self-organizing, and dynamic system. This system does not necessarily, and usually does not, follow the dictates of the presumed "will of the government" or that of a particular singular collective actor. Policies are complex systems that are embedded in larger interlocking social and natural systems. Like other complex systems, they emerge, change, and sometimes dissipate. There is no central regulator or master. This complexity view of public policy is obviously contrary to the liberal-democratic ideal, which is based on the imagery of a linear set of actions: that policies are made by elected representatives of people and then turned over to the executive branch to be implemented as intended through a bureaucratic chain of command. More sophisticated theories of public policy (e.g., advocacy coalition framework, institutional rational choice, network governance approaches) acknowledge that the liberal-democratic ideal is not the picture of how real policy processes work. Complexity theory contributes by bringing in a system's perspective, a self-organizational and dynamic view.

I propose particularly that public policies should be conceptualized as *systems* that are comprised of "situated activities of human agents, reproduced across time and space" (Giddens, 1984, p. 25).[2] In other words, a public policy is not merely what is spelled out in legislations, nor is it a tool used by a government. A public policy does involve legislation, an articulation of abstract principles, and concrete rules, but from the complexity perspective I propose here, there is more to it. There is no direct causal link between the legislation, or the abstract principles and concrete rules it spells out, and "policy outcomes." A lot happens in between. A public policy is better conceptualized as the whole of the activities of and relations among self-conscious, purposeful, and interdependent actors. Many individual and collective actors act upon their interpretations of the principles and rules—interpretations that are influenced by social construction processes and self-interests of actors—in such a manner that together their actions constitute a policy system.

Policy actors are interdependent. From their relations emerges a system, which is more than a simple sum of the effects of their behaviors. The concept of *emergence* is based on the systems theory notion that a whole is more than the sum of its elements. As I will discuss in Chapter 3, emergence is a controversial concept, and there are multiple interrelated issues/question in its conceptualization.

Self-organization is a concept that suggests that public policies should be conceptualized less in terms of command and control. The systemic relations among a group of human actors may be so integrated, so dense, that they resist command and control by external forces.[3] The question is, to what extent policy systems are integrated. If they are highly integrated systems, then they will be resistant to "external" attempts to control by governments or others. There are two main issues in this conceptualization. First, we should address the issue of how a system is, or can be, defined so that we can identify what is "internal" and what is "external" to it. For instance, are governmental actors internal or external to these systems? I address this issue in Chapter 2. Second, what is the "self" in self-organization? Does it constitute a totality that defines itself? I will address this and related issues in Chapter 4.

A precautionary note: The notion of self-organization may connote self-management, local control, decentralization, and perhaps more democracy. As such, it may be interpreted as the theoretical basis of the arguments against centralization and authoritarian political tendencies. As I discuss in Chapter 4, there are those who do interpret it this way. The problem with this interpretation is that self-organization and centralization are not necessarily opposites; in fact, self-organizational processes can create hierarchical structures. Self-organization, therefore, should not be interpreted to mean that complexity theory is a basis of the normative argument that social and political systems should be decentralized and self-managed. I elaborate on these concepts and issues in Chapter 4.

An actor may not be able to control a system using linear mechanisms and tools, because the relations among actors and between actors and policy systems are mostly nonlinear. Remember the liberal-democratic ideal of public policymaking and implementation: The legislative branch of the government makes the rules, the executive branch implements them, and it is expected that the policy outcomes is exactly as the lawmakers intended. This is a depiction of a linear process. Linearity means proportionality: Give one, take one. Policy theorists and practitioners know that this is not the way it works. The relationships among the actors in a policy system and the effects of the movement of the system as a whole are mostly disproportionate, i.e., nonlinear. *Nonlinearity* is a key concept of complexity theory, and I will expand on it later in this chapter.

Policy systems are dynamic. Most policy theories recognize this, and some study policy dynamics particularly (e.g., punctuated equilibrium theorists). Complexity theorists view these dynamics as coevolutionary processes. *Coevolution* occurs at two levels: (a) between policy actors and policy systems and (b) between policy systems. The acts of governments coevolve with those of other actors. A policy system in one area (e.g., environmental policy) coevolves with a policy system in another area (e.g., economic policy). Policy systems, which are human systems, also coevolve with natural systems. I discuss coevolution in Chapter 5.

POLLITT'S CHALLENGES

Christopher Pollitt (2009) is a skeptic of complexity theory, particularly of its usefulness for studying public administration, public policy, and

governance. He poses a series of challenges to those theorists and researchers who want to apply complexity theory to these fields of study. His critique appeared in the volume *Managing Complex Governance Systems:
Dynamics, Self-Organization and Coevolution in Public Investments*
(Teisman, van Buuren, and Gerrits, 2009b) and is directed specifically to its
contributors, but it has broader implications. I take up his challenges in this
book. I summarize his arguments and specific challenges and answer some
them briefly in this section. Pollitt poses three sets of challenging questions
to complexity theorists and researchers:

1. What kind of animal is complexity theory—epistemologically and
   ontologically?
2. How is one supposed to "do" complexity theory? What are the most
   typical and appropriate methods?
3. What is the added value of complexity theory—how and for what
   does it generate more powerful explanations than the alternative theories which are already available? (p. 213)

His first challenge ("what kind of an animal is complexity theory") has
multiple dimensions. The first of these dimensions is about the abstractness
and generality of complexity theory. His criticism is that "It is a theory
about almost everything, rather than a theory about some specific sector,
process or problem" (p. 213). Consequently, the claims complexity theorists make are beyond empirical verification, he points out (p. 214). He
contends that complexity theory is not a coherent theory, but "a bunch of
descriptive concepts" (p. 222). Pollitt's points and arguments do have some
validity. Indeed, the concepts of complexity theory are quite abstract, and
they have not been articulated in a framework; therefore, one cannot derive
specific claims (hypotheses) to verify them empirically.

However, the concepts that are associated with complexity theory do
have some coherence. Although there is no unified theory of complexity
yet, these concepts have congealed at an abstract level to such an extent that
they have challenged some long-held scientific views, like reductionism and
linearity. My goal in writing this book was to take a step toward articulating a theoretical framework from the existing concepts and tools of complexity theory, within the context of understanding policy processes. With
similar efforts, complexity theorists can develop a more articulate theory.

Pollitt inquires about the position of complexity theory on the issue of
the relative influences of *structure* and *agency* in social processes (p. 215).
This indeed is a critical question, and not many complexity theorists have
addressed it directly. Pollitt observes that complexity theory is structuralist, because it is about systemic relations and their evolutions and notes that
the theory does not say anything about the nature of the agency. I think this
is only a partly valid observation. Complexity theory is a systems theory; as
such it is concerned primarily of systemic relations (i.e., structures). As the

following chapters will demonstrate, many of the concepts and applications of the theory are about structures and dynamics of structures.

There are also complexity theorists and researchers who did attempt to understand the nature and behavior of agents and the agent–structure (micro–macro) relations in social processes. The micro–macro relations in policy processes are at the core of the framework I propose in this book. I address the issue of agents and structures in Chapter 2 and elaborate specifically on the processes of *emergence*, which involve agents and structures, in Chapter 3. I propose a framework for the methods of investigating complexity in Chapter 8 and discuss these methods within this framework in the following chapters. Pollitt rightly argues that complexity theory does not offer a specific conceptualization of agents or methods of investigating agents; instead complexity theorists have borrowed theoretical assumptions about the properties and behavioral tendencies of agents (e.g., "bounded rationality"). I propose that complexity theorists can legitimately adopt methods of investigation developed by others (see the chapters on methodology).

Pollitt critiques complexity theorists for not proposing a unified and coherent ontological and epistemological position. He asks where does complexity theory stand: Is it positivist, critical modernist, or postpositivist? Then, based on his observations that complexity theorists use mainly the methods developed by natural scientists, he reaches the conclusion that complexity theory is actually positivist (p. 216). I agree with his observation that complexity theorists do not have a unified or coherent ontological and epistemological position. The applications of the theory are quite diverse, and there are different kinds of knowledge claims its proponents make, as I demonstrate in the chapters of this book. But I do not agree with his assessment that complexity theory is necessarily positivistic simply because it uses the concepts and methods of natural sciences. There are complexity theorists who are natural scientists, like Ilya Prigogine, who take phenomenological positions on the fundamental questions of reality and knowledge, as I discuss particularly in Chapter 7. Also, as the discussions in Part III will demonstrate, many of the methods complexity researchers use were developed by social scientists, not natural scientists.

Pollitt asks, does complexity theory have its own methodology, or are its methods an eclectic mix? There are multiple methods complexity researchers use and could use, as I discuss in Part III. I agree with Pollitt that these methods are not necessarily used in a coherent fashion by complexity researchers. However, these tools of investigation are not an eclectic mix. They can help us understand different aspects of complex systems: macro structures and processes, micro–macro processes, and micro properties. The taxonomy I propose in Chapter 8 can help researchers identify the specific roles of the complexity theory methods in studying these aspects of complex systems.

Pollitt's third question, the one about the "added value" of complexity theory is also important. He observes that complexity theorists have not differentiated theirs from other theories clearly. For it to be a viable theory, its proponents have to differentiate complexity theory from other theories of governance/policy processes and demonstrate that it can explain these processes better than its rivals, Pollitt argues. In his view, the explanatory value of complexity theory is not very high because it does not describe any causal mechanisms and it neglects power relations in social processes (p. 227). He also argues that many of the concepts of complexity theory are not new. Self-organization, for example, is an old concept; endogenous change has been explored in many other theoretical perspectives (p. 227).

I agree with Pollitt in principle that complexity theorist should demonstrate that their theory has an added value by first articulating it clearly and coherently and then comparing its propositions and their empirical validity against those of other theories. Complexity theory and its implications and propositions should be compared particularly with those theories that acknowledge the complexity of policy processes and conceptualize policies as multi-layered systems. These theories are the institutional analysis and development (IAD) framework (Ostrom, 1990, 2005, 2007b), advocacy coalition framework (ACF) (Sabatier and Jenkins-Smith, 1993), and the network governance theories (e.g., Adam and Kriesi, 2007). In this book, I include in network governance theories in my discussions and argue that actually network theories in general should be considered complexity theories (see particularly Chapter 2). I do make occasional references to the IAD framework in this book (e.g., in Chapter 3). However, it was not my goal in writing this book to make comprehensive and systematic comparisons with IAD and ACF; they will be the topics of future studies.

I want to address three of Pollitt's criticisms here: that complexity theory neglects power relations, that it does not offer causal mechanisms, and that its concepts are not original. Although it is true that complexity theory does not emphasize social power relations particularly and that it does not offer unique conceptualization of power, it is not correct that that power is completely ignored in the studies of complex systems/networks. I address the issue of power in social network analyses in Chapter 10.

It is correct that complexity theory does not offer any specific causal mechanism, but it does not have to do so in order to be a viable theory anyway. The notion of "causal mechanisms" is pertinent in the context of *critical realism*, or *theoretical realism*, whose foundations were laid out in the 1970s by Keat and Urry (1975) and Benton (1977). From this perspective, the task of a scientific theory is to conceptualize and help discover the inner (invisible, but foundational and necessary) casual mechanisms of the phenomena under study.[4] I do not think that it is necessary for a theory of social processes to explain them in terms of inner causal mechanisms. Complexity theory does not have to be critical realist.[5]

The best way to designate complexity theory, as it stands now, is to call it a "metatheoretical language," in the sense Ostrom (2007b, p. 25) uses the term. Ostrom views her own IAD framework as a metatheoretical language, from which one can draw conceptual tools to investigate different realms of social life. Complexity theory is not as detailed or articulate as Ostrom's framework, but, like hers, its concepts can be used to identify patterns in different realms of study.

Pollitt is correct that many of the concepts of complexity theory are not original. They are borrowed from other theories. But that is true for most, if not all, of other theories of natural and social processes as well. Theorists learn from each other; they adopt the concepts of other theories and adapt them to fit their own frameworks. Old concepts in new frameworks can help advance our understanding of phenomena.

The complexity concepts I use in this book are not original either. I borrowed them from the numerous books and articles I had read and re-interpreted them. In the following chapters I give credits to the original authors of the concepts I use. Here I want to recognize specifically the book-length contributions made by complexity and network theorists to the fields of public policy, public administration, and governance. I already mentioned the books by Teisman, van Buuren, and Gerrits (2009b) and Geyer and Rihani (2010). I also want to cite the following books that laid the groundwork for mine: Kiel (1994); Kiel and Elliott (1997); Elliott and Kiel (1999); Byrne (1998); Koliba, Meek, and Zia (2011); and Rhodes, Murphy, Muir, and Murray (2011).

CHAPTERS OF THE BOOK

This book is organized in three parts. In Part I (Chapters 1 through 5), I discuss the core concepts of complexity theory. In Part II (Chapters 6 and 7), I discuss the epistemological implications of complexity theory. In Part III, I describe the methods complexity researchers use in a particular framework.

In Chapter 1, I present my understanding of the key concepts of complexity theory: complexity, nonlinearity, complex systems versus complicated and simple systems, and complex systems versus complex adaptive systems. I make the argument that complexity is both in the nature of things and in our knowledge of them. I elaborate on the argument in Chapter 1 by first laying out different ways of defining complexity and pointing out that nonlinearity is the primary source of complexity. I argue that the categorical distinctions some theorists make among "complex systems," "complicated systems," and "simple systems" are not sustainable and that the commonly used term "complex *adaptive* systems" is not useful, because not all systems have to be adaptive. I prefer using the term "complex systems" instead. My intention is not to designate certain kinds of systems and separate them from others ("simple systems") but to underscore the inherently complex nature of systems, including public policy systems.

Chapter 2 is about systems thinking: its history and different conceptualizations in it. I first summarize the reductionist/mechanistic and holistic conceptualizations of systems and demonstrate that complexity theory is actually a more advanced form of the holistic system conceptualizations, particularly general system(s) theory. Then I clarify the conceptualizations of open and closed systems and argue that openness and closeness of systems should not be viewed as categories; instead they should be treated as abstractions whose applicability can be verified empirically. Another clarification I make is that although system and network theories have developed separately, there are close parallels between the two and their concepts can be synthesized to gain better insights into the phenomena under study. This is why I use the terms "networks" and "systems" interchangeably in this book. In this chapter I also propose that Anthony Giddens' theory of structuration can be adopted to deal with the issue of stability versus change in complex systems. Finally, I address the issue of who defines the boundaries of a system and stress that both actors and the observers of systems define them.

The topic of Chapter 3 is emergence, a crucial, but also problematic concept. There are disagreements about its role in complexity theory and how it should be defined. The problem of emergence is the problem of micro–macro relations in social systems. This problem involves three related questions: (a) (How) Do macro-level properties emerge from micro-level properties/behaviors? (b) Once emerged, are those properties irreducible? (c) Once emerged, (how) do macro-level properties affect micro-level behaviors? Complexity theorists' answer to the first question is that macro-level structures emerge from the interactions at the micro level that are determined by simple rules and once they emerge these structures persist despite the changes at the micro level. I discuss the implications of this view of emergence for public policy and compare it with the aggregationist view of neoclassical economics/rational choice theory. I also discuss the mechanisms of how structural (macro) properties emerge. I highlight the disagreements among complexity theorists on the second question (the issue of whether macro properties are irreducible). I also point out that the question of whether macro properties affect micro behaviors is important, but more conceptual clarification will be needed and the methodological challenges should be addressed. In this chapter I return to Giddens' structuration theory to resolve the conceptual issues in emergence.

In Chapter 4, I address the issues in self-organization. This concept has attracted the attentions of many public policy scholars, because it connotes self-governance, decentralization, democracy, and the like. The discussions in this chapter show that the concept itself is highly complex. I first discuss the issues in defining the "self" in self-organization and the nature of those agents who play roles in systemic self-organizational processes. After summarizing the well-known conceptualizations of self-organization by Prigogine, Kauffman, and Strogatz, I focus on autopoiesis theory, which offers a unique perspective on self-organization: Autopoietic systems are self-referential. I illustrate the applicability of self-organization with examples from the management, urban planning, and public policy literatures. Finally, I address the issue of the contribution of complexity theory to our understanding of self-organizing policy systems from my perspective by posing and answering series of questions.

The topic of Chapter 5 is systems dynamics. I first summarize four models/theories of system dynamics that have been formulated by complexity theorists: self-organized criticality, dissipative structures, self-referentiality, and coevolution. Then I discuss the applications of dissipative structures and coevolution in the public policy literature. My discussions in this chapter are organized around the five propositions that I think frame complexity theory's view of system dynamics. I propose that Anthony Giddens' structuration and Niklas Luhmann's social system theories can be sources of future conceptualizations of policy system dynamics.

In the second part of the book, I discuss the epistemological implications of complexity theory. In Chapter 6, I compare its implications with the deterministic assumptions of the Newtonian/positivist science. Although complexity theorists do not have a common epistemological position, a general conclusion can be drawn from the literature: Complexity theory challenges the Newtonian/positivist assumptions that the universe is an entirely deterministic system and that it is entirely knowable, at least in theory. Different complexity theorists question the Newtonian/positivist notions of objectivity and generalizability of knowledge in their own ways. The knowledge of complex systems is contextual, because of the limitations in the predictability and generalizability of their behavioral patterns and because of the a priori cognitive schema observers of systems use in their observations. After discussing the implications of autopoiesis theory and second-order cybernetics for the relations between systems and their observers, I address the issues of the generalizability of the knowledge of complex policy systems and the predictability of their behaviors.

These implications have been interpreted somewhat differently by different complexity theorists. They articulated three epistemological alternatives to the Newtonian/positivist determinism and objectivism: pluralism, phenomenology, and postmodernism/post-structuralism. I summarize and discuss these three positions in Chapter 7. I reach the conclusion that phenomenology provides the most solid grounding for complexity theory. The implications of complexity theory make us acknowledge the contextuality and exophysicality of the knowledge of complex systems, but at the same time they suggest that a new form of objective scientific knowledge is possible. In this chapter, I also discuss the interpretations of phenomenology and post-structuralism in the public policy literature.

Several methods and methodological approaches have been employed by researchers of complex social systems. In Part III (Chapters 8, 9, 10, and 11), I describe and discuss these methods. In Chapter 8, I first discuss the issue of quantitative versus qualitative methods and argue that both are necessary to gain a better understanding of complex systems. In this chapter, I also propose a taxonomy of methods complexity theorists use and could use, based on the micro–macro conceptualization I put forth in Chapter 3: (a) methods that are used to measure structural (macro) properties of systems and the evolutions of these properties, (b) methods that are used to study the micro–macro relations in systems, and (c) methods that can be used to study the micro level (i.e., the mindsets, values, or preferences of actors/agents of a system).

I describe the first groups of methods in Chapter 9: the macro methods. They are regression analysis, fractal geometry, phase diagrams, Fourier spectrum analysis, Lyapunov exponents, spatial correlation analysis, and system dynamics modeling and simulations.

In Chapter 10, I discuss the methods of studying the micro–macro relations and processes in complex social systems: social network analyses, agent-based simulations, and qualitative case studies. Researchers use social network analyses to investigate structural properties of systems and properties (attributes, choices, and relations) of individual actors. Agent-based simulations are used to simulate the evolutions of systemic relations of individual agents. I discuss agent-based simulations in comparison with social network analyses and stress the dynamic and "artificial" nature of the former and the different kinds of units of observation and measurement the two methodological approaches employ. I highlight the epistemological and methodological issues in agent-based simulations and in studying the emergence. In the chapter I also argue that qualitative case studies are important and necessary, but they should be used together with quantitative methodologies, like social network analyses and agent-based simulations, to gain a better understanding of complex policy systems.

In Chapter 11, I describe and discuss four micro-level methods. The first of these methods is the experiments some agent-based researchers use to determine agent attributes to be entered into simulations. I also propose three other methods that have not been used by complexity researchers but could be used to elicit individual actors' values, perceptions, and preferences to be put into simulations. These are Q methodology, concept mapping, and repertory grids. These three methods are based on a half-century of developments in understanding how the human mind works and how this understanding can be used in individual and collective problem solving.

In the concluding chapter I reiterate the point that complexity theory poses a challenge to the deductive-nomological understanding of science and that it points to a contextual understanding of realities. I revisit the proposition that policies should be understood as systems and summarize the implications of the concepts of emergence, self-organization, and system dynamics for understanding policy processes.

Part I

Concepts

1 Fundamental Concepts of Complexity Theory

The purpose of this chapter is to lay the groundwork for the conceptual elaborations and discussions in the following chapters. I discuss the key concepts of *complexity* and *complex systems* in this chapter. I begin with a clarification of the concept complexity: Is it in large numbers or in the nature of relationships? Is it in the nature of things or in our knowledge of things? *Nonlinearity* is the most fundamental concept in complexity theory; it is considered the primary generator of complexity. This term does not signify merely a lack of linearity, but it can be defined positively. I address the theoretical issues in the commonly concepts of "complex systems," "complicated systems," and "simple systems." My argument is that the distinctions made among them are not sustainable. I also discuss the concepts of "complex systems" and "complex *adaptive* systems" and explain my preference for the former.

WHAT IS COMPLEXITY?

What do we mean by "complexity"? Is it in the nature of things? Or is it a function of the way human beings know the things in their worlds? In other words, is it ontological or epistemological or both? Do we call a situation (e.g., a policy problem) complex because that is the way policy problems are? Is it complex because perhaps it is beyond the comprehension of our cognitive capabilities? Alternatively, is there a mismatch between the way our minds work and the way things are?[1]

In my earlier discussions on the social constructionist views of public policy, I mentioned that those theorists attribute the complexity of public policies to social construction processes. If the policy process is complex, this is because of the myriad of ways human beings construe realities around them. This is not necessarily incorrect, but it reflects only a partial understanding of complexity. Complexity theorists suggest that policy processes are complex not only because policies are social constructions but also because the natural processes that public policies interact with are also complex.

Take the global warming issue as an example. It is complex, not only because there are many interpretations of it, which are related to individuals' and groups' perceptions of their self interests (such as, automobile manufacturers' and oil companies' interests in keeping up oil consumption) and dominant value systems in advanced industrialized countries (such as, the attachment of Americans to their cars, not only as vehicles of transportation, but also as symbols of a lifestyle). It is complex also because the natural processes that generate the global warming (atmospheric conditions, interactions between the levels of greenhouse gases in the atmosphere with temperatures, etc.) are complex. Therefore, a good understanding of natural complexities should be part of understanding the complexities of public policies.

Complexity theory can help us define complexity in a new way. Before I describe that new way, however, I should note, once again, that there is no unified complexity theory, yet. Complexity theorists do not even offer a definition of complexity that they agree on (see Rescher, 1998, pp. 2–3; M. Mitchell, 2009, pp. 96–111). What I propose in the following sections is my understanding of complexity, a synthesis of these definitions and conceptualizations.

Complexity is usually associated with large numbers. Although this is not incorrect, complexity theory shows that complexity is not always a product of large numbers. It is primarily a product of nonlinear relations. It is also an emergent property and a product of coevolutionary processes. All these (nonlinearity, emergent properties, and coevolution) are characteristics of all complex systems, natural or social. In social systems there is also the complexity that is a product of social construction processes.

Complexity in Large Numbers

It makes intuitive sense to define complexity in terms of large numbers: the higher the number of elements, the higher the degree of complexity. This commonsense numerical definition of complexity has some validity, but it is not always correct. Large numbers of uniformity do not generate complexity. If one has a large number of boxes of the same shape and size, for example, stacking them up is not a complex task. It may be a hard, backbreaking job but not a complex one. One can easily define how this job needs to be done and repeat the procedure as many times as needed to complete the job.

Sharkansky (2002, p. 1) applies this numerical definition of the complexity to policymaking. He says that policymaking is complex, because there are numerous governmental units and non-governmental organizations that are involved in it. For instance, in the US there are about 90,000 governmental units. Boris (1999, p. 6) notes that there are also about 1.5 million nonprofit organizations with a variety of public service delivery functions. Of course, there are also tens of thousands of for-profit organizations that may be involved in policy processes, one way or the other. It makes intuitive sense that with so many units involved, the policy process in the US must be very complex. Because of these high numbers, it is not possible to comprehend the policy processes in the US in their entirety, one might argue.

However, if they all are organizations operating under a common rule, the description of their interactions will be simple. It is not merely the number of units/elements in a system, or the number of the types of those units/elements, but also the number of the types of interactions among them that make a system simple or complex. A policy system is complex if there are multiple kinds of interactions among its elements/units. This could happen when there are different rules governing different kinds of organizations. For example, for-profit organizations are different from public organizations in that the former function is to maximize profits, but the latter are formed to serve the interests of their respective publics. Then the question is this: Can we reduce the number of the rules governing these different kinds of organizations? To the extent that they are subjected to the same rules, and to the extent that they actually operate according to these rules, we can simplify the system. This can be done only partially. All public, nonprofit, and for-profit organizations can be subjected to the same laws of non-discrimination among its employees, such as the Americans with Disabilities Act rules. But this is only one small aspect of the rules under which they operate. The US Environmental Protection Agency and a hedge fund firm operate under very different formal and informal rules, for example.

To further stress that there is no proportionate (linear) relationship between large numbers and complexity, I want to point to the example of sequencing the human genome. In his *New York Times* story on the first ten years of the Genome Project, Wade (2010) notes that scientists were surprised to find out that the number of genes in humans are not much larger than the number of genes in species that are much less complex. For instance roundworms, which are at a very low level of biological evolution and much less complex than human beings, have 20,000 genes that make proteins. Humans have 21,000 genes. So there is only a 5% difference between the number of genes these two species have. But the difference between the complexities of the two species is much more than this 5% obviously. Humans are far more complex than roundworms. Scientists note that it is not only the numbers of genes, but the ways these genes are connected to each other and the ways they are regulated that make the difference in the degrees of their complexity (see Szathmáry, Jordán, and Pál, 2001).

Complexity Theory and Complexity Reduction

As I argued in the introduction to this book, we, human beings, have the propensity to simplify; that is the way our cognitive system works. Complexity theorists are not immune to this human propensity; they too simplify, as I will show with multiple examples in the following chapters. But they do not agree with the Occam's razor principle; they do not think that the simplest explanation is always and necessarily the best explanation.

There is no commonly accepted definition of complexity in complexity theory, as I mentioned earlier. M. Mitchell (2009) identifies nine different definitions articulated by complexity theorists (pp. 96–111). She points out that there is a commonality among six of these definitions: They define complexity and simplicity in terms of the nature of *information content*. Complexity is defined as "entropy" (the degree to which a message is orderly), "algorithmic information content" (number of steps it takes to describe a system), "logical depth" (measure of how difficult to reconstruct an object), "thermodynamic depth" (amount of information required to reconstruct an object fully), "statistical complexity" ("minimum amount of information about the past behavior of a system that is needed to optimally predict the *statistical behavior* of the system in the future"), and "fractal dimension" (to the extent that an object can be reconstructed in fractal dimensions, rather than Euclidian discrete dimensions).[2] One of the definitions Mitchell identifies is about the "computational capacity" of the receiver of the information (e.g., a human brain); so it is also information related.[3]

Mitchell's observation that most definitions of complexity are information related has important implications. If complexity is in the information content, then it involves both the "sender" of the information and its "receiver." In other words, complexity is in both the nature of the reality that is "sending" the information and the receiver that receives and interprets it. This receiver may be a human being, a group of human beings, an animal, a plant, or a computer. Then the respective natures of both the sender and receiver determine to what extent the information is complex. In other words, *complexity is partly in the eye of the beholder.* I will discuss the general epistemological implications of this in Chapter 6. Here I want to address a specific implication: The complexity of a system can be defined in degrees, depending on the information-processing capacities and modes of the receiving system. I will intentionally ignore the problem of the nature of the receiving system here and postpone a discussion on it until Chapter 6.

Let's take the definition that *complexity is algorithmic information content*, otherwise known as the "algorithmic complexity" or "computational complexity" approach in defining complexity. In this approach, the complexity of an object, or a system, is defined in terms of how long, or how many steps, it would take to carry out a computation to describe the object, or the system, fully (Casti, 1994; Gell-Mann, 1995; Dooley and Van de Ven, 1999). In Casti's words, in this approach, "complexity is directly proportional to the length of the shortest possible description of [an] object" (p. 9). If we can find an algorithm, a rule, to simplify counting, or describing, the units in a system (rather than counting, or describing, them one by one), we can reduce the description of the system. The shorter the algorithm, the simpler the description of the system. In this definition, the complexity of a system varies from "maximal complexity" to "orderly behavioral regimes"; in between the two extremes one can find different degrees of complexity (Dooley and Van de Ven).

In the case of maximal complexity the description of an object, or the pattern of its behaviors, is the object or pattern itself: A maximally complex object or pattern is "incompressible," or "irreducible." Orderly behavioral regimes, on the other hand, are completely describable with simple rules, formulas: They are "compressible," or "reducible." Linear mathematical models are well suited for this purpose. They can be used to reduce the complexity of the relations between elements and describe them in simple formulas. All the other forms in between these two extremes are partly describable (compressible, reducible) at varying degrees. It takes higher-order descriptions, nonlinear equations and multidimensional attractors to describe them.

Then, the question would be *to what extent* can we simplify when describing a policy system? In other words, to what extent can we simplify the counting, or categorization, of its elements and/or their relationships with a formula, and algorithm, or a verbal description? If the relationship among the elements of a system cannot be defined with a common algorithm, then a simple rule cannot describe the system. If a system is perfectly orderly, this means that there is a simple rule that can explain all properties of the system. In other words, the description of the system is completely compressible. Einstein's formula of $E = mc^2$ is an example of this.

But Einstein's formula describes a physical system, which is simpler than a social system. Now consider the earlier example I gave for multiple types of organizations operating in the policy processes in the US. To the extent that they operate according to the same set of rules, we can simplify the description of the policy system. Consider the hypothetical possibility that each of the 90,000 governmental units, 1.5 million nonprofits, and millions of for-profits is entirely unique and each one relates to others in a unique manner. Then there would be no rule that could help us describe the entire system. If each unit has a unique set of characteristics and relates to each other in a unique manner, then there will be as many descriptions as there are units and their relations. This would be an example of maximal complexity. Alternatively, consider the hypothetical possibility that there is only one rule that can describe it all. Everything we may possibly want to know about all governmental units, nonprofits, and for-profits is described with that one rule. For instance, "They are all organizations, and all organizations have the exact same characteristics. All organizations relate to one another in a single manner." This would be an example of ultimate simplicity.

The fundamental assumptions, the ideals, of the classical management theorists of the early 20th century were very close this notion of ultimate simplicity. They aimed to reduce the complexities of organizational management by defining it in terms of a few principles. Luther Gulick's and Lyndall Urwick's (1937) POSDCORB model and Henri Fayol's (1963) fourteen "principles of management" were both aimed at finding a limited number of rules and abstractions that were supposed to define all organizations everywhere and at all times. Similarly, Frederick Taylor's (1947) "scientific management" was supposed to define a universal science of management that would reduce the complexity of managing work into a few simple rules.

The "human relations" revolution of the 1930s and the subsequent psychological and social psychological theories of organization suggested that there were actually many types of organizations and that the effectiveness of managerial methods would depend on the particular type of the organization under consideration. The contingency theories were good examples of this (Morgan, 1997, pp. 44–50). By pointing out that there were actually several categories of organizations, these theorists increased the complexity of our understanding of organizations. They also stressed that some commonalities could be found among organizations. In other words, the knowledge of organizations was "compressible" to a degree, in their view, but not to the degree that classical management and scientific management theorists had suggested earlier.

Richardson (2010) brings up an important issue in regard to the notion of the compressibility of information about a system's components. Richardson argues that it is the *description of the behavior of a system*, not that of its components, that determines the degree of its complexity. Richardson points out that "complex systems" are complex because they are incompressible "in *behavioral* terms but not necessarily in *compositional* terms" [emphasis added] (p. 21). In other words, we may have the complete knowledge of the components of a system and their composition, but even then we cannot predict the future behavior of the system "without running the system itself" (p. 21). No "algorithmic shortcut" is available for a complete description of the future of the system.

An important issue in the "complexity as algorithmic information content" approach is whether or not maximal complexity means randomness. In Casti's (1996) and Dooley and Van de Ven's (1999) views, these concepts are one and the same thing: If a system is incompressible, or irreducible, it is random (i.e., complex). Richardson (2010) agrees that incompressibility is closely related to randomness, but makes a differentiation between the complexity of a system and randomness. He notes

> . . . whether a complex system is random or not depends strongly on one's tolerance for noise. If one demands complete understanding, then the system of interest needs to be expressed in its entirety and knowledge could only be obtained by running the system itself. However, if one was less stringent in one's toleration of "noise" then maybe patterns could be found that in a rough and incomplete way allow for a description to be extracted that would indeed be less than the total description and yet still contain useful understanding. (p. 22)

In Richardson's view, randomness is a function of the "degree of tolerance" of a receiver of information. In other words, randomness is epistemological. I will return to the issues of the knowledge and the relations of knowledge and the relations between complex systems and their observer in Chapter 6.

Kauffman (1993, 1995) offers an alternative to the conceptualization of the continuum of maximal complexity–maximal simplicity. In his view systems' behaviors can be described "chaotic," "complex," and "orderly." In this conceptualization, complexity is not equated with randomness; it is placed somewhere between "chaotic" (random) and "orderly" behavioral regimes. More specifically, complexity occurs at a point he calls the "edge of chaos" (1993, p. 30). This is a critical state for behavioral regimes, according to Kauffman (1995, p. 26). Life emerged from organic molecules at the edge of chaos. This is a state that is essential for maintaining life and its evolution. Kauffman also notes that at the edge of chaos systems are unstable and dynamic. That is where they self-organize and go through phase transitions.

I will discuss concepts like emergence, self-organization, and (co)evolution in the coming chapters. Here I want to turn to a key concept in complexity theory: nonlinearity.

Complexity in Nonlinear Relations

At the most basic level, nonlinearity is another name for disproportionality in relations. It is the opposite of what we were raised to believe: Every act should receive a proportional response. This principle of proportionality is the basis of our legal systems. A thief who stole an apple should not be executed, for example. It is at the foundation of our sense of justice in social relations as well: Every worker should be compensated in direct proportion to the amount of his/her work, for example. We know from our experiences in life that disproportionalities exits in relations, but we treat them as anomalies. When observe a disproportionate reaction from someone, we call it an "overreaction," for example. Such reactions are not considered "appropriate," and they should be kept in check.

Proportionality is expressed as "linearity" in mathematical relations, and it is foundational in scientific/analytical thinking. Linear thinking is expressed succinctly in Newton's Third Law of Motion: "For every action there is an equal and opposite reaction." It is the basis of the mainstream thinking in public policy as well. Policies are put in place with the expectation that they will generate proportional effects. To deal with a massive problem of crime in a city, for example, policy makers need to introduce a massive amount of resources (e.g., a large number of police officers) into the system.

Linearity may be commonsensical, and it is pervasive in our daily and scientific/analytical thinking, but it is not natural. As Strogatz (2003) puts it, "linear equations describe simple idealized situations" and as such they may merely approximate reality (p. 181). Nonlinearity is the norm in nature, and most natural systems behave in a linear fashion only under specific conditions. Life depends on nonlinearity, as Strogatz puts it.

Complexity theorists do not attempt to explain away nonlinearity as "error terms"; they use it as a core concept in their explanations. They see it as an inherent property of systemic relations. They recognize that not only large numbers of elements, but also small numbers of elements and types of relations may generate complexity. Systems with a small number of elements and types of relations may behave in a complex manner. This happens because of the nonlinearities in the relations among the system's elements.

The authors of the Organisation for Economic Co-operation and Development's (OECD's) Report on the "Applications of Complexity Science for Public Policy" illustrate the effects of nonlinearity as follows:

> In a complex system, it is not uncommon for small changes to have big effects; big changes to have surprisingly small effects; and for effects to come from unanticipated causes. Thus, for example, a continent-wide electrical power grid can suffer massive cascading malfunctions after the breakdown of a single transformer in a small substation; an elaborate multi-year health education programmer may yield no discernable effect on health behaviours in one community while having a major impact in another; the emergence of a new pathogen in a remote village can sicken just a few individuals, or give rise to a devastating global epidemic; the adoption of an exotic new financial instrument can eventually contribute to a chain of stock market collapses and business failures. (OECD Global Science Forum, 2009, p. 2)

Nonlinearity is so central in complexity thinking that it will come up frequently in the discussions of the key concepts of complexity the following chapters: systemic holism, self-organization, dissipation, emergence, and uncertainty/unpredictability. According to M. Mitchell (2009, p. 23) systems have holistic properties because of the nonlinear relations among their components. She adds that "[l]inearity is a reductionist's dream, and nonlinearity can sometimes be a reductionist's nightmare" (p. 23).

Prigogine and Stengers'(1984) account of how open systems work in the universe captures the role of nonlinearity in systemic relations. According to Prigogine and Stengers, most systems in the universe are open systems. They exchange energy, matter, and information with their environments. Often they tend not settle in equilibria; to the contrary, they have the tendency to drift toward "far-from-equilibrium conditions." Under far-from-equilibrium conditions, systems are unstable and sensitive to external influences, and their behavioral patterns are nonlinear: Small changes in a component of the system may lead to large-scale changes. Under these conditions, systems often reach certain bifurcation points, where their trajectories are nonlinear. After small, incremental changes in its trajectory, a system experiences a sudden change at a bifurcation point: It may disintegrate into chaos or leap to a new, more differentiated, higher degree of order.

The central role of nonlinearity in complexity theory is well established. But what specifically is it? When we define *non*linearity as *dis*proportionality, this is a definition in terms of what it is not. Nonlinear relations are not proportional. But what are they? Are all kinds of relationships that are not linear nonlinear? Is there a positive definition of nonlinearity? Yes. And its roots are in mathematics.

John Holland (1995) points out that nonlinear mathematical functions entail the "products of two distinct variables instead of their sum" (p. 16). In other words, nonlinear equations have exponential (second- and higher-order) terms. But this is only the beginning of a definition of nonlinearity. Exponential terms may be used in so many different forms, and they describe so many different families of mathematical relations that it is best to define nonlinearity as a type of mathematical relationship between variables. A comprehensive discussion of all different types of relationship is beyond the scope of this book. I refer the reader to technical books like Kaplan and Glass' (1995) for such discussions and illustrations. Instead, I will cite a few well-known examples.

Before the examples, a conceptual clarification will be useful. Nonlinear mathematical relations can be grouped into two: functional and longitudinal (temporal) nonlinear relations (Stroup, 1997; Richards, 2000). Functional nonlinearity is a static description of relations between variables in an equation. Longitudinal (temporal) nonlinearity, on the other hand, is dynamic; it is a description of the behavior of a dynamical system. So it includes a time dimension. Descriptions of longitudinal nonlinear relations are generated by iteratively solving equations. The significance of this time dimension and the dynamic processes will become apparent after the examples below.

As I mentioned above, nonlinearity can be defined in positive terms, but it still can be illustrated best in reference to what it is not: linearity. The following is a linear equation; it expresses a simple relationship between two variables.

$$Y = kX$$

We can assign different values to the constant k in this equation. I will use the values of 1 and 3 in my examples. For each value of k, we can calculate the values of Y that correspond to the values of X. When we plot both sets of values on a two-dimensional plane, we will obtain a straight line (see Figure 1.1). This is linearity.

In both equations I used first-order terms only: X and Y. The relationship between X and Y is linear in both charts in the sense that for every unit of increase in X, the increase in Y is proportional: It is either 1 (Figure 1.1a) or 3 (Figure 1.1b). If I use second- or third-order terms in the equations, I will enter the realm of curvilinearity, a form of nonlinearity, more specifically a form of "functional nonlinearity." The following examples are of this kind. In these equations I will assign the value of 1 to the k coefficients.

$$Y = kX^2$$
$$Y = kX^3$$

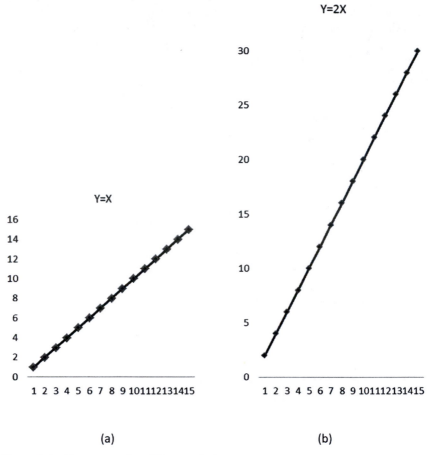

(a)   (b)

Figure 1.1   Two examples of linear relations.

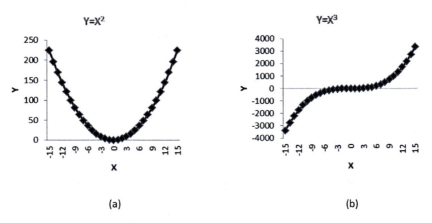

(a)   (b)

Figure 1.2   Two examples of curvilinearity.

We can observe curvilinear relations between X and Y in both examples. The relations between X and Y in Figures 1.2a and 1.2b are different from the linear relations in Figures 1.1a and 1.1b in this sense: This time the unit increases in X do not lead to fixed number of increases in Y. For example, in Figure 1.2a an increase in X from 1 to 2 generates an increase in Y from 1 to 4 (3 unit increase). In the same equation an increase in X from 2 to 3 generates an increase in Y from 4 to 9 (5 unit increase). In Figure 1.2b, an increase in X from 1 to 2 generates an increase in Y from 1 to 8 (7 unit increase). In the same equation an increase in X from 2 to 3 generates an increase in Y from 8 to 27 (19 unit increase). In other words, the unit increases in Y accelerates as the value of X increases in these curvilinear relations, and they accelerate even faster in Figure 1.2b than in Figure 1.2a. This is the nature of curvilinear relations. They do not fit into our commonsense notion of proportionality. But at the same time, there are observable patterns in the relations in these figures; they are not random.

It is important to note that these functionally nonlinear equations are not time dependent. In that sense they are static. Longitudinally (temporally) nonlinear relations are time dependent. Nonlinear equations that describe such relations are solved iteratively: The output of the solution in the first step is fed into the equation as the input in the second step and so on. This way, changes in a system that are defined in mathematical terms are observed over time.

The most well-known example of longitudinal nonlinearity is the logistic equation. Although it is a seemingly simple equation, when it is run iteratively and under different assumptions, it generates a variety of outputs, some of which are chaotic and unpredictable. The most generic form of the logistic equation is as follows:

$$Y = kX - kX^2$$

In this equation the value of the k makes surprising differences when the equation is solved iteratively. I will illustrate a non-iterative example first. Assign the values of 0.5 and 2 to *k*, the equation will be as follows:

$$Y = 0.5X - 0.5X^2$$
$$Y = 2X - 2X^2$$

Both are ordinary curvilinear equations. When we plot their outputs, they will generate the curves in Figures 1.3a and 1.3b. They are similar to the curves in Figures 1.2a and 1.2b.

Now I will enter a time dimension to the equation. Then the equation will looks like this:

$$Y_{t+1} = kY_t - kY_t^2.$$

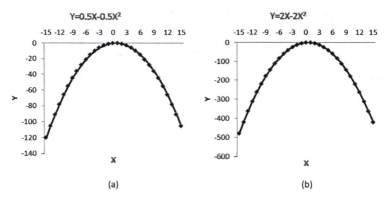

(a)   (b)

Figure 1.3   Two more examples of curvilinearity.

In this formula, *t* represents the time period, and k represents the coefficient assigned to X. When the output of the first iteration in solving this equation is fed as the input into the next iteration, and the output of the second iteration is fed into the third, and so on, a mathematical dynamic system is created. From this dynamic system complex patterns of behavior emerge. I solved the equation iteratively, using an Excel spreadsheet. I used the seed value of $Y_t = 0.5$ and plotted the outputs of 50 iterations for four different values of k: 2.3, 3, 3.5, and 3.7. I selected these particular *k* values,

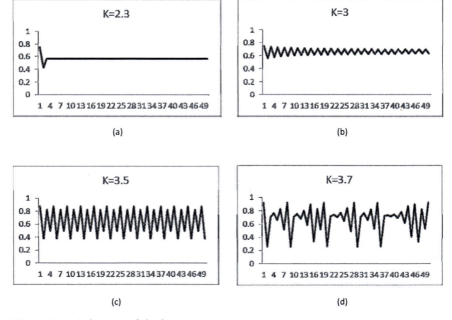

Figure 1.4   Solutions of the logistic equation.

because they are known to generate qualitatively different solutions.[4] Figure 1.4 displays the plots of the solutions for different k values.

The first thing that is noteworthy in these charts is that the same type of formula generated remarkably different patterns. In Figure 1.1 we saw that linear formulas of $Y = X$ and $Y = 3X$ both generated linear plots. Because of the change in the constant of X, the slopes of these lines are different, but they still are straight lines. Same is true for the plots in Figure 1.2. Because of the differences in the constants, the curves are different from each other, but they still are curves. The same is true for the plots of non-iterative solutions of the logistic equation in Figure 1.3: They both generated curves. When the logistic equation is solved iteratively, however, different constants (k values) generated qualitatively different patterns. When $k = 2.3$, the plot settles into is a straight line, after a brief fluctuation. This is called a "steady state" in the language of complexity theory. When $k = 3$, a periodic oscillation is plotted. This is called "period doubling." When $k = 3.5$, there are oscillations among four distinct points. This pattern is called "period quadrupling." The formula "behaves" most interestingly when $k = 3.7$: There is no seeming pattern; it is "chaotic."

The plot in Figure 1.4d does not seem to have a pattern, but does this mean that it is random? Not quite. Although the plot looks random, one can find a pattern in it using another analytical tool: "return maps," otherwise known as "phase diagrams," "phase space portraits," or "attractors." To generate the patterns in Figures 1.5a and 1.5b, I used the scatterplot option of Excel and plotted the differences between time intervals t and t+1 against each other. Figures 1.5a and 1.5b are two different views of the same pattern; I used two different options in Excel to generate them. Figure 1.5a illustrates the discrete values of t and t + 1. Figure 1.5b tracks the movements from one discrete data point to the next. There are recognizable

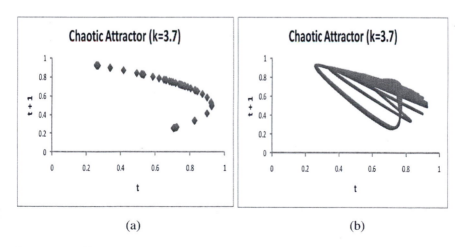

(a)   (b)

Figure 1.5   Chaotic attractors.

shapes in both. These shapes are quite abstract obviously, but they demonstrate that there is a pattern behind the seemingly random plot in Figure 1.4d. Whether there is a pattern in data or not depends on how you look at it and how you analyze it.

All these examples of linearity and nonlinearity illustrate some of the key concepts and themes I will discuss in the coming chapters. First, they show that nonlinearity is not just a negation of linearity. It is not a merely negative category. It does not mean randomness. Nonlinear relations can generate patterns. The movement of the system whose behavior is depicted in Figure 1.5 is not precisely predictable, but what is predictable is that the system will move around in a particular pattern, as described within the shape in the figure.

Second, the logistic equation example in Figures 1.4 and 1.5 illustrates that one's perspective and the analytical tools one uses matter in an inquiry. When the data are plotted like the way they are in Figure 1.4d, they look random. But when they are plotted as in Figures 1.5a and 1.5b, one can discern patterns.

Third, the example also illustrates that simple systems, like the simple logistic equation, can generate complex patterns. Complexity does not arise only from large numbers. It can arise from the nonlinear relations of a small number of elements or variables. In such relations initial conditions matter. Small changes in them may make big differences in future patterns.

Fourth, time also matters. When solved functionally, the nonlinear logistic equation generated only curves; the changes in its k constants (we can call them initial conditions) did not make any qualitative difference in the outcomes (Figure 1.3). But when time entered the equation (the iterative solutions in Figure 1.4), small changes in the constant k made all the difference.

One might ask: Does the logistic equation have any relevance to natural or social complex systems? It does. Ecologist Robert May demonstrated in his classic 1976 *Nature* article that the growth of an insect colony follows the "logistic rule," as defined by the logistic equation (cited in Casti, 1994, pp. 93–94). He used the equation to explain the fluctuations in the population of the colony. The logistic function has been applied in many other areas as well. Priesmeyer (1995) developed a logistic regression model and Comfort (1999) used it in her analysis of the nonlinear dynamics in the disaster response system in the 1994 Northridge, California, earthquake.

COMPLEX, COMPLICATED, AND SIMPLE

Nonlinearity is a key property of complex systems; that much we know, but beyond that there still is an ongoing discussion on what is a complex system. In this section I summarize the conceptualizations of "complex systems," "complicated systems," and "simple systems" and offer my take on them. In the next section, I will address the issue of whether or not we should use the term "complex *adaptive* systems."

A group of theorists and researchers make a distinction between "complicated systems" and "complex systems" (Cilliers, 1998; Newell and Meek, 2000; Newell, 2001; Taylor, 2001; Miller and Page, 2007; OECD Global Science Forum, 2009; and Richardson, 2010). This distinction, in my opinion, is difficult to sustain.

Paul Cilliers' (1998) conceptual distinctions between simple, complicated, and complex (pp. iix, 2–7) are one of most articulate ones, and most others refer to his when they make similar distinctions. I must note here that the distinction he makes between simple and complex systems is not as sharp as the one he makes between complicated and complex systems (p. 2). The distinction between complex and complicated systems is often a function of the distance one may have from the system, he observes. In other words, it depends on the viewpoint of the observer.

He posits that a system is "complicated" if it can be described completely in terms of its individual constituents, regardless of the number of the constituents. In other words, he is referring to the issue of the reducibility, or compressibility, of information about a system, which I discussed earlier in this chapter. Complicated systems are reducible, primarily because the interactions among their components are linear, according to Cilliers. Examples of complicated systems he cites are jumbo jets, computers, CD-players, and snowflakes. A system is complex if it cannot be described fully by analyzing its components. In other words, the information about a complex system is irreducible, or incompressible. That is primarily due to the nonlinear nature of the interactions among its components. Examples of complex systems, according to Cilliers are the human brain, bacteria, social systems, language, and economic systems.

The examples he cites and the reasoning he uses to differentiate complicated and complex systems are quite problematic in my opinion. Note that what Cilliers calls complicated systems are inanimate objects/systems and what he calls complex systems are animate or social systems. In other words, he considers only biological and human/social systems as complex systems: the human brain, bacteria, social systems, and language. He considers physical and chemical system as complicated: jumbo jets, computers, CD-players, and snowflakes.

The first problem with this distinction is that, as Ilya Prigogine and his colleagues illustrated with numerous examples, physical and chemical (inanimate) systems can also be, in fact many of them are, complex systems. Prigogine and his colleagues do not specifically use the term "complex systems," but this theory of "complexity" traces its roots to the basic laws of nature. The irreversibility of time, according to Prigogine and Stengers (1984), is at the core of the "evolutionary thermodynamics," which is the driving force of complexity in nature (pp. xxviii–xxix). "Thermodynamic objects" (i.e., complex systems in nature) display many of the properties of complex systems I will describe and discuss in the coming chapters. They are open systems that evolve. The general tendency of these objects is to move toward far-from-equilibrium conditions, not toward equilibrium. There are both linear and nonlinear relations among the elements of thermodynamic systems. There are physical processes like turbulence they may appear irregular or chaotic, but they are highly organized. Phase transitions in systems are self-organizational (pp. 141–142). Nicolis and Prigogine (1989) explicitly make the point that the gap between "simple" and "complex" and between "order" and "disorder" is much narrower than previously thought and that self-organizational phenomena are not limited to biology, but it is pervasive in physic-chemical phenomena as well, as it is "deeply rooted in the laws of nature" (p. 8).

Another problem with Cilliers' examples of complicated systems is that the boundaries he implicitly draws around them are quite artificial and static. What is missing in his examples is the fact that none of these objects is completely isolated from their environments all the time. They are either manufactured by human beings (jumbo jets, computers, and CD-players) or they come into being through natural processes (snowflakes). When they are isolated from their environments, they are not functioning. When they are not functioning, they may look perfectly orderly. This orderliness might be erroneously perceived as linearity.

When they interact with other systems, particularly human beings, *these systems of interaction* are highly nonlinear. Jumbo jets may fall off the sky, unintendedly of course, because of pilot errors, mechanical errors, or unanticipated weather conditions. In the case of a pilot error, there is a nonlinear process of human-machine interaction. In the case of a mechanical error, another nonlinear process of human-machine interaction occurs: Maybe airline mechanics did not do their maintenance jobs well, or the manufacturer of the plane makes errors in the process of building it. In the case of unanticipated weather conditions, like turbulence, there is a nonlinear process of machine-nature interaction. Computers can crash because of viruses or other software interactions. They may also malfunction if they are left under conditions of extreme heat. CD-players may not play the tunes as expected because of the scratches the child of the household or the dog of the household inflicted on them. In all these examples of machine-human and machine-nature interactions, there are numerous forms of nonlinearities, which by Cillier's definition, makes these systems of interactions complex.

The authors of the OECD's Global Science Forum (2009, pp. 2–3) make a similar distinction between complicated and complex systems, and in doing so they draw artificial and static boundaries around systems. They argue that an automobile is a complicated system, whereas an ensemble of automobiles travelling down a highway is a complex system. In their view, the automobile is a complicated system, because its parts obey precise mechanical cause-and-effect rules, whereas the ensemble of automobiles in a highway is a complex system because they are driven by drivers whose perceptions, expectations, and habits generate nonlinear behaviors. As in the cases of jumbo jets and CD players, automobiles do not function in isolation, however. To begin with, they are manufactured by human beings whose perceptions, expectations, and habits generate nonlinear behaviors and unexpected and uncontrollable outcomes, such as mechanical malfunctions. Think of the malfunctions in Toyota-brand automobiles that resulted in massive recalls in 2009 and 2010, as an example. Even when they are not in direct interaction with human beings, automobiles are in interactions with natural systems that can affect the functioning of their mechanical parts in nonlinear ways. Think of what extreme heat and humidity in the air can do to the functioning of an automobile.

Cilliers' example of snowflakes is also problematic. He observes that the structure of a snowflake has "remarkable detail," and each snowflake is unique, despite the similarities among the structures of all snowflakes. Snowflakes have multiple components that interact through a crystalline structure. He further asserts

> Each molecule is influenced only by local information (there is no external decision as to what the position of the molecule must be in a snowflake), but the relationship between the molecules are fairly fixed. There are no real feedback loops and there is no evolution (except perhaps decay). As far as its structure is concerned, it is not really an open system. It is in temporary equilibrium, cannot adapt to its environment, and therefore quickly loses its structure. (p. 5)

Cilliers assumes that a snowflake is a complicated system, because it is in a perpetually steady state and a closed system with no history or future. But his own description contradicts this assumption. A snowflake is in fact a temporary structure that comes into being as a product of chemical and physical processes that surrounds it, and it decays as a result of its interactions with its environment. Snowflakes are formed, and they melt under certain temperatures and humidity conditions. As Cilliers admits, a snowflake is in a "*temporary* equilibrium." So a snowflake does change.

He notes that a snowflake is not an evolutionary system, because it cannot "adapt to its environment"; it loses its structure eventually and decays. What Cilliers seems to be saying is that a snowflake is not a complex system because although it changes, this is only a process of decay. It does not have adaptive or self-organizational capabilities. Adaptation and self-organization are considered by many complexity theorists as two key characteristic of complex systems. Therefore, according to Cillers, a system that does not have the capabilities of adaptation and self-organization cannot be a complex system. I will discuss the issue of adaptation in the next section. I will argue that adaptation does not have to be an element of defining complex systems. I will discuss the issue of self-organization in Chapter 4. There I will argue that self-organizations should be conceptualized in terms of degrees, not in categorical terms. All in all, my argument is that the lack of adaptive or self-organizational capabilities is not a disqualifier for considering a system a complex system.

Miller and Page (2007, pp. 9–10) also make a distinction between complex and complicated systems. The main problem with their distinction is that it is quite vague. Components of complicated systems "maintain a degree of independence from one another" (p. 9), they say, without specifying what "degree" they mean. Is the suggestion that below a certain degree of independence systems are complex and above it they are complicated? They also state that in complicated systems removing one part of the system does not alter the behavior of the system's behavior, whereas in complex systems, dependencies among their elements make sure that removing an element "destroys the system's behavior" (p. 9). Once again, they do not specify what they mean by "destroying a system's behavior." As I will show in my discussions and examples in the coming chapters, complex systems do change their behaviors at different degrees and in a variety of ways (e.g., self-referential and/or adaptive), and some systems may disappear and other will emerge in evolutionary processes; it is not easy to make a categorical distinction what constitutes the "destruction of a system's behavior." Unless more clearly defined, these metaphors are not useful conceptual tools.

Richardson (2010) points out that despite his efforts to do so, he found that it was hard to maintain a distinction between complex and complicated systems. A distinction can be made based on the differences in how systems are connected, he argues: Complicated systems have simpler and linear connections. But, he admits, a few additions to the connections in a complicated system may transform it into a complex system. He emphasizes, like other complexity theorists, that nonlinearity is the key to understanding complex systems, but he notes that complicated systems may include nonlinear components as well. For instance, a computer is mostly a linear system, but it has nonlinear components like transistors. He also says that complicated systems may even exhibit "limited nonlinear behaviors." (p. 12). He concludes that the main distinction between complex and complicated systems is that the former can emerge into states that are not apparent from their constitution, but the latter cannot (p. 13). All in all Richardson's conceptualizations are useful for thinking about the nature of complexity and complex systems, but, as he also admits, complex and complicated systems may not be distinct forms.

Newell (2001) makes a tri-partite categorization of systems: simple, complicated, and complex. According to Newell, a simple system "may have multiple levels of components and connections arranged in a hierarchy, but the relationships among those components are predominantly linear" (p. 8). An example is a state road map. A complicated system is a system of simple systems in Newell's view. They are "loosely and linearly linked" simple systems. An example is a road atlas that links together state maps into a national system. A complex system, on the other hand, "links together combinations of components, simple systems, and even complicated systems using predominantly nonlinear connections" (p. 8). A geographic information system (GIS) map that overlays the maps of roads, water and sewer districts, fire districts, school districts, police precincts, rapid transit, regional planning administration, political wards, ethnic enclaves, the county, watersheds, soil profiles, water quality indicators, etc., is an example of the representation of a complex system, according to Newell. All these levels of services and structures interact in a nonlinear fashion and together constitute a complex system.

Newell's example of a GIS map is a good illustration of the complexities public policymakers and administrators face, but his tri-partite distinction is artificial; it artificially defines boundaries between these different kinds of systems. The state and national maps in his examples are arbitrary abstractions. A state's roads are always connected with other states' roads and multiple layers of activities take place in and multiple districts and agencies are involved in every given segment of a state road. People drive on them, passing from one state's road system to another's. Service stations cater to the needs to drivers. Plans are made for roads and surrounding areas by federal, state, and local governments. Accidents happen, and fires break out on or around the roads and fire departments react to them. Many of these interactions are obviously nonlinear.

Is it meaningful to make a distinction between simple and complex systems? As a linguistic shortcut, the term "simple" may be meaningful. We may want to simplify reality by segmenting it into parts for our convenience or for some practical utility. Remember from the discussion in the introductory chapter that human beings have the tendency to simplify, and this tendency has its roots in the human evolution. Simplification has some practical utility in our daily lives. Even when we conduct scientific inquiries and think philosophically we simplify. Our theories and models are abstractions (simplifications), and they can be useful. But a system can be viewed as a simple system only as an abstraction, as in Newell's (2001) description of a state road map in isolation as a simple system.

Organisms, even the conceivably simplest ones (e.g., bacteria) are not so simple. They may be simpler than higher organisms (animals and human beings) but not categorically "simple." Consider viruses, which are merely strings of DNA. They can be considered simple only if we ignore the fact that they are involved in immensely complex processes when they are formed and when they interact with host organisms to survive and perpetuate themselves. How about, one might ask, the basic building blocks of matter: atoms and subatomic particles? Are they not simple systems? The world of subatomic particles is not completely understood, but to the extent that quantum mechanics tells its story, there are no simple systems in this realm. No particle exists eternally or in isolation. They come into and go out of existence constantly; some particles take longer than others to do so.

The processes at the subatomic level are infinitely complex and unpredictable (for details, see Morçöl, 2002, chap. 5).

In sum, I do not think it is not meaningful to make a categorical distinction between simple and complex systems. Simplicity may be a useful concept when we understand that what we are doing is simplifying an inherently complex world. This brings us to an important question: If the distinctions between complex, complicated, and simple are not meaningful, is it meaningful at all to use the term *"complex* systems"? Why not simply use the term "systems" only? After all, some early systems philosophers used the terms "system" and "complex" interchangeably.[5] I will cite von Bertalanffy's definition of systems in the next chapter. There the reader will see that in his view only the group of elements that are related to each other in a nonlinear fashion and have holistic properties together should be considered as systems and assemblages of elements without holistic properties, what Cillers and others seem to be calling as "complicated systems," are not systems at all.

I think that the term complex system is still useful to underscore the nature of systems study. Complexity is an important natural characteristic and social phenomenon. Complexity is a meaningful and powerful concept. It counters the basic human propensity to simplify and opens up a new way of thinking. When I use the term complex system, I do not use it to differentiate certain kind of systems but to stress that complexity is in the nature of the systems we study.

COMPLEX SYSTEMS OR COMPLEX ADAPTIVE SYSTEMS?

Before I close this chapter, I want to clarify my position on one more terminological issue: Should we use the term "complex systems" or "complex adaptive systems"? This latter term is quite commonly used in the literature (e.g., Holland, 1995; McMillan, 2004; Miller and Page, 2007; Rhodes, Murphy, Muir and Murray, 2011). I prefer the term "complex systems" for two reasons. First, the term "complex adaptive systems" is used rather casually, without a clear differentiation from "complex systems" in the literature. Second, the term "adaptive" may have misleading theoretical implications.

I could not find any convincing arguments in the literature as to why complex systems should also be called "adaptive," nor could I find any convincing arguments as to how we can make a conceptually sound distinction between the two. Take as an example Miller and Page's (2007) usage of the terms interchangeably and rather casually. At one point in their discussion, they even introduce the term "adaptive systems" but do not offer a guidance as to how one can make a differentiation between "adaptive systems" and "complex adaptive systems" (p. 3). Holland (1995) does define the term "complex adaptive systems," and he uses the abbreviation *"cas"* for it, but his definition is not much different from M. Mitchell's (2009) definition of "complex systems."

As background information, I should note here that John Holland and his colleagues at the Santa Fe Institute, which is the leading institution of complexity studies, coined the term complex adaptive systems. In his historical account of the birth and evolution of the institute, Waldrop (1992) cites John Holland's definition of *cas* as a network of many agents with no central node or mechanism of control (i.e., it self-organizes). The system constantly learns from its environment, anticipates its future based on its "internal models of the world," and revises and rearranges its building blocks (pp. 145–147). In his own book, Holland (1995) describes complex adaptive systems in similar terms. It is apparent in Holland's descriptions in this book that when he uses the term *cas*, he means a system that has an internal picture of its environment and organizes itself and acts on its environment according to this internal picture. Melanie Mitchell, an external faculty member at the Santa Fe Institute, defines "complex systems" in a way very similar to Holland's definition of *cas*. Mitchell's complex systems have multiple components with no central order or leader; they use both internal and external stimuli to change their behaviors (to evolve; M. Mitchell, 2009, pp. 12–13). In both Holland's and Mitchell's definitions, the self-organizational capabilities of the systems are underscored. In both the systems have abilities to use their "internal models" or "external stimuli" to "adapt." So there is not difference between the complex systems and *cas* in these definitions.

McMillan (2004, pp. 29–32) makes another distinction: between "self-organizing systems" and "complex adaptive systems." Her distinction is insightful, but it may be problematic as well. She cites the brain, agents in an economy, and biological organisms in general as examples of complex adaptive systems and points to the following as their characteristics: (a) There is no controlling feature in them, (b) they have many levels of organization, and (c) they learn from their experiences and adapt. She stresses that the first two are common with self-organizing systems and the last characteristic is the one that differentiates complex adaptive systems. She points out that complex adaptive systems "do not respond passively to events, but they actively seek benefits from any situation" (p. 30). How do they do that? McMillan does not answer this question, but it can be inferred from Holland's and Mitchell's points above that they do so by using their "internal models" of the world.

The notion that systems use "internal models" to "adapt" to their environment is both insightful and problematic. The reader will remember the brief discussion earlier on Prigogine and his colleagues' observations on the complexity of physical and chemical systems. These systems do not have any internal models of their environments, and yet they are organizing, and they act in complex manners. Prigogine and Stengers say that they act in complex manners because the laws of nature are nonlinear. These are

McMillan's self-organizing systems. Her conceptualization and examples indicate that she makes a differentiation between these self-organizing (physical and chemical) systems on the one hand and biological systems on the other and uses the term complex adaptive systems for the latter. That is fine, except that we should be careful in applying this characterization to social systems. Could such a conceptualization be a misguided application of organismic metaphors to social systems, particularly policy systems? Would it anthropomorphize social systems? Do social systems learn through their "internal models," for example? Where does such a model reside in a social system? There are views of social systems that come close to this organismic view of socials systems, for example, autopoiesis theory, and more specifically Luhmann's social systems theory. There are conceptual issues in these theories, as I discuss in the following chapters.

Another problem in the complex adaptive systems conceptualization is with the term adaptation. This is an important but problematic concept. The emphasis Holland (1995) and M. Mitchell (2009) assign to adaptation in their respective definitions of *cas* and complex systems may be unnecessarily restricting and even misleading. The notion of adaption connotes a process of change, a rather smooth change, to fit or conform to external environments and accommodate the demands from the environment. There are three problems with this notion.

The first problem is that not all complex systems fit into, conform to, or accommodate the other systems in their environments. Some systems do not change, at least for a while, in face of external pressures. Others collapse or "dissipate" after certain periods of internal conflicts and/or conflicts with other systems. Some species do not fit well to their environments, and they go extinct. Social systems get involved in fights with each other, and some of them die or get transformed into other systems. Think of the many examples of empires, nation states, and political-economic systems. Think of the collapse of the Soviet Union, for example. It was a complex system that did not adapt well and then collapsed. Also think of North Korea as a complex system that has not collapsed, as of the time of the writing of this book. It did not adapt either; it survived by isolating itself from its environment. North Korean society is known to be one of the most isolated in the modern world. Of course, each of these cases is more complex than the brief description here. I will discuss the mechanisms and processes of transformation in Chapter 5. For our purposes now, it will suffice to say that not all social systems adapt, or adapt effectively. Then should we not call them complex systems? All in all, adaptation is not a necessary condition for considering a system a complex system. I agree with Axelrod and Cohen (2000, pp. 18–19), who state that it is an empirical question whether a complex system is adaptive or not or to what extent it is adaptive.

The second problem with the notion of adaptation is that the term connotes *change in response to external stimuli*. This was the view of some of the older "open systems" theories. I will discuss the evolution of systems thinking in the next chapter. In these theories the assumption was that systems were passive and only reactive to the changes in their environments. This is not what either Holland (1995) or M. Mitchell (2009) means when they use the term adaptation; they both emphasize that the change in a complex system may be stimulated by internal as well as external factors. In other words, change in complex systems could be, at least to an extent, an endogenous change. Complex systems have some self-organizational capabilities. Even when a system reacts to external stimuli or force, it does so in its own way. Particularly biological complex systems use their internal pictures of the external world to interpret the stimuli in their own ways. External stimuli to biological systems are not "objective information"; they are subject to interpretation by the receiving system. This is an important mechanism of self-organization in complex systems, which I will discuss in Chapter 4. In that chapter, I will also discuss *autopoiesis* theory, which posits that biological systems have self-referential knowledge of their environments, and this self-referentiality determines how they react to external changes and stimuli. The question will be to what extent social systems, like policy systems, are self-referential and/or react to external stimuli using their "internal pictures." This also is an empirical question.

The third problem with the notion of adaptation is that it implies that the change process in the relationships between a system and its environment is only one way: The environment demands, or pushes, and the system react by changing. As I will demonstrate later in Chapter 5, actually as a complex systems changes—whether in response to the stimuli from its environment or endogenously—it changes its environment, which is composed of other systems, as well. In turn, these changes in the environment will facilitate the way the system changes in the future.

In summary, I do not think that the term "adaptive" serves any useful purpose in naming or defining complex systems. Systems do change—if not immediately, but eventually—but whether a particular complex system is more or less effectively adaptive is an empirical question. And a system's evolution is not driven solely by external stimuli, or forces; biological and social systems use their internal mechanisms to interpret external stimuli, and these interpretations play important roles in systemic change. To what extent a particular system's evolution is internally or externally driven are empirical questions. As a system changes, it changes its environment, which in turn will affect how the system changes in the future. Once again exactly how this happens in a particular case is a question that can be answered only empirically.

Given all the conceptual problems in the distinctions made between complex systems and complex adaptive systems or between self-organizing systems and complex adaptive systems (McMillan, 2004), I will leave aside such distinctions in my discussions in the following chapters.

CHAPTER SUMMARY

Complexity is both in the nature of things and in our knowledge of them. It can be, and usually is, associated with large numbers, but defining complexity merely on the basis of large numbers would be incomplete and even misleading. Complexity is in the types of relationships among elements, more than in the number of elements. Some complexity theorists conceptualize complexity as information content and define different degrees of complexity; others view it as a state of being. There is an agreement, however, that complex systems have properties like nonlinearity, emergence, self-organization, and coevolution.

Nonlinearity, arguably the most fundamental concept in complexity theory, signifies disproportionality in relations. It is not merely lack of linearity but can be defined positively, particularly in mathematical terms. The logistic equation examples I gave in this chapter illustrate that because of the nonlinear relations in them simple equations can generate complex patterns. Small changes in such equations may make big differences in future behaviors of systems.

I argued that the categorical distinctions some theorists make among "complex systems," "complicated systems," and "simple systems" are not sustainable. I also argued that the term "complex system" is still meaningful, not as the signifier of a categorical distinction, but to stress that complexity is in the nature of the systems we study. I concluded the chapter by making the case that the designation "adaptive" in the commonly used term "complex adaptive systems" is not useful, because the usages in the literature are quite casual and because it would be misleading to suggest that all complex systems are adaptive.

2   Systems and Systemness

Complexity theory is a systems theory. Complexity theorists and research-ers call their subject matters "complex systems" or "complex adaptive systems," as I pointed out in the previous chapter. In this chapter I first trace the roots of systems thinking briefly. The systems thinking has at its core the notion of relatedness among a group of elements. Systems theories are theories attempt to explain how these elements are related to each other, how they together constitute a whole, and how this whole relates to other wholes. These are the core issues/questions in complexity theory as well.

To prepare for the discussions in the following chapters, in this chap-ter I address some key issues/questions in systems conceptualizations. The first issue is systems and networks. Although systems and network theo-ries come from different theoretical traditions, there are strong similarities between their conceptualizations. Second, I address the issue of open and closed systems. I also discuss the how systemic wholes change. One impor-tant question, particularly for complexity researchers studying human/social systems, is who defines a system and how? This is not only an episte-mological discussion but also a practical one too. In understanding policy systems, complexity theorists will need the help of social science theories. I propose to bring Giddens' concepts of systemness and system integration into the discussion in doing so.

WHAT IS A "SYSTEM"?

Although the term system does not have a universal definition, it usually connotes relatedness, togetherness, and integration. At the most basic level, a system is a collection of related elements. But related in what sense? "Rela-tionship" is a foundational concept in systems thinking and understanding what different theorists mean by it will help us understand how systems thinking is relevant to complexity theory.

This would be somewhat of a simplification, but one can observe that there are mainly two schools of thought in systems thinking: the reductionist/

mechanistic school and the holistic school. It is the latter school that is relevant to complexity theory. I begin with the reductionist/mechanistic school.

Terms like "systems design," "systems engineering," and "systems analysis" were all popular in the 1960s and 1970s. They still have some applicability. In many popular applications of "systems design," "systems engineering," and "systems analysis," the term "system" is used in a *reductionist and mechanistic* way. Van Gigch's (1978) definition of a system illustrates this: "A system is an assembly or set of related elements" (p. 2). A system is a "set" and an "assembly." The elements in a set are related to one another in a sense that they can be classified based on certain characteristics (a "set of apples" versus a "set of oranges," for example). A system in this definition is also an "assembly" of parts, as in a machine that is composed of parts that work together. This is a reductionist and mechanistic view of systems, because the underlying assumption is that a set of apples can be described as a sum of the individual apples (i.e., the sum can be reduced to the parts) and the relations among the parts can be described in mechanical terms (e.g., they fit together properly to make the machine work). In the rest of his book, Van Gigch offers several descriptions and illustrations that represent this reductionist and mechanistic understanding of systems: input-output models, decision trees, cost-effectiveness analysis, trade-off analyses, and the like.[1]

There is another aspect of Van Gigch's view of systems. Although it is not evident in the definition I cited above, in the rest of his book he promotes a "big-picture view" of planning and management. When solving a problem, he suggests, a manager or engineer should look at multiple aspects of it and its relations with other problems. He suggeststhat these parts should be "assembled" to solve problems. This *assembly view* is different from the *holistic* understanding of systems, which is represented in von Bertalaffy's and Capra's conceptualizations of systems.

Ludwig von Bertalanffy's (1968, 1972, 2008) and Fritjof Capra's (1996) conceptualizations are important partly because von Bertalanffy is "commonly credited with the fist formulation of a comprehensive theoretical framework describing the principles of organization of living systems" (Capra, p. 43). Capra is a well-known author who is credited with re-interpreting scientific theories and evidence in a holistic manner in his books *Tao of Physics: An Exploration of the Parallels between Modern Physics and Eastern Mysticism* (1975), *The Turning Point: Science, Society, and the Rising Culture* (1982), *The Web of Life: The Web of Life: A New Scientific Understanding of Living Systems* (1996), and others. This holistic view is important also because it is directly relevant to the complexity theory view of systems.

In von Bertalaffy's "general system theory" and Capra's "systems thinking," a system is an irreducible whole.[2] This whole is composed of elements that are related to one another not merely in the sense that they have similar characteristics or that they fit together mechanically but in the sense that they are *interdependent*. In their view, a system is also interrelated with other systems. In his discussion of the etymology of the term, Capra points out that the word "system" derives from the Greek *synhistanai* ("to place together") and adds that the term connotes a holistic understanding (pp. 17–35). He notes "to understand things systematically literally means to put them into a context, to establish the nature of their relationships" (p. 27).[3]

Von Bertalanffy (1968) does not offer a specific definition of a system. Instead, he elucidates its meaning step-by-step (pp. 54–57). He begins with the concept of "complexes of elements" and describes two types of these complexes. In the first type, the elements can be *isolated* and their relations can be characterized in a *summative* manner. Also in this first type, all the elements may be alike in some fashion (e.g., all are apples), or there may be differences among them (e.g., half are apples, and the other half oranges). In either case, the elements can be isolated in the sense that their properties (e.g., atomic weights and colors) and behaviors can be defined in categorical terms, regardless of the context. In other words, their properties and behaviors will be the same, regardless of whether they are placed in systemic relations or not. For instance, when four apples sitting on a tabletop are still apples when they are removed and placed on four different tabletops.[4] The same is true for two apples and two oranges sitting on a tabletop: Their properties will not change if each one is moved to a separate tabletop. The characteristics of these "complexes" (four apples and two apples-two oranges) are summative in the sense that if we add up the numbers of their elements, we will always come up with the same total, regardless of whether they are sitting on the same tabletop or separate ones. The reader will notice that this description fits nicely with Van Gigch's above-mentioned definition of a system (that a system of apples is actually a set of apples).

Von Bertalanffy's (1968) second type of complexes of elements is different from the first in the sense that the types of relations among their elements are different. He calls this second type of complexes "systems." By inference, then, the complexes of the first type are "non-systems," although he does not use this term. In this second type, systems, the elements do not exist in isolation. Their properties and behaviors are dependent on their relations with each other (they are interdependent). He also points out that the relations among the elements of a system are "strong" and "nonlinear" (p. 19). He does not elaborate on what he means by strong relations. We know what nonlinear means from the discussions in the previous chapter of this book: disproportional relations that can be expressed in a variety of mathematical equations.

The reader will remember the discussions on complex versus complicated systems in the previous chapter. There I made the point that the distinction some authors make between these two kinds of systems is not sustainable. Under the light of von Bertalanffy's conceptualizations of systems, I can add that what is defined as complicated systems by these authors are

actually not systems. Cilliers's (1998) example of jumbo jets as "complicated systems" is not meaningful in von Bertalanffy's conceptualization.
When a jumbo jet is not functioning, its elements exist in isolation. They
can be taken apart and put back together. Then it is not a system. When
it is functioning, it is in potentially nonlinear interactions with inanimate
systems, such as weather conditions, and animate systems, such as its pilots
and passengers. Then it is a system.

Because of the interdependencies among their elements, systems exhibit
"emergent" (holistic, irreducible) properties, according to von Bertalanffy.
I must note here that he uses the terms, emergent, holistic, and irreducible interchangeably. Von Bertalanffy's (1968) observation on holism is
important. He points out that systems are holistic not only spatially (that
the properties of a particular whole at a given time are irreducible to the
properties of its elements at that time) but also temporally (i.e., the present
behavior of the whole depends on its past behavior; pp. 56–57). The present
behavior of a particular societal whole is dependent on its past behavior,
for example.

It is important to note that in von Bertalanffy's (1968) conceptualization
the differentiation between the two types of complexes—non-systems and
systems—is not absolute. The difference actually is temporary and transitions from one type to the other can occur. He uses two terms to signify
these transitions: "progressive segregation" and "progressive centralization." Progressive segregation occurs when a system passes "from a state of
wholeness to a state of independence of the elements. . . . [when] a unitary
system splits up gradually into independent causal chains" (p. 68). In other
words, a system becomes a non-system, and the holistic properties of the
complex turn into summative properties. Progressive centralization is the
opposite: Independent elements, whose relations are summative, become
interdependent; a holistic complex of elements, a system, emerges. Biological organisms go through progressive centralization in natural evolution. In
the evolutionary process, according to von Bertalanffy, as certain elements
become more central in their relations with others, the complex becomes
more unified and "indivisible"(p. 73). In other words, when certain organic
molecules in a collection of molecules become more central, this collection
turns into an organism.

I conclude from Capra's and von Bertalanffy's conceptualizations that
(a) a system is a group of elements that are interdependent and that the
properties of a system are not a mere sum of the properties of its elements,
but they are holistic; (b) systemic relations are nonlinear; and (c) transitions
can occur between systems and non-systems. At this point the reader may
think that this conceptualization of a system is not much different from
the conceptualization of complex systems in the previous chapter. Indeed,
they are not different. That is why I mentioned in the previous chapter that
we could use the term *system* in place of the term *complex system*, but I
preferred the latter term to emphasize the complex properties of systems.

Systems are complex. They are composed of nonlinear relations, and they have holistic properties.

The similarities between the conceptualizations of systems and complex systems are not accidental. If one looks at the history of the ideas of systems, holism, and the like, one can easily see that there is continuity in the progression of these ideas. Von Bertalanffy's was obviously an important articulation of systems concepts. In Capra's words, he "established systems thinking as a major scientific movement" (p. 46). There were others—his predecessors and contemporaries—who contributed to the progression of ideas as well. In his own account of the evolution of system concepts, von Bertalanffy (1968) cites Leibniz's natural philosophy, Ibn Khaldun's view of history as a sequence of cultural entities, Hegel's and Marx's dialectics, and some others as early articulations of systems thinking (p. 11). Capra reminds us that Russian philosopher Alexander Bogdanov's (1873–1928) long-forgotten works on systems preceded von Bertalanffy's. Bogdanov's book *Tectology: Universal Organization Science* was published in 1928, when von Bertalanffy was beginning his career as a biologist in Vienna.[5]

I focused mainly on von Bertalanffy here, because he articulated the concepts of wholeness, irreducibility, and nonlinear relationships coherently and placed them under the umbrella concept "system." His conceptualization resonates with complexity theory. Complexity theory is a descendent of systems theories. Complexity theorists have contributed to this tradition with a new articulation of concepts and new methods of investigating systems. I will discuss these concepts and methods in the rest of this book.

SYSTEMS AND NETWORKS

Before I go any further in my discussion on the conceptualizations of systems, I need to interject another concept here: networks. This term has been used frequently in the public policy literature in the last few decades. The literature on "policy networks," "governance networks," "public service delivery networks," and the like has grown considerably in this time period. This literature has developed in a parallel track with the literature on complexity theory. Only recently the two intersected (for discussions and examples, see Mischen and Jackson, 2008; Koliba, Meek, and Zia, 2011).

One can observe strong parallels between the conceptualizations of networks and complex systems in these literatures. I think cross-fertilization between the two will be useful conceptually and methodologically. Complexity theory has its roots in the natural sciences, mathematics, and information sciences. Network theories have some of their roots in mathematics and information sciences, particularly graph theory, as well. This is why the two can easily communicate with each other. *Social* network theories have some of their roots in sociology and social psychology. Their history can be traced back to Moreno (1953) and his colleagues' works on "sociometry" and "sociograms," graphical illustrations of relationships among individuals in groups. As such, social network theorists are more informed about social problems and the applicability of network concepts, compared to complexity theorists.

The most important commonality between the two literatures is in their core concepts: system and network. Although this is rarely recognized by network or systems theorists, the commonalities in the descriptions of networks and systems are obvious. *Systems are networks, and networks are systems.* Systems theorists say that elements of a system are interdependent, systemic relations are nonlinear, and systems have holistic properties. In other words systems are complex. The definitions of networks by network theorists have close parallels to these characterizations.

Barabási (2002), a prominent network theorist, views networks as "skeletons of complexity" (p. 222). Governance network theorists emphasize that complexity is the major characteristic of networks.[6] Public service delivery networks are structurally complex, according to Klijn (1997). He points out that institutional or policy network theories, whose roots are in Allison's, Lindblom's, Cohen's, Kingdon's, and March and Olsen's process models of policymaking, which recognize the complexity of policy processes. Bresser and O'Toole (1998) argue that networks may be relatively more or less complex and the degree of complexity of a network is determined by the degree of cohesion and degree of interconnectedness among its elements.

Both network and complexity theorists recognize that there are interdependency relations among the actors of a social network and the elements of a system. O'Toole (1997b), for example, defines networks as "structures of interdependence involving multiple organizations or parts thereof, where one unit is not merely the formal subordinate of the others in some larger hierarchical arrangement" (p. 45). Bresser and O'Toole point out that interconnectedness refers to (a) the contacts between actors within the relevant policy formation process and (b) the relationships between them outside the policy process.

In Chapter 4 I will discuss self-organizational properties of complex systems. In network theories, governance is defined as a self-organizational, endogeneous, and even self-referential process as well (Schaap and Van Twist, 1997; Frederickson and Smith, 2003, pp. 207–227; Rosenkopf and Padula, 2008).

From this point on I will use the terms system and network interchangeably.[7] I will also use the terms system elements and network actors, or agents, more or less interchangeably, unless there are context-specific differences in the meanings of these terms.

OPEN AND CLOSED SYSTEMS

Quite often systems are classified as open and closed systems. These are potentially useful abstractions, as long as they are not conceptualized as distinct categories. In this section I briefly discuss where these concepts came from and how they can be useful.

Von Bertalanffy (1968) and Capra (1996) use the term "closed system" to signify the scientific approach in classical (Newtonian) physics and to contrast it with their own approach.[8] Von Bertalanffy points out that conventional physics and physical chemistry deal with closed systems (p. 32), those systems that are isolated from their environments and those systems whose behaviors tend toward equilibria (p. 39). These systems tend toward equilibria because of the second law of thermodynamics. The second law states that the differences that exist among the elements of a physical system (e.g., molecules) in terms of their physical properties (e.g., temperature) will even out over time if the system is isolated from its environment, i.e., if it is a closed system. This process of evening out is called "entropy." As the elements become more and more alike, the system comes closer to an equilibrium point. For example, all molecules will have the same temperature. The process of entropy is also depicted as a process of "decay" and "disorganization," because the very term "organization" is associated with the elements of a system being differentiated. If they all are like, then there is no organization. More important, if they are all alike, then there is no dynamism. When different molecules have different temperatures, they transfer heat among themselves, from the hot (more agitated) molecules to the cold (less agitated) molecules; this is the source of the dynamism. When they all are at the same temperature, there is no heat transfer or any activity. Because the second law is considered by many as a fundamental law of physics, it has some grim implications for the universe: It will come to an end because all the physical properties of all of its elements will even out and all activity will cease to exist eventually.

There is a key element in the second law view of physical systems: They are isolated (closed) systems—systems that do not exchange materials or energy with other systems. If there is energy or material exchange among the elements of systems, then we are talking about open systems. Because of these exchanges, open systems can defy, or even reverse, entropic tendencies. As von Bertalanffy (1968) puts it, open systems have the tendency to move toward higher order, heterogeneity, and organization (p. 41). This is what Darwin and other biologists observed in biological systems: There is an evolution from disorder to order and to increasing complexity in the living world (Capra, 1996, p. 46–49). Therefore, all biological systems are open systems. Are physical systems open or closed? Before addressing this issue, I want to make one more clarification about the behavior and evolution of open systems.

Can we say that open systems evolve away from equilibrium, unlike closed systems, which evolve toward equilibrium? If open systems keep moving more and more in the direction of disequilibrium, what happens? Do they end up in a state of ultimate differentiation, ultimate complexity (randomness or chaos), and ultimate dynamism? Does this mean that everything will blow up as a result of this ultimate dynamism? Von Bertalanffy's answer is that actually living open systems do not end up in ultimate dynamism; instead they maintain themselves in a "steady state," where they can avoid entropy and they do not decay; they may even organize themselves at a higher level (p. 41). Living systems maintain themselves in continual flow and change. Dynamism and steadiness together characterize open systems.

Von Bertalanffy's main contribution was to articulate a conceptual framework of open systems and expand its applications beyond living systems. He believed that this open systems approach could be used to unify different scientific disciplines (pp. 48–49). If the open systems approach is applicable to all sciences, does this mean that classical physicists' view of closed systems is wrong? Von Bertalanffy does not have an answer to this question.

How would complexity theorists Ilya Prigogine answer the question? The reader will remember that in Chapter 1, I briefly referred to his contributions to our understanding of complexity. His conceptualizations have important implications for the discussion of closed and open systems. In Prigogine and Stengers' (1984, pp. xxviii–xxix) view of "evolutionary thermodynamics," "thermodynamic objects" are open systems that move toward far-from-equilibrium conditions. One important implication of this is that not only living organisms but also many, if not all, physical and chemical systems are open systems. Prigogine and his colleagues also remind us that the conceptual distinction between open and closed systems should at least be softened, if not dissolved. This is because first the distinction between order and disorder is not as sharp as it may first appear. Physical processes like turbulence demonstrate this: There is order in the seeming disorderliness in turbulence. Second, not all physical or chemical systems obey the principle of entropy: movement from order to disorder. Chemical systems may evolve from a disorderly initial state toward a state of orderly but dynamic motion.

Although Prigogone and his colleagues do not answer the question "Are there no closed systems in the universe?" directly, it is evident in their conceptualizations that they think that openness and closedness of systems is a matter of degree. No *categorical distinction* between open and closed systems is sustainable. To what extent a particular system is closed or open is an empirical question. No system in the universe can be completely and eternally isolated from its environment. Perhaps the only possible closed system is the universe itself. And that is only if there is nothing else beyond the universe. All other systems must be open in the sense that they exchange matter and energy with each other. Some systems may be closed to their environments in certain respects and to an extent. They may be partially closed in the sense that they can be selective in allowing external materials and energy into them. A biological organism selects a certain kind of food to ingest and processes it in a way it will be useful to the organism, for example.

In Prigogine's perspective, completely closed systems exist only in our abstractions, with which I agree. Experimental designs are examples of such abstractions. When a researcher designs an experiment, he/she makes the assumption that he/she can isolate the factors affecting the dependent variable in the experiment. In this case, the issue is not closedness or openness of an experimental system in terms of exchanging matter or energy, but the closedness or openness of the system in terms of the relationships among the variables that are affecting it. In experimental research designs, the researcher assumes that he/she can isolate a system of variables from "external variables." Is this a plausible assumption? It is more plausible in physics and chemistry experiments than it is in public policy experiments.

Think about a physics experiment. When it is cooled to the 0 °Celsius, or 32 °Fahrenheit degree temperature, water molecules experience a phase transition from liquid to solid: They freeze. This happens regularly when a researcher conducts this experiment. Then is this experimental system a closed system, a system that is not affected by external conditions? To be able to reach that conclusion, we must first assume that the change in the temperature (cooling) is not an external factor. Having made that assumption, could this experiment be considered a closed system? There is another factor we should consider: atmospheric pressure. The higher the pressure, the lower the freezing temperature (University of Illinois, n.d.). The effect of atmospheric pressure is quite negligible at the point of freezing: Water freezes at 0 °Celsius pretty much at all elevations, under different atmospheric pressures, on our planet. So, atmospheric pressure is a small factor, but it is a factor. There is another complicating factor: Under some controlled conditions liquid water can be cooled to temperatures under 0 °Celsius without immediately forming ice. The reason for this is that "for liquid water . . . to form ice crystals, there must be a site for the formation of the ice to begin. When that does ice formation is very rapid" (Argonne National Laboratory, n.d.).

I can go on and on with citing other complicating factors, but I will stop here. My point in citing these factors is that if we ignore external variables like the effects of air pressure and the site of ice formation, the phase transition of water from liquid to ice can plausibly be considered a closed system. Under those physical conditions most of us experience most of the time, liquid water turns to ice at 0 °Celsius. This is a simplification, but it can be a useful simplification. However, one should not draw the conclusion from such simplifications that that physics experiments can be closed systems.

If it is difficult to create closed systems in physics experiments, it is even more so in social experiments. Consider an experiment in public policy: the "negative income tax" (NIT) experiments that were conducted between 1968 and 1980 in the US, particularly in New Jersey/Pennsylvania, Seattle/Denver, Iowa/North Carolina, and Gary, Indiana, and Canada, particularly in Manitoba. These were among the most sophisticated large-scale public policy experiments ever conducted in history. They were well funded and designed and executed by top-notch researchers. Both in the US and Canada, federal governments funded the experiments. Researchers from the University of Michigan and the Institute for Research on Poverty at the University of Wisconsin conducted them (Levine, Watts, Hollister, Williams, O'Connor, and Widerquist, 2005).

In these experiments the researchers wanted to test the effects of NIT on participants' conditions and behaviors in several areas. The most important question was whether or not NIT would cause participants to withdraw from the labor force. In other words, the question was, is NIT a work disincentive? The thinking was that because they were getting money without working, participants in the experimental group might not be motivated to work. The researchers also wanted to test the effect of the experiments on the health indicators of the participants, level of homeownership among participants, divorce rates among them, weights of their new born babies, school performances of their children, and a set of other indicators of well-being.

In his meta-analysis of the studies on these experiments, Widerquist (2005) notes that more than 200 studies had been published on the NIT experiments at the time of the writing of his article. After his analyses of a sample of these studies, he observes that the results are inconclusive and all the studies conclude by making comments about the context of each experiment and with some other caveats. He concludes: "the findings of the NIT experiments are far more complex, subtle, and ambiguous than one might be led to believe" (p. 66).

Widerquist identifies a group of methodological problems in the NIT experiments that are typical of the problems in all social experiments. He notes that the researchers had disagreements about the level of the precision in the measurement of the main dependent variable: rate of withdrawal from the labor pool (as a result of receiving NIT). The generalizability of the experiments was questionable for several reasons. First, the samples selected for the experimental and control groups were not random. Second, the NIT levels used in the experiments were not the ones used in real public policies at the time. Third, the experiments were artificial in the sense that they did not measure the effects of the employers' demand for labor in real markets. They were artificial also in the sense that the participants knew that these were experiments only and they would return to their regular lives after the experiments were over. Fourth, the researchers measured only short-term responses to policy changes, not long-term changes, which were actually of interest. Fifth, there were Hawthorne effects (reactivity) on the participants in the sense that they knew that they were being experimented on.

All these methodological problems allude to one key issue: In social experiments it is very difficult, if not impossible, to ignore those "contextual," "complicating," or "external" factors. The experimental conditions and the variables that are supposed to be controlled cannot be controlled.

That is because experimenters cannot create the conditions for isolating the systems they want to study. People participating in experiments cannot be isolated from their daily lives. Even under the most conducive conditions, it is impossible to avoid the "complex, subtle, and ambiguous findings." Social systems are open to the influences of all sorts of "external factors." Trying to turn them into "closed systems" artificially in experiments does not bear the expected fruits.

Social systems in general and policy systems in particular are definitely open systems. The notion of closed systems may have more applicability for physical and chemical systems, although Prigogone and his colleagues' studies cast some doubts about that too, as I mentioned earlier. In Chapter 4 I will address the issue of closednesss and openness again but in a different conceptual framework: autopoiesis and self-referentiality. In that framework closedness will be a meaningful concept in characterizing at least some social systems.

SYSTEM STABILITY AND DYNAMICS: STRUCTURES AND PROCESSES

Systems are complexes of interdependent elements, and they have macro properties that cannot be reduced the properties of their elements. These conclusions can be inferred from the earlier discussions in this chapter. These conclusions evoke two groups of questions. First, do these elements remain interdependent, and does the system keep its irreducible properties forever? Put in other words, how long do these elements hang together in such a way that they can be recognized as a whole? Do systems and their elements change? Second, if systems do change, how can their boundaries be defined? Who defines the boundaries of a system anyway? This is a particularly important question for social systems. Do external observers (e.g., social researchers, policy analysts, etc.) or the actors who play roles in a social system or whose acts and relations together constitute a social system contribute to the definition of that system? I address the first set of questions here and the second set in the next section.

Systems change. So do networks. For a system to be called a system, or a network to be called a network, it should have some stability. The nature of the relations among its elements, their interdependency relations, should be stable, at least for a while. Otherwise, the relations among this collection of elements would be in flux. A collection of elements that are in a state of eternal and ultimate flux cannot be considered a system. To the extent that the relationships among the elements of a system are stable, we can say that they have a "structure." Structure signifies stability. But structural relations change as well. They change because of external forces or internal dynamics or both (see Chapter 5). They may change slowly and gradually or abruptly and in a transformational manner.

Both systems theorists and network theorists recognize that stability and change—structures and processes—are characteristics of systems and networks. Capra (1996, p. 42) stresses that systems thinking is process thinking. He observes that there are stable relationships in nature, but there are also processes of change and transformation. There are forces and mechanisms that facilitate the interactions of structures and thus transformations of them into other structures. Mathematical network theorists acknowledge that networks have both structures and dynamics (e.g., Barabási, 2002; Newman, Barabási, and Watts, 2006). Policy network scholars also recognize the two faces of policy networks: They are stable to an extent (otherwise they would not be recognizable), but they also do change (e.g., Milward, 1996; de Bruijn and ten Heuvelhof, 1997). Bresser and O'Toole (1998) define policy networks as social systems "in which actors develop comparatively durable patterns of interaction and communication aimed at policy problems or policy programs" (p. 218). O'Toole and Meier (1999) observe that networks have "structural fluidity" (dynamism), compared to stable hierarchies.

The problem of structure versus process is not new or unique to systems or network theorists. This has been a major underlying dimension in sociological theorizing since the early days of sociology, when Comte, Durkheim, and Weber theorized how societies are held together. Their primary focus was on the stability of social structures and functions. Marx and other critical thinkers, on the other hand, focused on understanding the processes and mechanisms of social change. So it is appropriate to call in sociological theory for help to understand how the structure–process transformations occur in systems, or networks. I will cite Anthony Giddens' theory of structuration for this purpose later in this chapter.

WHO DEFINES A SYSTEM?

It is one thing to conceptualize a system as an abstraction, but it is quite another to identify a particular system empirically. The questions are, where does a system begin, and where does it end? Is there a beginning and an end? Are there "boundaries" of a system? And who defines these boundaries? These questions have kept systems theorists busy early on, and there still are no clear answers that all theorists can agree on.

An important issue is, whether social systems are different from natural systems. The elements, or actors, of social systems, or social networks, are conscious and reflective human beings. Do these actors know that they are elements of a social system? Do they define their own systems? Put it another way, is a social system still a system if its actors do not know that they are its elements? Or, does it take an external observer to identify such a system? I will address these ontological and epistemological questions in more detail in the coming chapters. This section is a preview.

Donella Meadows (2008) provides the most generic answer to the question: Are there boundaries to a system? She posits that systems rarely have real boundaries. Because everything is connected to everything else, there are no "clearly determinable boundaries" between systems. So goes on to say "There are only boundaries of the word, thought, perception, and social agreement—artificial, mental-model boundaries" (p. 95). She notes that we do need to draw boundaries "for clarity and sanity" should not "forget that we've artificially created them" (p. 97). She re-asserts that *"boundaries are our own making, and . . . they can and should be reconsidered for each new discussion, problem, and purpose"* [emphasis in original] (p. 97).

It is not clear who the "we" are in Meadows' conceptualizations of a boundary definition. She seems to be suggesting that boundaries are either personal or social constructs and that they exist in the minds of the construers (boundaries are "of the word, thought, perception, and social agreement"). Who are these construers? She does not say this clearly, but it can be inferred from her words that these are observer (researchers) of systems. Then, how about the constructions of the participants of systems? Do they matter? Do they contribute to the definition of a system's boundaries? She does not seem to have considered these questions.

Similarly, Koliba, Meek, and Zia (2011, pp. 168–171) posit that the boundaries of governance networks are defined in social construction processes, but they do not specify who defines them or how they are defined. They stress that the boundaries of governance networks are defined by constitutional rules and "policy tools," such as grants, contracts, regulations, etc. (pp. 168–170).

Fuchs (2002), Gerrits (2008), and Gerrits, Marks, and van Buuren (2009) look into the social construction process more closely. Fuchs acknowledges that the dynamic developments in and around a social system influence the way it is defined, but he emphasizes that participants of these systems, or "agents," are the ones who actually define them: "[A]gency is the decisive factor in deciding to which extent the self-reproduction of a social system is shaped by internal and external factors" (p. 26). Gerrits argues that the boundaries of policy action systems are defined by the interpretations and representations of agents and that not only what is included in the system but also how the agents act accordingly are determined by such definitions. Defining a system is a dialogical act, or a social construction process, in his view (pp. 15–16).

Do external observers play any roles in defining the boundaries of a system? Gerritts, Marks, and van Buuren recognize that both actors and observers contribute to the definition of the boundaries: A system's boundaries "do not exist a priori. What constitutes a system is a matter of judgment by the actors comprising the system as well as by observers" (p. 137). They add that a system's boundaries are defined by "the analytical questions" and the "focus of attention" of the observers (p. 137).

There are ontological and epistemological questions that underlie the issue of boundary definitions. Is it at all possible for the observers of policy systems (policymakers, policy analysts, and social scientists) to define them objectively? Can they discern and study a policy system more or less objectively, independent of the constraints of (their own) social constructions? To what extent are these observers at the same time policy actors who contribute to the definition of a system they study? These questions will come up again in different chapters of this book (Chapter 3, 4, 6, and 7), as they are pertinent to the issues in emergence, self-organization, and epistemology.

SYSTEM INTEGRATION AND SYSTEMNESS

Social systems pose specific conceptual problems to theorists. In addition to the problem of who defines a social system, there is the problem of how to define a social system. In other words, what should an observer of a system look at to recognize a system? I propose Anhony Giddens' (1984) conceptualizations of *system integration* and *systemness* as useful tools in defining social systems.

According to Giddens, systems are comprised of "situated activities of human agents, reproduced across time and space" (p. 25). It is not merely how actors see themselves and others, but, more importantly, how they act will determine if there is a system or not. He stresses that activities of human actors are the bases of defining a system and that such activities must be situated and reproduced across time and space. A system is a system only when it is situated within its environment. Its behaviors depend on this situatedness; they can be understood in the context of its relations with its environment. This environment is defined both spatially and temporally. The activities we call systems happen in relation to their geographic and social environments. They also happen at given time frame. This pattern of relations is not eternal, it may be fleeting, but for us to identify a pattern of relations as a system, they must have some durability.

Giddens differentiates "structure," a core concept in sociology, from the concept of "system." Structure refers to macro-level social phenomena in general. When he uses the term structure, Giddens refers to rules, principles, and values that are accepted commonly by the members of a society (pp. 174–186). In his usage of the term, structures are different from social systems in the sense that the former are ideas, social constructions that reside in the minds of individual participants, whereas the latter signify situated activities. In Giddens' view, structures do not exist separately from individuals' minds. Systems, which are situated and reproduced activities of individuals, do exist separately. But they are not completely disconnected from structures. Rules, values, and principles, can influence a system's behaviors through influencing the behaviors of individuals. These influences can be observed in the "structural properties of systems."

The conceptual distinctions Giddens makes among structures, systems, and structural properties of systems will be important in the understanding of policy systems from a complexity theory perspective. This differentiation will help us sort out some of the concepts I will introduce in the coming chapters. It will also be important in devising appropriate methods to study and understand complex policy systems.

Another important concept Giddens uses is *systemness*. This term connotes that a system should not be defined in dichotomous terms—either there is a system or not—but as a variable: To the degree that the activities of human actors are situated in an environment and to the degree that these activities are reproduced across time and space, we can say that they constitute a social. Therefore, a collection of relationships among a group of human actors may be more or less systemic. Then how do we determine to what extent they are systemic? To what extent is there a system?

Giddens' two other concepts, *social integration* and *system integration*, enable researchers to discern the degree of reproduction of actors' activities in a given situation. He defines social integration as "reciprocity between *actors in contexts of co-presence*" and system integration as "reciprocity between actors *or collectivities across extended time-space*" [emphasis added] (p. 28). In his definition, social integration signifies the co-presence of actors in the form of face-to-face relations (p. 28). Note that in his usage of the term, reciprocity does not signify direct "give and take" relations; he uses it in a broader sense: both the autonomy of actors vis-à-vis each other and their interdependence. In other words, to the extent that a group of actors are in the presence of each other and maintain interdependent relationships, we can talk about social integration. Family relations and kinship relations are typical examples of social integration. System integration differs from this in the sense that it does not require face-to-face presence of actors, but it still does require sustained interdependency relations over time, whether these relations are direct or indirect. National economies and societies are examples of this.

The concepts of social integration and system integration are tools we can use to observe the degree of systemness in a given situation. To the extent that the relations of actors in a given situation are interdependent and to the extent that they are sustained, we can say that they are integrated and that there is a system. Both social integration and system integration are useful concepts, but the latter is more important and meaningful in defining public policy systems. The face-to-face and co-presence relations (i.e., social integration) are not typical of policy systems. Actors in a policy system are not necessarily all in one place or in direct contact with each other. System integration is more typical for policy systems: Actors usually are in different locations, and yet they are in interdependent relationships. Most typical of these are resource interdependence (see Compston, 2009, pp. 18–19). To the extent that the activities of individual actors and organizations are integrated (i.e., reciprocated and reproduced across time and space), they constitute a policy system or policy network.

An obvious question at this point is this: Are there methodological tools that an observer can use to observe/measure the degree of integration in a system and thus determine the level of systemness in policy situations? The answer is yes. Some of the conceptualizations and tools of social network analysis can be used for this purpose. Social network analysts define networks in relational terms: The unit of analysis is not an individual actor, but the relations among actors. And they look for patterns that emerge from such relationships. Likewise, Giddens defines social integration and system integration, and thus systemness, in terms of reciprocities between actors. Social network analysis tools like centralization, density, fragmentation, and clustering coefficient are meant to measure different levels of integration, or cohesion, in networks (Wasserman and Faust, 1994; Knoke and Yang, 2008). I will discuss these methods and measures in detail in Chapter 10.

Another obvious question is this: To what extent should the reciprocal activities of individual and collective actors be integrated to be considered a policy system? Is there a threshold level of integration to be used in defining policy systems? Gerrits' (2008) conceptualization is helpful in answering this question. He does not suggest a threshold value but proposes that we can define "policy action systems" in two broad categories, based on the degree of their integration: *singular* and *composite policy action systems.* These are two different responses to the uncertainties policy actors face, according to Gerrits. In the case of a singular policy action system, multiple policy actors coalesce around common and few goals and engage in coherent patterns of action. In the case of a composite policy action system, actors are not united in their goals, the scope of their activities is open, and the system is dissipative (pp. 209–214). Singular systems are highly integrated, or they have higher degrees of systemness, and composite systems are less integrated, or they have lower degrees of systemness.

Arguably composite policy action systems are the norm, and singular systems are exceptions in increasingly networked societies of our times, but in rare occasions actors can coalesce around single goals. Only when there are strong challenges to the collective well-being of a pluralistic society (e.g., a war and unique challenges like the September 11, 2001, attacks in the US), singular policy systems emerge. To what extent a particular policy action system is composite or to what extent it is singular an empirical question.

Giddens' conceptualizations have important implications, and they are highly compatible with complexity theory. So far I have addressed only the implications of his concepts of systemness and system integration. I will come back to Giddens in the next chapter to seek his help with clarifying an important and controversial concept in complexity theory: emergence.

CHAPTER SUMMARY

At the most basic level, systems are defined in relational terms. The question is: What is the nature of these relationships? I summarized the views of two schools of thoughts on the nature of relationships. The reductionist and mechanistic school of thought views systems as assemblies of mechanical parts. Von Bertalanffy and others' holistic school stresses that (a) that a system is a group of elements that are interdependent and that the properties of a system are not a mere sum of the properties of its elements, (b) that systemic relations are nonlinear, and (c) that transitions between systems and non-systems occur. These characterizations show that the characterization of systems by this school is not much different from that of complex systems. Complexity theory is a more advanced form of general system theory and earlier systems conceptualizations.

I made a few conceptual clarifications about system thinking. First, I made the point that although system and network theories developed separately, there are close parallels between them and the concepts of the two can be synthesized for better theoretical insights. I will use the terms networks and systems interchangeably in this book. The concepts of open and closed systems are potentially useful abstractions, but they should not be used categorically in studying real systems. Complexity theorist Prigogine and his colleagues' works show that even in the natural world there is no categorical distinction between open and closed systems. I conclude that the openness and closedness of social systems should be verified empirically. Systems and networks are both stable and dynamic wholes. To what extent there is stability in a system of relationships is an empirical problem. Who defines a system? This is an important question, especially when understanding social systems. Their boundaries are defined in social construction processes, by both actors in systems and the observers of systems. I proposed that Anthony Giddens' concepts of systemness and system integration as useful concepts particularly in defining policy systems from a complexity theory perspective. I will return to these concepts later in the book.

3　Emergence

Emergence is a key concept in complexity theory, but it is vaguely defined and somewhat controversial. Emergence can be a useful concept for complexity researchers, but its history and the controversies surrounding it should be understood and it should be carefully conceptualized before it is applied to specific situations.

In this chapter, I first summarize the definitions and conceptualizations of emergence and their historical backgrounds. Then I proceed with a discussion of its potential and problems. I ask three groups of questions about emergence: (a) Do macro-level (i.e., systemic, structural) properties emerge from the interactions among actors? If yes, how? (b) Once emerged, do these emergent properties exist separately from the properties of individual actors? Are they reducible in any way to those of individuals? (c) Do these emergent properties have causal effects on the behaviors of individuals? I propose Giddens' structuration theory as a promising framework for answering these questions.

EMERGENCE, MICRO–MACRO RELATIONS, AND AGENTS AND STRUCTURES

To understand the issues the conceptualizations of emergence, we should look into some of the established theories of public policy processes and one of the key problems in sociology. The theories of policy processes can be grouped into two: those theories that conceptualize macro-level processes and those theories that conceptualize the relations between micro-level processes, such as individual and group behaviors and macro-level policy processes. The punctuated equilibrium theory, policy diffusion models, and large-n comparative studies fall into the first category and institutional rational choice theory and advocacy coalition framework into the second.[1] This second group of theories address what sociologists call the "micro–macro problem" or the "agency–structure problem." This problem is alternatively known as the "transformation problem" in European sociology, the "problem of aggregation" in economics, and the "problem of social (or "public") choice" in political science (Coleman, 1986, p. 1321).

Coleman (1986) traces the roots of the micro–macro problem to the philosophies of Hobbes, Smith, Locke, Rousseau, and Mill in the 17th, 18th, and 19th centuries. In all these philosophies the central question was how purposeful actions of individuals were connected to macrosocial phenomena. How do the acts of individual political and economic actors lead to macro events in politics and economy, for example? Coleman describes the micro–macro problem with the following examples:

> It is the process through which individual preferences become collective choices; the process through which dissatisfaction becomes revolution; through which simultaneous fear in members of a crowd turns into a mass panic; through which preferences, holdings of private goods, and the possibility of exchange create market prices and a redistribution of goods; through which individuals' task performance in an organization creates a social product; through which the reduction of usefulness of children to parents leads families to disintegrate; through which interest cleavages lead (or fail to lead) to overt social conflict. (p. 1321)

Coleman (1986) notes that sociologist Talcott Parsons posed this problem as the central problem of sociology and attempted to solve it with his theory of action in the 1930s, but then he gradually abandoned his efforts. Most sociologists after Parsons just ignored the problem and either focused on individual actions and adopted methodological individualist positions (i.e., behaviorism) or studied and theorized macro structures and processes only. But others did continue working on the problem coming from different theoretical backgrounds. Rational choice theorist in political economy continually worked on the "aggregation problem" (e.g., Olson, 1965; Ostrom, 2005). From a critical theoretical perspective, Jessop (1990, 2001, 2004, 2008) made the "agency–structure problem" a core problem of his theorization of the state and state power. Despite all the efforts, Coleman (1992) argues that the micro–macro problem remains the "central intellectual problem of the social sciences" (p. 269).

What can complexity theorists offer to help solve the problem? Emergence is complexity theorists' solution to the micro–macro problem. But this solution is not necessarily original, and there are controversial and unresolved issues in it. The concepts of emergence, systems, and holism go hand in hand. Capra (1996) points out that systems thinking is deeply rooted in holistic understanding in which a system is defined as an "integrated whole whose essential properties emerge from the relationships between its parts"; these properties are not reducible to the properties of the parts of the system (p. 30). Systems are multi-leveled hierarchies, according to Capra, and unique systemic properties emerge at each level. Complexity theorists adopted the ideas of holism and emergence. To gain an understanding of the specific issues in and controversies surrounding the concepts, a brief history would be useful.

A HISTORY OF THE CONCEPTS OF HOLISM AND EMERGENCE[2]

Von Bertalanffy (1972) traces the history of the dictum "the whole is more than the sum of its parts" to the holistic and teleological philosophy of Aristotle. After Aristotle, this holistic view was abandoned for a long time in Western philosophy and science, as the reductionist philosophies and practices gained ground and eventually became dominant. Descartes' and Newton's works in the 17th century contributed to the development. In his book *A Discourse on the Method* (1637), Descartes formulated the principles that every problem could be divided into as many elements as possible and that scientific problems should be analyzed sequentially, starting with the simplest elements and progressively proceeding to the more complex, and that every problem could be solved using mathematical methods (Murray, 1997, p. 12). Newton further developed Descartes' reductionism by developing experimental methods as the primary methods of reductionist science and by inventing calculus as the main tool of reductionist science (Morçöl, 2002, pp. 59–61).

The 19th century was an important period of time in the development of science and philosophy of science. One of the big philosophical debates of the times was the debate between reductionists and holists. Reductionism was the dominant philosophy in this century because of the earlier successes of the Cartesian and Newtonian science. A holistic critique of the perceived shortcomings reductionism arose in the forms of "vitalism" and "organicism" in this century.[3] Reductionist science was clearly materialistic; it was grounded in material and observable facts. Vitalists countered this reductionist tenet by arguing that those facts that were not immediately observable should be the subject of scientific observation as well. They proposed a dualist ontology particularly for biology. Vitalists contended that living organisms were not made up only of their materially observable organs and body parts but also of a "vital force" inside them. This vital force was a valid area so study for scientists, as well, according to vitalists. Organicists carried this view over into understanding social phenomena. They argued that social realities also had dual ontological existence: They were composed of both material and visible individuals and organism-like structures, which were not always visible entities.

Vitalism and organicism inspired an early 20th-century philosophical movement called emergentism. John Stuart Mill's and George Henry Lewes' refinements of the concepts of vitalism and organicism in the 19th century were major ingredients in the appearance of emergentism on the philosophical scene later. Both Mill and Lewes are credited for coining the term "emergence" (Sawyer, 2005).[4] Sawyer cites Lewes' example of the emergence of the water molecule as the first articulation this concept. A water molecule, as we know, is composed of hydrogen and oxygen atoms, but it has properties that cannot be traced to those of either atom. Particularly, water molecules have the property of liquidity, which emerges from

the properties of its atoms, but is different from them. Lewes conceptualizes emergence thusly:

> *Although each effect is the resultant of its components, the products of
> its factors, we cannot always trace the steps of the process, so as to see
> in the product the mode of operation of each factor.* In this latter case,
> I propose to call the effect an emergent. It arises out of the combined
> agencies, but in a form which does not display the agents in action.
> [emphasis added] (quoted in Sawyer, p. 32)[5]

The emergentist philosophers of the 1920s defined two levels of existence:
the individual/physical and structural levels. They argued that higher-level
structural (emergent) properties are determined by the properties of basic
physical matter, but still these two constituted two separate levels. The
logical empiricists of the early 20th century, like Bertrand Russell, strongly
argued against this two-level conceptualization of reality and claimed that
what emergentists called emergent properties were actually mere epiphenomena of physical properties. The idea of emergence lost prominence after
the 1920s, but became fashionable again with the advent of general system
theory in the 1960s and complexity theory later.

Capra's (1996, pp. 30–32) narrative of the history of holistic thinking in the first half of the 20th century sheds light on this re-emergence
of the idea of emergence. He notes that holism appeared as a reaction to
the dominant reductionism in in biology, psychology, ecology, and quantum physics in this period. Biologists had to contend with this question:
Since the genetic information is identical in all cells, why do they spe-
cialize into muscle cells, blood cells, nerve cells, etc.? Many biologists
rejected the mechanistic/reductionist thinking in their explanations of
biological organisms and attempted to understand them in terms of their
own "organizing relations" (p. 25). Gestalt psychologists formulated the
principle that all living beings perceive the world as integrated perceptual
patterns and that human psychology is an irreducible whole. From its
beginnings, ecology was built on a holistic understanding of the relationships of animals and plants. Quantum physics demonstrated that matter
is an integrated whole at its most fundamental (subatomic) level. Von
Bertalanffy notes that when he began developing his system theory in the
1920s, parallel developments were taking place in cybernetics, information theory, game theory, decision theory, mathematical topology, and
statistics, all of which affected his thinking (pp. 89–91).

Holism has been a strong undercurrent in sociology since the 19th century. Auguste Comte and Emile Durkheim, the founders of sociology,
espoused holistic views. Arguably, they had to do that, because they wanted
to create a science whose subject matter would be distinct from psychology.
They had to define society as a whole, a separate level of existence, not a
simple aggregate of individuals. Comte did not use the term emergence, but

his thinking that society had a separate level of existence influenced Mill's and Lewes' philosophies (Sawyer, 2005, p. 39). Comte posited that higher levels of phenomena in societies were irreducible to lower levels and that higher levels had causal power. Durkheim developed the notion of social emergence further. He noted

> Whenever certain elements combine and thereby produce, by the fact of their combination, new phenomena, it is plain that these new phenomena reside not in the original elements but in the totality formed by their union. (quoted in Sawyer, p. 40).

Later Talcott Parsons defined sociology as the study of emergent phenomena and formulated the problem of micro–macro connections, as I mentioned earlier. Contemporary "sociological realists" Russel Keat and John Urry, Roy Bhaskar, and Margaret Archer continue the tradition of conceptualizing "the social" as an emergent phenomenon (Sawyer, p. 49). In their conceptualizations, emergent social structures have holistic properties—properties that are irreducible to the properties or actions of individual actors. Bhaskar argues, for example, that "although social structure is dependent on individuals' actions, it is irreducible to them and ontologically autonomous from them" (quoted in Sawyer, p. 80). As we shall see later in this chapter, irreducibility is a contentious issue among social theorists.

EMERGENCE AND COMPLEXITY THEORY: AN OVERVIEW

Complexity theory's version of emergence builds on the tradition I summarized in the previous section. Complexity theorists offer more specific descriptions and illustrations of the emergence process, and in doing so they encounter difficult and controversial conceptual and methodological problems. There is an agreement among complexity theorists that emergence is a very important concept, but there does not seem to be a uniform understanding of emergence among complexity theorists. They do not necessarily agree on some the terms they use. I discuss the agreements and agreements and disagreements on the concepts of emergence in this section.

Is Emergence Real?

In his book *Emergence: From Chaos to Order*, arguably the most authoritative source on the conceptualization of emergence in the complexity theory literature, John Holland (1998) does not offer a definition of emergence, because, he says, emergence is a complicated and even "enigmatic" concept (p. 3). It is so enigmatic that some complexity theorists, like Epstein (2006), do not even consider emergence as a scientific concept, as I will discuss later in this chapter.

To understand better the problems in defining emergence, we should go back to the quote from Lewes: "Although each effect is the resultant of its components, the products of its factors, we cannot always trace the steps of the process, so as to see in the product the mode of operation of each factor" (quoted in Sawyer, 2005, p. 32). If we cannot "always trace the steps of the process," does this mean that there is a practical difficulty in doing so, or is there a fundamental, ontological, boundary that prohibits us from accessing the information about the steps of the process? In Miller and Page's (2007) view, there simply is a practical problem: "Emergent behavior is simply reflective of scientific ignorance rather than some deeper underlying phenomenon" (p. 46). In other words, we call what cannot understand or explain "emergent." If we can come up with a better scientific explanation of the subject matter under study someday, what we think as an emergent phenomenon today will not be so then. This is what the logical empiricists of the early 20th century, like Bertrand Russel, meant when they said that emergent phenomena were merely epiphenomena (i.e., not real phenomena, but merely shadows).

Holland (1998) does not think so. He argues and illustrates with examples in his book that emergence is real. It is natural; it is ubiquitous in nature and does not go away once the phenomenon is understood (p. 5). Therefore, emergence has an ontological status. Then what is it? How does it happen?

Complexity theorists follow Lewes' conceptualization of emergence in their conceptualizations: Emergence is a "process whereby the global behavior of a system results from the actions and interactions of agents" (Sawyer, 2005, p. 2), and emergent structures are "stable macroscopic patterns arising from *local interactions of agents*" [emphasis added] (Epstein and Axtell, 1996, p. 35). Then the natural question would be this: Can we characterize these local (micro) interactions and the process of macro structures emerging from them? Can we decipher the mechanisms of emergence? If we can, we should be able to rebuff the assertion that emergence is merely a reflection of our scientific ignorance at this time. If we cannot, then maybe we should concede that science cannot figure it out, yet.

Complexity theorists also stress that simple rules at the micro level can generate complex emergent patterns at the macro level. Macro patterns emerge "from the interaction of agents that follow *relatively simple rules*" [emphasis added] (Anderson, 1999, p. 218). We saw the connection between simple rules and complex patterns in Chapter 1, particularly in the example of computing the X_{t+1} in the logistic equation ($X_{t+1} = kX_t - kX_t^2$) iteratively. As we observed in this example, the iterative solutions of this simple equation at different levels of k generated a variety of patterns: linear, oscillating, and chaotic. We observed that when seemingly chaotic outcomes are plotted on a phase plane, a discernible pattern emerged.

The logistic equation is not the only example of complex patterns emerging from simple rules. This is illustrated in the applications of agent-based simulations, as well. Epstein and Axtell (1996) demonstrate with their simulations that the "spatio-temporal interaction of autonomous agents" operating under simple rules can generate complex macro-emergent patterns, such as skewed wealth distribution and cultural rules.

But, how do we know that a macro pattern is really emergent? Every time we see a macro pattern (e.g., mob behavior, stocks markets swinging upward or downward collectively, people acting out cultural norms), should we call it emergent? Or do emergent patterns have a more specific signature? In other words, can we tell emergent macro patterns apart from non-emergent macro patterns? The most important characteristic of emergent patterns is that once emerged, they persist, or they are "robust." There is more, according to Holland (1998): *Emergent macro properties persist despite continual turnover in their constituents* (p. 7).

Biological organisms are good examples of this. They have persistent collective structures and behavioral patterns, despite the fact that they are open systems—that they constantly exchange matter and energy with their environments. They breathe air in and out, drink water and perspire, and ingest and excrete food. Although an organism exchanges molecules with its environment constantly through these processes, it maintains its integrity—remains an organism—for some period of time. Between its birth and death, we can recognize an animal as the same animal. It gets older, and its body and behavioral patterns change over time, but it is recognizably the same animal during its life time, despite its constant exchange of molecules with its environment. After its death the body decomposes, and this biological system dissipates.

The question is this: Do these observations apply to social systems as well? Can we observe such persistent macro-level properties of social systems, despite the turnovers in their constituents? This is a key question complexity researchers should explore in their studies. I will come back to this issue in the concluding chapter.

Aggregation or Emergence?

Aggregation is another term complexity theorists use, sometimes interchangeably with emergence. Complexity theorist do not seem to have a common and clear understanding of these terms and whether or not they are different from each other. On the one hand, there are those who use them interchangeably. For example, Holland (1995) states that *aggregation* "concerns the *emergence* of complex large-scale behaviors from the aggregate interactions of less complex agents" [emphasis added] (p. 11). Similarly, Axelrod (1997) uses the terms vaguely and interchangeably. For example, in presenting the results of one of his simulations, he poses the question: "How can new political actors *emerge* from an *aggregation* of smaller political actors?" [emphasis added.] (p. 124). Miller and Page

(2007) define emergence in terms of aggregation of localized behavior that is disconnected from its origins (p. 44).

On the other hand, Sawyer (2005, pp. 95–97) differentiates aggregation and emergence specifically. Citing the work of Wilmsatt (1986), who equated emergence with "nonaggregativity," Sawyer stresses that whereas aggregative properties are reducible to the properties of components, emergent properties are not. Sawyer elaborates that complex systems are emergent, not aggregated, and that their properties are *nondecomposable* in the sense that "the system's organization has a significant influence on the functions of its components" (p. 96). They are *nonlocalized*, in the sense that "the system's properties cannot be identified with components, but are . . . distributed spatially within the system" (p. 96); and the interactions among the system's components are nonlinear and complex. The first two characteristics of emergent properties—decomposability and nonlocalization—are actually other names for irreducibility. In essence, Sawyer seems to be saying that emergence differs from aggregation in the sense that emergent properties are irreducible, whereas aggregate properties are reducible.

Public Interest: Aggregated or Emergent?

The issue of aggregation versus emergence is directly relevant to the theories of public policy and administration, particularly the conceptualizations of public goods and public interest.

There are roughly two positions on public interest: the position of the "traditional public administration" theorists versus that of the theorists of neoclassical economics, rational choice, and public choice. Traditional public administration demarcates public interest and private interests as separate realms and claims the former as its own territory. In Tullock's (1979, p. 31) words, this traditional view defines public interest as an abstraction that is reflected in the intentions and behaviors of selfless and altruistic men and women in government. Rational choice theorists are critical of this view. They argue that the behaviors of these men and women are actually "self-seeking," just like the behaviors of all other individuals. Thus the proponents of public/rational choice theories blur the line between the public and private realms.

The blurring of the line by rational choice theorists forces us to question what we mean by "the public" and inquire whether and how collective, or public, actions are related to private actions, the actions of individuals. Then the next question is this: Does public interest aggregate or emerge? In other words, is public interest a mere sum of private interests? Or, is it more than this sum and irreducible to those of private interests?

Neoclassical/rational choice/public choice theorists are not unanimous or clear in their answers to these questions. In fact very few of them, if any, make any differentiation between aggregation and emergence in their usages of thee terms. This lack of differentiation has its roots in Adam Smith's vague conceptualization of the relations between individual wealth and societal wealth and that of "invisible hand." Smith (1902) states

> As every individual . . . endeavors as much as he can both to employ his capital in the support of domestic industry [i.e., the economy of his household], and so to direct that industry that its produce may be of greatest value; every individual necessarily labors to render the annual revenue of the society as great as he can. He generally, indeed, neither intends to promote the public interest, nor knows how much he is promoting it. By referring the support of domestic to that of foreign industry, he intends only his own security; and by directing that industry in such a manner as its produce may be of the greatest value, he intends only his own gain, and he is in this, as in many other cases, led by an invisible hand to promote an end which was no part of his intention. . . . By pursuing his own interest he frequently promotes that of the society more effectually than when he really intends to promote it. I have never known much good done by those who affected to trade for the public good. (pp. 160–161) [6]

Three points can be observed in this quote. First, Smith wants to show that private interest, or private wealth production, is at the core of how public goods are generated. Second, he argues, individuals do not need to be intentional to contribute to public goods/public interest; they do so simply by acting in their own interests. They do not even know that they are contributing to something other than their own interests. Third, he points out that there is an "invisible hand"—a hidden social mechanism that works independently of the intentions of individuals—that ties the products of individual actions to societal goods and interests.

Smith does not tell us more about how that invisible hand works, but one might possibly find some elements of the idea of emergence in it. The notion that individuals unintentionally contribute to a greater good, or a collective outcome, is a component of emergence thinking. So is the notion that there are some mechanisms of emergence—mechanisms that bridge the divide between individual actions and collective outcomes—which I discuss in the next section. But it is not clear whether in Smith's view public goods/public interest are mere sums of private interests—that they are decomposable. Nor is it clear whether the "the whole is more than the sum of its parts," and it is irreducible. In other words, it is not clear whether in his view public goods/public interest are aggregated or emergent in the sense Sawyer (2005) makes the differentiation between the two.

The prevalent view among Smith's followers, contemporary neoclassical economists/rational choice theorists, seems to be that individual interests aggregate into a public interest. Public interest is conceptualized as a stable state, where different interests in the economy and society are in equilibrium.

In this aggregation process the whole equals to the sum of its parts. In Cochran and Malone's (1995) words, "'public interest' may be understood as the entirety of . . . individual preferences expressed as choices" (p. 5). Macro-level entities, such as society and culture, do not have "independent status[es] apart from the individuals who constitute them," as rational choice theorist Lichbach (2003, p. 32) put it. Perhaps the best popular expression of this position was what the then British Prime Minister Margaret Thatcher said in her interview with *Women's Own* magazine in 1987: "There is no such thing as society. There are individual men and women, and there are families."[7]

MacDonald (2003) puts this in more theoretical terms: In rational choice theory "macrosocial outcomes are the sum of discrete, intentional acts by preconstituted actors" (p. 558). Note that in this view, individual acts are intentional, but not in the sense that actors intend to generate a macrosocial outcome. Instead actors intend to maximize their own benefits and own utilities. Also note that these are actors with fixed interests and preferences. I underscore these two assumptions because they have implications not only for the issue of emergence versus aggregation but also for the issue of downward causation, which I will discuss later in this chapter.

THREE QUESTIONS FOR EMERGENCE

Earlier in this chapter I mentioned that emergence is the complexity theorists' solution to the micro–macro problem. Emergence involves transformations between micro and macro levels. These transformations can be understood better in responses to three questions: (a) Do macro-level (i.e., systemic, structural) properties emerge from the interactions among actors? If yes, how? (b) Once emerged, do these emergent properties exist separately of the properties of individual actors? Are they reducible in any way to those of individuals? (c) Do these emergent properties have causal effects on the behaviors of individuals? The discussions in the rest of the chapter are organized around these questions.

CHARACTERISTICS AND MECHANISMS OF EMERGENCE

Earlier discussions in this chapter show that complexity theorists think that macro properties do emerge from the interactions at the micro level, although they may not have a clear and uniform understanding of how this happens. There are some complexity theorists who proposed and studied a group of characteristics and mechanisms of the emergence of macro-level properties from micro-level actions and interactions. In this section, I summarize these characteristics and mechanisms.

There are five groups of characteristics and mechanisms of emergence one can identify in the complexity theory literature: context, nonlinearity, self-organization, differential persistence, and preferential attachment. The first three of these were either discussed in an earlier chapter or will be discussed in the following chapters of this book. I focus on differential persistence and preferential attachment in this section.

In the common view of complexity theorists, patterns emerge within their specific *contexts*. As Holland (1998) puts it, "Emergence is above all a product of coupled, context dependent interactions" (pp. 121–122). Therefore, it is important to understand the specific context of an emergent complex system in order to understand the system itself. The histories of its components and the paths they have taken matter. So do their current environments. If context is so important, it should have significant implications for epistemology, particularly for the generalizability of the characteristics and behavior of a complex system. The question is this: If an emergent system is a product of context dependent interactions, can we in any way generalize (a) how components of systems interact and (b) how systems behave in general? I will come back to the generalizability question in Chapter 6.

Nonlinearity, a concept I discussed in Chapter 1, is one of the most recognizable mechanisms of emergence, according to complexity theorists. Holland (1998) states that context-dependent interactions among the components of a system are nonlinear, and such interactions are the generators' emergent properties at macro levels (p. 122). This, of course, is a generic statement. Much more needs to be done by complexity theorists to clarify how nonlinear interactions become mechanism of emergence.

Self-organization also is a characteristic of emergence. The emergence of macro processes is self-organizational by definition. Complexity theorists observe that the self-organizational tendencies of elements, components, and individual actors of systems are at the source of the processes through which systemic properties emerge and once emerged, systems have self-organizational tendencies. There are a variety of specific self-organizational mechanisms, which I will discuss in the next chapter.

Differential Persistence

In Holland's (1998) view, *differential persistence* is the primary mechanism of the emergence of hierarchical organizations. The basic idea is that persistence pays in determining what comes out next. Those components of a system whose properties and behaviors made them more successful in the past will persist and play a larger role in shaping the future patterns in the behavior of the system. The source of this understanding is the Darwinian evolutionary theory: "[T]he patterns that persist long enough to collect resources and produce copies are the ones that generate new variants" (Holland, p. 227). Likewise, Holland points out, in neural networks persistent patterns in relations among nerve cells become cell assemblies with more sophisticated behaviors.[8] Different patterns persist at different rates. Holland notes

Some patterns persist only as long as they do not encounter other patterns. Others persist through some interactions, while undergoing dissolution or transformation in others. Still other persistent patterns interact with only a few other patterns, simply maintaining their form in all other contexts. (p. 227)

Obviously those patterns that maintain themselves are the ones that will play the most significant roles in emergence processes—processes through which macro structures and patterns emerge. "[I]n Darwinian evolution, the patterns that persist long enough to collect resources and produce copies are the ones that generate new variants" (p. 227).

Then what makes a particular pattern more or less persistent? To answer this question, Holland uses the analogy of the rules that guide the behaviors of living beings. With his example of the behaviors of ants, he illustrates that "generalist rules" are more persistent than "specialist rules" (pp. 228–229). Therefore, generalist rules play more roles in the emergence of complex behavioral patterns.

The analogs of the generalist and specialist rules in public policy processes are what Ostrom (2005) calls "constitutional rules" and "operational rules" (pp. 58–62). Constitutional rules, like the articles in a national constitution (e.g., the basic rights of citizens), are generalist rules. The First Amendment of the US Constitution guarantees the rights of citizens to free speech and assembly in a generic manner, for example; it does not specify under what conditions and how these rights may be regulated or restricted.

Operational rules do specify how they may be regulated and restricted. For example, the "City of Cincinnati Safety Department Rock Concert Guidelines" regulate and restrict the rights and movements of rock concert attendants at the city's Riverfront Coliseum as follows:

1. The doors would be opened 90 minutes prior to the scheduled concert.
2. At a point of time to be determined by the Police Officer in charge of the detail, when the plaza area has been secured, and check points established, no ticket sales can be made from ticket windows on the plaza level surrounding the Coliseum.
3. No seat would be sold to any patron or given free of charge to any patron that had an obstructed view of the stage or platform area where the performers were to perform the concert. ("Crowd Management" at http://www.crowdsafe.com/taskrpt/chpt8.html; accessed on April 12, 2011).

These rules were set after 11 people were killed in a crush when people were trying to get into a concert by the rock band The Who at Riverfront Coliseum on December 3, 1979. The rules are specific to the city and the coliseum. The First Amendment, on the other hand, was passed in 1791 and still is in effect. This "generalist rule" is certainly more persistent than the "specialist rules" like Cincinnati's Rock Concert Guidelines. Also, arguably, the First Amendment has played a much more important role, compared to specific rock concert guidelines, in the emergence of the patterns of behaviors of US citizens in expressing themselves in assemblies.

Holland's adaptation of differential persistence to explain the emergence process attracted the critical attention of others (e.g., Lane, 2006). Lane argues that the ontological status of the persistent patterns is not clear and that Holland's concepts has not yet led to the creation of successful models that could illustrate how specifically collective behaviors emerge in nature or society. Indeed, although it makes sense to think of the persistence of the generalist rule of the First Amendment as playing a major role in the emergence of the collective behaviors of US citizens, we do not have any models that would specifically demonstrate how this happens.

Preferential Attachment

Network theorists Albert-Lazslo Barabási and Réka Albert (1999) developed a similar concept: *preferential attachment*. In their research they identified the mechanisms of the emergence of a specific kind of network, "scale-free network." This is the kind of network in which some nodes are more connected to others. The degree distribution of a scale-free network follows a "power law." A generic example of the distribution that follows a power law is in Figure 3.1. In a power-law distribution, a few nodes have a large number of connections to other nodes, whereas a large number of nodes have very few connections. An important characteristic of scale-free networks is that

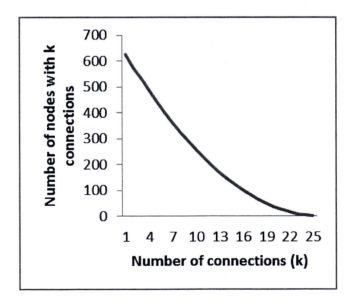

Figure 3.1   A power-law distribution.

the shape of the power-law distribution that represents a network remains the same regardless of the scale used to measure its elements.

Scale-free networks are ubiquitous in nature and societies, Barabási, Albert, and several other researchers found. [9] The connections among the Web sites in the World Wide Web and the citations of journal articles in the academic literature are examples. Another example of scale-free networks is the "hub" system in the flight connections of an airline (Barabási, 2002, pp. 70–71). For example, the Atlanta, Memphis, New York, Cincinnati, Detroit, Minneapolis/St. Paul, and Salt Lake City airports serve as the hubs in the Delta Airlines system. More Delta flights land in and depart from these airports; travelers make their connections to hundreds of other airports in the US and the rest of the world at these airports.

Barabási and Albert posit that two genetic mechanisms are responsible for the emergence of power-law distributions and scale-free networks: growth and preferential attachment. In Barabási and Albert's words: "Networks expand continuously by the addition of new vertices and *new vertices attach preferentially to sites that are already well-connected*" [emphasis added] (p. 509). Barabási (2002) notes

> Why do hubs and power laws emerge in the scale-free model? First, growth plays an important role. The expansion of the network means that early nodes have more time than the latecomers to acquire links: If a node is the last to arrive, no other node has the opportunity to link to it; if a node is the first in a network, all subsequent nodes have chance to link to it. Thus growth offers a clear advantage to the senior nodes, making them the richest links. Seniority, however, is not sufficient to explain the power laws. Hubs require the help of the second law, preferential attachment. Because new nodes prefer to link to the more connected nodes, early nodes with more links will be selected more often than their younger and less connected peers. As more and more nodes arrive and keep picking the more connected nodes to link to, the first nodes will inevitably break away from the pack, acquiring a very large number of links. They will turn into hubs. Thus preferential attachment induces a *rich-get-richer* phenomenon that helps the more connected nodes grab a disproportionately large numbers of links at the expense of the latecomers. [emphasis in original] (pp. 87–88)

Barabási later realized that what determines how many links a particular node gets is not only its prior links but also its "fitness." Those with better fitness attract more new connections (Bianconi and Barabási, 2001). They call it the "fitter-gets-richer" phenomenon. Bianconi and Barabási note that the cumulative effects of these processes at the individual node level "determine the system's large-scale topology" (p. 436). They cite the studies by others that showed that their model explained the distributions of connections among the sites on the Internet and the sources used in academic citations. M. Mitchell (2009, pp. 253–255) notes that the applicability of the concepts of scale-free networks, preferential attachment, and power-law distributions have been criticized by some. The critics argue that too many phenomena are described as scale-free or power law and that preferential attachment may not be the mechanism of emergence even in the networks that are actually scale free.

These critics may be right, but still these concepts can open up possibilities for policy researchers. They have not been explored fully yet, but the few existing examples can help show their potentials. In their studies of German cities, Helbing and his colleagues (2009) identified power-law distribution of connections in urban supply networks—numbers of doctors, pharmacies, and petrol stations—and traffic flows. Rosenkopf and Padula's (2008) review of the literature on the alliance networks among private businesses shows that preferential attachment is an important mechanism in the evolutions of these networks. Their review suggests that alliance networks become ever more self-reproducing and centralized, as more and more dense webs of relationships are developed among familiar and well-allied firms.

Holland's differential persistence and Barabási's preferential attachment are examples of simple mechanisms of emergence. In both cases the rules lead to the emergence of stable structures. Differential persistence leads to the emergence of hierarchical structures. Preferential attachments likewise lead to the emergence of a special kind of hierarchy: a scale-free network; the distribution of the connections of these nodes is a power-law distribution.

The preferential attachment concept can also be synthesized with Holland's concept of persistence: Those nodes that are well-connected are so because of the persistence of their prior behaviors or characteristics. In other words, persistence may be the reason for their fitness, which will eventually lead to their centrality in a network. For example, certain actors in formal organizations or policy networks may be well-connected—they may know a large number of other actors—and hence they can be more influential. The large number of their connections may have developed, because they have been around for a long time. Certainly one can argue otherwise as well: Their fitness in the first place may determine their degree of persistence. For example, these actors have been around for a long time, perhaps because they were "fit" to begin with: They had the requisite skill set for the organization or the policy network in which they operate. These hypothetical possibilities make intuitive sense, and one can draw examples from their own experiences in organizations and networks, but they also need to be empirically studied and tested.

IRREDUCIBILITY

The second set of questions I asked in conceptualizing emergence was the following: Once emerged do these emergent properties exist separately of the properties of individual actors? Are they reducible in any way to those of individuals? One can find partial answers to these questions in the previous sections. The question of whether macro properties are reducible to micro properties is the flip side of the question: Do macro properties emerge from micro properties? In fact, for many theorists these two questions are one and the same. The question of emergence is the question of irreducibility, they would say. From their perspective the issue of irreducibility is the issue of holism: The properties of a holistic system are irreducible. Indeed there are close connections between the concepts emergence, holism, and irreducibility. There are some disagreements on whether the concept of irreducibility is a necessary component of complexity theory.

I noted earlier in this chapter that rational choice theorists subscribe to the view that individual properties aggregate to macro properties. Then macro-level properties should be perfectly reducible to micro-level properties: If one understands how (boundedly) rational individuals maximize their utilities, then one will understand that an economy or society is made of the total of these utility-maximizing behaviors.

Most complexity theorists disagree with this aggregationist view and take the position that systemic properties are emergent and irreducible. One of the most classical examples of this position is expressed in Anderson's 1972 article "More Is Different," in which he states that systemic properties are irreducible in nature; not all phenomena can be explained in terms of the fundamental laws of lower level phenomena (pp. 393–396). In his interview with Waldrop (1992, pp. 82–83), Anderson cites Lewes' water molecule example to illustrate the irreducibility of systemic properties. When billions of water molecules are put together, they will collectively acquire a new property: liquidity. The property of liquidity is irreducible to those of the properties of hydrogen or oxygen molecules.

Kauffman (1995) observes irreducibility in the emergence of life: Once live organisms emerge, their complexity cannot be understood in terms of the rules governing the functioning of the molecules they are made of.

> Life . . . is an *emergent phenomenon* arising as the molecular diversity of a prebiotic chemical system increases beyond a *threshold of complexity* [edge of chaos]. . . . [L]ife is not located in the property of any single molecule—in the details—but is a *collective property of systems* of interacting molecules. Life . . . emerged whole and has always remained whole. *Life . . . is not to be located in its parts, but in the collective emergent properties of the whole they create.* . . . No vital force or extra substance is present in the *emergent,* self-reproducing whole. But the collective system does possess a stunning property not possessed by any of its parts. It is able to reproduce itself and evolve. The collective system is alive. Its parts are just chemicals. [emphasis added] (Kauffman, 1995, p. 24)

The view of irreducibility Anderson and Kauffman endorse is the most common view among complexity theorists, but not everybody agrees with this view. Epstein (2006) has deep reservations about the whole concept of emergence because it is closely related to irreducibility. His objection is that emergence in the sense of irreducibility is rooted in the emergentist philosophy and the mysticism that underlies this philosophy. He argues that the British emergentism of the 1920s is "unmistakably anti-scientific—even deistic." These philosophers, according to Epstein, "claimed *absolute unexplainability* for emergent phenomena" [emphasis in original] (p. 32). He specifically singles out the deist philosopher Lloyd Morgan, who said, "Emergent evolution is from first to last a revelation and manifestation of that which I speak of as Divine Purpose" (quoted in Epstein, p. 3). Therefore, Epstein argues, emergentism is not scientific.

He also points out that emergentism is not compatible with agent-based modeling, considered by some as the primary methodological tool of complexity theory. He puts it thusly:

> Classical emergentism holds that the parts (the microspecification) cannot explain the whole (the macrostructure), while to the agent-based modeler, it is precisely the generative sufficiency of the parts (the microspecification) that constitutes the whole's explanation! In this particular sense, *agent-based modeling is reductionist.* Classical emergentism seeks to preserve a "mystery gap" between micro and macro; agent-based modeling seeks to demystify this alleged gap by identifying microspecifications that are sufficient to generate—robustly and replicably—the macro (whole). [emphasis added] (p. 37)

Is there really a "mystery gap" in the concepts of emergence and irreducibility? Does irreducibility necessarily mean that natural systems, at least some of them, are unexplainable and therefore they should be the products of a divine purpose and intervention? These are, of course, philosophical questions. Some complexity theorists answer them directly or indirectly. Kauffman (1995), for example, says that "fundamental holism and emergence are not at all mysterious" (p. 24). According to Sawyer (2005), emergentism does not have to be deistic. In his view, the emergentism of most sociologists, particularly that of who founded the discipline, is nonreductive and ontologically materialistic (p. 29). He calls this understanding "nonreductive materialism" (p. 65). In this view both the macro- and micro-level properties are real; one is not an epiphenomenon of the other. There are micro–macro–micro transformations, but each level maintains its separate existence.

But then, one might ask, (how) do macro and micro levels maintain their separate existences while interacting with each other? Holland (1998) proposes an answer. He first recognizes the separation of micro and macro levels: Because the whole is not a simple sum of its parts, the "regularities in a system's behavior . . . are not revealed by direct inspection of the laws satisfied by the components" (p. 225). In other words, persistent macro patterns obey macro laws, and they "do not make direct reference to the underlying generators and constraints" (p. 239). Then he addresses the question, whether or not the properties of a system cannot be reduced at all to those of its components. Holland suggests that "we *can* reduce the behavior of the whole to the lawful behavior of its parts, *if* we take the non-linear interactions into account" [emphasis in original] (p. 122). Reduction is possible in science; after all it has worked for centuries. But he offers a different version of reduction.

> The laws of chemistry are indeed *constrained* by the laws of physics and, in this sense chemistry is reducible to physics. . . . [But, on the other hand,] [t]he macrolaws that govern the interactions of molecules are formulated and used without reference to the laws of particle physics. [emphasis added] (p. 245)

It can be concluded from Holland's conceptualization that the lower-level laws still do apply at a higher level, but only as constraints. For example, if we want to understand social phenomena, we cannot reduce it completely to biological laws, but biology will be a constraint in human social behavior. The fact that human beings biologically need to consume food works as a constraint: We cannot ignore an individual's biological urge to eat. Food is a crucial component of social and economic life. We cannot imagine a social system in which food does not play any role. It logically follows, and is empirically observable, that societies have developed mechanisms and rules of food production and distribution because of this fundamental biological need. But this does not explain how food is produced, distributed, and consumed in a particular society in a particular time period. It does not explain, for example, why the producers of certain food crops—for example, corn—are subsidized in the US, whereas others are not. We need different—historical and more complex—explanations for them, such as the corn farmers have a strong political influence on the US government.

Another answer to the question, "(how) do macro and micro levels maintain their separate existences while interacting with each other?" can be found in complexity and network theorists' works on the mechanisms of emergence, which I summarized in the previous section. If the mechanisms of emergence are identified, then they can be used to trace back the sources of emergent properties. Could this be considered a form of reduction—explaining systemic properties in terms of individual properties? My short answer is not a reduction in the sense of an additive aggregationist sense of the term., which is that a society, or an economy, is a mere sum of the activities of utility-maximizing and rational individuals. One can still maintain the differences between the properties of social systems and individuals, or between macro- and micro-level properties in general, and try to find the connections between them. After all, there are examples in nature like the distinct properties of water molecules than those of hydrogen and oxygen atoms and the distinct properties of life than those of organic molecules.

But we should take seriously Epstein's reminder that we may create a "mystery gap" between individual actions and systemic properties and behaviors by using the concept of irreducibility, particularly when we do so in explaining social phenomena. Whether "the social" has a distinct level of existence from "the individual" is an unresolved issue. I cannot offer a definitive resolution, but I continue the discussion with the topic of "downward causation" next and then propose Giddens' theory of structuration as a possible resolution.

DOWNWARD CAUSATION

Downward causation, or *social causation*, is a core concept in sociological theory and has direct implications for a complexity theory of public policy. S. Mitchell (2009) notes that the term downward causation was coined by the noted social science methodologist Donald Campbell, and it refers to the "causal efficacy of emergent properties" (p. 123). In Mitchell's words, downward causation refers to how "[t]he higher level properties that naturally emerge . . . place constraints on the behavior of their constituent parts" (p. 33).

Downward causation is relevant to public policy theory, because it is about whether, to what extent, and how the macro properties of policy systems affect the actions of policy actors. We can put the question as follows: How do social rules established by governmental acts, such as legislation, ordinances, executive orders, etc., affect the beliefs/values and/or behaviors of individuals?

There is a specific conceptual problem in conceptualizing downward causation. This may be called the *constraint versus internalization problem*. For instance, does the governmental rule "do not discriminate against minorities in employment decisions" influence individual behaviors merely as a *constraint*, or does it influence such behaviors because it is *internalized* by individuals and becomes part of the belief systems and values systems? Arguably such rules can influence individual behaviors as constraints, because if they are not obeyed, punitive actions can be taken against the violator. A discriminating human resource manager may be removed from his/her job, for example. That much is obvious. A more important issue is this: Are macro-level rules internalized by individuals and thus they become his or her own "values"? In other words, do macro-level properties causally affect the behaviors of individuals through influencing their values?

Another example of the problem would be how macro-level rules such as social/cultural norms affect individual behaviors? Some social norms are enforced by laws. For example, stealing is both a culturally unacceptable behavior—with the possible exceptions societies may make for special conditions—and penalized by law enforcement. Others are not enforced by law, but they still can influence individual behaviors. In many human societies, respecting the elders is a social norm. Do people respect the elders because they have internalized this norm—this has become part of their belief/value systems—or are they afraid to be ostracized, or frowned upon, if they do not do so?

The answer may be both. Or, it may be that some individuals may have internalized the norm, while others obey it out of the fear that they would be ostracized if they did not do so. It is not my goal to propose universal answers to the constraints versus internalization problem, but I want to highlight its significance for public policy theory.

Utility-Maximizing Rational Actors

The significance of the problem for public policy theory can be illustrated best with the example of rational choice theory's notion of *utility-maximizing rational actors*. These utility-maximizing rational actors do not have any histories or cultural affiliations that would affect their beliefs/ values the way they make their decisions or their behaviors, according to rational choice theory. In other words, there is no downward causation in rational choice.

There is a pair of core assumptions in neoclassical economics/rational choice theory. First, economic, political, and bureaucratic actors are uniformly self-interested. Second, the tastes and preferences of the actors are fixed in the sense that the specific social or historical conditions in which they exist do not have any influence on their preferences and behaviors. [10] In rational choice proponent MacDonald's (2003) words, they decide and behave as "preconstituted actors": "[It] is the purposive, intentional, self-propelled behavior of individuals that aggregate into outcomes; structures neither constitute this behavior nor constitute the actors" (p. 558).

The assumption that individuals are utility-maximizing rational actors has been criticized from different angles. Behavioral and cognitive psychologists critiqued it by pointing to the behavioral and cognitive biases and predispositions in the human cognitive processes.[11] Simon's (1979) theory of "intended and bounded rationality" is the most well-known critique and revision of the utility maximization assumption. The gist of his critique is that individuals cannot be rational entirely because of their cognitive limitations. Simon stresses that these cognitive limitations are not "imperfections"; they are actually "ineradicable." Rationality, in other words, is inherently bounded.

An increasing number of rational choice theorists (e.g., Ostrom, 2005) have adopted Simon's notion of bounded rationality. These theorists do not give up entirely on the utility maximization assumption, however. There is a tension on this issue in institutional rational choice theorist Elinor Ostrom's writings, for example. On the one hand, she stresses that the bounded rationality assumption should be substituted for the "extreme assumptions such as unlimited computational capability and full maximization of net benefits" (1999, p. 45), that the results of her and her colleagues' research are consistent with the assumption of bounded rationality (2005, p. 118), and that individuals may behave in ways that do not fit into the rational egoist model (2005, p. 113). On the other hand, she emphasizes that she used and will continue to use the basic assumptions of rational choice theory (p. 99) and that she found those assumption as "useful starting points" for her analyses (p. 103).

Ostrom (2005) acknowledges that the messiness of reality forces theorists to modify the assumptions of rational choice (p. 103) and points out that because of the different mental models individuals use, various feedbacks they receive from the world, their shared culture, and the emotional states they are in, their behaviors are more complex and context dependent than these assumptions suggests (pp. 105, 112, 119). The "attributes of a particular community" (i.e., culture) and institutional structures constitute the context in which complex individuals make their decisions and act, according to Ostrom (1990, pp. 57–58; 2005, passim). But this context is external to individual actors. They are only "external inducements for action" (Ostrom and Parks, 1999, p. 292). In other words, they do not shape individual preferences or values. Individuals do not internalize them. The relationship between an individual actor and an institution may be one of mutual influence, according to Ostrom and Parks, but even then the two are external to each other.

Ostrom's conceptualization is consistent with Simon's (1986), who also stresses the role of social context in human decision making. He says the rationality of a certain behavior can be judged only in the context of its premises, or "givens," which include its social situation, the goals of the decision maker, and the computational means available to him/her. This description suggests that in his view these social factors are external to the decision maker. In other words, in the bounded rationality view individuals do not internalize society.

All in all, rational choice theorists either completely ignore the possibility of downward causation or, as in the case of Ostom, acknowledge it and adopt the view that macro properties, or social structures, affect micro behaviors only as constraints and external inducements.

Complexity Theory on Rational Actors and Downward Causation

What are complexity theorists' views on the rational actor assumption of rational choice and on downward causation? Are there unified or common views on these issues among complexity theorists? The short answer is no, but one can discern some patterns in the conceptualizations by complexity theorists.

The rational actor assumption of rational choice has been adopted by many complexity researchers, particularly those who use agent-based simulations as their primary methodological tool. These researchers accept Simon's notion of bounded rationality concept in general terms, but they modify it by suggesting that agents are heterogeneous, adaptive, and interactive as well (e.g., Holland, 1995; Axelrod, 1997; Cohen, Riolo, and Axelrod, 2001; Epstein, 2006; Bednar and Page, 2007; Miller and Page, 2007).

Like Simon, most complexity theorists critique the pure and complete rationality assumption. According to Epstein (2006), complexity theory undermines the complete rationality assumption, because it shows that "optimization is computationally intractable" and, even if it were, the cost of computing it would be so large that such an attempt would be overwhelmed by the cost (p. 26). Therefore, according to Epstein, the agents in simulations are best conceptualized as bounded rational (p. 27).

Epstein, together with other complexity theorists, such as Holland (1995), Axelrod (1997), and Miller and Page (2007), add that these agents are also heterogeneous and adaptive. Their motivations and behaviors are not all the same or fixed, contrary to what rational choice theory assumes. Holland points out that each agent has its "internal model," or "schema," which helps it anticipate future events and thus guide their actions (pp. 31–34). The internal models of agents are different from each other. Miller and Page stress that agents learn from their experiences, use "nonlinear algorithms to recognize key opportunities for action," and adapt their actions accordingly (p. 180). These characterizations do not contrast with Ostrom's conceptualizations. Ostrom (2005) acknowledges that individual actors have different mental models (p. 105), that their motivations are learned and developed over time (p. 132), and that they are adaptive (p. 137).

Downward causation can be inferred from the recognition that actors are heterogeneous and adaptive: Because they are different and because they adapt differently, these differences may be influenced by some macro-level structures. Axelrod (1997); Cohen, Riolo, and Axelrod (2001); and Bednar and Page (2007) applied the concept of downward causation in their simulations. I will discuss these applications in Chapter 10.

There is a paucity of theoretical discussions on downward causation among complexity theorists. Sawyer (2005) is among the few exceptions. I will discuss his views, in contrast to Giddens', in the next section. It is worth noting here that he stresses that downward causation means individuals "*contain representations* of the emergent macropatterns" (p. 26). In other words, the question is not how macro patterns constrain micro properties, but it is how they are internalized by individuals. This explicit emphasis on the internalization of macro patterns is missing in other complexity theorists' conceptualization of downward causation.

In his theory of social systems, Luhmann (1995) takes the concept of downward causation one step further. In his view it is not that individuals internalize macro- (system level-) properties. Instead, individuals are *subsystems* of social systems, and as such their behaviors are completely determined by the system. Individuals do not even have independent ontological existence. They are constituted by their social systems. In his words, "the element is constituted as a unity only by the system that enlists it as an element to use it in relations" (p. 22). In the debate on whether a the unity of an elements emerges from below or constituted from above, he says, he opts "decisively for the latter" (p. 22). "Elements are elements only for the system that employs them as units and they are such only through this system" (p. 22). One might argue that Luhmann's view goes beyond the original conceptualization of downward causation: "causal efficacy of emergent properties" (Campbell, as cited in S. Mitchell, 2009, p. 123). I think his theory is an important perspective on how the causal processes from the macro to the micro levels work. I will discuss Luhmann in more detail in next chapter.

STRUCTURATION

Complexity theorist Simon Levin (2009) observes that the process of emergence is a full circle in both ecological and social systems: Macro patterns "emerge from the collective actions of individuals, and feed back to influence those behaviors" (p. 143). Anthony Giddens (1984) provides a framework for understanding this full circle of emerge in social systems: from the emergence of macro structures to downward causation.[12] In this section I want to show how.

The gist of Giddens' theory can be summarized as follows. The reproduced *actions of intentional and knowledgeable actors* constitute *social systems*, which exhibit *structural properties*. Social systems are created and reproduced through the practices of actors and structures are "recursively organized sets of rules and resources" (p. 25). As such structures do not exist independently of actors; a structure exists "only in its instantiations in such practices and memory traces orienting the knowledge of human agents" (p. 17). Social systems are created and reproduced through social practices, but this is not a one-way relationship; it is rather a structuration process in which structural properties of systems in turn enable or constrict the future behaviors of actors (p. 25).

The importance and implications of Giddens' theory for conceptualizing the full circle of emergence can be understood better in Sawyer's (2005) critique of it. Sawyer's arguments are important particularly because he associates emergence closely with structural sociology and attempts to show that Giddens' theory is incompatible with both structural sociology and the notion of emergence. Whether Giddens' theory in general is incompatible with structural sociology is beyond the scope of this book, but I will elaborate on Giddens' compatibility with the notion of emergence.

Sawyer criticizes Giddens for his idea that structures exist only in the practices and memories of human beings. This way, according to Sawyer, Giddens ends up rejecting the independent existence of social structures all together. Structural sociologists like Durkheim attribute an ontological status to "social structures" in the sense that structures have existence that are independent of the individuals who populate a particular geography. Then social structures should be conceptualized with a theory that aims to explain macro patterns separately, not in relation to the behaviors of agents. Giddens, on the other hand, conceptually closes this micro–macro gap with his two propositions: that reproduced *actions of intentional and knowledgeable actors* constitute *social systems*, which exhibit *structural properties*, and that structures do not exist independently of actors. This is not only an outright rejection of structural sociology, according to Sawyer, but it also a denial of the notion of emergence.

To better understand Sawyer's concerns, we need to look more closely into Giddens' theory. He defines the domain of the social sciences as *social practices ordered across space and time*. Social systems are created and reproduced through these practices, but this is not a one-way relationship. It is a structuration process in which structural properties of systems emerge from the behaviors of actors and in turn the structural properties enable or constrain the future behaviors of actors. He puts it thusly:

> Analyzing the structuration of social systems means studying the modes in which such systems, grounded in the *knowledgeable activities of situated actors* who draw upon rules and resources in the diversity of action contexts, are produced and reproduced in interaction. Crucial to the idea of structuration is the theorem of the *duality of structure*. . . . The constitution of the agents and structures are not two independently given sets of phenomena, a dualism, but represents a duality. . . . [T]he *structural properties of social systems are both medium and outcome of the practices they recursively organize*. Structure is not "external" to individuals. . . . Structure is not to be equated with constraint but is always both constraining and enabling. [emphasis added] (p. 25)

Sawyer objects to Giddens' theory on three grounds. First, it ignores the fact that social structures can emerge from the actions of unknowledgeable actors. Second, it denies irreducibility, which is a basic tenet of the notion of emergence. Third, it denies downward causation, which is also a basic tenet of the notion.

Emergence of Social Structures

Sawyer takes issue with the notion that the structural properties of social systems are constituted by knowledgeable activities of actors. He argues that actors do not have to be knowledgeable about their environments or systemic processes at all for structural properties to emerge. Sawyer cites multiple agent-based simulations to back up his argument (p. 148).

In agent-based simulations researchers use two kinds of agents: "cognitive agents" and "reactive agents." Cognitive agents are intentional and deliberative agents who have beliefs about their environments, their actions, and their impacts. These are like Giddens' knowledgeable actors. Reactive agents" do not have any internal representation of the world. In various simulations researchers demonstrated that structures emerged from the activities of reactive agents. Sawyer points out that the findings of these simulations refute Giddens' claim that social structures cannot exist without knowledgeable and conscious actors: "Objective structures can emerge, and the existence of those structures can 'constrain' individual agents (via changes in patterns of local interactions) even when agents have no internal representations" (p. 161).

Indeed, agent-based simulations do show that structures can emerge even when agents are not cognizant of the emergence process or the emergent structure (see Chapter 10). The problem is that regardless of what these simulations show, real human beings are not reactive agents. They are not dumb machines or simple robots. They are more like cognitive agents, who are intentional and deliberative and have beliefs about their environments, their actions, and their impacts. So the results of simulations with reactive agents do not tell us much about the real mechanisms in human societies. I will come back to this issue of cognitive versus reactive agents in the next chapter.

Irreducibility

Giddens' (1984) concept of duality of structure dissolves the distinction between agents and structures: "The constitution of the agents and structures are not two independently given sets of phenomena, a dualism, but represents a duality" (p. 25). This is an outright rejection of the independent existence of social structures, which is the conceptual basis of sociology as a separate discipline, and a denial of the irreducibility of emergent social structures, according to Sawyer.

Giddens' position on this issue can be seen in his critique of Durkheim, one of the founding fathers of sociology (pp. 171–174). In his explanation of the emergent properties of social structures, Durkheim gives the example of the emergent properties of bronze. Bronze is made of copper and tin, but it does not have their properties. Once these malleable components are mixed, hardness arises as the emergent property of bronze. Durkheim likens the properties of a society to those of bronze: once emerged, they are not like the properties of individuals. Giddens argues that this analogy is false, because individuals never existed in a state of nature (they were never "untainted by association with others"). The individual and the society cannot be separated as bronze and tin and copper can. He also posits that society cannot be external to the individual the same way natural environment is. We cannot speak of the givenness, or facticity, of society in the same way as the givenness, or facticity, of nature. Giddens critiques structural sociology and contrasts it with his structuration theory as follows:

> [In structural sociology] [t]he structural properties of social systems ... are like the wall of a room from which an individual cannot escape but inside which he or she is able to move around at whim. Structuration theory replaces this view with one which holds that structure is implicated in that very "freedom of action" which treated as a residual and unexplicated category in the various forms of "structural sociology."(p. 174)

Sawyer sides with Durkheim and argues that society has a separate level of existence, like the walls of room that constrain individuals. He concedes that Giddens rightly emphasizes the role of individual subjectivities in a society (e.g., different perceptions of the existence of a wall) but argues that acknowledging an individual's subjectivity does not prevent us from accepting that "the emergent social fact is independent of any individual's internalization of it or subjective orientation toward it" (p. 110).

Sawyer's position is not the common position among complexity theorists on the issues of the separate existence of social structures and irreducibility. I mentioned earlier in this chapter that Epstein and Holland raised issues with the "mystery gap" the concept of irreducibility creates. Giddens' conceptualization of duality of structures removes this mystery gap.

Downward Causation

How do social structures affect individuals? Do they function like the walls of a room, to use Giddens' analogy? Sawyer notes that macrosociologists answer to this question by saying that "the individual deterministically internalizes society" (p. 142). Sawyer finds this an extreme position; society should not have such deterministic influence of individuals. He calls Giddens' duality of structure conceptualization the "other extreme."

Whether his position is extreme or not, Giddens indeed challenges the notion that social structures exist independently and they deterministically constraint individual actions on two grounds. First, he thinks that *structures not only constrain, but also enable actors' acts.* He gives the example of language to make his point: Language both constrains and enables individuals' thinking and actions (p. 170).

Giddens' second challenge is more important. He acknowledges that social structures can be constraining, but there is a considerable variation in the constraints on individual's behaviors. He defines three types of constraints: material constraints, (negative) sanctions, and structural constraints (pp. 174–179). Material constraints are imposed by the character of the material (physical and biological) world. Human beings cannot defy the laws of physics or stretch the limits of their biology. They cannot defy gravity and flap their arms and fly, for example. Negative sanctions are punitive responses to individual actions by authorized agents of a government (e.g., an arrest by a police officer) or by the representatives of social groups the individual belongs to (e.g., banishment by a leader of a religion). Negative sanctions involve application of power, either in the form of applying physical power or using the force of communally accepted authority. Structural constraints are different from negative sanctions in the sense that the former derives from the contextuality of an action, the characteristics of a given situation. Giddens cites Karl Marx's example of workers having no choice but to "sell their labors" to be able to earn their livings. The worker actually has only limited choices because of the fact that he does not possess a means of production—a factory, a business, equipment, etc. His only choices are to sell his labor to this employer or that one.

These three types of constraints are different not only in kind, but also in degree, according to Giddens. Material constraints are more constraining than sanctions or structural constraints. One cannot defy the law of gravity or grow wings so that one can fly. Negative sanctions and structural constraints are not constraining at the same degree as material constraints. It is not easy to escape the arrest by a police officer, but in some cases it may be possible to change the laws that one's arrest was based on; this way an arrest can be avoided the next time. If an individual is banished from a religious group, he/she may be able to join another group or live without joining one. Structural constraints may be extremely limiting under certain social and economic conditions, but those conditions may change or the individual may be able to change his/her status in the society. For example, it is very difficult to find any employment during a recession, but a worker may find a way to start his/her own business and thus free himself from the constraints of being a worker.

Giddens' term *span of time-space distanciation* can help us understand the different degrees of constrains social structures can impose. He posits that the greater the distanciation, the more resistant social structures are to change and they are more constraining for individuals (p. 171). In other words, those structural rules that are more distant, in terms of time and geography, to a particular individual will be more externally constraining to them. Those that are closer to the individual will be more internalized. This has implications for public policy in the sense that those structural rules that were made in a distant past or in a distant location will be more externally constraining to individuals. Many polls show that Americans find their local governments and the rules they make more acceptable, as opposed to the ones made by the federal government. This is an example of the space distanciation: Federal government is more distant to citizens than local governments. Giddens' concept of space-time distanciation also underscores the importance of participatory rule making. Conceivably, those rules that are made in a more participatory manner are internalized more, and they can be implemented more effectively and robustly. These implications of Giddens' concept are not sufficient to explain the entire policy process, but it can be helpful to understand it partly.

CHAPTER SUMMARY AND IMPLICATIONS FOR POLICY

In this chapter I summarized the issues in conceptualizing emergence, which is a crucial, but also problematic, concept in complexity theory. What it is and how it works are unsettled issues. Complexity theorists offer different conceptualizations of emergence. In this chapter I organized my discussion of emergence around three questions: (a) (How) Do macro-level properties emerge from micro-level properties/behaviors? (b) Once emerged, are these macro-level properties irreducible? (c) Once emerged, (how) do macro-level properties affect micro-level behaviors?

Complexity theorists' answer to the first question is, yes, indeed, macro-level structures emerge from the interactions at the micro level, from the applications of simple rules. Once they emerge, structural properties persist despite the changes at the micro level. Public policies, in this sense, are macro structures that emerge from the behaviors of individual actors. These behaviors do not have to be "rational" in any sense of the word for a complex system to emerge; no rational design is needed for the emergence of complex policy systems.

The most general implication of the emergence of complex policy systems is that there is no direct and linear causal link between governmental policy actions and outcomes. As Salzano (2008) puts it, the notion that there is a direct casual relation between policymakers' decisions and their outcomes is "in direct contrast with the complexity concept" (p. 186). Policies should be conceptualized, instead, as policy systems that come into being as consequences of the actions and relationships of multiple individual and collective actors. Governmental actors play important roles in policy systems, but they are among many whose actions influence policy outcomes.

Complexity theorists offer both conceptual tools, such as mechanisms of emergence, and methods of studying emergence processes, such as social network analyses, agent-based simulations, and case studies, which I will discuss in Chapter 10. They define four groups of factors and mechanisms: context, nonlinearity, persistence, and preferential attachment. They observe that the process of emergence is context dependent. Context-dependent interactions that lead to emergent outcomes are nonlinear. Holland (1998) defines differential persistence as the primary mechanism of the emergence of hierarchical organizations. Preferential attachment is the primary mechanism in the emergence of a specific kind of hierarchy: scale-free networks (Barabási and Albert, 1999).

The concepts of differential persistence and preferential attachment can be intuitively applied in understanding policy systems. I cited Ostrom's (2005) conceptualization of "constitutional rules" (e.g., articles of a national constitution) and "operational rules" (e.g., police guidelines for crowd control) as examples of "generalist" and "specialist" rules and noted that the former typically persist longer and contribute to the emergence of collective behaviors in a society, as Holland would predict. A certain policy actor may become more central—better connected and more influential—in a policy network because others may have prefer to "attach themselves" to him/her—engage in relations with him/her. They may prefer to attach themselves to him/her because of his/her persistence and longevity. It may also be the case that this actor has been preferred because he/she was more "fit" to begin with: He/she had the requisite skill set and assets to be useful to others in the policy network in which they operate. I suggested that these intuitive propositions can be empirically studied and tested. The methods of complexity I will discuss in Chapter 10 offer the tools that can be used in such studies.

Complexity theorists give different answers to my second question: Once emerged, are emergent properties irreducible? There is a general agreement among complexity theorists with the Aristotelian dictum "the whole is more than the sum of its parts." But when the question is formulated as "Is there a complete separation between the whole and the parts in the sense that the properties of the whole are completely detached from those of the parts and therefore the former are irreducible to the latter?" there are disagreements. Epstein (2006) raises deep reservations about the notion of irreducibility, because he argues that it creates a "mystery gap"; as such it is not scientific. Holland (1998) suggests that reduction is actually possible if nonlinear interactions are taken into account. He offers a special conceptualization of reduction: Lower-level laws still do apply at a higher level, but only as constraints.

The deep philosophical and methodological problems Epstein and Holland bring up to our attention apply to policy systems as well, but they have not been addressed directly. Policy theorists do not ask questions like "do structural properties of public policy systems have a separate level of existence from the properties, activities, and relationships of policy actors?" However, there are those who study macro-level properties as if they were separate from the properties, activities, and relationships of policy actors. The large-n comparative studies (Blomquist, 2007), punctuated equilibrium theory (True, Jones, and Baumgartner, 2007), and dynamic system simulations (Chapter 8 of this book) are examples of this approach.

The debates on the possibility of irreducibility have implications for the third question: Once emerged, (how) do macro-level properties affect micro-level behaviors? This is the issue of downward causation, or social causation: the manner in which systemic properties affect those of individuals. The question in the context of policy processes is, whether or to what extent do the macro properties of policy systems affect the actions of policy actors? Downward causation is a potentially useful concept, but partly because of the lack of clarity in its definitions and partly because of the methodological challenges it poses; there are not many applications of it in the complexity theory literature.

In this chapter I argued that downward causation is a relevant concept for public policy, although it is rarely recognized as such. Downward causation is not an issue for rational choice theorists, because they assume that all individuals are "preconstituted" utility-maximizing rational actors: They do not have any histories or cultural affiliations that would affect their belief/values, the way they make their decisions, or their behaviors. Complexity theorists do not pay much attention to the problem of downward causation either, but, I think, they should. Downward causation is about how macro-level rules, such as legislation, ordinances, and executive orders affect the beliefs/values and behaviors of individuals. Are macro-level rules are internalized by individuals and become his or her own values? In other words, do macro-level properties have causal effects on micro-level beliefs/value and behaviors. If yes, how?

I propose that the biggest challenge in policy studies is in understanding the micro–macro relationships and transformations. It is not reasonable to assume that emergent structural properties of policy systems are completely separate from those of individual actors. We can consider the separation between micro and macro levels in degrees. The following questions need to be answered conceptually and empirically in specific policy situations: To what are extent emergent properties external to individual actors? To what are extent emergent properties independent of the properties of individual actors? To what extent do they constrain or enable actors' behaviors? To what extent are social structures internalized by individuals?

I proposed Giddens' structuration theory as a framework that can help complexity theorists conceptualize the micro–macro transformations in policy processes. Giddens forces us to reformulate our understanding of emergence in a dynamic framework. Giddens states that reproduced *actions of intentional and knowledgeable actors* constitute *social systems*, which exhibit *structural properties*. These structural properties do not exist independently of actors but in their memories and knowledge. Systems are created and reproduced through social practices in a structuration process. In this process structural properties are both the media and outcomes of the practices they recursively organize. Structural properties both enable or constrain future behaviors of actors.

It remains a task for complexity and network theorists to articulate a synthesis of their and Giddens' theories. Klinj's (2001) and Zaheer and Soda's (2009) works are promising applications toward a synthesis. They illustrate how Giddens' theory can be applied in investigating policy and industry networks, respectively. Klijn cites Giddens to underscore the interrelationship between the stability (structure) and dynamism (process) of networks and the role of actors. Through their sustained interactions, actors create policy network structures: rules and resources that (will) have a structuring effect on future interactions in the network. Zaheer and Soda note that prior network structures both enable actors to create or recreate future structures and constrain their actions. Actors' purposive actions may form and dissolve network links and their experiences and knowledge of past network connections motivate and enable the actors to take such actions. Needless to say, much more work needs to be done in conceptualizing and empirically applying Giddens' theory in the context of complexity and network theories.

4 Self-Organization

Self-organization, like emergence, is a key concept in complexity theory, but its specifics are not all that clear or agreed upon among complexity theorists. One thing that is clear is that self-organization is a way of thinking. The term connotes, and is often used interchangeably with, spontaneity, endogeneity, and autonomy. And all these terms suggest that events and actions that take place in systems do not require external drivers, or a hierarchically superior force. They can happen for internal reasons, driven by the internal dynamics of systems. In contrast to the external cause–effect determinism of the Newtonian/positivist science (Morçöl, 2002, pp. 13–17), a self-organizational way of thinking is that systemic processes can fold back on themselves. In other words, the "causes' of systemic processes are within themselves.

A self-organizational way of thinking has historical and philosophical underpinnings and implications. It has close connections with the concept of emergence. In the previous chapter I cited self-organization as a group of mechanisms of emergence. In many conceptualizations in the literature, the authors do not make a distinction between emergence and self-organization at all. Self-organization is also considered a mechanism of systemic change, which I will discuss in the next chapter.

After summarizing the background and history of the concept of self-organization, I will address its different interpretations and the conceptual problems associated with it in this chapter. Then I will summarize and discuss its applications in organizational management, urban theories, and public policy.

A BRIEF HISTORY OF SELF-ORGANIZATIONAL THINKING

Knodt (1995) traces the roots of self-organizational thinking to the notion of teleology in ancient Greek philosophy. She notes that Aristotle's notion of "purposive finality of nature" was its beginning. Purposive finality is the idea that causes of events in nature exist in final purposes. In other words, things do not happen in response to external forces, but they are driven by internal and pre-given purposes.

This teleological thinking was later rejected by the Cartesian and New-tonian view of science (Morçöl, 2002, pp. 59–61). Descartes articulated analytical/reductionist thinking, which set the stage for Newton's grand synthesis of a philosophy of science that is still dominant in science today. In this Newtonian view the order of the universe could be understood by reducing observations to their essential elements and establishing the causal relations between them. In this view causes are external: Events are caused by other events, not by any internal final purposes in nature. Newton not only articulated the principles of external causality but also developed the experimental method that could be used to establish the causal relations.

Later, Immanuel Kant re-invigorated Aristotelian teleology and posited that organisms could be understood by understanding their "inner teleol-ogy" or "internal purposes" (Taylor, 2001, pp. 84–93). This was not appli-cable to physical objects and chemical compounds though. Kant argued that organisms, unlike machines, could self-organize and self-produce because of their inner teleology.

The Newtonian synthesis continued to hold sway after Kant. Auguste Comte, one of the founders of sociology, followed the Newtonian path. He suggested that social events could be explained, not teleologically, but as results of a coalescence of external forces. The logical positivists of the early 20th century further refined the Newtonian notion of causation by external forces and made this the core of their vision of scientific explanation. Carl Hempel, for example, posited that to establish a good causal explanation for an event, one has to demonstrate that there are "antecedent conditions" for it and that there is a logical and temporal connection between those conditions and the events.

Hempel's model, which is also known as the "covering law model," is commonly used in empirical studies today. In this model the correlations observed between the variations in an independent variable and a dependent variable is attributed to a causal relationship between the two variables: The independent variable is the cause and the dependent variable is the effect. This could be represented symbolically as follows: $X \rightarrow Y$, or $Y = kX$.

The notion of self-organization became popular again in the middle of the 20th century. In this period, concepts like "self-organization," "sponta-neous emergence," and the "emergence of order from noise" were refined and applied in general systems theory, cybernetic studies, mathematical models of neural networks, and the models of the nervous system (Capra, 1996, p. 22). During this time, the earlier teleological underpinnings of self-organization were dropped.

Take the example of the logistic equation I discussed in Chapter 1, par-ticularly its iterative version: $Y_{t+1} = kY_t - kY_t^2$. In this equation there is no independent or dependent variable; the output of the equation is fed back into the same variable (Y_t) over and over again. There is no teleology in this logistic equation in the Aristotelian or Kantian sense, because there is no final purpose in solving the equation. But there is an inner logic that regulates the input and output of the system. The system does not require an external intervention, an independent variable. The equation regulates itself.

The iterative solutions of the logistic equation illustrate both the potential of self-organizational thinking in understanding phenomena and the conceptual issues in it. The illustrations of the iterative solutions of the logistic equation in Chapter 1 indicate that complex patterns can emerge from simple rules, and there is no need for an external driver for them to emerge. The illustrations may also bring up questions: Was the equation not set up by an external designer? Who decides what k constant is going to be? So the process of solving the equation was not completely self-organizational, after all. As I will explain later in this chapter, there is no such thing as a complete self-organization anyway.

Complexity theorists' views of self-organization are not uniform. There are unresolved conceptual issues. I turn to these issues next.

ISSUES IN SELF-ORGANIZATION

Self-organization is an attractive concept. It is a way of thinking that vaguely connotes spontaneity, endogeneity, and autonomy, as I mentioned earlier. There are multiple conceptual issues complexity theorists deal with in making this concept operational. In this section I bring up these issues and summarize the thinking on them in the complexity theory literature. One of the big issues is the relation between self-organizing systems and their environments. Another one is the level of self-organization: Does it happen at the system level, the level of its components, or both? A more specific issue is the nature of the components: agents. Are they self-organizational? Another issue is this: Are there mechanisms and preconditions of self-organization in systems? I leave the thorniest conceptual issue to last: What is "self" in self-organization anyway? Complexity thinking is more advanced and articulate on some of these issues, as the following summaries and the discussions in the following sections in this chapter will show, but more work remains to be done on all of them.

Self-Organizing System and Environment

What is the *relationship between a* self-organizing system and its environment? Self-organization does not necessarily mean that an internal mechanism or process works in a completely closed, isolated system. I addressed the issue of open and closed systems in Chapter 2 and said that the openness and closedness of a particular system is a matter of degree. Then, the issue is to what extent a system is closed to its environment and to what extent it is self-organizational.

According to Cilliers (1998), "The capacity of self-organization is a property of complex systems which enables them to develop or change internal structure spontaneously and adaptively in order to cope with, or manipulate, their environment" (p. 90). He goes on to point out that a self-organizing system is neither active nor passive in its relations with its environment. It reacts to it environment but also transforms itself as a result and also affects the environment. (p. 108). "Self-organization is a self-transforming process; the system acts upon itself" (p. 108). So, in his view, complex systems reorganize their internal structures in order to adapt to their environments.

In Chapter 2 I argued that adaptation was a problematic concept because it could mean that a system adapts to fit, conform to, or accommodate its environment in response to external stimuli and that this is a one-way relationship between the environment and the system. I argued that these were not realistic assumptions. Cilliers' description of self-organizational adaptation is obviously more sophisticated than the concept of adaptation I criticized in Chapter 2. He suggests that the system adapts "to cope with" its environment. So is this a one-way relationship? He suggests that the system's internal dynamics work in their own way, not in direct, one-to-one, reaction to the stimuli from the environment. So there is some autonomy; it is not just a simple reaction to the stimuli from the environment. Also, he notes, the system self-organizes to "manipulate" its environment. So the relationship is not one way; the system can have, or at least tries to have, some effects on its environment. Niklas Luhmann's interpretation of autopoiesis theory for social systems, which I discuss later in this chapter, echoes this two-way conceptualization of self-organization and takes it to a particular direction.

Cilliers' description brings up two issues that complexity theorists deal with conceptually and empirically in their studies: (a) To what extent is a system open or sensitive to external stimuli/forces? In other words, to what extent can it be closed to them? (b) Does the system or its environment have the upper hand in their relations? In other words, which one is more accommodating in this relationship? There are no final, or common, answers to these questions. From my perspective, these are open questions. Instead of trying to find a final answer to them, we should empirically investigate to what extent a particular system is open or closed to external stimuli under different conditions and to what extent the system influences its environment.

Levels of Self-Organization

Another issue in the conceptualizations of self-organization is the level of self-organization. Does the system as a whole self-organize? Are there also subsystem level self-organizational processes? If self-organization takes place at both the system and subsystem levels, what is the nature of the relationships between the two levels (or perhaps among even more levels)? The reader will recognize that these questions, particularly the last one, are about the micro–macro relationships I discussed in Chapter 3. The question was this: If both policy systems and agents have self-organizational capabilities, then how do these levels affect each other? Complexity theorists do address these questions in general terms, but there is no framework they commonly use.

In his characterization of self-organization, Cilliers (1998, pp. 91–95) asserts that self-organization is an emergent property of the system as a whole. In his view self-organization is a process in which a structure emerges through the activity of initially undifferentiated "large number of microscopic elements" (p. 94). Thus, in his conceptualization, self-organizational processes take place between the micro and macro levels of a system.

If self-organization involves both the micro and macro levels, then how does it happen at both levels and between them? Many questions can stem from this question. I will address three questions/areas of conceptualization complexity theorists have worked on: self-organization at the micro (agent) level in social systems, preconditions and mechanisms of self-organization, and directions of self-organization.

Self-Organizing Agents

Socials systems, including policy/governance systems, are composed of, or constituted by the practices of, individual and organizational actors. When we say that self-organization occurs at both the micro and macro levels, do we mean that these actors are self-organizational? Teisman, van Buuren, and Gerrits think so. In their book on managing complex governance systems, they state: "Self-organization is the reflexive capacity of actors and (sub)systems who are able to receive, encode, transform and store information and use this to consider actions." (2009a, p. 9). This implies that the self-organizational capacities of actors are directly linked to their having information-processing capabilities and reflective capacities.

This proposition needs to be refined and tested empirically. As I noted in the previous chapter, in the applications of agent-based simulations, there are two traditions: those simulations that use "reactive agents" or "behavioral agents," which do not have any internal representation of the world, and "cognitive agents," who are intentional and deliberative agents and have beliefs about their own actions and their environments. It has been shown empirically in agent-based simulations that artificial social structures emerge through self-organizational processes regardless of whether the agents were reactive or cognitive (Sawyer, 2005, p. 148). So, information processing and the reflective capacities of agents are not the preconditions for self-organization in systems. At least, agent-based simulations indicate that. Also, as I discuss in the next section, the theorists of complex natural systems show that self-organizational processes can be observed natural systems as well, which indicate that their inanimate components, which do not have any capacity to process information or reflect, can self-organize as well.

It is reasonable to assume that in real human societies agents have internal representations of their worlds and of the systems in which they participate. They do have worldviews that help them make sense of their worlds. They are cognitive agents in that sense. So Teisman and his colleagues' observation that information processing and reflexive actors have self-organizing capacities is quite relevant for social systems. There is an issue: What do we mean when we say agents have information-processing capacities? Should we consider, for example, how accurate and comprehensive their internal representations and decisions are when assessing their capacities? This, of course, brings us back to the issue I discussed in Chapter 3: To what extent are policy actors rational? As I mentioned there, many theorists of economic, political, and policy systems acknowledge that the rationality of human actors is limited, and they adopt Simon's notion of bounded rationality. But nobody suggest that actors are "reactive" in the sense that they do not have any internal representations or intelligence.

Then could the term reactive agent still be useful? Yes, if the cognitive and reactive agents are not conceptualized as two dichotomous categories, but as characterizations of different degrees of human agents' capacities to understand their systemic relations. In this conceptualization, the term "cognitive agent" or "knowledgeable actor" would not mean that an agent is fully knowledgeable of all of the environment and the social structures that emerge as a result of his/her behaviors, but different actors are knowledgeable at varying degrees. The concept of reactive agent could be used to mean that an agent does not have an accurate and complete representation of the social system in which he/she participates. Individuals do have internal representations of his/her worlds and the systems in which he/she participates. They do have worldviews that help them make sense of their worlds. They are cognitive agents in that sense. But the comprehensiveness and accuracy of their internal representations obviously vary. Then it would be an empirical question to what extent the actors in a particular policy system are cognitive and reactive.

Preconditions and Mechanisms of Self-Organization

Self-organization does not happen in a vacuum. Complexity theorists understand that there are variations in the capacities of systems and their components to self-organize, as the above discussion illustrates. Then what are conditions conducive to elements of a system to self-organize? Cilliers (1998, pp. 94–95) and Meadows (2008) address this issue at two different levels. Cilliers looks at the self-organization of micro units in the process of the emergence of macro patterns. Meadows highlights a mechanism of self-organization at the system (macro) level.

Cilliers provides a list of preconditions for self-organizations in neural networks. Initially neural network models were developed to simulate and understand the workings of the human brain. Later this modeling approach became the basis of developing artificial intelligence. True to their legacy in brain research, neural network models include "neurons" (nodes) connected by "synapses" (links). The researcher defines these neurons and synapses by assigning initial values to them and runs simulations to observe how they change over time. Researchers have shown using neural network models that macro patterns (structures) can emerge self-organizationally.

Cilliers stresses that for self-organizational processes to happen, there should be a series of conditions. The nodes should have *local information*—information about their immediate environments—but not global information—information about the systemic relations in which they are embedded. In terms of the reactive versus cognitive agent dichotomy, these nodes are closer to being reactive but do have some cognitive capabilities so that they can process information about their immediate environments. The *"memory of the system"* should be stored in a *distributed* fashion, meaning that each node should have some information about a part of the systemic relations it is in, but none should have the complete information about the system. There should also be *competition* and *cooperation* among the nodes, according to Cilliers, and their interactions should be *nonlinear*. One important precondition is *entrainment*, the ability of the nodes to synchronize their actions with each other. (I will discuss the synchronization issues in the next section.) Although no initial structure of the relations among the nodes is required, they should not be too homogenous or too much alike in the beginning. Small initial differences among them will be sufficient to "break the symmetries" in the system and lead to the emergence of complex macro patterns.

Whether or not and to what extent Cillers' preconditions are applicable to social systems, particularly policy systems, are open questions

Meadows points to the feedback loops in systems as the primary mechanisms of self-organization at the system level. Because of these loops, systems regulate themselves. To understand the function of feedback loops in self-organization, we should understand two key concepts in systems thinking: stock and flows. Systems, according to Meadows, are made up of *stocks*, and they change through the actions of *flows*. Stocks are the "elements of a system that you can see, feel, count, or measure at any given time" (p. 170). Examples are population of a species in an ecosystem, volume of water in a reservoir, or amount of money in a bank account. Stocks change over time through flows. Examples of flows would be births and deaths in the species, inflows and outflow of water, and deposits to and withdrawals from a bank account. Meadows points out "[A] stock . . . is the present memory of the history of changing flows within the system" (p. 18).

Systems display persistent behaviors, which are created by feedback loops. "A feedback loop is formed when changes in a stock affect the flows into or out of that same stock" (p. 25). In other words, a feedback loop is a "chain of causal connections from a stock . . . and back again through a flow to change the stock" (p. 27).

There are two kinds of feedback loops: negative and positive feedback loops. A negative feedback loop is the "balancing feedback loop," according to Meadows. They keep systems balanced and stable. An example of a negative feedback loop is regulating a room's temperature with a thermostat. The thermostat regulates the room's temperature by activating the heating or cooling system. Meadows notes that negative feedback loops may also be "goal seeking" in the sense that through negative loops a system's behavior tends toward a preset goal. Room thermostats are set at certain levels of temperature, for example.

Positive feedback loops are "reinforcing feedback loops" (p. 31). They have amplifying, self-multiplying, or snowballing effects. Positive feedback loops are among the sources of nonlinearities in systemic relations. An example is the growth in bank savings: A small incremental change in the interest rate can cause exponentially higher growth in the savings (p. 32). They can cause runaway growth in systems. In an economic system income growth stimulates higher inflation, which in turn stimulates income growth; for a while and to an extent, this may be healthy and desirable, but at one point this positive feedback loop can cause the behavior of the economic system to run out of control, and the system may crash.

In real-life systems, both negative and positive feedback loops operate together, Meadows points out. If negative feedback loops are predominant, a system will be more stable. If positive feedback loops are predominant, the exponential growth or decline in a system can create crashes and transformations from one set of systemic relations to another set of relations. In other words, these two kinds of feedback loops are the engines of self-organization and system dynamics. In Meadows' words, because of these loops "a system can cause its own behavior" (p. 34).

Complexity theorists Ilya Prigogoine and Stuart Kauffman describe specific forms of feedback mechanisms in physical, chemical, and biological systems. I discuss some of these mechanisms later in this chapter.

Direction of Self-Organization

One of the issues complexity theories discuss is the *direction of self-organizational processes*: Do self-organizational processes create *order* or *disorder*? A common view among complexity theorists is that self-organizational processes are the engines of the emergence of systemic properties, the evolution toward more and higher-level order. As Anderson (1999) puts it: " . . . complex systems exhibit 'self-organizing' behavior: starting in a random state, they usually evolve toward order instead of disorder" (p. 218).

In Prigogine's view (Prigogine and Stengers, 1984; Nicolis and Prigogine, 1989; Prigogine, 1996) the self-organizational process is actually more complex than what this description suggests: Systems spontaneously evolve toward "far from equilibrium" conditions under which either systemic properties break down—there is some disorderliness—or new systemic properties emerge. So, self-organization can create both orderliness and disorderliness.

What Is Self?

What is the "self" in self-organization? This is one of the most difficult questions to answer in understanding systems in general, and complexity theory in particular. A definition of self depends on the definition of a system.

As Fuchs (2002) puts it, in the social sciences theoretical discussions on self-organization and related concepts—endogeneity versus exogeneity, autonomy versus dependence—are all related to how systems are defined. This definitional issue has implications in the context of public policy. If we take local economic development as an example, a pertinent question would be how to define a "local economic development system" and then ask what is external and what is endogenous to this system. The question can be put thusly: Do "external governmental interventions" determine the level of economic development in a particular community, or is it an endogenous, self-organizational, process?

Fuchs would object to this dichotomous conceptualization. He points out that "the modern world is a global, networked one. . . . Only at the level of the world social system can causality be described as to a large extent endogenous" (p. 26) Therefore, we cannot demarcate policy systems clearly, nor can we say that certain factors or elements are completely endogenous (self-organizational), or exogenous, for a policy system. It is indeed difficult and problematic to demarcate social systems with clear boundaries, but does it mean that we should abandon the notions of self and self-organization together with it? Not necessarily. I take his observation as a call to use the terms self and self-organization more carefully.

How can self be defined? An approach one can take is that systems, and thus "selves," are defined in social construction processes. Fuchs (2002), Gerrits (2008), and Gerrits, Marks, and van Buuren (2009) all suggest that social systems are socially constructed. They are defined jointly by their participants and their observers, researchers. This social constructionist approach is insightful but not adequate. It is not adequate first because it may imply that social systems are merely the products of the conjectures of their participants and/or observers. It may also mean that a social system is merely an imaginary entity that exists in some people's minds.

I propose that we improve on the social constructionist view in two ways. First, we should bring in Giddens' (1984) conceptualization to the discussion. He posits that systems are not as mere conjectures but are "situated activities of human agents, reproduced across time and space" (p. 25). So, regardless of human agents' conjectures about themselves and their relationships, what matters more is that they engage in certain tangible activities that researchers can identify as social systems.

This activity-based definition of a system is adopted by Moreno and Ruiz-Mirazo (2007) in their discussion on the autonomy of systems. They state, "When the maintenance of a system is more a consequence of its own organizational dynamics than of the structure and conditions of its external environment it can be considered autonomous" (p. 66). Then they say that autonomy happens through "self-encapsulation": sharply differentiating the organization of the system—the set of relations that constitute it as a distinct unity—from the environment. Thus, through establishing a distinct set of relationships among themselves, a group of elements define a system, a self. Moreno and Ruiz-Mirazo note that the best example of this is the process of developing the membrane of a living cell. Through this act of self-encapsulation, a group of molecules become a cell.

We can think of social systems in a similar way: a group of human beings establishes a distinct set of relations among themselves and thus differentiate themselves as a system. A religious group, for example, differentiates itself though the routinized relations among its members, such as going to church, mosque, synagogue, or temple routinely and conducting ceremonial acts during their special religious days. By doing so, they establish a self, a group identity, for themselves.

There is a conceptual and empirical problem with Moreno and Ruiz-Mirazo's conceptualization: Human beings are not encapsulated in any particular physically distinguishable system, unlike organic molecules, which can get encapsulated within the membrane of a cell. Even when a person becomes an "element" (a member) in the system of a religious group by participating in the routinized relations among group members, he/she is not detached from his/her other relations. He/she participates in other routinized relations as well: relations with their family members, professional associations, political parties, and the like. This is why I argued in Chapter 2 that instead of using the term "system," it is better to use "systemness" and conceptualize systemic relations in terms of the degree of systemic integration. One person may belong to multiple systems at the same time and the degree of systemness of each depends on the degree of integration.

There is another issue Moreno and Ruiz-Mirazo's conceptualization reminds us: Did the molecules that self-encapsulated themselves into a cell know that they were doing that? Probably they did not, at least not in the sense we normally use the term "knowing" by intelligent beings. As I mention in the next section, complexity theorists show that in the natural world self-organization happens, and systems are formed, naturally (i.e., those natural elements know that they are forming a system. Neither intelligence, nor knowledge, is a precondition for self-organization.

SELF-ORGANIZATION IN NATURE

Why should we assume that for something to happen in nature something else has to cause it? The origin of this understanding is in the Newtonian scientific understanding of natural phenomena. Complexity theorists Ilya Prigogine, Stuart Kauffman, and Steven Strogatz counter this understanding, each in his own way.

Prigogine

Earlier in this chapter, I mentioned Ilya Prigogine's view that the self-organizational process is not merely a movement from disorder to order, but instead it is a dynamic process through which some systemic properties may break down and others emerge. Prigogine's view of self-organization is one of perpetual dynamism: Systems are born and transformed, and they dissolve so that other systems can be born. For all these to happen, no external forces are needed.

In Prigogine and Stengers' (1984) view, self-organization happens in open systems that operate at far-from-equilibrium conditions, and it is propelled by the nonlinear interconnectedness of the components of a system. Self-organizational processes create new structures and new modes of behavior for systems. They note that the Newtonian science makes the assumption that natural objects in their motions tend toward equilibrium. In fact, they argue, the tendency in nature is toward far-from-equilibrium conditions, under which systems are not stable and they are open to change. Systems do not need external causal factors to change; they are self-propelled to change. This self-organizational tendency does not mean, however, that they are closed systems. They change and evolve in interactions with their environments, and environments influence these systems. But the effects of the environment are not as they are conceptualized in the Newtonian view of the universe.

In Prigogine's (1996) view, being open to the environment and being self-organizational are not mutually exclusive. Neither are stability and adaptability of systems. He puts it thusly:

> Self-organizing systems allow adaptation to the prevailing environment, i.e., they react to changes in the environment with a thermodynamic response which makes the systems extraordinarily flexible and robust against perturbations from outside conditions (p. 71).

In his books Prigogine describes and explains specific nonlinear feedback mechanisms of self-organization in a variety of physical, chemical, and biological systems (Prigogine and Stengers, 1984; Nicolis and Prigogine, 1989; Prigogine, 1996). Most of these feedback mechanisms are specific to the contexts of physical, chemical, and biological processes, and they are not directly relevant to my discussions in this book. One of these mechanisms is autocatalysis, and it has broader applicability, as Kauffman illustrates.

Kauffman

Stuart Kauffman's (1995) view of self-organization has some similarities with Prigogone's, but Kauffman's is more specifically focused on biological systems. Kauffman draws on Darwin's theory of evolution but modifies it with a holistic understanding of self-organization. Unlike Darwin, Kauf-mann does not think that life emerged and biological organisms evolved accidentally. Life, according to Kauffman, is an "emergent, self-producing whole," and "it is able to reproduce itself and evolve" (p. 24).

In his interview for Waldrop's book (1992, p. 102), Kauffman says that both self-organization and random mutation are the mechanisms of bio-logical evolution. "We are not here as the result of divine intervention, or even space aliens." But evolution is not as accidental as Darwin's theory suggests. Darwin theorized that random mutation was the primary mech-anism of mutations in species. But he did not know that self-organization is a primary mechanism too. Self-organization, in Kauffman's words, is "matter's incessant attempts to organize itself into ever more complex structures, even in the face of the incessant forces of dissolution described by the second law of thermodynamics." The story of life, he points out, is "indeed the story of accident and happenstance. . . . But it is also the story of order: a kind of seep, inner creativity that is woven into the very fabric of nature" (p. 102).

The order in the biological world arises spontaneously because of the laws of complexity. He declares, "order raises spontaneously, order for free" (p. 75). The emergent biological whole may exhibit collective properties that are not readily explained by understanding the parts. The laws of the emergent whole should be understood in their own right (pp. vii–viii). The laws of complexity generate much of the order in the natural world; then natural selection comes into play, further molding and refining. In other words, life's patterns are generated by endogenous and natural processes, not caused by exogenous impacts. Kauffman's notion of endogeneity is not dualistic; it does not isolate a system from its environment. Like Prigogine, Kauffman views systems, particularly biological systems, as open to their environments. Differently from Prigogine, he suggests that biological sys-tems and their environments *coevolve*. Species live in the niches afforded by other species, he observes: "We all have made our worlds together for almost 4 billion years" (p. 73).

An important concept in Kauffman's conceptualization is the *threshold of complexity* or *edge of chaos*. This threshold is the point where systems are in an unstable, agitated state. This is where they self-organize through phase transitions. At this threshold, matter springs into life. This does not happen as an accident of random variation, but it is inherent in the very nature of life (p. 43). In other words, life emerges naturally, without an external intervention.

Kauffman cites *autocatalysis* as a primary mechanism of self-organi-zation in nature. Catalysts are molecules that speed up chemical reac-tions. They initiate a chemical reaction, but in the end they come out intact. Enzymes are examples of catalysts. Autocatalysis is a mechanism of "molecules speed[ing] up the very reactions by which they them-selves are formed" (p. 49). Kaufmann stresses that this is a catalytically closed—self-organizing—system, because it does not need an external input—for example, another molecule—to happen. A living organism is such an autocatalytic system, a "system of chemicals that has the capacity to catalyze its own reproduction" (p. 49). This "collective catalytic closure" is the secret of life, according to Kauffman (p. 48).

Nicolis and Prigogine (1989) note that autocatalysis is not only the primary mechanism of the emergence of life, but a more general chemical mechanism. Autocatalysis is based on the "seemingly exotic phenomenon" that "the presence of a product may enhance the rate of its own production" (p. 17). Actually the phenomenon is not exotic at all:

> [It] happens routinely in any combustion process, thanks to the presence of free radicals, those extremely reactive substances containing one unpaired electron, which by reacting other molecules give rise to further amounts of free radicals and thus to a self-accelerating process. In addition, *self-reproduction*, one of the most characteristic properties of life, is basically the result of an autocatalytic cycle in which the genetic materials are replicated by the intervention of specific proteins, themselves synthesized through the instructions contained in the genetic material. [emphasis in original] (pp. 17–18)

Kauffman (1995) proposes a model to show that mechanisms like autocatalysis are in the nature of things and that they can be reconstructed mathematically. He calls it the "NK model." He observes that when the number of complex molecules passes a certain threshold, "a collectively autocatalytic system snaps into existence. A living metabolism crystallizes" (p. 62). A key condition for the autocatalytic process is that a sufficiently diverse mix of molecules should accumulate. Then an autocatalytic system will emerge with certainty. The NK model shows how this happens.

A lengthy description and explanation of the NK model is beyond the scope of this book. I refer the reader to Kauffman's own books (1993, 1995) for that. I briefly illustrated the NK model as follows in an earlier work (Morçöl, 2002).

The N in the NK model represents the total number of elements, and the K represents the number of connections each element has with other elements. This can be illustrated with the example of 100 light bulbs (N) connected with each other via wiring. Each bulb may be connected to one other bulb (K = 1), three other bulbs (K = 3), or all other bulbs (K = 100). Kauffman shows that different combinations of Ns and Ks generate different behavioral regimes. The connected bulbs in my example would show different patterns of illumination, when the power is turned on. For instance, when K = 1, it is "steady-state regime"—like the straight line in the solution of the logistic equation with k = 2.3 in Figure 1.4a in Chapter 1. When N = K, the system displays chaotic behavior—as in the solution of the logistic equation with k = 3.7, Figure 1.4d. When K = 2, cyclical orderly behaviors emerge, and the magnitude of N determines the specific nature of this cyclical orderliness. These cyclically ordered behavioral systems are complex.[1]

With his NK model, Kauffman shows that right combinations of numbers can generate order through self-organization. In other words, self-organization and emergence of order are inevitable under right conditions. What kind of an order will emerge depends not only on the numbers but also the type of the connections between elements (Kauffmann, 1995, p. 81). In the bulb example, there was only type of relationships: turning the switch on and off uniformly. Certainly in biological and social system there are many types of connections, relationships, which make them highly complex.

Strogatz

Steven Strogatz (2003) describes another mechanism of self-organization in nature: "mutual cuing." He makes the observation that there is a tendency among the elements of a system to synchronize without an external control or direction. As an example of this phenomenon, he cites the studies that show that fireflies flash in unison, rhythm, and constant tempo. This does not happen through centralized planning or direction. Instead, he observes "In a congregation of flashing fireflies, everyone is continually sending and receiving signals, shifting the rhythms of others and being shifted by them in turn. Out of the hubbub, sync somehow emerges spontaneously" (p. 13). This synchronization occurs through "mutual cuing." It is the same mechanism with which the members of an orchestra can keep perfect time even without a conductor. He explains: "Each firefly contains an oscillator, a little metronome, whose timing adjusts automatically in response to the flashes of others" (p. 13).

Strogatz further argues that his and his colleagues' studies show that the phenomenon of synchronization is pervasive in nature. "For reasons we do not understand, the tendency to synchronize is one of the most pervasive drives in the universe, extending from atoms to animals, from people to planets" (p. 14). He cites examples of female coworkers spontaneously synchronizing their menstrual periods, sperms swimming in a synchronized manner, and millions of brain cells discharging in pathological lockstep and thus causing epileptic seizures, and the coherence of trillions of atoms pulsing together and thus creating laser beams.

LIMITS OF SELF-ORGANIZATION IN NATURE

From the above descriptions of Prigogine's, Kauffman's, and Strogatz's works, one should not draw the conclusion that self-organization is an endless process. Moreno and Ruiz-Mirazo (2007) reminds us that actually there are limits to self-organization. They point out that at the physical level of existence, systems cannot keep self-organizing toward more and more orderliness. They dissipate at certain points. This is because the self-organizational ability of a physical system depends on its external boundary conditions (p. 63).

They cite the example of hurricanes for this. Hurricanes cannot maintain themselves forever; they dissipate after a while. This is because they cannot control the material-energetic resources around them that are necessary to create complexity. To maintain their own structures, it is necessary for systems to have some capacity to change the processes and boundary conditions around them. Moreno and Ruiz-Mirazo call this "progressive take-over of the external conditions required for their viability" (p. 65). Systems should have the capability of actively restructuring/redefining themselves. To the extent that a system can restructures itself, it can overcome the perturbations that threaten its persistence (p. 64). Moreno and Ruiz-Mirazo stress that this can happen only at the chemical level, not at the physical level.

The question of whether and to what extent physical and chemical systems are capable of self-organizing is for scientists to determine. But two of Moreno and Ruiz-Mirazo's observations are important to highlight our understanding of social systems. First, self-organization does not always lead to more orderliness or a higher level of order; it may also lead to dissipation of systemic relations. This is valid for socials systems as well. Second, a system is capable of self-organizing, and self-producing, to the extent that it has the capacity to change the processes and boundary conditions around itself. Autopoiesis theory, which I discuss next, describes the processes and mechanisms of systemic self-production.

AUTOPOIESIS AND SELF-REFERENTIALITY

Autopoiesis theory deserves a separate discussion in this chapter, because the theory describes self-organization in a special manner.[2] Autopoiesis theory depicts autopoietic systems as self-referential and self-producing wholes. The Chilean biologists Humberto Maturana and Francisco Varela (1980) formulated autopoiesis theory to explain the nature of living systems. Later the theory was applied to social systems, most prominently by Niklas Luhmann (1995).

Maturana and Verala ask this question: What makes a living being, such as a cell, an autonomous living whole? Living beings continually exchange materials (food, water, air, and excretion) with their environments. Their molecular structures and cells are continually replaced by new ones. A living being is not the same in consecutive time periods, because of this constant replacement of its constituent molecules and cells. Then how does it keep its identity intact and its components together in a particular organizational form over time? The answer is in the self-referential and holistic nature of the production and reproduction of the components of living systems. Maturana and Varela (1980) define these living systems as follows:

> An autopoietic [system] is . . . organized (defined as a unity) as a network of processes of production (transformation and destruction) of components that produces the components which: (i) through their interactions and transformations continuously regenerate and realize the network of processes (relations) that produced them; and (ii) constitute [the system] as a concrete unity in the space in which they (the components) exist by specifying the topological domain of its realization as such a network. (pp. 78–79)[3]

Maturana and Varela note that autopoietic systems are autonomous systems (p. 81) and closed systems (p. 88).[4] They are autonomous and closed in the sense that these systems define their own *identities* and *boundaries*. Autopoietic systems, they argue, actively define and maintain their *identities* and keep it independent of the definitions by external observers. Autopoietic systems also define their own *physical boundaries* through their operations. They are different from "allopoietic systems," like cars or other mechanical machines, whose identities and boundaries are defined by outside independent agents.

Autopoietic systems are not isolated from their environments, however. They do change in response to their environments but on their own terms. The independent events in its environment can only "perturb" an autopoietic system. Once it is perturbed, the system undergoes internal changes to compensate for these perturbations. The system does not change its organization or structure following the instructions coming from its environment. To the contrary, it makes internal changes to maintain its unity, and, in doing so, it uses its self-image as the template.[5] In this sense an autopoietic organization is self-referential.

Maturana and Varela use the term "structural coupling" to describe the situations where an autopoietic system maintains its organization in congruence with it environment (pp. xx–xxi). To maintain congruence with the environment the system must be "plastic"—capable of changing its components and their relations accordingly. When the system and its environment are in congruence, they are structurally coupled. It is highly likely that the system's environment is composed of other autpoietic systems, such as other organisms. What happens when a system encounters other autopoietic systems that may be hostile to them? Then either the systems will find a way to be in congruence with them, or, if it cannot do that, the system may disintegrate.

Maturana and Varela's conceptualization of autopoietic systems is holistic and self-organizational. In their view, a biological organism should be understood as an autopoietic whole that does not need a central regulator. Nor is there a need for teleology or telenomy for autopoiteitic systems, according to Maturana and Varela. An autopoietic system can maintain its unity without having an overall ultimate purpose or without its components having a purpose guiding their actions (p. 86).

In his interpretation of autopoiesis theory, Mingers (1995) points out that each cell in an organism is an autonomous entity and that these autonomous components do not have the complete knowledge of their system. They cannot explain or describe the system. The components of the system can only have the local knowledge of their immediate environments and they can only respond to the actions of other components (pp. 10–11). The reader will recognize that this is similar to Cillers' description of self-organization in neural networks: Nodes have only local knowledge. Autopoiesis theory sides with the view that comprehensive knowledge of the system at the local level is not necessary for the system unity to be maintained. The system as a whole maintains its unity.

Autopoiesis and Social Systems

This autopoetic holistic view of systems has two important implications for social systems. The first implication is that social systems are self-organizational in a particular way: They are self-referential wholes that define their "selves" and maintain a *radical autonomy* against other systems in their environments. The second implication is that as they define themselves, social systems define the identities of their own components. This second one suggests that there is *strong downward causation* between a system and its components, for example, between a social system and individual actors (see Chapter 3). Both implications deserve serious consideration by students of policy systems. Are policy systems radically autonomous in the sense that they are self-referential? And, while maintaining their unities, do they shape the identities of their actors?

A few theorists applied autopoises theory or some of its components in their theories of social systems and governance networks. Its applicability to social systems has been a subject of controversy. Maturana (1980, pp. xxiv–xxx) himself thinks that it is possible to apply some aspects of the theory in the social domain, but only in a limited fashion. He points out that socials systems are composed of autopoietic systems, such as individuals are biological organisms, and this obviously has implications for the functioning of social systems, but social systems themselves are not physically or biologically produced or reproduced. Similarly, Varela argues that not all principles of autopoiesis theory are applicable to social systems, but the broader concept of "organizational closure" may be applicable (cited in Capra, 1996, p. 122).

Bob Jessop (1990) used autopoiesis theory in his interpretation of the "radical autonomy" of social systems. Autopoietic social systems define their own boundaries, develop their own codes, reproduce their own elements, and obey their own laws of motion, according to Jessop. These systems are not governed from outside or from a superordinate center, a government, for example. In Jessop's conceptualization, societies are networks of closed systems that coevolve.

Network theorist Rhodes (1997b, pp. xi, 3) observes that governance networks are centerless. There is no sovereign authority in such networks. Networks and their members are autonomous from the state, and they are not accountable to it. Schaap and van Twist (1997) also observe that governance networks are closed, and they are maintained partly through self-referential dominant frames of reference: network cultures, rules, and customs. These frames are used in shaping the networks by making selections in including or excluding new members and procedures.

Could governments be self-referential and self-producing as well? In Kickert's (1993) interpretation, autopoiesis theory means that governments reproduce themselves and that bureaucracies never die, regardless of the needs of the society or signals they receive from the society. Little (2000) points out that Kickert's interpretation has disturbing implications for democracy: If bureaucracies are self-referential and self-producing, they will not be responsive to citizens' needs, let alone being controlled by them through electoral mechanisms.

Niklas Luhmann's (1995) is the most comprehensive application of autopoiesis theory to social systems. Luhmann offers a solution to the problem Maturana and Varela posed: that social systems themselves are not physically or biologically produced or reproduced. Knodt (1995), who wrote the foreword to Luhmann's book, notes that he solved the problem by defining social system as systems whose elements are *communications*, not physical or biological entities. Communications are events that occur temporarily and vanish over time. As they come into and go out of existence, they reproduce the systems in which they are generated. In Knodt's own words, they "constitute emergent orders of temporalized complexity" (p. xxiii). According to Luhmann, the elements of communication are produced and reproduced in social systems autonomously from their environments. The meanings of communications are made and sustained within the social contexts of these systems. Because they are organizationally closed, a system of beliefs, explanations, and values is continually sustained through communications within these systems. It is not physical barriers, but these beliefs and values that bound social systems.

Social systems are self-referential, according to Luhmann. He defines self-referentiality as follows: "One can call a system self-referential if it itself constitutes the elements that compose it as functional unities and runs reference to this self-constitution through all the relations among these elements, continuously reproducing its self-constitution in this way" (p. 33). Self-referential systems are closed systems in the sense that "they allow no other forms of processing in their self-determination" (p. 34).

More specifically, systems define their identities and thus demarcate themselves self-referentially. Luhmann argues that how a social system defines itself matters more than how it is defined by its observers. He also posits that self-description of a system is what differentiates it from its environment. This is what he calls "self-referential closure" (p. 9). Through self-referential closure, a system defines its boundaries.

Boundaries are not simple demarcation points, according to Luhmann. Self-referential systems "constitute and maintain themselves by creating and maintaining a *difference* from their environment, and they use their boundaries to regulate this *difference*" [emphasis added] (p. 17). More specifically, self-referential systems differentiate the interdependencies inside and outside: "Using boundaries, systems can open and close at the same time, separating *internal interdependencies* from *system/environment interdependencies* and relating both to each other" [emphasis added] (p. 29).

This conceptualization can help us understand the boundaries of social systems. Once an individual becomes a member of a social system (e.g., a social club), he engages in some sort of interdependency relations with other members, but he/she does not suspend his/her interdependencies with non-members. The interdependencies within the system (among the club's members) and outside of it (with non-members) are different in kind. Luhmann stresses that this differentiation of interdependencies constitute a system's boundaries. He also stresses that boundaries do not close systems to their environments physically or in other ways; in fact, they cannot exist without their environments. The members of the social club do not cease their relations with others; they need to maintain these other relations. The system needs its members to maintain their "outside" relations, because without them the members and eventually the system cannot survive. The members need to be in relationships with their organizations of employment and their grocery stores to maintain their lives. Therefore, social systems need to be open to their environments. But they maintain their identities by differentiating the type of relations their members have inside and outside.

I will come back to Luhmann's interpretation of autopoisesis theory, particularly in understanding system dynamics, in the next chapter.

APPLICATIONS OF SELF-ORGANIZATION IN MANAGEMENT, PLANNING, AND POLICY

Self-organization is an intriguing and attractive concept. It has used by several theorists of management and policy. Some think of self-organization as a conceptual basis of the liberal-democratic and egalitarian ideals. In this perspective, self-organization connotes an egalitarian system of relations, a self-governing polity, participatory democracy, decentralization, and the like. But the discussions in this chapter so far has shown that self-organization is not necessarily compatible with some of these concepts and that its implications are broader. In this section, I review the literature on self-organization in management and policy. This literature shows that self-organization is not a straightforward process; it has multiple facets and forms.

Self-Organization and Management of Organizations

In its applications to the management of human organizations by Goldstein (1994), and Kiel (1994), and Stacey, Griffin, and Shaw (2000), self-organization is closely associated with decentralization, democracy, and participation. Stacey, Griffin, and Shaw argue that self-organizing interactions are the "transformative cause of emergent new directions in the development of an organization." This contrasts the dominant discourse on management, which attributes a central role to the manager in removing ambiguity and securing consensus in organizational processes (p. 123).

Goldstein (1994, pp. 33–52) interprets self-organization as another name for participatory and democratic management practices. He advises managers that they should give up on the notion that they can control their organizations centrally and they should let the underlings decide for themselves and organize to do tasks on their own volition. Managers should not be afraid of uncertainties that will be unleashed by letting employees decide and act for themselves. Uncertainty is inevitable. Also, letting employees self-organize unleashes their creativities and energies. He advises that managers create the space for nonlinear interactions, which will generate dynamism and uncertainty and help transform organizations in a positive manner.

Kiel's (1994, pp. 173–199) vision for a self-organizing government agency is similar to Goldstein's description of a self-organizing organization. Such an agency should maintain a "dynamic instability" to attain new forms of order and structure in an environment that is increasingly complex, according to Kiel. A self-organizing agency should be in constant renewal and receive feedback continuously from both internal and external sources. Its leaders should recognize instability and chaos as sources of creative renewal and act as "catalytic managers," rather than trying control their organizations authoritatively. They should not view change as a problem or resist it. They should not be seeking certainty and order all the time; instead they should be tolerant of uncertainty and they should be risk takers and able to discover new ways of problem solving. They should also strive to create a diverse work force; this is necessary to instigate fluctuations and instability that would eventually contribute to organizational renewal. The leaders should also bring the agency closer to their clients (e.g., parents at schools) and allow citizens to participate in the renewal of the agency.

The core messages in Goldstein's and Kiel's descriptions of existing practices of self-organization and prescriptions for the future are that managers should be not be afraid of uncertainties or letting their employees take their own initiatives and that planning for the future should be an ongoing and adaptive process. I should insert a note of caution here, however. Self-organizational processes do not necessarily lead to democracy, equality, and participation. Instead hierarchical organizational forms may emerge through self-organization as well, as I discussed in the previous chapter.

Self-Organization and Urban Planning

The idea that cities are self-organizing systems has a long history. As early as in the 1960s, self-organization, spontaneity, and organic growth were in the lexicon of urban theorists. Lewis Mumford (1961) found examples of spontaneous and organic economic and social processes in the cities of ancient Greece and medieval Europe.

There were those who theorized that urban systems were self-organizational, unpredictable, and uncontrollable and that their forms and functions resisted to external interventions, such as central planning. Jane Jacobs (1993) argued that modernist urban planning practices of her times were counterproductive because they were based on top-down designs and ignored the self-organizational capacities of cities.[6] Jay Forrester (1961, pp. 108–122) agreed with this from his system dynamics perspective. He observed that urban systems were mostly closed and self-organizational systems and that the multiple-loop alignments in them made them highly resistant to external interventions. There were certain points in urban systems that were highly sensitive to changes, but "corrective programs" that are aimed at these points may have unanticipated, even adverse, effects. Forrester cited the tax structure and zoning regulations in the US as examples of programs contributing to the degeneration in urban areas: Tax policies that favored the poor contributed to the urban decline, and zoning practices segregated economic activities and prevented interactions between them (p. 12).

Allen (1982) makes a similar observation about the unpredictability and uncontrollability of the future behaviors of self-organizing urban systems. He draws the conclusion that instead of attempting to design urban systems, urban planners should focus on describing how these systems "fold" and what types of structures emerge. Then they should facilitate these processes, rather than trying to control them. In his illustration of self-organizational dynamics in cities and metropolitan areas with system dynamics models, Allen (1997) shows that urban forms and dynamics emerge from the cross-catalyzation of the demand for skilled workforce and economic investment.

Portugali (2000) takes a similar approach to urban planning: Instead of adopting specific land-use plans, city planners and policymakers should adopt general planning principles and let urban agents plan for themselves. He calls this approach "parallel distributed planning." In this approach, private and public actors would engage in planning activities from which planning parameters emerge. All agents and agencies would plan by themselves. Each agent (individuals, families, planning agencies, etc.) would be a self-organizing system, but there would be interplays among them. In the bottom-up approach of parallel distributed planning, ideas would enter the process from the people. Planners would only provide information to the public, and there would be constant re-evaluation, updating, and re-interpretation of plans.

Buijs, van der Bol, Teisman and Byrne (2009) and Pel (2009) describe case studies of the specific processes self-organization in urban areas. These studies show that self-organization is a highly complex process.

For their case analyses of the evolution of the polycentric Randstad Holland metropolitan region in the Netherlands since the 1960s, Buijs and his colleagues developed and applied a conceptual framework of self-organization. This region is composed of multiple municipalities, including major cities like Amsterdam and Rotterdam. The issue is that the polycentric administrative organization—i.e., the self-organizational processes—in the region led to urban sprawl over decades. To curb this trend, the central government attempted to create structures to force or encourage local governments to collaborate in issues like land-use planning. These central measures met the resistance of people in these local communities because they were fearful of losing local control.

To illustrate the complex processes that took place in the region over five decades, Buijs and his colleagues first adopt Jantsch's (1980, 1981) "conservative" and "dissipative" forms of self-organization and then develop their subtypes for the Randstad Holland case. Conservative self-organization "comes down to the capacity of a system to govern itself and focuses on the self-referential character of the system" (p. 99). Buijs and his colleagues propose subtypes of conservative self-organization: "structure-oriented conservative organization," in which the organization restructures itself (e.g., a new regional governmental structure was created), "content-oriented conservative self-organization," in which a new leadership is created to carry out already determined plans. Dissipatively self-organizing systems, on the other hand, seek dynamic order and maintain themselves though continuous exchange with their environments. Dissipative self-organization has two subtypes as well: "structure-oriented dissipative self-organization," exemplified with the partnerships and alliances are formed among multiple organizations, and "content-oriented dissipative self-organization," which involves exchanging project ideas and developing joint programs among local governments.

Buijs and his colleagues' case study is interesting because it underscores two important aspect of self-organization. First, self-organization is not a generic process; it can have multiple types, shapes, and forms, and new concepts are needed to understand these multiple forms. Second, self-organization happens in broader contexts. Their case descriptions show that the self-organization of the local governments took place in the broader frameworks drawn by the central government.

The contextuality of self-organization is illustrated also in Pel's (2009) observations on the traffic management systems in the Netherlands. Pel notes that traffic management can be a highly centralized system: All traffic lights can be centrally controlled based on predetermined and fixed optimizing rules, such as what time each light will turn green or red. But it can also incorporate some elements of self-organization. For example, the "dynamic traffic management" systems let traffic lights self-organize to an extent. They set up some simple rules for each light (e.g., keep count of coming cars to a red light and when the number reaches a threshold, switch to green) and let each light make a decision based on that. The feedback mechanisms in the system regulate themselves. The system is not completely self-organizational however: Designers of the system set the parameters for switching the traffic lights. Pel calls this a "conservative self-reproduction" system. It is dynamic, but the rules set by the designers keep the overall system within certain boundaries.

Pel also makes the point that complete self-organization may be counterproductive. Using the example of the "open process design" (relying on citizen self-organization entirely) in a Dutch city, he demonstrates that the selective and self-referential perceptions of participants may lead to failures in these self-organizational schemes. Citing Luhman, Pel argues that there is a practical need for citizens to reduce complexity, and they use self-referential boundary judgments to demarcate themselves and their environments. When this happens, people perceive selectively and their perceptions differ from each other. They may not even be aware of each other's boundary judgments. Then they are bound to misunderstand each other. A traffic system requires coordination, but actors with different boundary judgments tend to fail coordinating their actions.

A few lessons can be drawn from all these observations made by urban scholars. First, urban systems are self-organizational; ignoring this and forcing to change them with central planning and policy interventions may be counterproductive. Second, self-organization is not a uniform process. There are different types of self-organization and the specific contexts of self-organizational process make differences. Third, self-organization is not a panacea when it comes to solving urban problems. Self-referential and selective perceptions of urban actors may lead to failures when they are left to self-organize.

Self-Organization and Policy Processes

Self-organization, self-regulation, and self-referentiality are popular concepts among policy and governance theorists. Even those who did not adopt complexity theory as their frameworks use these concepts (e.g., Ostrom, 1990, 2005; Rhodes, 1997a; Kettl, 2002; Koppenjan and Klijn, 2004; Agranoff, 2007). Then what would be the contribution of complexity theory to our understanding of self-organizing policy systems? This is the question I will address in this subsection.

Stewart and Ayres' (2001) conceptualization of public policy is the best expression of the complexity theory perspective. They posit that policy interventions should be viewed as *self-organizational* processes. A public policy is not a linear process that could be directed or controlled by a central authority, a government; instead it is a self-organizational process in which *self-conscious policy actors* play roles. Therefore, according to Stewart and Ayres, the aim of a policy intervention should not be to reach a predefined goal, but to enable the "target system to enhance its modes of reflexivity, so that its capacity for self-steering is enhanced" (p. 87). Consequently, the success of a policy can be judged not on the basis of whether or not a preset goal has been reached, but of how much this *self-steering capacity* of the target system has been enhanced.

A series of questions should be asked and answered to elaborate on this general conceptualization. I propose the following questions. Some of these questions are broader in focus; others are more specific to public policy. Some of the questions have been addressed, though not answered completely, in the literature, and others are yet to be addressed in future theoretical and empirical studies.

1. The general view of self-organization is that it negates the notion that complex social problems can be solved with linear interventions that are carried out by hierarchically ordered bureaucratic structures and thus it may connote a democratic image of governance. Does self-organization automatically mean democracy and participation?

Godlstein's (1994) and Kiel's (1994) applications of self-organization to organizational management reflect this image of self-organization. But, others show that self-organizational processes can generate inequalities and hierarchies. This is an issue that needs to be investigated more systematically and extensively with empirical studies.

2. What is the role of the government, or governmental agencies, in self-organizing policy systems? Is the government merely one of the multiple actors in a policy system? Or does it play a special and different role from the roles other actors play?

The studies on network governance (e.g., Koliba, Meek, and Zia, 2011) suggest that the role of governments in policy processes has diminished in recent decades. In his theory of the state in the late 20th century, Jessop (1990) argues that our societies have become "centerless," as self-organizing and self-governing entities proliferated.

Klijn and Snellen (2009) underscore the difficulty in governing or influencing self-organizing systems. Buijs and his colleagues' (2009) "guiding ability of governmental agencies" have become questionable. Governmental decision making is still possible, but "the effects of governmental actions are highly influenced by the spontaneous actions of many other agents," they observe (p. 97). As I mentioned in the previous subsection, many urban scholars share a similar perspective and stress the counterproductive nature of top-down urban planning schemes.

Rhodes (1997a, p. 57) notes that in the new era of governance what we call "the state" is actually composed of interorganizational networks that are made up of governmental and societal actors. The state is no longer the sovereign and its new role is to seek out new forms of cooperation. Kettl (2002) observes that in the governance process both governmental and non-governmental actors play roles. Governmental actors still have special roles in this process, according to Kettl: They have the "responsibility to law and public interest" and therefore should have the "capacity to steer behaviors of policy systems" (p. 161). Similarly, Agranoff (2007) views government's role as guiding, steering, controlling, and managing a wide range of non-governmental actors (p. 192).

3. How can "self" be defined in self-organizing policy system? Is self defined self-referentially or externally?

Luhmann's theory of social systems can be useful in conceptualizing policy systems, with some caution and modifications. The reader will remember that there are two interrelated propositions in his theory: (a) that social systems are self-referential and they are radically autonomous from other systems in their environments and (b) that social systems determine the identities of their members by differentiating the interdependencies within and outside themselves. These propositions may be applicable to social systems like religious cults, which separate themselves radically from their environments and shape the worldviews and lifestyles of their members strongly. Policy systems are not like religious cults. However, if Luhmann's characterizations of social systems are applied to policy systesm, not in absolute terms, but as reference points against which a particular policy system is compared, then they can be a useful. Then the questions would be these: To what extent is a policy system self-referential and thus autonomous and to what extent does it determine the identities of its members? These questions can be answered empirically by studying the cohesion of the self-images of the members of a policy system and the differentiations in the interdependencies of its members within and outside the system.

Luhmann's conceptualization can be considered together with Giddens' concepts of systemness and social and system integration. Giddens conceptualizes systemic relations in terms of degrees of "systemness" (Chapter 2), which is better than Luhmann's categorical view. Giddens' conceptualization can be used to "soften" Luhmann's image of social systems that they have a grip of over their members' relationships by injecting the idea that systems are integrated at different degrees. Systemness is a variable. In Giddens' view, to the degree that the activities of human actors are reproduced across time and space and to the degree that they are integrated socially and systemically, we can say that they constitute a social system.

By combining the conceptualizations of Luhmann and Giddens, we can ask two questions: To what degree the reciprocity between actors is reproduced across time and space? To what degree the system is capable of differentiating the relations among its members from those with others? This way, we can differentiate between those strongly integrated, strongly self-referential, and strongly demarcated systems and those weakly integrated, weakly self-referential, and weakly demarcated systems.

Some social systems may indeed be strongly integrated, strongly self-referential, and strongly demarcated. Think of religious cults again. They self-referentially define and demarcate themselves and differentiate the relations among their members from those relations with outsiders. They have strong grips over their members' lives. They are integrated in the sense that the reciprocated relationships among their members are reproduced across time and space. Policy systems, obviously, cannot demarcate themselves and control the relationships of their members at the level religious cults do. They are not "strong systems" in the manner cults are. But it is conceivable that there are differences among different policy systems. It is important to ask the question to what extent a particular policy system is "strong" in the sense that it is self-referential, that is, can differentiate the relationships among its members from those with outsiders, and that the reciprocal relations among its members are reproduced across time and space. The question of how strong a policy system is can be answered empirically. Understanding the strength of a policy system may be important in understanding its capacity to reproduce itself, its durability, and its effectiveness.

4. How do self-organizing systems relate to each other? For instance, what is the relationship between a policy system with other policy systems, other social systems, and natural systems?

Some of the concepts I discussed in this chapter provide clues to answering these questions. Strogatz's "sync" and Maturana and Varela's (1980) "structural coupling" both describe the situations in which a system is in congruence with others in its environment. Two or more systems may be synchronized spontaneously through "mutual cuing" according to Strogatz. Does this happen in public policy processes? Coevolution is another pertinent concept in answering the questions, and I will discuss it in the next chapter.

5. I made the point earlier that self-organization is not a uniform process. Not all systems are equally self-organizational. Then the questions are these: Do some systems have more *self-organizational capacity* than others? If so, what are the characteristics of those systems with more self-organizational capacity?

Ostrom's (1990, 2005) Institutional Analysis and Development framework offers some answers to these question. She describes a set of specific conditions that are conducive to self-organization in common-pool resource management systems.[7] She observes that when there is a good chance to improve the common resources and when good indicators to measure and assess improvements in conditions are available and outcomes are relatively predictable, individual actors are more likely to self-organize. Other conditions that increase the likelihood that they will self-organize are that the issue of improving the conditions of common resources should be salient to participants, that they should have common understanding of how the resource system operates, that they should be allowed to decide on their own by external authorities, and that there should be prior experience and local leadership (2005, pp. 244–245).

Geyer and Rihani (2010, pp. 131–137) answer the question of self-organizational capacity from their complexity theory perspctive. They argue that developed nations are developed because they developed more self-organizational capacity than underdeveloped nations. Geyer and Rihani cite primarily two conditions for the high self-organizational capacities of the developed nations: the existence of basic democratic and market structures and an appreciation of the value of "social capital." Geyer and Rihani argue that the "massive freedom deficit" in the underdeveloped countries is the primary source of the lack of self-organization. This results in too few interactions among individuals and organizations and a "state of stultifying order" (p. 135). Geyer and Rihani also make the point that both too much order and too little of it can be detrimental; both lead to developmental dead ends. What is needed is a dynamically structured situation for success, they argue.

CHAPTER SUMMARY

The view that public policy processes are, or can be, self-organizational has an intuitive appeal. The discussions in this chapter show that the concept of self-organization is complex. It has many interpretations and implications.

In this chapter I first traced the history of self-organizational thinking. Then I discussed the primary conceptual issues in defining self-organization. I raised the following questions and summarized the answers given by complexity theorists to them. What is the relationship between a self-organizing system and its environment? Does the system as a whole self-organize? Are there also subsystem level self-organizational processes? If self-organization takes place at both the system and subsystem levels, what is the nature of the relationships between the two levels? If self-organization occurs at multiple levels in systems, are the actors in social systems self-organizational as well? Are there variations in the capacities of systems and their components to self-organize? If yes, then what are conditions conducive to elements of a system to self-organize? Do self-organizational processes create order, disorder, or both? What is the "self" in self-organization?

I also summarized Prigogine's, Kauffman's, and Strogatz's conceptualizations and models of self-organizations. Autopoiesis theory offers a unique perspective on self-organization: autopoetic systems are self-referential.

I summarized its interpretation for social systems by Luhmann and discussed the issues in his theory.

In the final section of the chapter, I summarized the literature on the applications of self-organization in management, urban planning, and policy processes. The literature on self-organization and management provides prescriptions for managers: managers should be not be afraid of uncertainties or letting their employees taking their own initiatives and that planning for the future should be an ongoing and adaptive process. I noted that self-organizational processes do not necessarily lead to democracy, equality, participation, however. Urban scholars observe that urban planning should not ignore the self-organizational nature of urban systems. They also suggest that there are different types of self-organization. Some studies show that self-organization is not a panacea when it comes to solving urban problems. Finally, I summarized the implications of all the discussions in the chapter in five sets of propositions and questions in this section.

5   System Dynamics

What makes a complex system change? In the common view of complexity theorists, change is natural. Then, the question is not why systems change, but how they do. The task of complexity theorists is to describe the patterns and mechanisms of change. There is no unified view of system dynamics among complexity theorist, but one can find four distinguishable models of change in the literature: self-organized criticality, dissipative structures, self-referentiality, and coevolution. In this chapter I first describe these four models and then discuss the applications of dissipative structures and coevolution models in the public policy literature. I also make five propositions for future applications of these change models in policy studies.

MODELS OF CHANGE

Self-Organized Criticality

Self-organized criticality is the name Peter Bak and Kan Chen (1991) use for their description of a form of self-organizational mechanism of change in large systems. These are systems like the movements of tectonic plates that lead to earthquakes, crashes in stock markets, and extinctions of species like dinosaurs. They observe that large-scale changes in such systems can be triggered by small events, and these changes are self-organizational. Actually all complexity theorists would agree with this statement. What Bak and Chen add to this is that large-scale changes happen at certain critical states: "Large interactive systems perpetually organize themselves to a critical state in which a minor event starts a chain reaction that can lead to a catastrophe" (p. 46). In traditional analyses of these systems, it is assumed that the "causes" of the events are proportional to the magnitude, scale of the event: Big events cause big changes; small events cause small changes. Bak and Chen posit that there is no necessary proportionality between triggering events and the changes. More important, they argue, the mechanisms that lead to small and large changes are of the same kind.

Bak and Chen use a simple model, a pile of sand, to illustrate their points. In this model, grains of sand are dropped gradually on top of other grains on a flat surface. Initially sand grains stay at the positions they were dropped. Later, they form a pile with a gentle slope, and then the slope of the pile steepens. As the slope steepens, some grains begin to fall off the edge of the pile. When the slopes are steeper, larger numbers of grains fall off. Often when a grain is dropped, other grains make minor moves, but at certain critical points movements of grains turn into "avalanches" or "catastrophes." In other words, a single grain dropped on a pile may have both proportional (linear) and disproportional (nonlinear) effects; it can trigger small changes and big ones.

Then what is the mechanism of this process? In their own words,

> At the beginning of an avalanche, a single grain slides down the slope because of some instability on the surface of the pile. The grain will stop only if it falls into a table position; otherwise, it will continue to fall. If it hits grains that are almost unstable, it will cause them to fall. As the process continues, each moving grain may stop or continue to fall. The process will cease when all the active particles have stopped or have moved off the sand pile. (p. 46)

The pile maintains two of its macro properties—its overall size and shape—despite all the avalanches and catastrophic changes it has experienced. In this process there is a critical value of the slope of the pile, which regulates the behavior of the pile. When the slope is less than that critical value, avalanches stop; when it exceeds the value, avalanches occur.

The sand pile example brings together two seemingly incongruous observations, according to Bak and Chen: The sand grains are unstable at different locations on the pile (micro properties), but the size and the slope of the pile (macro properties of the system) are robust. The elements of the systems and their relations keep changing, but the system overall is in a "meta-stable state" (p. 46).

Bak and Chen's model illustrates four important characteristics of complex systems. First, small events can lead to large events—the cause–effect relation is nonlinear. Second, the process of transitioning from linear accumulation to nonlinear avalanche is self-organizational; it does not need an external design. Third, although the changes at the macro level (sand pile) emerge from interactions at the micro level (grains), these changes at the two levels are not synchronous. Fourth, once they emerge, the structural properties of the system are robust. These last two, of course, are characteristics of emergence (Chapter 3).

Dissipative Structures

Prigogone and his colleagues' model of dissipative structures (Prigogine and Stengers, 1984; Nicolis and Prigogine, 1989; Prigogine, 1996) has some similarities with and differences from Bak and Chen's self-organized criti-cality model. Similar to Bak and Chen's model, nonlinearity, self-organi-zation, and emergence play critical roles in Prigigone's, but unlike in the former, the systems Prigogine conceptualizes do not settle into a "meta-stable state." Stability, or equilibrium, is not the normal state of affairs in Prigogine; it is an exceptional state.

Stability is not a normal state, because most systems in the universe are open systems, and they constantly exchange energy, matter, and information with their environments. Dynamism is the normal state of open systems, not stability. Their motions do not tend toward equilibrium but toward *far-from-equilibrium* conditions. When they are far from equilibrium, sys-tems become sensitive to external influences. Under these conditions, sys-tems are dissipative; they dissipate, and new systems, new forms/structures, emerge. What specific form will emerge is not precisely predictable. Under these far-from-equilibrium conditions, the patterns of the motions of sys-tems are nonlinear and thus partly unpredictable. They are not completely unpredictable, however. They reach certain bifurcation points, where they may take one of two paths: Their motions may turn chaotic, and then the systems disintegrate, or they may self-organize at a higher level of organiza-tion, and a higher degree of complexity emerges. It is more likely that they will take the latter path than the former. A key notion in Prigogine's theory is that the motions of systems—typically toward far-from-equilibrium—are irreversible; systems cannot go back to their earlier states.

There are three important points in Prigogine's model. First, he observes that most systems in the universe are open systems, which exchange energy, matter, and information with their environments. They are dissipative in this sense. This is important because both the open system and closed sys-tem concepts are used by policy scholars. For instance Buijs, Eshuis and Byrne (2009) contrast "conservative self-organization" and "dissipative self-organization" in their discussion of complexity-based research methods that could be used in public management studies. Gerrits (2008) proposes a similar conceptualization for understanding "policy action systems." He suggests that "singular policy action systems" are closed and self-referen-tial, whereas "composite policy action systems" are open and dissipative (p. 213). I will come back to Buijs and his colleagues' and Gerrits' dichotomous conceptualizations later in this chapter.

Nicolis and Prigogine (1989) use the term "conservative systems" and note that the two main characteristics of such systems are that they are isolated and they tend toward equilibrium (p. 121). Probably the most well-known example of conservative systems is the conjecture of a har-monic oscillator in a frictionless environment. It can be mathematically shown that in such an environment the oscillator keeps returning to its original position when removed from its original equilibrium position. The oscillating motions in its return journey can be represented with sinusoi-dal functions. The problem is that other than strictly controlled labora-tory conditions, it is hard to find frictionless environments. This is why the oscillator example is an abstraction and the "conservative system" is an abstraction, an approximate description of some observable phenomena in nature. Nicolis and Prigogine say that the concept of conservative systems applies only to a narrow range of phenomena in classical mechanics and quantum mechanics (pp. 46–50). Most systems in nature are not conservative; they are open and dissipative. Because of its limited and abstract nature, the concept of conservatives systems should be handled with extra care when it is applied to social and policy systems.

The second important point in Prigogine's dissipative structures theory is that dissipative systems have the tendency to move away from equilibrium— toward what he calls "far from equilibrium"—not equilibrium. Prigogine and Stengers (1984) note that dissipation of energy creates instability and the conditions for nonlinear relations among unequal elements (pp. 12–13). This is why open systems are inherently dynamic. This dynamism is not necessarily destructive though. It may lead to the system's disintegration, but even then, through a self-organizational process, this dynamism can lead to the emergence of higher-level order. The spontaneous dynamism of dissipative systems is uncontrollable in principle, according to Prigogine and Stengers, but it can be partially controlled by controlling the initial conditions (p. 120).

The third point in Prigogine's theory is that time is irreversible. Irreversible time is why dissipative systems are dynamic and self-organizing. It is the basis of the notions that systems *evolve* and that the *history* of a system matters in understanding their current behaviors. Irreversible time is also the basis of the unpredictability of the future behaviors of systems. To understand his point better, we should consider the notion of reversible time first. In Newtonian mechanics time is reversible. It can go either way, to the future and to the past. This is because the motion trajectories of Newtonian objects go back and forth. And the solutions of the Newtonian equations that describe them can be reversed in direction. Because of the reversible nature of time in their trajectories, the behaviors of these systems are considered deterministic and universally generalizable. I will come back to the issue of generalizability in Chapter 6.

As an example of the Newtonian system with reversible time, again consider the motion of the harmonic oscillator in frictionless space. It goes back and forth indefinitely. And every time its swings, it goes back to its past. But remember that the pendulum in frictionless space is an abstraction. Prigogine and Stengers (1984) argue that in reality we cannot go back in time, because the second law of thermodynamics prohibits it. The second law states that because of the infinite entropy barrier, which we will never be able to overcome, we cannot go back in time. Therefore, time is irreversible. Prigogine (1996) concedes that only under certain conditions, on certain islands of reality, Newtonian notions of reversible time and deterministic relations may be applicable. Because of the fundamental irreversibility of time, unlike in the idealized conservative systems like the oscillator in frictionless space, the behaviors of (dissipative, open) systems are open ended; they are not deterministic or predictable.

I will return to the issues of determinism and unpredictability in Chapter 6. For now, I want to note that Prigogine's notion that time is irreversible has the implication that the history of a system's behavior matters. For an abstract conservative system, like the oscillator in frictionless space, the history of the system does not have anything to do with its future behavior. In a manner of speaking, the system "forgets" its past. Dissipative systems, on the other hand, "remember" their pasts in the sense that the past behavior guides and constricts the future evolution of the system.

This is particularly important for social systems, which do not have any resemblance to the abstraction of conservative systems. They are open systems. This makes the evolutionary path of each social system is unique and its future behavior dependent on the path it travelled in the past: "The system builds up a unique and irreversible history, and the structures that emerge build on preceding complexity and interactions" (Engelen, 1988, p. 55). This is the notion of "path dependence," which complexity theorists often apply in their studies.

Self-Referentiality

In his application of autopoiesis theory to social systems, Luhmann (1995) argues that change and stability are two complementary characteristics of systems. Change and preservation cannot be explained with two separate theories, according to Luhmann; a single theory must explain both. The theory of autopoiesis is that theory, he argues. That is so, because an autopoietic social system "is confronted at every moment with the alternative of ceasing or continuing. Its 'substance' continually vanishes, so to speak, and must be reproduced with the help of structural models" (p. 347). Structural models are the models of the system's self-image, from which an autopoietic system reproduces itself. In this process of reproduction, actually the *relations among a system's elements are reproduced*. If they can be reproduced successfully, the system will be able to maintain itself. If not, the system ceases to exist.

To better explain Luhmann's theory of systemic change, I will elaborate on three key concepts he uses—time, process, and structure—and two key issues he addresses—system's relations with its environment and its own elements.

Time is an important concept in Luhman's theory, because it is the source of systemic change. Systems change because under the pressure of time, they make selections in their environments and themselves. They adapt through these selections. In Luhmann's theory, systems adapt by making selections in its environment and its elements. If the time available to all the systems in the universe were infinite, the systems would make selections both internally and externally to bring "everything . . . into tune with everything else" (p. 42). At that hypothetical point, there would be no need for change anymore.

Process is another important concept in Luhmann's theory. According to Luhmann, not all successions of events should be considered processes. A succession of events is a process only if "it fulfils the characteristic of increasing selectivity" (p. 355). Increasing selectivity can occur in two ways. It may be anticipatory (teleological, goal directed) or morphogenetic (i.e., connecting one structural change to another without a sense of direction in the overall change). An example of teleological selectivity would be the rational model of decision making. In this model the assumption is that the decision maker sets his/her ultimate goals a priori and makes his/her selections among the alternatives to reach those goals. This process is intentional and goal directed. To what extent these teleological assumptions are realistic is debatable. Morphogenic selectivity is more "natural," as it is the case of natural selection in Darwin's theory of biological evolution. In a morphogenic selection process, the next step is selected by the system without a sense of what the ultimate goal would be. This is the view underlying incrementalism in policymaking.

An example of morphogenic selectivity would be the way reactive agents are set up in agent-based simulations. As I mentioned in Chapter 3, reactive agents know only their local environments, not the whole system or the larger environment (they have only local knowledge), and they can make selections for their next moves only, without an overall goal. Despite this lack of an overall vision or goal, structural properties can emerge, and they can evolve as a whole. Cognitive agents have more knowledge of their environments, and they are reflective, but even they do not act teleologically. They do not have the full knowledge of their system or its environment, nor can they set an overall goal for the system.

Luhmann stresses that when he speaks of social change, he means *structural change*. What changes and to what degree are questions of the *time frame*. Structures can be continued, kept constant, or changed relative to this time frame.[1] He underscores that the structural properties of a system change, not the system itself. This is because systems are

> composed of immutable elements, namely, events. Yet systems are identified by structures, which can change. To this extent, one is justified in saying that the system changes when its structures change because, after all, something that belongs to the system (i.e., what makes its autopoietic reproduction possible) changes. (p. 345)

In Luhmann's view social systemic change should be understood in terms of the system's self-reproduction through its definition of itself and its environment. He notes that there is a question commonly asked in both the biological evolution literature and the social change literature: Do systems adapt to their environments, or do environments adapt to systems? This is not a relevant question for self-referential systems, according to Luhmann. Instead, the questions should be this: How does the system define "itself" and its boundaries with "its environment"? And how does its semantic differentiation affect information processing among the components of the system, regarding what adaptations are necessary (pp. 349–350). In his own words

> Self-referential systems are closed systems in the sense that they pro-duce their own elements and thus their own structural changes. There is no direct, causal intervention of the environment on the system without the system's cooperation. That is why the system endows its own structure (although it is no event) with causality. . . . This latent causal contribution, which must be triggered, can adapt to changing requirements by structural change. Without such cooperation from the system, the environment would remain merely the possibility of destroying autopoietic reproduction. (p. 350)

There are two implications of this view of self-referential systems. The first one is about the synchronization of the relationship between the sys-tem and its environment. Because complex social systems "must adapt not only to their environments but also to their own complexity" (p. 31), it is a challenge for them to seamlessly follow the changes in their environments. A complex system cannot be in full synchronization with its environment (p. 43), according to Luhmann. This, of course, creates the conditions for further change within the system. It has to keep redefining the relations among its elements and its boundaries with its environment.

The second implication is that the system, to reproduce itself success-fully, has to replace its elements and the relations among them. He uses the term "temporal complexity" to signify the temporally transient nature of the elements of a system. The system reproduces itself by "decreasing the temporal duration of its elements or even reducing them to evanescent events" (p. 47). He further argues, " . . . an adequately stable system is composed of unstable elements. It owes its stability to itself, not to its ele-ments" (p. 48). Because of the constant replacement and destabilization of its elements, a self-referential system is in a state of dynamic stability all the time. Change and stability are not mutually exclusive.

Coevolution

Prigogine's dissipative structures and Luhmann's self-referential social sys-tem models look at the problem of systemic change from the perspective of the system. The coevolutionary models suggest a different kind of look, a look at the relations between the evolutions of different systems.

The roots of the idea of coevolution were in evolutionary biology, primar-ily in the reactions to and revisions of the Darwinian notions of *evolution through random mutation* and *survival of the fittest*. The notion of coevolution presupposes that there are relationships between autonomous, self-organizing, and purposeful systems. This presupposition was expressed in an elementary form by von Bertalanffy (1968), who criticized the notion of random mutations in Darwin's theory and posited that biological evolution must have been purposeful, not accidental. He also argued that the notion of the survival of the fittest is in contradiction with that of random mutations. For an organism to survive, it has to be a self-maintaining and purposeful system, and thus it must be in control of its destiny, at least partly; therefore, evolution cannot be the result of random mutations (p. 152).

Ehrlich and Raven (1964), who coined the term coevolution, built on these notions of autonomy and purposefulness and stressed the mutuality in systems' relations. They posited that species do not simply adapt to their environments, but different species are in reciprocal responses to each other, and they coevolve together. Stuart Kauffman (1993, 1995) developed a more elaborate theory of coevolution. His is a three-level conceptualization (1995, pp. 207–208). At the first level, a species evolves to adapt to its environment; its survival depends on its ability to adapt. His conceptualization at this level is not much different from Darwin's theory. At the second level, the environment evolves, together with, or in response to, the evolution of the species; there is mutuality, i.e., coevolution. The key to his understanding of coevolution is that the fitness of an organism to its environment depends on the characteristics of other organisms in the environment. "Each organism lives in the niche created by other organisms, each seeking its own living blindly creates the modes of living for the others . . ." (p. 207). Therefore, other organisms may change as the organism changes. At the third level, the mechanisms and patterns of coevolution evolve.

A key metaphor Kauffman uses in his conceptualization of coevolution is "fitness landscapes"—that the species must fit to the landscapes around them. He points out that during the billions of years of the existence of life on our planet, complex organisms have been "climbing up fitness landscapes toward peaks of high fitness" (p. 161). Those landscapes themselves have also changed, partly in response to the evolution of the species. So, fitness landscapes coevolve with species (the second level of coevolution). And in the long run, the way a particular landscape and the species interact (mechanisms of coevolution) changes (the third level of coevolution). In Kauffman's words,

> The coevolution of organisms alters both the organisms themselves and the way organisms interact. Over time, the ruggedness of the fitness landscapes changes, as does their resiliency—how easily each landscape is deformed by the adaptive moves of the players. The very process of coevolution itself evolves! (p. 208)

What are the characteristics of coevolution, according to Kauffman? First, it is a self-organizational process; coevolution does not need an external choreographer (Kauffman, 1995, p. 246). Second, self-organizational coevolutionary processes happen at the "edge of chaos" (p. 302).[2] Biological systems have the tendency to evolve to the edge of chaos, at which point they undergo phase transitions into more complex states. Third, coevolution does not signify a harmonious relationship between a system and its environment (p. 216). In fact, the coevolutionary relations between systems may not be mutually beneficial; they may even be destructive. Kauffman gives the examples of viruses that destroy their host bodies. For instance, the HIV virus coevolved with the host human bodies—both the human immune systems and the virus itself changed in reaction to each other—but they did not coevolve in synchrony. The HIV virus evolved faster than the body's adaptation to it. In the end, in most cases, the virus causes full-blown AIDS and kills the body. There are, of course, exceptional cases of individuals who continue living with the virus, without developing AIDS; the mechanisms of these mutually non-destructive relationships are not yet known.

There are a couple of models developed by complexity theories to describe the mechanisms of coevolution. The first and the most generic mechanisms are feedback loops between coevolving systems. Gell-Mann points out that complex adaptive systems are bound to their environments through feedback loops; through these loops systems modify their behaviors and reorganize (cited in Taylor, 2001, pp. 166–168). So systems give each other feedbacks. Gerrits (2008) reminds us that this is not a mere information exchange between systems, but it is a reciprocal and selective interaction between them (p. 36). I will come back to Gerrits' conceptualization later in this chapter.

The second and more specific mechanism is Kauffman's NK model, which I described in the previous chapter. The reader will remember that the NK model describes a self-organizational process of the emergence of macro structures from the interactions of micro units. The NK model is relevant to coevolution, because it describes the emergence of fitness landscapes and their coevolution with species. More specifically, the NK model shows how different degrees of "ruggedness of landscapes" emerge (McKelvey, 1999). McKelvey observes that ruggedness is a function of the number of parts constituting the evolving organism (N) and the amount of interconnectedness among the parts (K). When $K = N-1$, the landscape is very jagged. As K increases from 0 to $N-1$, ruggedness increases. (pp. 301–302).

APPLYING MODELS OF SYSTEM DYNAMICS TO PUBLIC POLICY

Two of these four models of system dynamics—dissipative structures and coevolution—have attracted the attentions of management, planning, and policy scholars. I summarize these applications in this section. I discuss the application of feedback loops in the policy change literature in a separate subsection. Although the self-organized criticality model has not been applied fully in the management, organization, or policy literatures, it is used as analog in one source, which I mention in the feedback loops subsection. Luhmann's self-referential systems model does not have any applications that I am aware of, but I propose that it deserves serious consideration.

Dissipative Structures

In Chapter 4, I highlighted the self-organizational nature of dissipation and mentioned Gemmill and Smith's (1985) and Goldstein's (1988) applications of Prigogine's theory to organizational management. It should be obvious from the discussions so far that self-organizational and evolutionary processes are inseparable in complexity theorists' understanding of systems. This is evident Gemmill and Smith's and Goldstein's interpretations of dissipative structures. Their message is that because change, even transformational change, is endogenously driven, and thus inevitable, managers should be open to it, even embrace it. These authors also emphasize that an awareness of dissipative processes can help increase the probability of successfully guiding transformational changes in organizations.

Dissipative structures theory has been adopted by urban planning scholars as well. Batty (2007) and Portugali (2000) use it to underscore the perpetual dynamism of urban systems. These two authors apply different approaches in measuring or understanding this dynamism. To discern the patterns of urban dynamics, Batty applies quantitative modeling techniques, particularly cellular automata, agent-based simulations, and fractal geometry. In contrast to Batty's exclusively quantitative approach, Portugali's approach is qualitative and descriptive. In Portugali's view cities are dissipative structures, because of the parallel and overlapping plans created by multiple actors in different time periods. Because of this, the city is in a perpetual far-from-equilibrium state. Each plan participates in a process in which various configurations compete and cooperate until one of them wins and becomes the order parameter of future plans. These new order parameters are emergent structures, and they "enslave" future activities of agents in the sense that they are reproduced in the future actions. From this observation Portugali draws the conclusion that long-term and top-down urban planning is a fruitless effort. Instead, he proposes a "parallel distributed planning" approach. In this approach, specific land-use plans would not be adopted; cities would regulate general planning principles and let local actors self-organize. There should be constant re-evaluation, updating, and re-interpretation of plans.

These applications of dissipative structures theory in management are insightful and rightly suggest that we should look at managerial and planning processes in a way to understand their inherent dynamism. But the applications of coevolution in public policy, which I discuss next, are more specific and hence offer potentially more useful conceptualizations to guide future studies.

Coevolution

Kauffman (1995) thinks that his conceptualization of coevolution is applicable to economic, cultural, and technological systems as well. In his view, "Goods and services in an economy live in the niches afforded by other goods and services. . . . [We] make a living by creating and selling goods and services that make economic sense in the niches afforded by other goods and services" (1995, p. 240). Therefore the evolutions of goods and services are interconnected; they coevolve. The "complementarities" in an economy, such as the consumption complementarities between cars and gasoline, are coevolutionary patterns, according to Kauffman. Technologies also coevolve. The developments in the hardware technology of desktop personal computers enabled the Internet to evolve from a limited network of communications into a World Wide Web. In turn, the capabilities of the Internet, such as electronic mail and electronic commerce, provided the niche for the hardware of personal computers to evolve into hybrids like the wireless telephone and handheld devices (and now a hybrid of telephone; 1995, pp. 279–284).

Gerrits and his colleagues (Gerrits, 2008, 2010, forthcoming; Gerrits, Marks, and Van Buuren, 2009; Van Buuren, Gerrits, and Marks, 2009), Dutch scholars of governance systems, use coevolution as the core concept in their analyses. Van Buuren, Gerrits, and Marks' work is particularly important for their conceptualization of coevolution within policy systems. They identify three different "tracks" in policy processes: fact-finding track (producing policy-relevant information), framing track (actors' interpretations of reality and their own systems), and will-formulation track (finding an acceptable selection of concrete ambitions). These tracks are interdependent, and they coevolve. Policy decisions form temporal equilibria in the coevolutionary processes among these three tracks. They illustrate their conceptualization in a case study of the spatial reallocation of a polder, a low-lying piece of land gained from the sea in the Netherlands.

Gerrits and his colleagues (Gerrits, 2008, 2010; Gerrits, Marks, and Van Buuren, 2009) expand the scope of the application of coevolution in policy processes to focus on the coevolution of *policy action systems* and *physical systems*. They provide refined conceptualizations of the mechanisms of coevolution. At the core of their conceptualization is the notion that both natural and policy systems should be considered self-organizing and coevolving systems. These two types of systems do not self-organize independently, but their self-organizational processes are interdependent. In these coevolutionary processes, physical and policy action systems "reciprocally select each other" (Gerrits, 2008, p. 199) and their mutations affect each other (p. 36).

The most important implication of this coevolutionary perspective is that physical (natural) systems cannot be controlled by policy systems. This may sound obvious, especially in the face of increasingly common large-scale natural disasters that overwhelm human response capabilities around the world—hurricanes, earthquakes, tsunamis, and the like—but policy analysts and policymakers have not stopped assuming that they can subjugate and control natural forces at least to an extent. This control-oriented approach to natural systems has had adverse consequences, Gerrits (2008) argues. He illustrates his points in his case study of the Unterelbe estuary in Germany and the Westerschelde estuary between the Netherlands and Belgium. He observes that as the policymakers tried to deepen these estuaries to allow larger ships access to the ports around them in the late 1990s and early 2000s, the natural systems responded by creating unexpected problems, such as increased sediment accumulation and oxygen depletion in the basins (pp. 103–107).

Gerrits makes the point that although each was different in some other ways, the common problem was that the policymakers ignored the fact the natural systems they were trying to control were actually self-organizing systems. The reader will remember that complexity theorists Prigogine, Kauffman, and others have already demonstrated the self-organizing capabilities of natural systems with ample evidence. So Gerrits' point is not particularly novel in that sense. But what is novel is that he brings this insight into understanding the relationships between policy systems and natural systems. Gerrits astutely observes that because of their self-organizing capabilities, natural systems act "as much . . . agent[s] in a policy process as . . . the human agents" (p. 14). Therefore, he suggests, the anthropomorphic view that nature is nothing but a collection of objects that can be subjugated to policy objectives should be abandoned. Instead, policy analysts and policymakers should try to understand not only the respective self-organizational characteristics of natural and policy systems, but also the specific mechanisms of their interactions, their coevolutions. This requires a shift in the way policymakers and analysts think about nature. It also requires a close collaboration in policymaking between natural scientists and social scientists/policy scholars. Furthermore, it requires that complexity theory concepts are refined and applied in understanding the coevolutionary relations between the two kinds of systems.

Gerrits and his colleagues offer a conceptual outline for such an understanding. The two primary mechanisms of coevolution are *mutual feedback loops* and *reciprocal selection* between systems. It is not merely an information exchange between the systems, but their mutual selections that determine the path of the coevolutionary process. Gerrits (2008) observes in the case of the Unterelbe that the efforts to deepen the estuary triggered a positive feedback loop. They shifted the tidal regime in the harbor basin, which partly determined sediment transportation. The increased upstream transportation of the sediments resulted in increased sedimentation; consequently a need emerged for increased dredging to maintain the harbor basin at the desired depth (p. 108).

An important conceptual contribution Gerrits and his colleagues make is the typology of policy action systems—singular versus composite policy action systems—which I introduced in Chapter 2. They observe that when policy action systems make their selections in their interactions with natural systems, they use one of these two strategies. Singular policy action systems are self-referential, and thus they respond by re-connecting with those actors who already support the goal of the system. In other words, the leading actors in such systems keep reinforcing their beliefs about the way things work in their policy environments and their policy goals by communicating only with those actors who support their views and goals.[3] Composite policy actions systems are open and dissipative. They respond by redefining their system's boundaries and connecting with other actors who were not in the system and thus expanding the variety of ideas and goals in the process. Gerrits (2008) observes that the singular policy action system in the Unterelbe case tried to maintain its structural stability by allowing only those who agree with their goal, which was opening up the harbor by dredging the basin, into decision-making processes and excluding the opponents of this goal—environmentalists and fishermen. The decisions and actions of this policy action system ended up triggering adverse effects in the basin. In the Westerchelde case the policy action system was "composite," i.e., open to alternative views, including the views of the opponents of opening up the harbor by dredging the basin. This openness resulted in the development of a more comprehensive and long-term plan for the estuary with less adversarial consequences.

Like Kauffman (1995), Gerrits (2008) points out that coevolution does not mean a harmonious relationship between the coevolving systems (p. 51). It is possible that coevolving systems develop a symbiotic relationship. But it is also likely that one of the systems will benefit from their relationships, and the other one will suffer losses. This is a parasitic relationship, an example of which is the relationship between the HIV virus and the human body. Another possibility is that none of the systems will benefit from their relationship, and both systems will be compromised.

Gerrits and his colleagues' conceptual refinement of coevolution for policy systems and their case illustrations open up new perspectives and provide guidance for future empirical studies. Their fundamental insights that natural and *policy systems are both self-organizing and coevolving systems* should be not only the basis of empirical scholarly studies but also a guiding principle in policymaking. Policymakers should not assume that nature is merely an object that can be subjugated to their will and policy goals. It is important for policy scholars to try to understand the relations between policy and natural systems in terms of their "mutual selections" and feedback loops. The specific selection mechanism and rules of feedback in specific policy domains should be investigated in future studies. Their conceptualization of *singular versus composite policy action systems* should be a topic of further empirical studies. It is important to investigate to what extent specific policy systems are singular or composite and to what extent these types are related to policy effectiveness.

Feedback Loops and Policy Change

Negative and positive feedback loops are generic mechanisms of systems dynamics. Baumgartner and Jones (2009) use these in their conceptualizations of policy change.

In Baumgartner and Jones' *punctuated equilibrium theory,* the American system of policy making is described as a complex interactive system. This system is mostly static, but at times it undergoes large-scale changes. The system is in a state of equilibrium most of the time, but occasionally an issue is forced into the national policy agenda, and this may "punctuate" the equilibrium with a drastic change. In this process of punctuated equilibrium, both negative and positive feedback loops, but primarily the former, play roles. The fragmented and overlapping institutions of the US political system and the relatively open access of policy actors to the system create the conditions for "a dynamic that usually works against impetus for change but occasionally reinforces it" (True, Jones, and Baumgartner, 2007, p. 157).

The separation of the political institutions in the US usually reinforces the existing system of relations. Entrenched interests capture "policy subsystems" (systems of relationship around particular policy issues) and form "policy monopolies." These monopolies constitute negative feedback loops in the sense that they "systematically dampen pressures for change," and if there is any change, that takes place incrementally (True, Jones, and Baumgartner, p. 159). However, policy subsystems are vulnerable to large-scale changes as well, because they are open to new policy actors. These newcomers usually are not powerful enough to instigate any changes in the system, but they may be able to do so through nonlinear positive feedback loops— processes in which small changes are amplified. They can put enough pressure on the system over time, which may trigger massive interventions by powerful previously uninvolved actors (e.g., governmental institutions) and lead to major changes (pp. 159–160).

Then why does a particular small change lead to major changes through positive feedback loops, while other small changes do not? Baumgartner and Jones (2002) cite two mechanisms to explain this: attention shifting and mimicking. People have limited attention spans, and therefore they can focus on certain policy issues at a time and use information shortcuts in decision making. Their attentions and or informational shortcuts may shift at those times when salient policy issues change due to triggering events. Policy venues and policy images change during those times. Because people also tend to mimic others' behaviors, this can have an amplifying effect during the times when attentions are shifted. Mimicking can lead to fads, "feeding frenzy," and "bandwagon effects." True, Jones, and Baumgartner

(2007, p. 160) cite Bak and Chen's sand pile analogy to illustrate the point that relatively minor events can accumulate over time and thus lead to major policy changes.

In their characterization of governance networks, Koliba, Meek, and Zia (2011) build on Baumgartner and Jones' conceptualizations of negative and positive feedback loops. Their emphasis, however, is on negative feedback. Koliba and his colleagues view negative feedback as the reason governance systems can be resilient. Through negative feedback mechanisms like sanctions and punishment for deviant behaviors, governance systems, such as emergency management systems, can be kept in their proper courses. They specifically cite "written rules, laws, strategic or action plans, standards, contractual agreements, and performance measures" as "manifestations" of negative feedback (p. 178).

One gets the impression from Baumgartner and Jones' descriptions that in the American political system negative feedback loops and the equilibria created by them are the norm and positive feedback loops and large-scale changes are exceptions. This is a reasonable observation of the system. From Koliba and his colleagues' descriptions, one gets the impression that negative feedback is also desirable, and positive feedback is undesirable for the resilience of governance systems. Indeed, negative feedback is a course-correcting mechanism ,and as such it is necessary to keep a system intact. However, it is not necessarily desirable under all conditions from the perspective of complexity theory.

As I mentioned earlier in this chapter, in Prigogine's view complex systems are self-organizationally dynamic. Systems are born, transformed, and dissolve so that other systems are born. In his critical assessment of the mainstream views on policy systems, Brem (2000) points to the dangers of artificially stabilizing these systems. He argues that large-scale systemic changes, such as collapses, are not only normal, but also desirable:

> Collapse and instability are in fact beneficial to long term system vitality in a dynamic cycle of emergence, collapse, and re-emergence. In this fashion, a process of evolutionary development takes place as systems change over time and adapt to new temporal and spatial realities. However, when the cycles and dynamics of emergent order, increasing complexity, bifurcation, and reordering are artificially stabilized beyond natural parameters, the potential for dysfunctional or catastrophic collapse is increased. (p. 125)

Brem mentions a variety of situations in which negative feedback loops stabilize systems artificially, which eventually lead to catastrophic collapses. Policymakers may develop over-attachment to particular belief systems or simply may fear change and stick to their routines emotionally. They may tweak systems to make them continue to work. As a result, they overload the systems, which eventually collapse.

Five Propositions

The implications of the four models of system dynamics for policy studies can be summarized in five propositions.

    1. The natural tendency of a system is not toward stasis, or equilibrium, but away from it. Equilibrium is not the end state of a dynamic process, but it may be a phase in ever-changing systemic processes.

All complexity theorists would agree with this proposition. It suggests there is no ideal and stable state of societies where all problems are solved. There is no final "solution" to policy problems in the sense that the problem would disappear and the policy system would reach a state of equilibrium. Public policy processes are dynamic; new problems are created as others are solved. These assumptions are accepted by most, if not all, public policy theorists, implicitly, if not explicitly. So, complexity theory reaffirms and strengthens the accepted wisdom in the policy thinking. The other four propositions are the more specific and important contributions to our understanding of policy processes.

    2. Systemic change is self-organizational for the most part. External events can certainly trigger changes, but the existence of external events is not a necessary condition for change.

This is the common theme in all four models I discussed in this chapter: Bak's, Prigogine's, Luhmann's, and Kauffman's models. They all stress that systemic change does not require an external force. It is internally driven. But the questions of what is internal and what is external to a system and how is "self" defined and by whom are open (see Chapters 2 and 4).

Luhmann's theory of self-referential social systems is particularly noteworthy here. The self of a system in Luhmann's theory is so strong and cohesive that it determines its boundaries with its environment and thus it defines its "self" and "environment." On the basis of this definition, the system preserves its structural integrity and replaces or reorganizes its own elements. This is a view of a closed system. Prigogine's theory of open systems offers a different view of self-organization. In Prigogine's view systems exchange energy and information with their environments constantly, and yet their behaviors are not determined by external forces. Prigogine's is a self-driven dynamism.

Gerrits and his coleagues' conceptualization of singular and composite policy action systems are applications of Luhmann's and Prigogine's ideas in comparison to each other in understanding policy systems. Gerrits' dichotomous conceptualization is insightful, and it can help us understand better the role of closeness and openness, or self-refentiality and dissipation, in policy systems. An important issue is, whether there is such a clear-cut dichotomy of singular versus composite policy action systems.

Or is the self-referentiality of a policy system a matter of degree? Gerrits (2008, p. 222) acknowledges that the dichotomy is not clear cut and the characteristics of both singular and composite systems can be observed in particular systems in empirical studies. Future studies can help us identify different configuration in policy systems.

3. Systems evolve together, not in isolation, but this does not mean that their coevolution is necessarily a synchronous process.

Gerrits and his colleagues' conceptualizations and case descriptions also illustrate that systems evolve together, not in isolation, but this does not mean that their coevolution is necessarily a synchronous process. Natural and policy systems coevolve, but not in synchrony. The nature and mechanisms of this asynchronous coevolution is illustrated in Koehler's (1999, 2003) conceptualization of adaptive governance. His basic insight is that as they coevolve, policy systems do not always do so in harmony, or synchrony, with natural systems or other policy systems. Neither do they have equal impacts on all actors. He uses the term heterochrony to signify the effects of governmental involvement in economic development. Such involvements tend to change both the nature of the relations among business and nonprofit organizations and future government actions by modifying the complex system in which they operate. Kohler's insights can be adapted for future empirical studies in other areas of public policy.

4. Although changes at the micro and macro levels of systems are related, they are not necessarily proportional, synchronous, or parallel. A system's structural properties may remain stable, despite the changes in its elements.
5. In a more generalized form, the proposition 4. can be restated as this: Change and stability are not mutually exclusive; they can be complementary.

These propositions are most clearly reflected in Bak's and Luhmann's conceptualizations. In Bak's observations while as a system's elements (sand grains) keep changing at differing rates, the system itself (sand pile) maintains its "meta-stability." Luhmann's theory suggests that stability and change are not mutually exclusive; in order for self-referential systems to maintain their structures, they need to replace and/or renew their elements and the relations among them. In other words, stability at the system level is ensured by change at the micro level. This process is driven by the system's tendency to reproduce itself in its own image.

Luhamnn's theory can be used in investigating policy systems. The questions would be: Do, or to what extent, policy systems develop self-images? Do, or to what extent, they reproduce themselves by replacing their elements at the micro level?

Gerrits' (2008) study indicates that singular policy systems try to maintain their structural stability by selecting the participants that "buy into" the pre-established self-image of the system, which is set by the leadership. They keep the members who support the pre-established views of the leadership and ignore and/or exclude those who have different views, whereas composite policy actions systems are open to differing views and dissent, and they are more dynamic in the sense that they change their structures to adapt external events. In Gerrits' view composite policy systems are more effective compared to singular systems.

The specifics of how singular and composite policy systems work and their effectiveness should be the topics of future studies. There are many examples of organizations, particularly private corporations, making personnel changes, restructuring their organizational relations, and "rebranding" themselves to maintain their viability in periods of turbulence and major change. The questions are, to what extent are these changes self-referential and to what extent are they actually successful in maintaining the integrity of their organizations. It is reasonable to ask similar questions for policy systems: Do they replace the actors involved in them? Do they change the type or style of the relations among their actors? Do they "rebrand" themselves? And, to what extent do these activities self-referential?

CHAPTER SUMMARY

In this chapter I summarized the four models of system change that have been developed by complexity theorists. The first of these is *self-organized criticality*. This model explains how small events lead to large events. It shows that systemic change is self-organizational. Small changes at the micro level can lead to changes at the system level, but the changes at the two levels are not synchronous.

The *dissipative systems* model suggests that change is natural and inevitable in nature. This is because most systems in the universe are dissipative (open) systems, which exchange energy, matter, and information with their environments. Dissipative systems have the tendency to move away from equilibrium and toward "far-from-equilibrium" conditions. The model also suggests that time is irreversible, which is why dissipative systems are dynamic and self-organizing. Irreversible time is also the basis of the unpredictability of the future behaviors of systems.

In the *self-referentiality* model of change, change and stability are two complementary characteristics of systems. Systems change because under the pressure of time, they make selections in their environments and themselves. In other words, systems self-reproduce through their definitions of themselves and their environments. Systems cannot be in full synchronization with their environments; this triggers further change within the system and changes in the system's relations with its environment.

Coevolutionary models are the models of systems' evolving together and in relation to each other. Changes in one system triggers changes in others it is in relationship with. Through feedback loops and mutual selection mechanisms, systems evolve together.

Of these four models only dissipative structures and coevolutionary models have been applied relatively extensively by policy theorists. I summarized these applications and made five propositions for future applications of the models in policy studies.

Part II
Epistemology

6 Epistemology of Complexity
Uncertainty and Contextuality

In the introduction to this book I mentioned that the first, and probably the most significant, contribution of complexity theory is to make us appreciate the complex nature of realities and the uncertainties that generates in knowledge processes. Then I noted that this appreciation is important, because complexity theory challenges the implicit simplifying assumptions of the Newtonian/positivist scientific methods, such as the universe is a clockwork mechanism, and therefore we can gain a certain and complete knowledge of it by breaking down the clockwork to its most basic elements. This Newtonian/positivist reductionist approach to scientific inquiry undergirds the mainstream methodologies of the natural and social sciences today.

The picture of complexity theory that emerges from the previous chapters confirms these observations and does more. Complexity theory suggests that we should question some of the commonly held assumptions in the social science research, including policy research, and the suitability of the tools of investigation we use in our inquiries. For instance, the problematic nature of the linearity assumption that is deeply ingrained in popular research methodologies like linear regression has been highlighted by complexity theory. Complexity theory also makes us question the assumptions that the sum of individual properties are equal to those of the whole, that events are caused by external factors, not endogenously (the assumption that underlies experimental designs), and that systems tend toward steady states (equilibria) and stay there unless disturbed.

Complexity theory also suggests that we should look for alternatives to these commonly held assumptions. The problem is that there is no alternative epistemology or methodology that is commonly adopted by all complexity theorists. As M. Mitchell (2009) reminds us, there is no unified theory of complexity. In this and the following chapters, I summarize the views of complexity theorists in their search for alternatives and interpret the implications of complexity theory for epistemology and methodology.

In this chapter, I discuss general ontological and epistemological implications of complexity theory: determinism, certainty, predictability, objectivity, generalizability, and contextuality.[1] In the next chapter, I will summarize and assess the three epistemological positions complexity theorists have espoused in their writings: pluralism, phenomenology, and post-structuralism. Part III of this book is about the methodological alternatives complexity theorists and researchers offer.

I want to clarify what I mean by "commonly held assumptions" in the social sciences, including policy research. In my earlier book *A New Mind for Policy Analysis* (2002), I demonstrated that the roots of the mainstream thinking and practice in policy research and policy analysis are in the Newtonian/positivist science, which is the dominant scientific framework today (see particularly Chapters 1 and 2 in that book). The term *Newtonian science* is usually used in reference to the developments in the scientific worldview in the 17th century. Although it is commonly known as the Newtonian science, others like Bacon and Descartes contributed to this scientific worldview. Bacon re-invigorated the Aristotelian legacy of empiricism—legacy of the belief that truth should be derived from experience and experimentation—and defined science broadly to include both the natural and social sciences. Descartes separated the mind from matter and defined the latter as the legitimate domain of science. He also developed the conceptual tools of breaking down realities into their units and measuring them and mathematically establishing their relations. Newton further developed the mathematical tools of scientific investigation and established experimentation as the main tool of science. *Positivism* is a term used interchangeably with "empiricism," "behaviorism," "naturalism," and "science" (Hughes, 1990, p. 16), but it mainly and more specifically refers to August Comte's positivist philosophy of the 19th century and the principles of the Vienna Circle of logical positivists of the early 20th century. Others who did not call themselves positivists, such as J. S. Mill and Durkheim, shared the foundational beliefs of positivism (Giddens, 1995 pp. 136–146). I will use the terms Newtonian science and positivism together, because their philosophical assumptions are the same or similar for the most part.

The Newtonian/positivist science depicts a clockwork universe that exists independently of the knowing subject and is deterministic. The entities that exist in this universe and the events that take place in it are knowable with certainty and in their entirety, *in principle*, by breaking them down into their basic units and gaining information about each unit and its relationship with other units. "In principle" is the key phrase here. For practical reasons scientists may not know reality with certainty or in its entirety at given moment, or they may not be able to predict future events in their entirety, but that would not be because of the inherent unknowability of events, but because of the limitations of their knowledge at the time. In other words, this is an epistemological limitation, not an ontological one. Future events are totally predictable in the Newtonian/positivist view: Given sufficient background information about the units and their relations, and if the proper analytical tools are used, scientists can predict everything that will happen. [2]

A core epistemological assumption of the Newtonian/positivist science is that scientists can remove themselves from the realities they study and, by doing so, gain an objective knowledge of them. Scientific knowledge can correspond to its objects of study on a one-to-one basis. A scientist can and should separate factual knowledge from his/her predilections, values, and preferences in this process of discovery. The Newtonian/positivist epistemology defines the goal of science as to discover the universal and timeless laws of the fully deterministic universe. Newtonian/positivist philosophers of science believe that the assumptions and methods of science should be the same in both the natural and social realms. They think that reductionist/analytical and quantitative methods suit all realms of study in science and consider holistic and qualitative approaches as inferior or unscientific. Complexity theory's challenge to this worldview is the topic of the following sections.

DETERMINISM, CERTAINTY, AND PREDICTABILITY

Complexity theory disagrees with the Newtonian/positivist science on the issue of determinism, inherent knowability of natural events, and the predictability of future events. To understand better the differences between the Newtonian/positivist and complexity perspectives, I propose using Kellert's (1993, pp. 49–76) conceptualization of the *three levels of determinism* as the framework for discussion. According to Kellert, determinists make the assumption at the first level that the world is composed of *discrete entities and events* that can be aggregated hierarchically to understand reality. Newtonian physics is based on the idea that the universe is made of discrete entities: Matter is composed of molecules, which are in turn composed of atoms, which are composed of subatomic particles, and so on. The nature of physical reality can be understood by breaking it down to these constituent parts. Examples of these assumptions can be found in the social sciences, primarily in J. S. Mill's view of society. He considered individuals as the elements of society and suggested that the laws of society could be deduced from the study of individuals (Keat and Urry, 1975, p. 76).

The assumption that entities and events are discrete was challenged by quantum mechanics in the early 20th century. Quantum physicists demonstrated with experiments that subatomic particles do not exist in discrete or definite forms. The uncertainty in the measurement of the positions of subatomic particles led to the quantum theoretical principle that they have probabilistic existence. The insights of quantum mechanics into subatomic particles do not have a direct bearing on the kinds of physical, chemical, biological, or social phenomena complexity theorists are concerned about, but they are important in the sense that they shake up the Newtonian assumption of determinism at the most basic level of existence, the level of the building blocks of all matter. [3] Quantum mechanical findings make us question this: If Newtonian determinism does not hold at the most basic level, can we assume that it does at higher levels?

Complexity theorists do not have a specific or coherent answer to this question. I have not encountered a direct answer to the question in the complexity theory literature, but from my readings of complexity theory writings, I can infer that complexity theorists generally would not dispute the Newtonian assumption that there are discrete entities and events in nature. At least, they would suggest that units of events and entities can be viewed as discrete for analytical purposes. In the literature on agent-based simulations, for example, "agents" are treated as if they were discrete units.

As a simplifying assumption, this may be acceptable. But, in my view, complexity theorists, particularly those who study social systems, should be cognizant of the theoretical problems this simplifying assumption could create.

The problem of unit of observation, or unit of analysis, has not been thought through in complexity theory, but there are some conceptualizations complexity theorist can adopt and build on. The most fundamental conceptual issue is that units of social systems are not merely discrete biological entities. Then what are they? Complexity theorists can build their answers on the conceptualizations by network theorists, Giddens, social constructionists, and Luhmann. In social network analyses, the units are *relationships* among actors (see Chapter 10 of this book). In Giddens' conceptualization the units are the "situated activities of human agents, reproduced across time and space" (1984, p. 25). Social construction theorists define systems as products of the collective constructions of individuals (see Chapter 2 of this book). Then *constructions* are the units. In Luhmann's theory, the perceptions and behaviors of individual actors are determined by the social system; therefore, it may not even be meaningful to talk about any "units." Regardless of which perspective complexity theorists adopt, the units these perspectives suggest are not discrete.

Kellert's second level deterministic assumption is that these discrete entities and events are *causally connected*. Philosophers conceptualized the nature of causality in a variety of ways, which are beyond the scope of my discussion here. It is important to reemphasize, however, that in the Newtonian/positivist scientific view *external events* cause changes in the positions and movements of objects. The Newtonian model of causality can be expressed as follows:

Independent Variable (X) $\rightarrow$ Dependent Variable (Y)

This model should be familiar to the reader, because it is the core model in many research methods social and policy researchers employ, from experimental and quasi-experimental designs to multiple regression models. The complexity theory notion of self-organization—that systemic dynamics are internally driven, endogenous—is in direct contrast with this model and the underlying assumption that causation is external.

The Newtonian/positivist notion of causality is also *linear*: that is cause–effect relations are proportional. Although the Newtonian science recognizes that there are some nonlinearities in nature, linearity is dominant in its mathematical models. Newton's second and third laws of motion are succinct expressions of the notion that causality is linear: A force that is applied to an object produces a *proportional* momentum (the second law). The object reacts to the source of the force with an *equal* and opposite force (the third law). Newtonian scientists do observe nonlinearities in the phenomena they study, but they view them as annoying disturbances in the perfectly ordered, clockwork universe. The "error terms" in measurement or "residuals" in regression analyses are examples of this Newtonian view. As I stressed in Chapter 1 and repeated in the following chapters, nonlinear relations are at the center of complexity theory; they are not treated as annoyances.

The Newtonian notion of causality also includes the assumption that there are *necessary* connections between events: that the relations between past and future events are fixed, and no alternative futures are allowed. William James calls this view the "iron block of universe." In this view, "The future has no ambiguous possibilities hidden in its womb: the part we call the present is compatible with only one totality. . . . The whole is in each and every part, and welds it with the rest into an absolute unity, an iron block, in which there can be no equivocation or shadow of turning" (quoted in Honderich, 1995, p. 194).

Another expression of this assumption is that *the universe is an entirely deterministic system*. This constitutes the third level of deterministic assumptions in Kellert's framework. Because the universe is an entirely deterministic system, it is possible to know it certainly and entirely: all of its details, both in the past and in the future. This model suggest that even if there are practical difficulties in knowing all the details of all the events in the universe, they are *predictable in principle* "by an all-powerful intelligence or computational scheme, given complete information of instantaneous conditions and the complete set of physical laws" (Kellert, 1993, p. 60).

I discuss complexity theory's response to this third level of deterministic assumptions next in a separate section.

UNCERTAINTY IN THE KNOWLEDGE OF COMPLEX SYSTEMS

Complexity theorists articulated two related, but distinguishable, positions on the relations between determinism, certainty, and predictability. The first one is that even though the universe may be deterministic in principle (Kellert's first two levels), the future behaviors of systems are not predictable, at least, not precisely. This position is expressed by chaos theorists like Lorenz. The second position is that indeterminism is the norm in nature, and this makes predictability of future behaviors impossible. This is Prigogine's position.

Chaos Theory

In his popular book *Chaos: Making a New Science* (1987), Gleick articulated the conceptualizations and propositions of chaos theorists. Chaos theory may be considered an earlier version, or a branch, of complexity theory.[4] Chaos theorists observed in the systems they studied—from atmospheric conditions to dripping faucets and heart rhythms—that even when the relations among the elements of a system can be expressed with deterministic terms—not probabilistic terms—the future behavior of the system cannot be predicted with certainty or precision.

This is because of the nonlinear relations among the system's elements. Linear relations make certain and precise predictions possible. Nonlinear relations do not allow that. Nonlinearity is the primary source of uncertainties and makes the trajectory of a system's future behavior unpredictable. As Goerner (1995) puts it, opposing tendencies are built into a nonlinear system: "Nonlinearity can produce either positive (amplifying) or negative (dampening) feedback. It can produce stability or instability. It may produce coherence . . . but it may also produce divergence and explosion" (p. 20). These tendencies make nonlinear systems versatile, and their behaviors and states unpredictable. Therefore, it is not possible to obtain the complete knowledge of a complex system or the precise knowledge of its parts. But even then some qualitative, less precise, predictions are possible.

Note that in this chaos theory view, the first two of Kellert's three levels of determinism are accepted, at least implicitly: Events may have distinguishable discreteness, and they are causally connected. However, because these causal connections are not linear, the third level of determinism—that all events are connected in an ironclad manner that makes total and precise predictability possible—is rejected.

Lorenz's (1963a, 1963b) studies on atmospheric flow and hydrodynamics were among the earlier and most significant studies that broke the connection between determinism and predictability. In these pioneering studies Lorenz showed that because of the irreducible nonlinearity in these systems, the predictability of their future behaviors is fundamentally limited. More specifically, Lorenz showed that atmospheric and hydrodynamic systems exhibit nonlinear behaviors under certain, but common, conditions. Under such conditions, the behaviors of the systems are not predictable quantitatively, or precisely, but when such behaviors are modeled using three-dimensional plots, their patterns can be discerned qualitatively.

A good illustration of the disconnect between determinism and predictability can be found in the logistic equation I described in Chapter 1, particularly in the solution of its iterative form of $Y_{t+1} = kY_t - k\,Y_t^2$ with $k = 3.7$ (Figure 1.4d). The relations in this deterministic equation are nonlinear.

This equation is considered deterministic, because there is no probabilistic term in it, and in that sense, the relations among its terms are determined. Figure 1.4d represents a system at far from equilibrium, where the iterative solutions to the equation do not settle into a straight line—they fluctuate in a seemingly random manner—which does not allow us make generalizations about its behavior or make predictions about its future behavior. One cannot predict where the next output is going to be from the position of the previous output.

In contrast to this, in the solutions of the equation with smaller values of k, for example 2.3, the next move of the system is precisely predictable (see Figure 1.4a). It is predictable, because we know that a perfectly linear pattern emerged after a few iterations. The iterative solutions of the equation settles into a straight line at a value close to 0.6 (0.565218 to be precise) and stays in this equilibrium state. This allows us to make a generalization about the pattern of the solutions—that it will be on a straight line—and thus make predictions for their future values (0.565218).

Although the chaotic pattern in Figure 1.4d does not allow any precise predictions, when the outputs are plotted on a two-dimensional attractor, we can observe that there is a discernible geometric pattern (see Figures 1.5a and 1.5b). Although we still cannot predict the "behavior of the system"— the movements of the outputs from one step to the next—precisely, we can predict that they will move within the boundaries of this geometric shape. This is where we can see a qualitatively discernible pattern, which represents a form of limited generalizability—generalizability in qualitative forms.

The conclusion we can draw from this example of the logistic equation is that the behavior of a nonlinear and chaotic system is not predictable precisely—meaning quantitatively—but we still can predict it geometrically— in a qualitative manner.

Prigogine

Prigogine (1996, pp. 5–6) questions the assumption that the future behaviors of systems are predictable at a deeper level. He posits that indeterminism reigns in the universe, and determinism is exceptional. This is because most systems in nature are open systems, and they endogenously drift toward far-from-equilibrium conditions where they are dynamic and their future courses cannot be predicted with certainty. There are only a few closed systems in the universe, and their deterministic characteristics allow us to make only limited generalizations and predictions.

Time is a core concept in Prigogine's understanding of the world. In his view time is irreversible. This view contrasts with the Newtonian view of reversible time. As I mentioned in Chapter 5, irreversible time is the basis of evolution and history, according to Prigogone, and it makes precise predictions about systems' future behaviors impossible. In Newtonian mechanics, because time is reversible, the motion trajectories of Newtonian objects go back and forth in time—they repeat themselves—and thus the directions of Newtonian equations that describe them can be reversed. This allows scientists to make generalizations about systems' behaviors, within the perspective of the Newtonian science. Prigogine and Stengers (1984) counter that in reality we cannot go back in time, because the second law of thermodynamics prohibits it. They also assert that the evolutionary, irreversible, nature of time lays at the origin of self-organization, which in turn nullifies the notion of determinism in the form of predictability of future behavior (p. 8). In other words, the existence of irreversible time is the source of indeterminism. Irreversibility and randomness—unpredictability of future behaviors—are the rules in nature, not exceptions. Reversible time and determinism, and thus predictable behavior, apply only to a limited number of cases (p. 9).

Note that with these arguments and observations Prigogine questions the second level of Kellert's three-levels of determinism. He underscores the fundamental nonlinearity of casual connections between the elements of systems and the self-organizational nature of systemic processes, which call into question the Newtonian model of causality: Independent Variable → Dependent Variable. The level of complexity generated by nonlinearities and self-organizational processes call into question the validity of this model.

Prigogine draws the conclusion that scientists cannot be external observers of natural systems, which are mainly indeterministic. He takes a phenomenological position and argues that the knowledge of a complex system is constricted and conditioned not only by nonlinearity and indeterminism but also by the situatedness, or embeddedness, of the observers in the world they observe. I will discuss Prigogine's phenomenological arguments in the next chapter.

OBJECTIVITY, GENERALIZABILITY, AND CONTEXTUALITY

Objectivity and Universality of Knowledge

As I mentioned earlier in this chapter, a core epistemological assumption of the Newtonian/positivist science is that scientists can remove themselves from the realities they study and, in doing so, gain an objective knowledge of them. In other words, the knowing subject can be separated from the object of his/her study. This is known as the *subject–object distinction*. The Newtonian/positivist science further assumes that scientific knowledge can correspond to its objects of study on a one-to-one basis and the truthfulness of any piece of knowledge can be determined by empirically testing its correspondence to reality. This principle is called the *correspondence theory of truth*. To make sure that knowledge corresponds to reality, a scientist should separate *facts*, which are empirically testable, from his/her *values*, which are predilections, subjective states of his/her mind or heart. This is the principle of *fact–value distinction*. This set of assumptions— subject–object distinction, correspondence theory of truth, and the fact– value distinction—together may be called *objectivism*. This is the set of assumptions that make objective scientific knowledge possible in the view of the Newtonian/positivist science.

In this view the goal of science is to discover the universal and timeless laws of the fully deterministic universe. This is the principle of *universalism,* and it applies to both the natural and social sciences. Consequently, it is assumed, the same set of reductionist/analytical and quantitative methods are suitable for both realms of study. This may be called *methodological unity.* In the Newtonian/positivist view, holistic and qualitative approaches are considered inferior to reductionist/analytical and quantitative methods.[5]

Complexity theory has implications for these assumptions of the Newtonian/positivist science. I discuss them next. At the end of the chapter, I will discuss the implications of these problems and the different positions on them for public policy inquiry.

Complexity Theory and Contextuality of Knowledge

Complexity theorists do not have a unified and coherent view of the generalizability or universality of scientific knowledge, but one can identify a couple of threads of thought in the literature: that *the laws of complexity are universal* and that *knowledge of complex systems is contextual*. The coexistence of these two threads generates a tension in complexity theory, but I will argue that the two can also be complementary.

On the one hand, complexity theorists suggest that the properties of complex systems—nonlinearity, emergence, self-organization, and coevolution—apply to all realms of reality—physical, biological, and social realms. On the other hand, and ironically perhaps, because of these common properties, each system has a unique structure and evolutionary history. Nonlinear relations among a system's elements and between systems, self-organizational systemic processes, the process of emergence, and coevolutions of systems are so complex that they together create a unique behavioral pattern for each system. Because of the uniqueness of each system, we cannot make precise predictions about a system's behavior or universal generalizations about systems' behaviors. This forces us to recognize that knowledge is contextual: Each system's behavioral patterns can be understood within the context of the system. The behavioral patterns of social systems are even less predictable and generalizable, and the knowledge of each system's behavioral pattern is more contextual, because they are constituted of the activities of purposeful and reflective actors.

What I just said in the previous paragraph is broad and vague. Because it is broad and vague, multiple and conflicting interpretations can fit into it. Complexity theorists would generally agree that there are limitations to the generalizability of our knowledge of reality and that knowledge is contextual, but there are also differences among them on the extent to which generalizations are possible and what should be the epistemological basis of the contextuality of knowledge. These differences emanate from the different epistemologies different complexity theorists adopt. For instance, Prigogine thinks that complexity theory supports a phenomenological view of the world. Cilliers makes the case for a post-structuralist interpretation of complexity theory. I will address these different interpretations in the next chapter.

A clarification of the concept of contextuality is necessary before any further discussions. There are two related, but conceptually distinguishable kinds of contextuality, or two reasons for the contextuality of the knowledge of complex systems. The first one is the *context of a complex system*. Because complex systems emerge through self-organizational and nonlinear processes and their structural properties change over time, each system has unique properties, as well as properties that are common with other systems. Universal generalizations about systems' behaviors are not possible, and their properties can be known only in their spatial and temporal contexts. In other words the contextuality of knowledge has an ontological basis; it is because of the nature of the way complex systems are. The second one is the *context of the observer*. This kind of contextuality has an epistemological basis: It is due to the positions of the observers of complex systems and the particular ways they process knowledge. I discuss each kind in a separate section below.

Context of a Complex System

Complexity theory is a scientific theory; therefore, complexity theorists make generalizations. Without generalization, there is no scientific knowledge. However, the structural properties and dynamical process of each complex system is unique. Then how is it possible to find commonalities and make generalizations about the properties and processes of complex systems? If yes, to what extent? Complexity theorists differ in their answers to these questions. I summarize the views of three theorists here: von Bertalanffy, Kauffman, and Prigogine.

Von Bertalanffy's work obviously predates what we call complexity theory today, but as I mentioned in Chapter 2, his general system theory provides an important background for understanding complexity theory. His description of systems is not much different from the later descriptions of complex systems by complexity theorists.

Von Bertalanffy, like many other philosophers of science of the first half of the 20th century, was concerned about how to unify scientific knowledge.

He aimed to unify scientific knowledge by finding out the general principles of systems that would be generalizable to all fields of science. His solution to the problem of unification of scientific knowledge was to identify the "isomorphic laws" that apply to all kinds of systems—systems that different fields of science study (von Bertalanffy, 2008, pp. 220–222). He cites examples from a variety of fields of science to show that the same differential equations apply to the behaviors of systems in all these fields. He mentions, for example, that the law of compound interest with negative exponent applies to diverse phenomena such as the decay of radium, the killing of bacteria by light disinfectants, the loss of body substance in a starving animal, and the decrease of birth rate when the death rate is higher than the birth rate. He acknowledges that the applicability of many natural laws to social systems is questionable, but expresses the hope that the principles of general system theory will be applicable to social sciences, and this would lead to the unification of science (p. 234).

When von Bertalanffy expresses this hope, he does not mean that one day all biological phenomena would be explained in terms of physics or all social phenomena would be explained in terms of biology. He rejects such reductionist views. Instead, he points to the "structural similarities"—"isomorphisms"—among the phenomena in physics, biology, and society. An example of such structural similarities is the scale-free networks and the power-law distribution of the nodes in them. As I mentioned in Chapter 3, Barabási and others found examples of scale-free networks in the World Wide Web, the citations of journal articles in the academic literature, the "hub" system in the flight connections of airlines, urban supply networks, and traffic flows. I also mentioned that these observations by Barabási and others, they were criticized for exaggerating the similarities among these systems.

The debate on the issue of isomorphisms has not been settled. A natural question would be this: If such isomorphisms are observed, are they expressions of natural laws that govern all realms of reality, including the social realm? This is an open question.

Kauffman (1995) is hopeful that the *laws of complexity* can be discovered but acknowledges that there are difficulties in such discoveries. Note that what he is referring to is not structural similarities observed in systems in different realms, but universal "laws," as in the laws of nature in the Newtonian view of science. But his notion of law has an important difference from the Newtonian notion of natural laws as well. According to Kauffman, order emerges in the biological world because of the laws of complexity, and the emergent biological whole exhibits collective properties that cannot be explained in terms the workings of the chemical and physical components of biological organisms; they should be understood in their own right (pp. vii–viii). In other words, the laws of complexity are not reductionist. He breaks up the Newtonian connection between the reductionist/analytical thinking and universal laws: Once the components of a system are understood, the whole system can also be understood by aggregating pieces of information.

Kauffman acknowledges that there are three kinds of difficulties in developing universal laws in science (p. 23). The first one is that quantum mechanics precludes the possibility of detailed description of molecular phenomena and the prediction of their behaviors. So, at least at the quantum level, universal generalizations based on detailed descriptions and predictions are not possible. Second, he cites chaos theory's finding that even in the deterministic macro-level phenomena very small changes in the initial conditions can lead to profound changes of behavior in chaotic systems. This precludes the possibility of making predictions in many systems.[6] Third, Kauffman points out, the complexity of systems is incompressible, irreducible. This precludes the possibility of finding simple and reproducible explanations of phenomena.

Despite these difficulties, Kauffman is hopeful that the "robust" features of organisms—those features that are stable and not sensitive to details—that emerged during the biological evolution will allow scientists to find *some* universal laws. Even if this is possible, it would be a scaled-back version of the universalism of the Newtonian science that the universe is a completely deterministic system whose behaviors are predictable and generalizable in principle—Kellert's (1993) third level of determinism.

Prigogine and Stengers (1984, pp. 60–61) take the most skeptical position on the Newtonian view of predictability and universality of laws. They argue that the irreversible nature of time is at the origin of self-organization, which in turn nullifies the notion of determinism in the form of predictability of future behavior. Therefore, universal generalizations about systems' behaviors are not possible; however, they point out, generalization can be made about the "islands of determinism" that exist within the mostly indeterministic universe.

Although the views of complexity theorists on universality vary, it is clear that the implications of complexity theory impose limitations on the extent to which knowledge is generalizable. This is because of the nature of complex systems—an ontological limitation. There are also limitations to generalizability of knowledge because of the positions of the observers of complex systems.

Context of the Observer

Is the knowledge of a system subject to epistemological limitations as well? In other words, is the knowledge of a system at least partly in the eye of a beholder? Complexity theorists Prigogine and Stengers (1984), Rössler (1986), and Casti (1994), and Gell-Mann (1995) answer the question affirmatively. Gell-Mann points out that when measuring the complexity of an entity, one has to take into account the level of the detail of its description, which depends on the previous knowledge and understanding of the observer of a system. Also the language employed by the observer will contribute to, or constrict, the perception and measurement of complexity, according to Gell-Mann. Prigogine and Stengers and Rössler and Casti agree that the knowledge of complexity, or reality in general, is constricted by the cognitive apparatuses and situatedness, or embeddedness, of an observer in the world he/she observes.

Casti points out that the knowledge of a system depends on the position of the knowing subject—whether he/she is inside or outside the system:

> . . . sometimes things look different if you're inside the system than if you look at what's happening from the outside. . . . And so it is when it comes to chaotic processes. We have an entirely different set of tests for identifying the presence or absence of chaos if we are given the vector field of the system (the insider's view) then if all we have to go on is the outsider's record of only the system's observed behavior (i.e., its output). (p. 98)

The knowledge of a system is not merely determined by whether the observer is inside or outside the system, according to Casti. The main issue is that the complexity of a system is not independent of the observer, it is partly determined by the subject: "[W]hatever complexity such systems have is a joint property of the system and its interaction with another system, most often an observer and/or controller" (p. 269). In other words, complexity is both ontological and epistemological. He goes on to say

> [J]ust like truth, beauty, good and evil, complexity resides as much in the eye of the beholder as it does in the structure and behavior of a system itself. This is not to say that there do not exist *objective* ways to characterize some aspects of a system's complexity. . . . The main point here is that these objective measures only arise as special cases of the two-way measures, in which the interaction between the system and the observer is much weaker in one direction than in the other. [emphasis in original] (p. 270)

Casti also posits that some observers may be more attuned to observing the complexities in phenomena better than others (p. 276). He gives the example of a stone. Whether it is a simple or complex system depends on if you are a layperson or a geologist. A layperson interacts with stone differently and is likely to see it as a simple object. A geologist sees it as a complex system, with an understanding of its molecular structure, its interactions with its chemical and physical environments, and the history of how it has become what it is.

Cognitive psychologists have recognized for some time now that the knowledge acquisition in human beings is facilitated by a priori cognitive conceptions, or filters, called "schemata" (Gestalt psychologist) or "constructs" (e.g., Kelly, 1955). The philosophical roots of the notion that the mind is proactive in knowledge acquisition and that prior conceptions exist in the mind can be traced back to Immanuel Kant's *synthetic a priori* and Husserl's consciousness, which I will discuss in the next chapter.

Some complexity theorists adopted this proactive view of the mind. Holland, for example, emphasizes that schemata are anticipatory and stresses that they evolve in interactions with external realities. He also points out that observers, who are complex adaptive systems themselves, make forecasts based on their internal models of the world, which are tested, refined, and rearranged as the system gains experience (Holland cited in Waldrop, 1992, pp. 145–147). Gell-Mann (1995) concurs with the notion that schemata evolve in interaction with their environments. Holland and Gell-Mann agree that although there may be accidental changes in them, the survival of a complex adaptive system depends on its fitness to its environment. Fitness involves both interrelations among the components of a schema and their relations with the systems they are observing. However, the experience of an observer is never raw; it is always screened by prior schemata and gathered into coherent objects. Thus knowing is an ongoing adaptive process in which objectivity and subjectivity emerge and continually evolve.

Maturana and Varela's autopoiesis theory offers a different view. They suggest that observing systems are themselves autopoietic—closed and self-referential—systems (Kickert, 1993). In Maturana and Varela's view, the nervous system works as a closed network of interactions, and it is a self-referential system. As such, it does not represent external realities but keeps reorganizing itself to accommodate incoming signals (Capra, 1996, pp. 96–97). In Luhmann's application of autopoiesis to social systems, each social system observes itself and its environment in a self-referential manner: It is selective in its observations and refers back to its schema/frameworks in selecting incoming signals. Both social systems and their observers are two separate autopoietic systems (Knodt's preface to Luhmann, 1995). In Luhmann's own words,

> No system can decompose another analytically to arrive at final elements (substances) in which knowledge could find an ultimate foothold and secure correspondence with its object. Instead, every observation must employ a difference schema whereby the unity of difference is constituted in the observing system and not in the observed one. (p. 35)

Second-order cybernetics, which Little (2000) introduced to the public administration and policy literature, has similar implications, but it takes the role of the observer one step forward: The observer not only observes a system but also participates in the construction, or constitution, of the system. Little notes that while first-order cybernetics is the science of observed systems and their circular causal interactions, second-order cybernetics is the science of observing systems. The term second-order cybernetics was coined by Heinz von Foerster in the 1970s (von Foerster, 1974). It is based on the assumption that the observer cannot be completely divorced from the system under consideration; in fact, the observer is a constitutive part of a circular organization. Observing systems are necessarily self-referential and self-producing. The realities they observe are their constructions (Little, pp. 153–154).

If the observer participates in the constitution of a system, would the actors of the system not do the same? In other words, do, or to what extent, the knowledge of actors in a social system constitute the system itself? The reader will remember from Chapter 2 that in Gerritts, Marks, and Van Buuren's (2009) view, both actors and observers contribute to the definition of the boundaries of a system; the boundaries do not exist a priori. "What constitutes a system is a matter of judgment by the actors comprising the system as well as by observers" (p. 137). If this is the case, then we are dealing with highly complex knowledge processes.

How does the knowledge—or beliefs, opinions, etc.—an actor has about him/herself, others, and their relations affect his/her actions and relations with others and the systemic whole? This is a highly pertinent issue for public policy. How do actors come together and form policy systems? This can at least partly be answered that policy systems are formed on the basis of the beliefs and opinions of actors about themselves and others.

IMPLICATIONS FOR PUBLIC POLICY

Determinism, Predictability, and Public Policy

The deterministic beliefs of the Newtonian science have penetrated the theoretical thinking in public policy and administration from the beginnings of these fields of study. I discussed this issue in some depth elsewhere (Morçöl, 2002). Briefly, Newtonian beliefs manifest themselves particularly in the theories of long-term planning and bureaucratic organization. In long-term planning, the assumption is not only that government actions and programs can cause desired effects, such as economic growth and manufacturing of goods at desired levels, but also that the relationship between cause and effect is linear and proportional. To obtain a desired amount of economic growth, a proportional amount of monetary or non-monetary incentives are injected into the economic system. It is also assumed that an all-knowing planner, or a group of planners, can predict the future of an economy or society and therefore plan accordingly.

Some policy theorists criticize the technocratic role this view of planning attributes to planners. Fischer (1990, pp. 355–377) argues that the policy analysis profession has become technocratic and undemocratic and is out of the control of the public it is supposed to serve. Fischer traces the roots of these undemocratic tendencies to the 17th-century philosopher Francis Bacon's empiricist epistemology—which is a foundational principle of the Newtonian science—and his dream that a technical elite should rule in the name of efficiency and technical order. The Baconian dream has resulted in supporting a technocratic and elitist political system, according to Fischer.

The institutions of public administration were formed based on bureaucratic principles. The bureaucratic organization is expected to be deterministic and linear in its functioning. It is deterministic, because an order given by a superior in a hierarchy is expected to go down the ladders and implemented as intended: order is the cause; implementation is the effect. It is linear, because it is assumed that a proportional relation exists between order and its implementation. Accountability mechanisms are set up to check whether the linear cause–effect relation is maintained. But as Pressman and Wildavsky (1984) showed with their empirical studies, the implementation process is not as linear as the policy makers intend it to be.

The issue of determinism and predictability is also relevant to the discussion on the rational choice framework and its applications in public policy: public choice, principal–agent theory, institutional rational choice, and the like. One of the fundamental assumptions of the rational choice framework is that rational actors compete in economic and other social arenas, including bureaucracies, to maximize their utilities. Whether or not they are actually capable of maximizing their utilities has been disputed by many. Behavioral and cognitive psychologists critiqued the utility maximization assumption by pointing out the behavioral and cognitive biases and predispositions in the human cognitive processes. Simon's (1979) theory of "intended and bounded rationality" is the most well- known critique and revision of the utility maximization assumption, as I mentioned in Chapter 3: Individuals cannot rank-order their decision choices consistently or predict the outcomes of their decisions entirely because of their cognitive limitations.

Simon's critique is epistemological in nature. Complexity theorists, particularly Prigogine, on the other hand, point to the indeterministic nature of reality itself as the source of the limitations in knowledge in general. What could make utility maximization possible is the potential for certainty in the knowledge of stable states and thus the predictability of future stable states. If reality is stable, then its precise knowledge will be possible, and future states will be predictable. Rational choice theorists assume that social and economic systems tend toward stable states. Prigogine and his colleagues show that the state of equilibrium is not the norm, but an exception, even in natural systems. The assumption that social systems tend toward equilibrium is harder to maintain. Therefore, uncertainty is inevitable in the knowledge of social systems.

This logical conclusion has been affirmed by many socials scientists. Particularly, network theorists acknowledge that uncertainties abound in the functioning of governance and policy networks. They point to the complex and self-organizational nature of these networks for the uncertainties in their behaviors (e.g., O'Toole, 1997a; Agranoff and McGuire, 1999).

Koppenjan and Klijn (2004) point out that the sources of uncertainties in networks are the complex problems dealt with in today's societies. They cite three types of uncertainties in networks: substantive, strategic, and institutional uncertainties. Koppenjan and Klijn explain and illustrate strategic and institutional uncertainties. They point out that strategic uncertainty is created intentionally by the actors who play strategic games to gain advantage in networks. Institutional uncertainty is created by the interactions among actors who have different institutional backgrounds.

Koppenjan and Klijn devote very little space to the discussions on substantive uncertainty. They simply state that substantive uncertainty is a result of the complexity of problems and perceptions of actors. This is where complexity theory can be helpful. From the perspective of complexity theory, substantive uncertainty arises from the nonlinear relations within and between complex systems. In public policy processes there are a variety of factors that increase complexity and add to the substantive uncertainty: the limitations of expert knowledge, interactions between scientific and knowledge and politics, and interactions between natural and social systems. Gerritts' case studies of the decision-making processes over the estuaries in Germany, Belgium, and the Netherlands illustrate these substantive uncertainties in policy processes. He shows that the decision makers in these cases, particularly in the Unterelbe case in Germany, failed to understand the nonlinear and coevolutionary nature of the relations between policy systems and natural systems and the inevitable uncertainties these relations generated for decision making.

Rational Choice and Universality

Both the rational choice critic Mirowski (1990, p. 305) and the rational choice proponent Lichbach (2003) agree that the ultimate goal of rational choice theorists is to develop a universal theory of human behaviors. This universalist aspiration is based on three key assumptions: the rational actor assumption, equilibrium assumptions, and the assumption that quantitative analyses are the best (or superior) methods in all fields of science.

If all individuals are uniformly rational in all societies and at all times and there is an "inborn and necessary human nature" (Lichbach, 2003, p. 29), then it makes logical sense that universal generalizations can be made about their behaviors in all realms of life: economy, politics, organizations, etc. Also, if all social and economic systems tend toward equilibria, then universal generalizations about their behaviors will be possible. The rational choice critics Green and Shapiro (1994, pp. 24–26) observe that there are strong connections between the search for universality and the search for economic and political equilibria. This is because, in equilibria systemic behaviors are repetitious, and, as such, they allow generalizations. The reader will remember from earlier discussions that the reversible time assumption in the Newtonian science allows going back and forth in the motions of objects and thus allows generalizations about their behaviors.

The universalist aspiration of rational choice is reflected also in its heavy reliance on quantitative methodologies. Rational choice theorists believe that theirs is the only true science of society, because they use mathematical models and see case studies and historical and cultural studies as lesser science or no science at all (Cohn, 1999). It is easy to understand why quantitative analyses are so central to this universalist aspiration. In my earlier discussions on the logistic equation and the illustrations of its outcomes in Figures 1.4 and 1.5, I noted that we could make generalizations when $k = 2.3$. This allows us to make quantitatively precise predictions. When $k = 3.7$, we can make only qualitative generalizations, which are less precise (see the attractors in Figure 1.5). We can describe the shape of the attractor but cannot say that there is a "universal" value that the solution settles into.

Although the assumptions that individuals are uniformly rational and that systems tend toward equilibria represent a strong tendency among rational choice theorists to adopt a universalist stance, not all of them believe that a universal theory of human behavior would be possible. Lichbach (2003) notes that there are rationalists who factor social and contextual determination of behaviors into their models (pp. 29–31). He also notes that some rational choice theorists think that they can develop only middle-range theories (p. 37), whereas others insist that rational choice can explain everything in all social sciences and aim to unify social sciences within the rational choice paradigm (p. 4).

MacDonald (2003), a rational choice proponent, points to a dilemma rational choice theorists face when it comes to the universality of their theories. He identifies two main schools of thought in rational choice—instrumental empiricism and scientific realism—and notes that both run into difficulties when they try to justify making universal generalizations. Instrumentalist empiricists do not make strong assumptions about the rationality of human behavior; they do not assume that all human behaviors are uniformly rational. They are more interested in making predictions about the outcomes of behavior. These predictions are more easily verifiable and therefore generalizations about the outcomes of human behaviors can be made more easily. However, because instrumental empiricists ignore the ontological status of rational behavior, they do not provide a credible foundation for a scientific understanding. (If it does not matter whether rationality really exists, how can one make credible generalizations about rational behavior?) Scientific realists do try to demonstrate that human behavior is rational, but by doing so, they limit the scope of their studies to only few observable cases or situations, and thus limit the generalizability of rational behavior.

Institutional rational choice theorists, particularly Ostrom (1990, 2005) are cognizant of the difficulties in making universal generalizations about human nature. They acknowledge the importance of contextual factors—institutional rules, rule configurations, and culture—in understanding human behaviors. These contextual factors make it difficult to formulate any universal rules of human behaviors. Ostrom concedes that the generalizability of her observations is limited. However, the ultimate goal of her and her colleagues' research program remains to develop empirically verified generalizations of human behavior. This goal creates tensions in her writings. On the one hand, Ostrom (2005) believes that there is an underlying universality in human behaviors: "my deep conviction . . . [is] that underlying the immense variety of surface differences, all repetitive situations faced by human beings are composed of nested layers composed from the same set of elements" (p. 185). She wants to discover the "universal building blocks" of "structured situations" (p. 5) or the "fundamental building blocks of organized human interactions" (p. 6). She also cites successful applications of the institutional rational choice models in vastly different contexts of several countries—e.g., Bangladesh, Bolivia, Brazil, Nepal, Nigeria, Norway, Poland, Uganda, Turkey, and the US—and in a wide variety of public policy areas—urban policies, education, health care, irrigation, fisheries, forest resources, etc. (Ostrom, 1990, p. 64; 2005, p. 9). On the other hand, she accepts the possibility that a "continuum of models of human behavior"—not a universal one—may be needed when analyzing different situations (p. 7) and criticizes the universal models of rational behavior (2005, chap. 4).

Complexity theory does not have a clear or coherent alternative to the universalism or qualified (limited) universalism of rational choice, as my discussions in this chapter indicate. Alternatives can be elicited from the epistemologies some complexity theorists propose. I discuss those alternative epistemologies in the next chapter.

CHAPTER SUMMARY

In this chapter I discussed some of the epistemological implications of complexity theory. The discussions in the chapter indicate that complexity theory challenges the deterministic assumptions of the Newtonian/positivist science, but complexity theorists do not have a unified and coherent alternative to these assumptions.

I constructed the discussion around the three levels in Kellert's (1993) framework of determinism: (a) the world is composed of *discrete entities and events* that can be aggregated hierarchically, (b) these discrete entities and events are *causally connected* (external and linear causation between entities and events), and (c) *the universe is an entirely deterministic system.* Complexity theorists challenge these assumptions in two distinguishable ways.

Chaos theorists like Lorenz argue and demonstrate that even though the universe may be deterministic in principle (Kellert's first two levels), future behaviors of systems are not predictable, not at least precisely. Prigogine and his colleagues question determinism at the second level as well.

The Newtonian/positivist science assumes that objective knowledge is possible and it is universally generalizable. Different complexity theorists question the objectivity and generalizability of scientific knowledge at varying degrees. There are two recognizable strains of thought among complexity theorists: that *the laws of complexity are universal* and that *knowledge of complex systems is contextual.* In von Bertalanffy's view isomorphic laws can be applied to systems in different fields. Kauffman also thinks that the laws of complexity apply in all fields, but he also points out the limitations in generalizing knowledge. Prigogine takes a more skeptical view and says that because of the indeterminism in the universe generalizations should be very limited at best.

Complexity theorists recognize that the knowledge of complex systems is contextual because of the limitations in the predictability ad generalizability of their behavioral patterns. Complexity theorists also recognize that observers utilize their a priori cognitive schema (frameworks) when they attempt to understand systems, but these schema also evolve as they learn from them. There are differences among complexity theorists in their conceptualizations of how these schema work. Autopoiesis theory suggests that observing systems are self-referential. Second-order cybernetics add that observing and observed systems are in a circular relationship: The way an observer knows a system can affect it.

There are implications of the discussions in this chapter for public policy. The deterministic assumptions of the traditional conceptualizations of public policy and administrations and the related assumption that the outcomes of policy actions are predictable have ben critiqued by several theorists. The ontological and epistemological implications of complexity theory lend support to those theorists who think that policy knowledge is contextual and its generalizability is limited. As such, the implications of complexity theory challenge the universalist aspirations of rational choice theory, but complexity theory does not have a clear or coherent alternative to universalism yet.

7   Phenomenology, Hermeneutics, and Post-Structuralism

Complexity theory brings the complex relations in nature to the center of our attention. With its holistic view of systems and the conceptual tools it uses—nonlinearity, emergence, self-organization, and coevolution—complexity theory forces us to revise our assumptions of determinism and predictability. It recognizes the uncertainties in and contextuality and limited generalizability of scientific knowledge. But does it offer a coherent epistemological alternative?

There is no commonly accepted epistemological or philosophical tradition among complexity theorists, but three strains of thought can be identified in the literature. Some complexity theorists suggest that given the uncertainties in and limited generalizability of the knowledge of complex systems, the best we can do is to adopt a "pluralist epistemology"—an epistemology that suggests that researchers should use multiple tools when trying to understand realities (Richardson, 2007, 2008, 2010; S. Mitchell, 2009). Prigogine and his colleagues articulated a phenomenological position for complexity theory (Prigogone and Stengers, 1984; Prigogine, 1996). Cillers (1998) finds parallels between some aspects of complexity theory and post-structuralism.

In this chapter I will review these three positions. Before I get into the specifics of the positions, I present brief background information on phenomenology, hermeneutics, and postmodernism/post-structuralism.

PHENOMENOLOGY

Phenomenology is a philosophical tradition that emerged in the 19th century in response to the rising popularity of the Newtonian science, particularly Descartes' articulation of its principles. In the Cartesian view of scientific knowledge, a scientist is a dispassionate and rational observer who can, and should, generate precise, eternal, and context-free rules that would capture the patterns in reality. To enable the generation of scientific knowledge, Descartes' separates the mind from matter. According to Descartes, matter was spatial and divisible, while the mind was non-spatial and indivisible. As such, the mind stands outside matter: The observer is external to the world he/she observes. This makes objective, external, knowledge possible. He also reasoned that because matter is spatial and divisible, it can be studied using analytical/reductionist and quantitative methods. He developed the foundations of the conceptual structure of using such methods, like Cartesian geometry. Using these methods, one can measure elements and their relations and explain them with certainty, in Descartes' view.

The point of departure for phenomenologists like Husserl, Heidegger, and Merleau-Ponty was the critique of Descartes' notion of decontextualized and disembodied knowledge. All phenomenologists espouse contextual, embodied, situated, and temporal notions of knowledge, but they differ among themselves in details. They all agree that knowledge is not generated by Descartes' detached mind, but it is a product of the mind's being in the world. This phenomenological notion disturbs the Cartesian certainties about knowledge. It does not offer an alternative resolution, however. In fact, it creates a tension. This is the tension between the premise that knowledge is embodied and contextual—therefore, it is too complex to be comprehended fully, and it is bound by the perspective, "subjectivity" of the knower—and the goal of establishing some sort of objective knowledge. If knowledge is bound and contextual, is there any room for objective knowledge? If not, then is science possible at all? In the words of the Dutch philosopher Radder (1996), in phenomenological thinking

> . . . an irresolvable but resourceful tension exists between two basic intuitions. On the one hand, human beings, necessarily, keep trying to grasp and control reality by interpreting it with the help of language and by working in and on it through action. On the other, reality—including natural, human, and social reality—appears to be essentially contingent, complex, and variable. Consequently, for reasons of principle it transcends any attempt at a permanent grasp and control. (p. 1)

The tension, according to Radder, is between the notions that knowledge *in* the world and that it is *about* the world at the same time (p. 2). This tension is expressed in somewhat different forms in the philosophies of Husserl, Heidegger, and Merleau-Ponty, all of whom influenced complexity theorist Prigogine's thinking, as I will discuss later in this chapter. I summarize Husserl's, Heidegger's, and Merleau-Ponty's philosophies briefly here.

Edmund Husserl

Husserl's phenomenology was a major challenge to the Cartesian science, or what he called the "Galilean science." According to Husserl, the Galilean science was objectivist, and it mathematized and geometrized spacetime. Husserl was critical of this view of science because it separated the knowing subject from his/her objects and would eventually lead to a loss of touch with the world humans actually lived in (Hummel, 1994, p. 18). Husserl's response to objectivism was to dissolve the dichotomy between the "epistemological subject" and the "objective world." He did so by positing that the relation between consciousness and reality is constituted by the former. In Madison's (1988) summary of Husserl's view, "Reality is nothing other than the ideal object of all possible conscious acts, and in this sense it is immanent to and inseparable from consciousness" (p. 11). In other words, objects are constituted by consciousness and could not exist without it. Husserl clearly assigns primacy to the consciousness in its relationship with objects: "[C]onsciousness is essentially *intentional*, that is, in relationship with an object, and hence it is unnecessary to inquire about objects outside of a relation to consciousness or about consciousness without an object of which it is conscious" [emphasis in original] (Van De Pitte, 1993, p. 363).

Therefore, "objective scientific knowledge" is not a true reflection of independently existing realities but a product of the consciousness of scientists. Does this mean that objective scientific knowledge is not possible at all? Husserl does not offer a clear or consistent answer to this question. He does not deny the existence of real objects, but he "simply avoids the complex of insoluble problems in justifying truth claims about objects considered outside of a relationship to consciousness" (Van De Pitte, 1993, p. 364). It is clear, however, that human consciousness has the primacy in a human being's relations with objects. In his review of Husserl's philosophy, Føllesdal's (1988) puts it thusly: "Our consciousness structures what we experience. How it structures it depends on our previous experiences, the whole setting of our present experience and a number of other factors" (p. 108). Husserl calls these previous experiences *noēma*, i.e., intended objects. His notion of noēma is somewhat similar to Kant's *synthetic a priori*. However, unlike Kant's fixed a priori categories, Husserl's noēma are malleable. Noēma anticipate, but they can be wrong—expectations may not be fulfilled—and the knower may have to revise his/her views and expectations (Føllesdal, p. 115).

In his later writings, Husserl's developed the concept *Lebenswelt*, or life-world, which is the "immediate flow of unreflective life. . . . It is the world as we actually live it" (Madison, 1988, p. 44). It is "the unproblematic and pre-scientific presupposition of any understanding and meaning" (Honderich, 1995, p. 488). Objectivist scientists do not recognize this, but their scientific knowledge in fact originates from Lebenswelt and is grounded in it, according to Husserl. The life-world is the "ultimate court appeal, behind which there is no point for further justification. . . . Every claim to validity and truth rests upon this 'iceberg' of largely unthematized prejudgmental acceptances" (Føllesdal, 1988, p. 129). In Husserl's own words, "Thus alone can that ultimate understanding of the world be attained, behind which, since it is ultimate, there is nothing more that can be sensefully inquired for, nothing more to understand" (Husserl; cited in Føllesdal, 1988, p. 129).

The relationship between the life-world and scientific knowledge is not a one-way-street, however: "[T]he sciences have the life-world as their evidential basis, and on the other hand, the sciences gradually change the life-world" in Føllesdal's (1988, p. 128) interpretation. People's prior experiences, explicitly held assumptions and beliefs, and what they learn from science "sediment" over time and become an implicit background, parts of the life-world.

Husserl projects a complex view of knowledge. It is not a one-way process or straightforward one. The knowing subject is embedded in the world he/she wants to know and his/her prior knowledge has the primacy when he/she attempts to know the world. The reader will remember from the previous chapter that cognitive psychologist have a similar view of prior knowledge, which they call "schema" or "constructs." In Husserl's view, prior knowledge is not merely imposed on the world; one's worldview is subject to change as it interacts with the world, with which cognitive psychologists agree. Husserl's framework has resonance not only with cognitive psychologists but also with Heidegger and Merleau-Ponty, who built on it and further specified it.

Martin Heidegger

Like Husserl, Heidegger sees the roots of all forms of human knowledge in the primordial, existential understanding, which is constitutive of being in the world. Husserl's life-world and his thesis of intentional consciousness are the starting points of Heidegger's ontology of *Dasein*, being there, or being-in-the-world. Like Husserl, Heidegger thinks that "human existence embodies in its ontic constitution, as part of its Being, a preontological understanding of self and of the world in which it finds itself" (Mueller-Vollmer, 1994, p. 33). All understanding flows from Dasein:

> Understanding constitutes rather the Being of the "there" in such a way that, on the basis of such understanding, a *Dasein* can, in existing, develop the different possibilities of sight, of looking around, and of just looking. In all explanation one uncovers understandingly that which one cannot understand; and all explanation is thus rooted in *Dasein*'s primary understanding. [Emphases in original] (Heidegger, quoted in Mueller-Vollmer, 1994, p. 32)

Heidegger's Dasein is situated, temporal, and self-realizing. The *situatedness* of a human being is in relation to other human beings, and it is historical. Heidegger thinks that we experience ourselves in the company of others; we are *co-beings* (Hummel, 1994). We share our co-being through communication, and through communication we understand our common situatedness (pp. 179–180). Heidegger sees a danger in individualism, because individualists ignore the fact that we are co-beings and as such they remove authenticity and create a crowd of anonymous "others" (p. 181).

The commonly situated understanding of human beings is *temporal.* It includes not only the past and present but also projects into future. As it projects future possibilities, Dasein calls for the realization of this possibility. Thus understanding is not merely reflective, but it is constitutive and oriented toward self-realization. Dasein is more than what it factually is "to its facticity its potentiality-for-Being belongs essentially" (Heidegger, 1994a, p. 218). As Hummel (1994) puts it, in Heidegger man becomes his own project; he becomes himself through his intentional acts. In doing so he does not only reveal himself to the world, but also his Being emerges (p. 273).

According to Heidegger, understanding pertains to being-in-the-world. Interpretation and meaning are derivatives of understanding. We must understand what is to be interpreted beforehand. Thus, philosophy and scientific knowledge are derivatives of understanding, hence Dasein. But is science not supposed to be independent of the observer? Is this circle of understanding not a vicious circle? Heidegger raises these questions and answers them as follows:

> This circle of understanding is not an orbit in which any random kind of knowledge may move; it is the expression of the existential *fore-structure* of Dasein itself. . . . In the circle is hidden a positive possibility of the most primordial kind of knowing. To be sure, we genuinely take hold of this possibility only when, in our interpretation, we have understood that our first, last, and constant task is never to allow our fore-having, fore-sight, and fore-conception to be presented to us by fancies and popular conceptions, but rather to make scientific theme secure by working out these fore-structures in terms of the things themselves. (Heidegger, 1994b, p. 226)

But then, how does one make sure that "fancies and popular conceptions" are not allowed in scientific thinking? And how does one make "scientific theme secure by working out these fore-structures in terms of the things themselves"? In answering these questions, Heidegger reiterates the circularity of scientific understanding but does not offer a way out of it.

It may not be possible to break the endless circularity Heidegger suggests, but his thinking is still important because he underscores the situatedness of a knower's knowledge in his/her relations to other knowers (i.e., the importance of social constructions in scientific knowledge processes, as well as in others). This is an important starting point for social constructionist and post-structuralist theorists, some of whom cite Heidegger among their intellectual predecessors. I will come back to post-structuralism in this chapter. Heidegger also underscores the temporality of knowledge (i.e., that it is dynamic; it evolves). This is an important notion that complexity theorists share. Merleu-Ponty took another aspect of Heidegger's *Dasein*, being-in-the-world as a body, and developed a philosophy around that.

Maurice Merleau-Ponty

Merleau-Ponty is known as the preeminent philosopher of the body, because of the primacy he attributes to the corporeal dimension of existence. Like Husserl and Heidegger, Merlaeu-Ponty targets the subject–object dualism of Cartesianism but somewhat differently and more specifically, develops "a description of the world as the field of experience" for the body (Honderich, 1995, p. 554). In his description, Merleau-Ponty is closer to Heidegger's notion of being situated in the world. He disagrees with Husserl's idea that Lebenswelt is the product of the constituting ego. There is no "inner man" that projects itself onto the world, according to Merlau-Ponty. Instead, he argues, "man is in the world, and only in the world does he know himself" (Madison, 1988, p. 60). He views the body as "a dynamic region of sensory awareness that is oriented toward the world" (Chamberlain, 1993, p. 424). The body is interdependent with its environment. Likewise, our language and lived experiences are interdependent: Language is expressive of the body's experience, but also "the lived experience of the body as motor subject transcends itself through language and enters a linguistic field beyond its immediate perceptual one" (Chamberlain, p. 424).

In his later works, Merleau-Ponty used the term *flesh*, which means more than the body:

> Being neither the objective body nor the body which the soul thinks of as its own, the flesh is rather the sensible itself, "the sensible in the twofold sense of want one senses and what senses." The flesh is the formative milieu of both the corporeal and the psychic, of object and subject; it is the undivided Being . . . existing before the consciousness–object split. (Madison, 1988, p. 64)

Merleau-Ponty's philosophy of embodied knowledge deeply influenced Prigogine, as well as some cognitive scientists, as we shall see later in this chapter.

HERMENEUTICS[1]

It is important to provide an overview of hermeneutics here, because post-structuralism has its roots in it, and phenomenology is closely intertwined with it. Heidegger is known to be the father of phenomenological hermeneutics, and, as mentioned above, he is cited as a predecessor of at least some post-structuralist thinkers.

Hermeneutics is concerned with the interpretation of meaning in communication, particularly written forms of communication. But it has broader implications. Hermeneutics started as a discipline of interpreting religious texts in the Christian tradition. Its particular source was the early Protestants who wanted to demonstrate that the scriptures were basically intelligible and self-sufficient and that they could be properly interpreted by lay people. In the late 19th century, hermeneutics was developed into a philosophy and methodology of textual interpretation. Martin Heiddeger, Friedrich Schleiermacher, Wilhelm Dilthey, and others established its fundamental principles. Contemporary hermeneutic scholars have expanded the scope of the interpretations of these founders to all linguistic forms—speech as well as written text—and other forms of symbolic interaction—rituals, architectural style, cultural artifacts, etc. This is relevant for public policy scholars in the sense that from the hermeneutic perspective, public policies are texts to be read and interpreted. Roe's (1994, 1998, 2007) narrative policy analysis, as well as Schneider and Ingram's (1997) and Stone's (2002) social constructionist interpretations of policy (see Chapter 1) have their roots in this hermeneutic understanding.

Then the problem for hermeneutics, in general, and the hermeneutic perspectives in public policy, in particular, is how to interpret these texts. The primary problem in hermeneutics is whether, or to what extent, there is a "true meaning" in the text. If there is one, can it be read and understood by the reader as it was intended by the author? Or, is the meaning a product of the reader's own interpretation? While the early Protestant hermeneutic philosophers intended to show that the meaning was in the text and that it could be interpreted correctly, their followers held a range of positions on this issue. Kerby (1993) identifies four schools of thought in hermeneutics: the original hermeneutic of authorial intentions, phenomenological hermeneutics, radical hermeneutics, and critical hermeneutics.

Dilthey represents the school of thought that aimed to uncover *authorial intentions* in texts. According to Dilthey, authorial meanings could be interpreted correctly if proper methods were used. Later, many others, like E. D. Hirsch, adopted this assumption and worked on developing methods of properly interpreting language. In this approach to hermeneutics, the scholars attempted to close the gap between positivism/empiricism—the notion that reality can only be known through empirical observation and verification—on the one hand, and interpretivism/constructionism—the notion that reality is always subject personal or social interpretation/construction—on the other. By devising the proper methods, they thought, it would be possible to interpret texts objectively, as intended by their authors.

For Heidegger and Gadamer, the foremost theorists of *phenomenological hermeneutics*, or *hermeneutic phenomenology*, the meaning of a text does not subsist apart from the consciousness of the reader (Madison, 1988, p. 11). According to Heidegger, meaning and interpretation cannot be separated from the situated and temporal existence of a human being. As human beings are situated in different societal and temporal contexts, they will have different interpretations of meanings. This makes understanding each other's meaning problematic but does not preclude the possibility of doing so. That is because we all have a tacit understanding that is based on our common situatedness and embeddedness in the world (Kerby, 1993). We do not know each other as external, independent objects, but we can know, understand, each other, through our common belonging to the world (Valdes, 1993). Gadamer, a student of Heidegger, proposed that hermeneutical understanding is the result of a dialogue between the past (authors) and present (us), and this dialogue can and should be authentic. With authentic intentions, one can understand others' meanings.

Stanley Fish represents *radical hermeneutics*. Fish posits that there is no predetermined meaning in a text; its meaning is totally a product of how we interpret it (Kerby, 1993, p. 93). This approach separates the reader/interpreter from the author completely. It does not allow any possibility of correct interpretation of a text. Note that many post-structuralists are criticized for adopting this view of hermeneutics and thus making scientific objectivity impossible. I will come back to that issue later in this chapter.

The fourth school of thought Kerby identifies in hermeneutics is Jürgen Habermas' *critical hermeneutics*, or *critical theory*. Habermas does allow the possibility of true/correct interpretation, like the first two schools of thought—the Dilthey/Hirsch school and the Heidegger/Gadamar school—but like the second school, he problematizes interpretations. Habermas is concerned about distorted communications, which not only deceives people but also can oppress them. It is possible to accomplish authentic communication, according to Habermas, through critically interpreting such distorted communications. He also believes that truth can be established through authentic communication/discourse. And this will lead to the emancipation from oppression. In public policy, Fischer (1990, 1995, 2003, 2009) applied Habermas' critical hermeneutics extensively.

POSTMODERNISM/POST-STRUCTURALISM

Postmodernism, or post-structuralism, is not a unified philosophical or theoretical position. It is somewhat simplistic to use the terms postmodernism and post-structuralism interchangeably, but following Madison (1988) and Rosenau (1992), I will use the terms interchangeably here. Although there are differences, they are not significant enough to mention, given the limited context of my discussion in this section.

In Rosenau's (1992) assessment, postmodernism offers indeterminacy, as opposed to determinism, diversity, rather than unity, difference, rather than synthesis, complexity, not simplification; it emphasizes uniqueness, more than generalities, intertextual relations , rather than causality, unrepeatable occurences, rather than recurring events; it promotes subjective knowledge, rather than objective truth, relativism, rather than objectivity, fragmentation, more than totalization; and has confidence in emotion, rather than in impartial observation. In this list of contrasts, one can see that there are potential parallels between postmodernist/post-structuralist assumptions and the core concepts of complexity theory (p. 8). Therefore, it is understandable that postmodernism and post-structuralism has some appeal among complexity theorists. I reserve my judgment on these parallels and this appeal until I discuss Cillers' (1998) position later in this chapter.

Madison (1988) notes that postmodernism rejects modernism's "logo-centric metaphysics," whose aim is to achieve a basic fundamental knowledge and discover grounds that will allow for certainty in the knowledge of "the external world" (p. x). If these goals are achieved, modernism assumes, a true "representation" of "objective" reality will be obtained. Modernist philosophy, therefore, makes a distinction between the subject and object and emphasizes method—as opposed to insight (p. x). The dissolution of the subject–object distinction in Husserl's phenomenology constituted the beginning of postmodernist thought, according to Madison. The reader will remember that Husserl posited that the subject and object are not only relational but also mutually constituted. There is no such thing as an "objective knowledge of the world," because what some may call an "objective reality" is nothing but the object of the intentional acts of human consciousness.

Post-structuralists take another step and dissolve the subject as well. They argue that there cannot be a coherent or unified subject. The modernist notion that the subject is an agent independent of social relations is a mystification, according to post-structuralists (Rosenau, 1992, pp. 42–46). Postmodernists think that the subject is a Cartesian mystification. Cartesianism presumes that the subject, or author, originates consciousness, meaning, and truth. Post-structutralists believe that the human subject does not have a unified consciousness, but it is structured through language (Sarup, 1989, p. 4). Once the subject–object distinction and the subject are dissolved, no objective knowledge is possible. According to post-structuralists, social reality is constituted as it is interpreted.

Like hermeneutic philosophers, post-structuralists consider social reality as nothing but a text to be interpreted. That is where the hermeneutic problem of how to interpret social realities as texts arises. Obviously, post-structuralists do not agree at all with the Dilthey and Hirsch school of thought in hermeneutics, because, they think, it is not possible to read texts objectively, as intended, by their authors. The common post-structuralist stance is that both what "the authors"—makers social reality—"mean" and how "the readers" interpret that meaning are structured within their respective cultural and historical contexts; therefore, the meanings interpreted by the readers cannot match the meanings intended by the authors.

This approach is evident in post-structuralist Madison's (1988) critique of what he calls the "objectivist" version of hermeneutics, i.e., Hirsch's hermeneutics. He critiques Hirsch for promoting the positivist dogmatism by equating knowledge with scientific knowledge and by erasing the differences between the natural and social sciences (p. 4). The problem of interpretation, according to Hirsch, is to understand "the author's meaning," which, for Madison, becomes an absolute object, a super-historical essence, a determinate, selfsame object accessible to everyone who approaches it scientifically (p. 6). According to Madison, Hirsch sets impossible criteria for obtaining true, objective knowledge of meaning, and thus he sets himself up for failure and consequently promotes cynical relativism in society (pp. 13–14).

Habermas' critical hermeneutics has some appeal to postmodernists and post-structuralists, because at least some postmodernists take critical stances as well (e.g., Miller, 2002; Miller and Fox, 2007), but in the end they disagree with his notion that some sort of commonly held truth can be established through communication. Postmodernists are drawn more to Heidegger's and Gadamer's phenomenological hermeneutics or and/or Fish's radical hermeneutics. It is difficult to tell which of these two versions of hermeneutics is dominant in postmodernist/post-structuralist thought, because of the wide variations in it. Madison sees Heidegger's phenomenological hermeneutics as an articulation of post-sructuralist phenomenology (p. xiii). Miller (2002) and Miller and Fox (2007) do not deny the possibility of understanding some realities, particularly in the contexts of public policy an administration—in fact they lament that "hyperrealities" have taken over social discourse in modern societies preventing us from accessing and establishing partial truths. They call for public discourses that would value perspectival and local nature of realities and particularistic nature of truths.

There are other versions of postmodernism/post-structuralism that not only view everything as a text but also every text as subject to private, multiple readings or interpretations (Rosenau, 1992, p. 37). Any form of social communication or action is considered a self-referential "language game" in this perspective. To understand this perspective, we need to look into the distinction made between the "signifier" and the "signified" by structuralist linguist Ferdinand de Saussure. Signifier is the word; signified is the concept. Signifier should refer to a concept. In post-structuralism the signified is demoted, signifier made dominant, and the proposition between the language and their referents in reality is broken. Post-structuralists argue that there are no extra-linguistic referents (Sarup, 1989, p. 3).

This is why post-structuralist Derrida declares that the text is all there is, and there is nothing outside it (Rosenau, p. 35). According to Derrida, meaning or value in a situation is determined completely within the language, and language does not refer to anything outside of itself. There are no rules governing the workings of a language; therefore, the interpreter cannot rely on a common methodology to discover, extract, and understand true meanings. Post-structuralism removes the "epistemological privilege" of the interpreter and levels the playing field for science and other forms of knowing. I will come back to the issue of signifiers and signified and the role of language when I discuss Ciller's (1998) interpretation that complexity theory has some parallels with post-structuralism later in this chapter.

Post-structuralists use *deconstruction* as a tool to expose the power bases of the seemingly rational and scientific discourses and to level the playing field for everyone involved. They attempt to delegitimize the socially constructed bases of authorities and to level the playing field for alternative, underprivileged discourses. Deconstruction aims to demystify texts by revealing the arbitrary hierarchies and propositions in them. Since all texts can be deconstructed, no privileged position is allowed to any.

Deconstruction is not only a method, but it also refers to Derrida's version of post-structuralism (Adamson, 1993). The method of deconstruction is used not only by post-structuralists, like Derrida and Lacan but also by Heidegger and structuralist Saussure. In Adamson's summary, deconstruction was historically based on scepticism of all entrenched "theological" securities of truth—including a monolithic, uniform understanding of science—and author-oriented and formalist approaches to literature, such as Hirsch's version of hermeneutics. Deconstruction rejects the notion of a correct or proper interpretation of literary texts. In Derrida's version, the aims of deconstruction are to expose the problematic nature of "centered discourses"—discourses that depend on concepts such as truth, presence, origin, etc.—and display its conceptual limits. Deconstruction suggests that interpretation should be limitless and it should be a semantic play with no referent outside the language.

COMPLEXITY THEORY: PLURALISM, PHENOMENOLOGY, AND POST-STRUCTURALISM

Intuitive parallels can be drawn between the concepts and insights of complexity theory on the one hand and the concepts and propositions of phenomenology, hermeneutics, and post-structuralism on the other. Some complexity theorists did exactly that. Given the current inarticulate state of complexity theory, it is normal that different complexity theorists drew different parallels. The question is this: Which of those parallels are justifiable? In this section I will summarize three views on the epistemological implications of complexity theory—pluralism, phenomenology, and post-structuralism—and indicate my preference among them.

Pluralist Epistemology and Complexity Theory

Both Sandra Mitchell and Kurt Richardson propose that complexity theory should adopt a pluralistic epistemology. Although there are differences between the two, their common understanding is that complexity theory projects a view that is neither naively realistic and positivistic, nor relativistic. In other words, complexity theory does not suggest that scientific knowledge directly corresponds on one-on-one basis to a simple external reality or suggest that any form of knowledge is equally valid. Both Mitchell and Richardson suggest that the scientific knowledge process is complex.

Sandra Mitchell (2009) calls for an epistemology that should be pluralistic and pragmatic and should recognize the dynamic character of realities (p. 13). She thinks that a pluralist epistemology is needed, because complexity theory shows that reality "is not beyond our understanding, [but] it requires new ways of understanding" (p. 13). It requires that we understand the contexts of events, accidents, and boundary conditions, which all play roles in the complexity of events. We should recognize that there are multiple ways of describing this multifaceted and complex reality. We should recognize that reality is dynamic and so should be our knowledge. Her pluralism is not an "anything goes" kind of pluralism, however; scientific claims must be empirically tested (p. 108).

Richardson proposes (2007, 2008, 2010) an epistemology he calls "critical pluralism" (2007, p. 193; 2008, p. 39), or "quasi-'critical pluralism'" (2010, p. 86). He compares his critical pluralism two other schools of complexity. The first school of thought is what he calls the "new reductionism" (2007, p. 191). This school is essentially positivistic, according to Richardson, because it uses the tools of complexity theory simply as another tool kit to make generalizations about complex realities, more specifically to discover the general principles of complex systems (2007, p. 191). This school is akin to the "theory of everything" in physics, he argues: It aims to make complexity theory the theory of everything. Richardson notes that the main tool of investigation this school uses is "bottom-up agent based modeling." The second school Richardson identifies is the "metaphorical school" (p. 192). This school is composed mainly of organization theorists who adapt some of the concepts of complexity theory—dissipative structures, emergence, coevolution—to metaphorically understand organizational processes (e.g., Goldstein, 1994; Kiel, 1994). This metaphorical school casually uses the concepts of complexity theory as metaphors. Because of this casualness, these theorists espouse a relativistic epistemology.

Richardson stresses that his pluralist epistemology is neither positivistic, nor relativistic; it not an "'anything goes' postmodernism" (2010, p. 84). It does not suggest a constructivist worldview either. Constructivism assumes that "all boundaries are created in our minds and as such do not correlate with objective reality at all" (p. 86). Contrary to this view, in his quasi-critical pluralism, the boundary definitions in our minds do correspond to the real ones but not in perfect one-on-one correspondence (p. 88). He recognizes that there are not an unlimited number of valid constructions of reality; there are only a limited number of "substantially real levels" (p. 82).

Phenomenology and Complexity Theory

Complexity theory suggests that the knowledge of complex systems is contextual and that participants and observers of complex systems cannot be detached observers, as the discussions until this point clearly indicate. Kauffman and Rössler are explicit in calling for a science that does not detach scientists from the world they live in. Kauffman (1995) is critical of the detached view of modern science, which, he says, leaves humans outside a lifeless universe. He calls for a science that would make them feel "at home in the universe" and connect back scientists with realities they observe. In his critique of the Newtonian objectivist paradigm of science, Rössler (1986) emphasizes that a new scientific paradigm is needed and that it should include a movement "from the usual detached, 'exophysical' way of looking at one's model worlds to an understanding, 'endophysical' one" (p. 320).

Kauffman's and Rössler's views are vaguely reminiscent of the phenomenologies of Husserl, Heidegger, and Merleau-Ponty. Prigogine embraces phenomenology directly. Like Kauffman and Rössler, Prigogine and Stengers argue that science should move away from the assumptions of the Newtonian physics, which presumes that observers are outside the physical realities they observe, and toward a new understanding in which the physicist is situated within the observed world (p. 218). They argue that the "classical notion of objectivity" is untenable (pp. 224–225). Newton's laws do not recognize the limitations of the observer as a physical being. And that is where it fails and should be replaced with a phenomenological view.

According to Prigogine and Stengers, the problem with the Newtonian science is its predilection for studying closed systems, equilibrium states, and linear relations, which are not the rule in nature, but exceptions. Because of this predilection, the Newtonian science tends to see the world as a deterministic system that can be observed from outside. Actually, the universe is composed primarily of open systems, which are dynamic, tend toward disequilibrium, and their behaviors are not precisely predictable. These characteristics of the universe do not allow scientists to make universal generalizations; only local and temporal knowledge is possible. Scientific knowledge is situated within the world it was generated.

The local and temporal situatedness of scientific knowledge is not a deficiency, according to Prigogine and Stengers. The objectivism and universalism of the Newtonian science was misguided to begin with. The implicit metaphor of the Newtonian science—"the clockwork universe"—suggests that the clockwork was set in motion by an external creator, and therefore it is possible to generate an objective and complete knowledge of it by stepping outside and observing it from this creator's external vantage point. This is not possible, according to Prigogine and Stengers, because there are no complete and precise boundaries of "the world" or reality; there is no such thing as "entire reality."

Prigigone (1996) notes that the deterministic and objectivist view of the Newtonian science emerged in a historical context. It was a response to the needs and dominant thinking of the rising industrial period and the search for order and stability in newly emerging industrial societies. Descartes formulated his thoughts in the tragic situation of the 17th century, when the wars between Catholics and Protestants created political instabilities in Europe. He aimed to reach order and stability through certainty in knowledge. Descartes' views found their realization in Newton's work. Newton described an orderly world, cosmic clockwork, which was put into motion by God and supposed to be ticking in perfect harmony.

This Newtonian view of science created a backlash in the form of the irrationalist philosophical movements in Germany in the 1920s, Prigogine and Stengers (1984) note. This irrationalism formed the cultural background of quantum mechanics. Quantum mechanical ideas embodied the "opposition to science, which was identified with a set of concepts such as causality, determinism, reductionism, and rationality," (p. 6) and quantum mechanics depicted a fundamentally irrational picture of nature. According to Prigogine and Stengers,

> Life, destiny, freedom, and spontaneity thus became manifestations of a shadowy underworld impenetrable to reason. . . . By admitting only a subjective meaning for a set of experiences men believe to be significant, science runs the risk of transferring these into the realm of the irrational, bestowing upon them a formidable power. (p. 6)

Prigogine and Stengers see the contrast between the Newtonian and quantum-mechanical visions as a product of the "schizophrenia of the European (Western) thought." They point out "Western thought has always oscillated between the world as an automaton and a theology in which God governs the universe. This is what Needham calls the 'characteristic European schizophrenia.' In fact, these visions are connected. An automaton needs an external god" (pp. 6–7). They question

> Do we really have to make this tragic choice? Must we choose between a science that leads to alienation and an anti-scientific metaphysical view of nature? We think such a choice is no longer necessary, since the changes that science is undergoing today lead to a radically new situation. (p. 7)

Prigogine and Stengers propose a synthesis, a new conception of objectivity, a new form of rationalism. This new conception would subject us to "intrinsic constraints that identify us as part of the physical world we are describing. It is a physics that presupposes an observer situated within the observed world. Our dialogue with nature will be successful only if it is carried on from within nature" (p. 218). They also assert, "We must accept a pluralistic world in which reversible and irreversible processes coexist" (p. 257). In this world the objectivist view of knowledge is replaced with a constructivist view:

As randomness, complexity, and irreversibility enter into physics as objects of positive knowledge, we are moving away from this rather naïve assumption of a direct connection between our description of the world and the world itself. Objectivity in theoretical physics takes on a more subtle meaning.

Whatever reality may mean, it always corresponds to an active intellectual construction. The descriptions presented by science can no longer be disentangled from our questioning activity and therefore can no longer be attributed to some omniscient being. (p. 55)

They use the experimental method to illustrate their new conception of objectivity. Experimentation is a dialogue with nature. "The experimental dialogue with nature discovered by modern science involves activity rather than passive observation. What must be done is to manipulate physical reality, to 'stage' it in such a way that it conforms as closely as possible to a theoretical description" (p. 41). This experimental dialogue requires a highly specific procedure. It is more of an art. Nature is not malleable in experiments, however, "Einstein used to say that nature says 'no' to most of the questions asked, and occasionally 'perhaps'" (p. 43). "However partially nature is allowed to speak, once it has expressed itself, there is no further dissent: nature never lies" (p. 44).

In Prigogine and Stengers' new conception of objectivity, one can clearly see the imprints of phenomenology. Like Heidegger, they stress the situatedness and temporality of scientific knowledge. Prigogine and Stengers argue that nature cannot be described from outside, as if by a spectator (p. 300). They refer to Merleau-Ponty's notion "truth within situations" and point out: "since we are inside truth and cannot get outside it, all that I can do is define truth within the situation" (p. 299). Like Merleau-Ponty, they argue that knowledge is both objective and participatory. Like Husserl and Heidegger they struggle with the possible implication of this situated and temporal view of scientific knowledge—that it may lead to a rejection of the possibility of objective knowledge—and stress that scientific objectivity is still possible in this indeterministic, nonlinear, and self-organizational world.

Prigogine and Stengers defend science and criticize both Husserl and Heidegger for creating an unnecessary contrast between Lebenswelt and Dasein, on the one hand, and the "objective world of science," on the other. They argue that the Lebenswelt versus objective science dichotomy is false; the developments in our understanding of nonlinearity, self-organization, and complexity nullified this dichotomy (p. 299). They critique Heidegger for directing his criticism "against the very core of the scientific endeavor, which he sees as fundamentally related to a permanent aim, the domination of nature" (p. 32). Heidegger was critical of this instrumentalist notion of domination of nature by the man. He ignored, however, how science, even in its flawed Newtonian form, contributed to improving human lives (pp. 32–33). They see Heidegger's position as an echo of some the themes of the anti-science movement of his times. They observe that some of the implications of relativity and quantum mechanics provided the ground for mysticism and parapsychology and argue that these implications must be rejected. According to Prigogine and Stengers, the emerging science eliminates the need to move away from science (pp. 33–36). Prigogine and Stengers' critique of Husserl and Heiddeger shows that their relationship with phenomenology is not entirely comfortable, but all in all they still see the new conception of objectivity within the realm of phenomenology.

It is worth noting that recent developments in cognitive science resonate well with Prigogine and his colleagues' phenomenological view of scientific knowledge. In their syntheses of the developments in cognitive science, Damasio (1994, 1999) and Lakoff and Johnson (1980, 1999) show that the human mind actively constructs knowledge and that human knowledge is necessarily embodied. Knowledge is a product of the interactions of the body and mind together with their environment. Damasio critiques Descartes' mind-body dualism and argues that the mind and the body constitute together an indissociable organism. The body, he points out, is the indispensable frame of reference for the neural processes that we experience as the mind. Also, cognition and emotions are not two separate realms, but they together constitute the human mind. Damasio points out that knowledge occurs in the relationship of the organism with its environment. The evidence from cognitive science shows, according to Lakoff and Johnson, that human ability to reason grows out of bodily capacities and the interactions of our bodies with our environments: "[H]uman reason is a form of animal reason, a reason inextricably tied to our bodies and the peculiarities of our brains. . . . Our bodies, brains, and interactions with our environments provide the mostly unconscious basis for our everyday metaphysics, that is, our sense of what is real" (1999, p. 17). And this is not a deficiency, but a capability our species acquired through its evolutionary experiences.

Postmodernism/Post-Structuralism and Complexity Theory

Some complexity theorists seek philosophical grounding for the theory in postmodernism/post-structuralism (e.g., Young, 1991a, 1991b; Cilliers, 1998). This positioning of complexity theory makes some sense, given that its philosophical implications challenge the Newtonian/positivist science, as I have argued so far, and this can be interpreted as a challenge to "modernism" all together. However, I argue that this distancing of complexity theory from the Newtonian/positivist science does not necessarily bring it close to a postmodernist/post-structuralist position. I concede that there are actually close relations between post-structuralism and phenomenology and that the roots of post-structuralist thinking can be traced back to Husserl and Heidegger. It still would be a stretch to place complexity theory in the postmodernist/post-structuralist camp.

My main argument is this: Whereas complexity theorists like Prigogine, Kauffman, and Rössler seek to establish a new form of objectivity in science—a situated and embodied objectivity—and seek to establish some truthfulness through scientific investigation, post-structuralists deny any "epistemological privilege" to the products of any form of investigation or interpretation, scientific or otherwise.

Young (1991a, 1991b) contends that chaos theory decenters all claims of perfection, finality, normality, or historical necessity and alters the mission of science to the extent that it is no longer a quest for universal laws yielding prediction, uniformity, certainty, and stability of findings. Thus, it provides a theoretical envelope for a postmodern science. This is a debatable claim.

Chaos theory, as I mentioned earlier in this book, can be considered either a predecessor or part of complexity theory. Chaos theory's main insights are that small differences in the initial conditions can make big differences in a system's future trajectory and that nonlinear deterministic relations may generate chaotic behaviors. As such, chaos theory challenges the reductionist, linear, and universalist assumptions of the Newtonian/positivist science, but it remains grounded in the scientific tradition. Postmodernism, at least some versions of it, rejects scientific and empirical methods all together. Complexity theory renders the Newtonian notion of universal laws questionable, but it still offers generalizations about natural and social phenomena. Postmodernism denies any "epistemological privilege" to scientific interpretations over others. Whereas, postmodernists stress the arbitrary, conventional, historically contingent, situationally specific, and linguistically constructed nature of social realities, complexity theorists aim to make sense of a world that exists beyond our language games, although they admit that the knowledge of this world should be contextual, situated, and embodied.

Cilliers (1998, p. 21) finds some "affinities" between complexity theory and postmodernism/post-structuralism. Cilliers finds parallels particularly between the connectionist models of the mind—neural network models—and Derrida's post-structuralist descriptions of language. He makes three main arguments (p. 37). First, complexity arises through large-scale, nonlinear interactions. Second, the dynamics of language post-structuralists describe can also be used to describe the dynamics of complex systems. Third, because connectionist models of the human mind share the characteristics of complex systems, these models can also be used as general models for describing complex systems.

Cillers' first argument is a restatement of the well-known observation of complexity theorists that nonlinearity is the primary reason for complexity (see Chapter 1). I take issue with Cillier's second and third arguments. I think the analogy he makes between language and complex systems is interesting, but it is a stretch to use language as the model for describing complex systems in general. Particularly his conclusion that complexity theory is compatible with Derrida's theory of language is a long stretch. Similarly, the parallels he finds between connectionist models and complexity theory are insightful, but the conclusion he draws—that these models are sufficient to describe all complex systems—is narrow and misleading.

Before I expand on my criticisms, I want to describe briefly what connectionism is and how it could relate to complexity theory.[2] As in the last five decades during which *cognitive science*, the composite science of how the human mind works, has developed and evolved, two theoretical orientations emerged: the *computational theory* and the *connectionist theory*.

> The computational theory was the framework of earlier cognitive scientists. It was inspired by [Noam] Chomsky's theory of generative grammar and was formulated first by Jerry Fodor . . . [The theory is based on two propositions:] that the mind works with abstract rules (e.g., propositions) to sort out the incoming information (signals) and that it is hierarchically structured (into short- and long-term memories, for example) to deal with such information. In other words, the mind is like computer software; it turns information into symbols and manipulates them. (Morçöl, 2002, p. 204)

> [Connectionist theories] suggest that information is not processed by hierarchically structured models in the mind; cognition is more like many independent computer processors' carrying out many independent tasks simultaneously (i.e., parallel processing). Memory and perception occur in a distributed fashion; many units in the brain operate simultaneously. . . . Knowledge simply inheres in the strength and appropriateness of the connections between simple neurons. (p. 205)

> [The mind] is a product of the coevolution of the neurons in the brain and the cultures of human societies. In this evolutionary process, synaptic pathways are formed in different regions of the brain. These regions specialize in different functions (e.g., perception of color, sound). Some synaptic pathways between neurons (i.e., patterns of connections between them) are "selected," because of their success in meeting the demands of the biological and cultural environments. Once the successful pathways are selected, they organize in more complex forms: "neuronal maps." Each neuronal map is connected to other maps to form clusters. These clusters of maps facilitate linking of the information the brain receives to produce cognitive or behavioural outcomes. (pp. 205–206)

The main contrast between the computational and connectionist theories is highlighted in these descriptions: The former projects a hierarchical view of the mind, and the latter a self-organizational view. Because self-organization is a key concept of complexity theory, Cilliers (1998) derives the conclusion that connectionist theories can be used as the primary models of complexity theory (pp. 11, 37). This may make intuitive sense, but if we look into it carefully, we can see a few problems.

I must note here that Cilliers offers a sophisticated view of self-organization in his book, which I cited in Chapter 4. He recognizes that self-organization is a process in which the system structures itself in response to the stimuli from its environment (p. 90), and by doing so, the system affects its environment as well (p. 108). He also asserts that self-organization is an emergent property of the system as a whole (pp. 91–95). These are also the characteristics of the mind as described by connectionist theories. In these theories, the structure of the mind (e.g., neuronal maps) emerges from the interactions among neurons in a coevolutionary process.

Note that this is the description of a unidirectional and perpetual self-organizational process, starting from scratch. The neurons keep self-organizing, without any interference of a prior structure every time an individual is born, in this view. Is this perpetual self-organization conceptualization a realistic description of the way the human mind works? This is a controversial matter. Cognitive scientist Pinker (1997) argues, for example, that this self-organizational view of connectionist theories cannot explain cognitive processes as a whole. There must be some inscribed rules of cognition—deep grammar and schema—that are inherited from generation to generation. Self-organization may occur within the framework defined by these rules, he argues.

Whether it is a good description of the human mind or not, a more important question for my discussion here is whether this view of perpetual self-organization is compatible with complexity theory. The reader will remember from Chapter 4 that there are multiple versions of self-organization that complexity theorists describe, and there are several open questions about self-organizational processes. Given this multiplicity of descriptions of self-organization and unanswered questions, it would not be reasonable to suggest that the connectionist models of the mind provide comprehensive and definitive descriptions of complex systems.

Cilliers draws parallels between the connectionist models, Derrida's version of post-structuralism (deconstruction), and complexity theory. This is quite problematic in my view. I want to note first that from the descriptions of hermeneutics and postmodernism in earlier sections of this chapter, it should be clear that there are different trends in hermeneutics and postmodernism. Some versions of these may be compatible with complexity theory but not Derrida's post-structuralism.

Cilliers describes Saussure's structuralism and Derrida's post-structuralism in some detail (pp. 38–47). He shows that in Saussure's theory language is a closed system in which meanings are generated. There are no external referents of Saussure's "signifiers"; nor is there a "natural link" between signifiers and concepts. In other words, the links between words and the concepts they are supposed to represent are arbitrary. All forms of metanarratives and discourses are generated solely within language: The mind, or language, is a closed system. Because language does not have any external referents (or "external telos" as he puts it, p. 40), it cannot be controlled from outside. Cilliers does not say this directly, but it can be inferred from his descriptions that he thinks that there is no commanding, organizing center of the language either. It is a self-organizational system in that sense. It is obviously tempting to find similarities between Saussure's structuralism and the self-organizational processes described by connectionist models, but the adequacy of the connectionist models in describing the way the mind works has been questioned, as I mentioned earlier.

Cilliers brings Derrida into his discussion to find similarities between post-structualism and complexity theory. Derrida revises Saussure's structural view of language. He posits that not only the relations between words and concepts are arbitrary, but also concepts do not have stable meanings. In Derrida's view language is a system of "unanchored"—i.e., indeterministic—relationships between signs. He dissolves the difference between the signifier and the signified. Derrida's dissolution is so complete that it does not allow making any distinctions between the language and the world it describes. Cilliers views Derrida's dissolution as an example "open systems," but I do not think this is the understanding of open systems most other complexity theorists would agree with.

Derrida's key concept is *différance*, which means differences between signs and their meanings. Because, according to Derrida, signs do not have inherent meanings ("The sign is an entity without any positive content," Cillers, p. 44); their meanings can be determined only when they are differentiated. In other words, the meanings of signs (words) can be determined only *in relation to* other signs. It is of course tempting to compare this with complexity theory's insight that *systems are made of relationships* (see Chapter 2 in this book). The problem is that in Derrida's view differentiation is an endless process; the process never stops to constitute a meaningful whole, even temporarily. It is an endless "play of signifiers" or a "language game" (p. 43). Cilliers argues that "Derrida's concept of *différance* can be used to describe the *dynamics* of complex neural networks" [emphasis in original] (p. 46). Cilliers recognizes that this play of signifiers does not constitute a meaningful whole: No recognizable and stable structures emerge from this play. He also recognizes that complex systems do have recognizable and relatively stable—emergent—structural properties. Then these two are in conflict: The description of language by Derrida, if true, is not a good description of complex systems.

There is another issue with the epistemological implications of structuralism and post-structuralism. Cillers comments: "The obsession to find one essential truth blinds us to the relationary nature of complexity, and especially to the continuous shifting of those relationships" (p. 112). Agreed. But the alternative complexity theory offers does not seem to be post-structuralism. The post-structuralist idea that language is nothing but a play of signifiers, with no external referents, is not what complexity theory suggests. Post-structuralism denies any "epistemological privileges" to any discourse, scientific or otherwise. This is not compatible with complexity theory, whose roots are in science. Because in post-structuralism no external referents are allowed, it is impossible to check the validity of any statements empirically. Cilliers recognizes that there is a relationship between language and the world it describes, albeit this is not a direct, transparent, or objectively controlled relationship (p. 125). Pluralists and phenomenologists recognize this too, as I discussed in the previous sections, but this does not necessitate that we deny any epistemological privilege to any form of knowledge, including a science of complexity.

Even if we assume that the post-structuralist argument is suitable for interpreting social realities, I do not think that it would be reasonable to suggest the same for natural phenomena. Even if we assume that all metanarratives of and discourses about social reality are equal, we cannot reasonably say that all metanarratives of and discourses about natural phenomena are equal as well. The notion of endophysical knowledge complexity theorists like Rössler (1986) espouse challenges the Newtonian/positivist correspondence theory of truth and the naïve notions of representation and objective knowledge and problematizes the relationship between knowledge and reality, but it does not suggest that the scientific discourse is not epistemologically privileged or that scientific signifiers do not have any referents in nature.

Cilliers (1998) has an important insight and reminder. He says, "When we deny the possibility of a theory of representation [as Derrida does], the question concerning the relationship between the distributed system and the world does not, however, disappear" (p. 83). Cilliers' answer to the question is that there must be a "generalized reference" to an outside world in the mind, or in the language (p. 82). This generalized reference can be in the form of a "simulation," according to Cilliers. "A simulation does not attempt to represent some essential abstraction of something real; it rather attempts to repeat it, thereby undermining the distinction between the real and the simulated" (p. 84). Simulations are important tools of complexity theory. I will discuss agent-based simulations in Chapter 10.

A Brief Assessment of the Three Interpretations

All three interpretations of the epistemological implications of complexity theory—pluralism, phenomenology, and post-structuralism—point to one important conclusion: that complexity theory forces us to at least question or even abandon Newtonian, Cartesian, and positivist assumptions about reality and knowledge. Under complexity theory it is no longer possible to assume that reality is stable, or always tends toward equilibrium, and that as external observers we can know the totality of reality objectively. The knowledge of a complex system is always contextual. It may be the biological context of the knowing body (Merleau-Ponty) or the temporal and cultural context of the knowing subject (Heidegger), or both, that shapes the knowledge process. One way or the other, knowledge is contextual.

Which of the three interpretations is the best interpretation? Based on the limited work done by complexity theorists so far, in my opinion, phenomenology provides the most solid grounding. Prigogine and his colleagues acknowledge the contextuality of the knowledge of complex systems but at the same time assert that a new form of objective scientific knowledge is possible. Their works show why phenomenology and complexity theory are compatible, but more work needs to be done to elaborate on the details.

The pluralist perspectives of S. Mitchell and Richardson are actually agnostic. Because reality is so complex, we do not know what the best way of knowing it is, they say. Therefore, we should be open to all interpretations. This pragmatic approach might be the best approach, unless and until a more coherent philosophical perspective is developed for complexity theory.

Post-structuralism is not quite compatible with complexity theory. The parallels Cillers draws between the connectionist models of the mind and post-structuralism and the inferences he makes for complexity theory are challenging intellectually. However, as I tried to show, his interpretations are quite selective and narrow. Post-structuralism, in Cillers' interpretation, reduces the knowledge process to a "language game," attributes equal standing to all kinds of knowledge, and makes it theoretically impossible to establish the validity of any knowledge claim. This is not compatible with complexity theory, which has its roots in science.

COMPLEXITY, EPISTEMOLOGY, AND PUBLIC POLICY

The reader may ask at this point: What is the relevancy of all these epistemological issues and discussion to public policy and administration? The answer is this: Many, if not most, of the foundational assumptions in the social sciences in general, and in public policy and administration in particular, have their roots in the Newtonian, Cartesian, and positivist worldviews, as I discussed in the previous chapter.

Briefly, once again, the Weberian model of bureaucracy and the scientific and classical management theories of the early 20th century were based on this Newtonian mechanistic image of organization. This model and these theories are based on the closed system and equilibrium assumptions, which the social sciences and biology adopted from the Newtonian physics of the 17th century (Prigogine and Stengers, 1984, pp. 207–208). The geometry of organizational charts and the mathematization of work relations in ergonomic studies are Cartesian. Adam Smith's classical theory of economics and its derivates, like neoclassical economics and rational choice, presume that self-interested individuals function in deterministic sets of relations in closed systems, which tend toward equilibrium conditions. In the minds of neoclassical economists, human beings are elementary particles that exist solely to maximize their utility functions. Neoclassical economists use mathematical equations to predict the behaviors of human elements, just like Newtonian physicist would try to predict the trajectories of moving objects (Waldrop, 1992, p. 22).

These Newtonian, Cartesian, and positivist assumptions have been challenged from phenomenological and post-structuralist perspectives. Phenomenological philosophers critiqued the Newtonian science for creating an objectified view of knowledge and thus alienating human beings. Both Husserl and Heidegger were concerned about this objectification and thought that it would lead to losing touch with the reality individuals actually live (Hummel, 1994, p. 209).

There are a few applications of phenomenology in public policy and administration: Harmon and Meyer (1986), Jun (1986), and Hummel (1994). These authors are concerned about the alienating effects of bureaucratic organizations on civil servants and the citizens they are supposed to serve. Jun (1986) notes that phenomenology emphasizes the role of qualitative understanding of people's experiences and suggests that problem solving must be relevant to the participants' realities. He argues that researchers of organizational processes must reflexive participants, not detached observers (p. 175). Similarly, in his works, Harmon critiques the reification of organizations and offers a pheneomenological alternative that recognizes the active and intersubjective nature of organizational activities and encourages participatory practices.

Hummel (1994) presents a thorough critique of the bureaucratic form of organization. The bureaucratic form of organization makes the behaviors of workers predictable for a capitalist or manager. Therefore it is valuable for capitalism, Weber observed (p. 96). But bureaucracy also has adverse effects. Hummel cites Husserl's view that bureaucracy has become distant from real life with its standardized modeling of life and its preoccupations with procedures (p. 213). As such, it has removed basic humanness of its participants by creating artificial patterns of behavior and a language that is disconnected from their daily lives. The bureaucratic form of organization is problematic also because it forces public administrators to know their clients and their actions only in bureaucratic terms and ignore their humanities (p. 16).

Complexity theory does not add any more details to the critiques by Jun, Harmon, Meyer, and Hummel, but it provides additional grounding for them. If the bureaucratic managerial practices of the 20th century were based on the 17th-century Newtonian science, the practices of future organizations can be based on complexity theory, which suggests a participatory and contextual view of knowledge.

I argued earlier in this chapter that post-structuralism is not compatible with complexity theory. Schram's (1993, 1995) works, the primary examples of postmodernism or post-structuralism in the policy studies literature, show why post-structuralism is not compatible with complexity theory. Like other post-structuralists, Schram denies any "epistemological privilege" to scientists or analysts in the knowledge process.

Denying any epistemological privilege to anybody or any form of discourse has significant implications in policy analysis. This goes beyond the participatory practices phenomenology suggests. These implications can be observed in Schram's (1995) arguments against critical theory. Schram argues that the prevailing paradigm in policy analysis and planning is grounded in a narrow, falsely objective, overly instrumental view of rationality and masks the biases of policy elites and technocrats. Schram acknowledges that Habermasian critical policy analysis, which suggests that we should engage in practical communicative action (i.e., a genuinely participatory policymaking process), is well intentioned, but not sufficient. Critical theorists are still modernists and Habermas' theory is not a radical departure from the positivist paradigm, according to Schram. Habermasian policy analysis maintains the notion that cogitating about a policy ahead of time is necessary, so it retains the old paradigm's prejudice of "epistemic privilege" for planners. Schram argues that policy struggle cannot be theorized ahead of time by analysts or planners. The implication is that because an analyst's knowledge is not any better than anybody else's, policy analysis is not a meaningful practice, and therefore all analysts should abandon policy analysis and join the political struggle for social change as policy activists.

Postmodern inquiry provides activists an important tool, according to Schram (1993). Postmodern inquiry into the "discursive construction of identity" makes a democratizing contribution. It does so by enabling us to rethink the questionable distinctions that privilege some identities at the expense of others. And it dispels the popular myth that policies and institutions exist as entities that are independent from the beliefs and rituals that make them real. Therefore, it makes possible to change policies and institutions.

The merits of policy analysts joining political struggles are debatable. But reducing all forms of policy-related knowledge to equal footing (denying any epistemological privilege to any form of knowledge) is harder to justify. At least that is not what complexity theory suggests.

CHAPTER SUMMARY

In this chapter I described and assessed the three epistemological positions complexity theorists propose as alternatives to the Newtonian/positivist determinism and objectivism: pluralism, phenomenology, and postmodernism/post-structuralism. To provide a background to the discussions, I summarized the general philosophies of phenomenology, hermeneutics, and postmodernism/post-structuralism in the first part of the chapter.

Phenomenology emerged in response to the Newtonian and Cartesian view of science, particularly its view that scientific knowledge should be context free and scientists should be external viewers of reality. The three phenomenologists whose views I summarized in this chapter—Husserl, Heidegger, and Merleau-Ponty—all object to this view of science and scientists in their own way. They all agree that knowledge is a product of the mind's being-in-the-world and therefore it is contextual. Hermeneutics is concerned with the interpretation of meaning in all forms of symbolic interaction: rituals, architectural style, cultural artifacts, etc. The problem for hermeneutics is how to interpret these forms of communications and discern the meanings in them. Postmodernist and post-structuralist scholars are quite a diverse group, but their interest and positions have varying degrees of overlaps with phenomenology and hermeneutics. Postmodernists/post-structuralists view the world as an indeterministic and diverse place and favor forms of knowledge that highlight differences, fragmentation, uniqueness, subjectivities, and relativities.

Different complexity theorists found parallels between phenomenology, hermeneutics, or postmodernism/post-structuralism and the implications of complexity theory. All these theorists agree that complexity theory forces us to at least question or even abandon Newtonian, Cartesian, and positivist assumptions about reality and knowledge. Under complexity theory it is no longer possible to assume that reality is stable, or always tends toward equilibrium, and that as external observers we can know the totality of reality objectively. The knowledge of a complex system is always contextual. Then, pluralist complexity theorist argue, we should be ready accept multiple forms of knowledge as valid, because no one form can capture the entire complexity of reality. Those who favor phenomenology argue that the complexity of the world cannot be known externally and that scientists and others are internal to the complex realities they study. Others find parallels between the post-structuralist interpretations of language and the self-organizational processes in complex systems. In my assessment of the three interpretations among complexity theorist, I critiqued the post-structuralists and favored the positions of phenomenologists. The agnosticism of the pluralists may be a practical position in the absence of a coherent epistemology for complexity theory.

Phenomenology and post-structualism have been applied in public policy and administration by those who aimed to counter the dominance of the assumptions of the Newtonian science. In the last section of the chapter, I assessed these applications and pointed to their relevance of complexity theory in this context.

Part III
Methodology

8 Methods of Complexity Research
An Overview and Taxonomy

QUANTITATIVE AND QUALITATIVE METHODS

Complex systems are only partly knowable; the knowledge of their micro- and macro-level properties is only partly generalizable, and their future behaviors are predictable only partly. As Capra (1996) observes, in general systems thinking, approximate knowledge replaces the notion of certainty, definitiveness, and completeness in knowledge (p. 41); this is true for complexity theory as well. The methods of inquiry that complexity researchers use fit this understanding of complex systems.

Capra also notes that the acceptance nonlinearity as a property of systemic relations leads to a recognition that a qualitative understanding of such relations is necessary (p. 123). Indeed, not only the recognition of nonlinearity but also the understanding of complex systems and the epistemological implications of complexity theory I discussed in the previous chapters lead to the methodological conclusion that qualitative methods are necessary, as well as quantitative ones. We can quantify and model the measurable aspects of systems' structural properties and their evolutions. We also should aim to understand the context of those properties and their evolution qualitatively. An understanding of the natures of the agents of social complex systems and their relationships requires both quantitative and qualitative methods.

There is a wide range of methods complexity researchers use. These are mostly quantitative methods, but some researchers use qualitative methods as well. In this and the following chapters, I will describe the methods complexity researchers use in a taxonomy and make suggestions for syntheses and refinements of some of these methods. I propose a taxonomy in the next section.

I want to clarify first what I mean by qualitative and quantitative, as there are different understandings of these terms. In their classic and intensely debated book on social science methodology, *Designing Social Inquiry: Scientific Inference in Qualitative Research* (1994), King, Keohane, and Verba, use the term qualitative to mean "small-n research" (research with small samples), and contrast it with "large-n studies" (research with large samples).[1] In large-n studies, statistical analyses are used to make inferences from selected samples to populations. According to King, Keohane, and

Verba, qualitative studies *should* use the same "logic of inference" as quantitative studies, with some modifications (p. 4), but they do not. Because of this, in their view, existing qualitative studies are typically deficient. The authors propose remedies to improve qualitative research methods, so that they would fit better the "universal logic of inference," i.e., the logic of inference used in quantitative (large-n) studies. They do so because they assume "that valid general knowledge follows directly from proper application of quantitative methods. . . . [T]he task at hand is to remake qualitative methods so that they are more consistent with the template of quantitative research" (Ragin, 2008, p. 50).

There are other conceptualizations of quantitative and qualitative methods as well. Marczyk, DeMatteo, and Festinger (2005) use the term "qualitative" in reference to categorical/nominal variables in statistical analyses and contrast it with "quantitative" ("continuous," "scale," "interval and ratio") variables. "*Qualitative variables* are variables that vary in kind, while *quantitative variables* are those that vary in amount" [emphasis in original] (p. 49). For instance, they say, the "helpful" versus "not helpful" dichotomy is a qualitative variable, because there is only a difference in kind between the two categories. The number of times someone is engaged in a particular behavior is a quantitative variable, because real numbers are attached to it. In their view, quantitative variables are considered superior to qualitative variables, because the former allow more precise measurements, analyses, and inferences, whereas the latter are limited in all these areas.

Note that in both King, Keohane, and Verba's and Marczyk, DeMatteo, and Festinger's conceptualizations, the implicit frame of reference is the "logic of inference" of the Newtonian/positivist science. The common assumption is that entities and events are measurable with certainty and precision and generalizations can be made from these measurements. The higher the precision and certainty, the more complete the generalization, and therefore the better the method. Because quantitative variables enable researchers to measure with higher precision and achieve more certainty, and because large-n studies allow more complete generalizations, they are preferable to their qualitative and small-n alternatives. In this view, qualitative methods are a lesser version of quantitative methods.

This view is not shared by Berg (1998). He stresses that qualitative and quantitative methods have fundamentally different purposes: Whereas the former is used to understand meanings in human communications and artifacts, the latter is used to measure tangible things and detect and explain the relations among them. Both are necessary; neither one of them is superior to the other:

> Quality is essential to the nature of things. On the other hand, quantity is elementally an amount of something. Quality refers to the what, how, when, and where of a thing—its essence and ambiance. Qualitative

research thus refers to the meanings, concepts, definitions, characteristics, metaphors, symbols, and descriptions of things. In contrast, quantitative research refers to counts and measures of things. (p. 3)

Yanow and Schwartz-Shea (2006) take a similar approach but use the term "interpretive research," instead of "qualitative research." They point out that the central problem of interpretive research is to understand the "meaning-making activity of human actors" (p. xii). They contrast this with "positivistic research," in which the goal is to make generalizations about objective phenomena. Even those researchers who use "qualitative methods" to make generalizations are positivists, according to the authors. The task of an interpretive researcher is to understand the meanings created by actors within their contexts, not to make generalizations about them.

In my view, Yanow and Schwartz-Shea's sharp contrast between "interpretive" and "positivistic" forms of research is too categorical, and their dismissal of the term "qualitative research" is not warranted. But their contrast between understanding human meanings versus making generalizations is important. This actually points to the different orientations of qualitative and quantitative research methods. These orientations should not be considered as categorical distinctions; however, particularly in studies of complex social systems, both orientations are necessary. Complexity researchers need to measure and make limited generalizations about the structural properties of systems and their evolutions, and they need to use qualitative methods to describe the contexts of systemic properties and evolutions, as well as the contexts and meaning-making processes of actors/agents of systems. I will discuss these uses of quantitative and qualitative methods in this and the next two chapters. I will also show that in some methodologies quantification and qualitative interpretation are or can be mixed.

I want to note here that Berg's and Yanow and Schwartz-Shea's definitions of qualitative, or interpretive, research methods are closely related to hermeneutics, which I discussed in the previous chapter. The reader will remember that the problem of hermeneutics was how to interpret meanings generated by human beings, individually and/or collectively. To understand the distinction Berg and Yanow and Schwartz-Shea make between quantitative and qualitative/interpretive forms of research, we should go back to the history of hermeneutics briefly here.

The distinction they make has its roots in the distinction hermeneutic philosophers like Wilhelm Dilthey of the 19th century made between the natural sciences (*Naturwissenschaften*) and the social sciences (*Geisteswissenschaften*). The question then was this: Can social realities be studied and explained the way natural sciences study and explain their subject matters? Dilthey reasoned that because their subject matters were of different kind, the natural and social sciences had to use different kinds of methods. The goal of the natural sciences was explanation (*Erklären*), and the goal of the social sciences was understanding (*Verstehen*). The natural sciences could explain the workings of the objects in nature, but the social sciences could not do the same for social realities, because they could not treat human beings as objects. Instead they had to aim to understand the meanings created by human beings and the meaning-making processes. Whereas the objects in nature could be measured and the relations among them could be generalized and explained, human meanings could not be measured. Instead meanings had to be understood in the contexts they were created and from the perspective of the meaning makers. This is the basis of the distinction Berg and Yanow and Schwartz-Shea make between quantitative and qualitative/interpretive methods.

The reader will remember from the previous chapter that the question of whether, or to what extent, a researcher can understand the meanings created by the human beings he/she studies remains an open question. The "objectivist" hermeneutic philosophers like Hirsch think that there are objective meanings in texts and other artifacts and they can be understood using proper methods. Gadamer thinks that hermeneutic understanding is possible, but it should be "an interaction between the historically grounded intentions of the author of a text or an artifact and the historically grounded interpretations of the reader" (Morçöl, 2002, p. 101). Fish takes the position that "there is no predetermined (true) meaning in a text; a meaning is a product of the reader's interpretation" (p. 101). Regardless of the specific position they take, these philosophers all agree that social/cultural/human sciences require different kinds of research methods. These methods range from case studies, to interviews, narrative/discourse analyses, dramaturgical methods, and others.[2]

The qualitative versus quantitative distinction hermeneutic philosophers make should be the basis of understanding why and how complexity researchers use both types of methods and under what conditions they use which methods. Complexity researchers use both qualitative and quantitative methods in their studies of natural and social systems, but quantitative methods are dominant in the complexity research literature. This is primarily due to the fact that complexity theory has its roots in the natural sciences and most of the systems complexity researchers have studied are natural systems. These quantitative methods have been carried over into the studies on complex social systems, but there are also methods that combine quantitative and qualitative tools.

An important issue is that complexity researchers should be clear about the ontological and epistemological underpinnings of the methods they use. The hermeneutic distinction I mentioned above should be taken seriously. Even though certain forms of quantification can be used in understanding meanings, possible repercussions of doing so should be understood clearly.

There is a potential problem in the applications of quantitative methods particularly in the social sciences, what Strauch (1976) calls the problem of *quantificationism*. Quantificationism is the belief that quantification is a value per se, and a quantitative answer to a scientific question is better than a qualitative one in principle. In the quantificationist view, because reality is assumed to be tangible and decomposable into discrete units, it is also assumed that scientific knowledge should be reductionist. Reality is reducible to small units that can be counted and analyzed quantitatively. For example, the number of molecules in a room can be counted—or, estimated, if exact counting is not possible for practical reasons—and the changes in the numbers can be traced. Quantitative analyses are considered more scientific than qualitative forms of inquiry, because it is assumed that quantification yields more precise knowledge.

These quantificationist beliefs are sometimes expressed openly, as in computer scientist Ron Graham's words: "As any science matures, its methods inevitably become quantitative. So mathematics, as the language of science, is ideally suited for a deeper understanding of the science" (Mahurin, 2000, p. 90). It is also expressed by von Bertalanffy (1968). In his view mathematics and formal models are essential for his general system theory. He says that a verbal model is better than no model and that some verbal models have been very influential and helpful and one may start with a verbal model, but ultimately all scientific models should be expressed in mathematical terms. He prefers mathematics over ordinary language, because the former is more precise than the latter (p. 24).

More often, however, quantificationist beliefs are expressed indirectly or they are subtly injected into analyses. Economist Brian Arthur observes this in neoclassical economics. In his view the rich complexity of the world is reduced to a set of abstract principles, and mathematics is elevated to the status of the mere arbiter of truth in neoclassical economics. He points out that mathematical economists describe the humans as elementary particles. This is the notion of the "economic man." "[J]ust as physicists could predict how a particle responds to any given set of forces, economists could predict how economic man will respond to any given economic situation: he (or it) will just optimise his utility function" (quoted in Waldrop, 1992, p. 22).

In policy analysis, quantificationism is manifested in the assumption that quantitative methodology is an extension of scientific method and rationality (Strauch, 1976). The late Edward S. Quade (1989) warned against quantificationist tendencies in policy analysis: "[A]n answer obtained by quantitative methods is not necessarily better than one obtained by qualitative arguments, for in order to quantify a model, too many aspects of the problem it seeks to illuminate may have to be suppressed or drastically simplified" (p. 170).

The discussions in the previous chapters demonstrate that although most of its applications are quantitative, complexity theory is not quantificationist. Complexity researchers who study complex policy systems are, or should be, aware that simplifications they make when they use quantitative methods and models are "suppressed or drastically simplified" pictures of inherently complex realities and that they should be complemented with contextual, qualitative understandings of systems and their actors.

In contrast to von Bertalanffy's view that all models of systems should ultimately be expressed in mathematical terms, Smith and Jenks (2006) argue, "All complexity is qualitative, because it is self-organizing" (p. 23). They go on to say

> [T]o treat complexity in a quantitative . . . sense becomes increasingly untenable: complex systems have histories and futures, paths by which they come into being and possible directions dependent on many factors. . . . They are not "things" in the noun sense but processes; nor are they "things" in the categorical sense because nothing underwrites the linguistic academic habit of collecting them together. (p. 23)

Although Smith and Jenks are right in stressing the histories of complex systems, with the multiple factors affecting their trajectories and the impossibility of delineating and categorizing them, I disagree with their conclusion that all understanding of complexity must be qualitative. Complexity researchers have developed multiple quantitative methods that are necessary to process and summarize massive amounts of information about complex systems. These quantitative methods model some limited aspects of complex systems and in doing so they simplify complexities. That is a deficiency, but the knowledge of complex systems has to be deficient, incomplete, and partial anyway. No model or simulation of reality can match its complexity. Smith and Jenks note "there cannot possibly be any direct one-to-one correspondence between the environment and the system as a whole" (p. 11). Qualitative descriptions cannot correspond to real complex systems on a one-to-one basis either. Both quantitative and qualitative methods are needed to understand complex systems better, although all forms of understanding would still be partial and incomplete.

METHODS OF COMPLEXITY RESEARCH: A TAXONOMY

A few other books describe and illustrate the quantitative methods complexity researchers use (Guastello, 1995; Kaplan and Glass, 1995; Batty, 2007; Gros, 2008). In this section I propose a taxonomy that can be used to understand the uses of both quantitative and qualitative methods in complexity research. The conceptual basis of this taxonomy is the micro–macro problem (Chapter 3). I group the methods into three categories: (a) methods of detecting and measuring macro patterns, (b) methods of understanding micro–macro relations, and (c) methods of understanding micro processes, particularly the cognitive processes of actors/agents. In my taxonomy I include not only the methods that have been actually used by complexity researchers but also those methods that I think complexity researchers could use.

The taxonomy is presented in Table 8.1 below. In this section I discuss the categories listed in the table briefly. In the following chapters, I will provide more details on each of these methods. I will emphasize all the methods equally, because I consider some of them more important than others. Some of the methods have technical details that would require lengthy descriptions and illustrations; I will refer the reader to the sources these methods are described and illustrated.

The macro-level methods listed in Table 8.1 are used to detect emergent patterns at the system level and their dynamics. I group these methods into two: methods of detecting emergent structural patterns and methods of detecting macro-level processes. The macro-level methods are discussed in Chapter 9.

Whereas the macro-level methods listed in the table are used quite extensively, not only by complexity researchers, but also many others, the micro–macro methods are more specific to complexity studies. These are the methods of detecting, measuring, and interpreting/understanding the relations between micro agents/actors and the structural properties that emerge from their interactions. In other words, they are the methods of understanding emergence and self-organization. I will discuss them in Chapter 10.

The micro-level methods in the table are actually not known to many complexity researchers, with the possible exception of laboratory experiments.

Table 8.1   A Taxonomy of the Methods of Complexity Research

Macro methods
    Methods of studying macro-level structures and processes
        Regression models
        Fractal geometry

    Methods of studying macro-level processes
        Time-series methods
            Phase portraits, attractors
            Lyapunov exponents,
            Fourier spectrum analyses
            Spatial correlations
        System dynamics modeling

Micro–macro methods:
    Social network analyses
    Agent-based modeling
    Qualitative case studies

Micro methods:
    Laboratory experiments
    Repertory grids
    Cognitive mapping
    Q methodology

I think they can make important additions to the complexity research tool chest. As I discussed in Chapter 3 and will do so again in the next chapter, complexity researchers who study micro–macro relations make assumptions about the minds and behaviors of agents (e.g., that they are cognitive agents or they are reactive agents). These assumptions are based on generalizations about the human mind and behaviors (i.e., "average" minds or "average" behaviors), not on an understanding of specific human minds or behaviors in particular settings. The micro methods I describe in Chapter 11 can be used to remedy this shortcoming in future studies.

CHAPTER SUMMARY

Because of the nonlinear, emergent, self-organizational, and coevolutionary properties of complex systems, no single method is sufficient to generate a complete knowledge of their structural properties or the properties of their components: actors/agents. Both quantitative and qualitative methods are needed to gain a better understanding of complex systems at both micro and macro levels. In this chapter I summarized the different notions of qualitative and quantitative methods. I adopted the notion that qualitative methods are needed to understand the meanings made by actors and the contexts of actors and their systemic relations, whereas quantitative methods can be used to make generalizations about measurable aspects of systemic properties. In some methodological applications both quantitative and qualitative approaches will be used together.

I also proposed a taxonomy of the methods complexity researchers use. In this taxonomy the methods are grouped into three: (a) methods that are used to measure structural (macro) properties of systems and the evolutions of these properties, (b) methods that are used to study the micro–macro relations in systems, and (c) methods that can be used to study the micro level (i.e., the mindsets, values, or preferences of actors/agents of a system). These groups of methods are discussed in the following chapters.

9   Macro Methods

In this chapter I describe and discuss macro-level methods in two groups: methods of studying macro-level structures and processes and methods of studying macro-level processes. Although it is not always clear where one should draw the line between structures and processes (see the discussions in Chapters 2, 3, and 4), I made this differentiation to indicate the different emphases in these two groups of methods. For example, in most of their applications, regression models are static: They are used to measure and sort out the cross-sectional relations between variables. Regression models are used in time-series analyses as well but less frequently. Fractal geometry is about self-similar (self-replicating) processes, and its tools can be used to detect macro patterns that emerge from these processes. The time-series methods are used to detect particularly the "chaotic patterns" in a system's behavior. System dynamics modeling is used to describe the patterns of systemic relations and their outcomes.

METHODS OF STUDYING MACRO-LEVEL STRUCTURES AND PROCESSES

Regression Analysis

Regression analysis is a family of methods. It is better to call it a methodological approach, rather than a particular method. Its various forms are known well and used extensively by a wide variety of researchers, including complexity researchers.

In its most basic form, regression analysis is used to identify the relations between a set of independent variables (causes) and a dependent variable (effect). This approach epitomizes the Newtonian/positivist view of experimental science. In this view, the researcher hypothesizes a relationship between a dependent variable (e.g., rate of poverty) and an independent variable or a set of independent variables (e.g., rate of unemployment in the community). The relationship between the dependent and independent variable(s) is/are not only external (no endogeneity, or recursiveness) but also linear.[1] The empirical data that do not fit into linear equations are considered "residuals" or "error terms" in regression analysis.[2] These two core assumptions of regression analysis—external causality and linear causality—directly contrast the assertions by complexity theorists that complex systems are self-organizational and that it is essential to understand nonlinearities in systemic relations.

Then why would complexity researchers want to use regression analysis? There are not many examples of complexity researchers using this method, and those who use regression models include nonlinear elements in their analyses. Regression analysis does allow the inclusion of nonlinear terms. For instance, instead of using the simple regression model ($Y = a + bX$) or a multiple linear regression model ($Y = a + b_1X_1 + b_2X_2 + b_nX_n$), a researcher may try to detect second-order or third-order relationships between variables (e.g., $Y = a + b_1X_1 + b_2X_2^2 + b_3X_3^3$). The curvilinear relations represented by the second- and higher-order terms are considered nonlinear.

In most of its applications, regression analysis yields cross-sectional snapshots of the relations between variables at the macro level; the aim of the researcher is not to understand micro–macro relations. In a few creative applications of regression methods, some aspects of micro–macro relations in systems are studied as well. Guastello's (1995) applications of regression analysis in combination with simulations in studying the labor force problems for small businesses in Wisconsin (pp. 285–292) and in creative problem solving among a group of social scientists (pp. 319–328) are examples. I refer the reader to Gusatello's book for elaborate descriptions of the mathematics of nonlinear regression analysis and rich examples of its applications.

Typically the relations between variables are simplified by linearizing them in regression analysis. Even when nonlinear terms are used in regression models, as Gastello does, the researcher has to make some simplifications by excluding data as residuals and error terms. Arguably, some simplification is inevitable in any modeling and analysis process. With that in mind, regression analysis, particularly its nonlinear forms may be useful in gaining insight into the structural properties of complex systems.

Although in most of its applications, regression analysis is cross-sectional—i.e., static—it is versatile enough to be used in longitudinal—time-series—analyses as well. However, such applications are highly problematic because of the nature of time-series data. Time-series data are *serially dependent*, or *path dependent,* as complexity theorists would call it. The value of the next data point cannot be independent of the previous data point. One of the best examples of this is the serial dependencies of budgetary allocations over the years. Although theoretically it is possible that the budgetary allocation for a particular agency or program each year would be independent of those in every other year, in practice this is determined incrementally, based on the amount in the previous year. Another example would be performances of school children in standardized tests: Later scores in these performance tests cannot be independent of earlier scores, because children's learning processes are cumulative.

These serial dependencies budgetary and cognitive processes are normal and expected. The problem is that when the serially dependent budgetary figures and test scores are used as dependent variables in regression analyses, this violates a cardinal assumption of this method: "the observations of the underlying behavior are mutually independent" (Suen and Ary, 1989, p. 213). When the assumption is violated, the results of the analyses will have serious validity problems. Particularly, the value of the inferential statistics used will be artificially inflated (p. 195). As Suen and Ary note, this is why methods that factor serial dependencies into account, such as autoregressive integrated moving average (ARIMA), are preferred over regression analysis when time-series data are analyzed.

I will not discuss ARIMA in this chapter, but I will summarize the time-series methods that are used by complexity researchers to investigate the changes in structural properties of systems later in this chapter: phase diagrams, Lyupanov exponents, Fourier analysis, and spatial correlation.

Fractal Geometry

Benoit Mandelbrot, the founder of fractal geometry, developed it in the 1960s and 1970s, but the roots of its principles can be traced back to German mathematician Georg Cantor's works on "Cantor sets" in the late 19th and early 20th centuries (Peitgen, Jürgens, and Saupe, 2004, pp. 65–75). A core concept of fractal geometry is *self-similarity across scales*. This concept refers to the idea that a simple geometric shape—a shape that can be generated using a simple mathematical formula, like a triangle—can be plotted repeatedly at different scales to obtain highly complex patterns. For example, one can generate the fractal geometric object called the "Sierpinski Gasket" by connecting the mid-points of an equidistant triangle iteratively and infinitely.[3]

Mandelbrot derived the name *fractal* from the Latin adjective *fractus*, which has its roots in a verb that means "to break" or "to create irregular movements" (Briggs, 1992, p. 61). The name fractal represents the contents of this type of geometry nicely; fractal geometry makes use of "irregular" dimensions, unlike the well-known integer dimensions of the Euclidean geometry. The Euclidean object the square is two dimensional, and the cube is three dimensional, for example. A fractal geometric object may have 1.3 or 2.56 dimensions, which indicate the degree of roughness, brokenness, or irregularity in an object. Although the fractal dimensions signify irregularity, these irregularities remain constant over different scales. This is the principle applied in plotting objects with self-similarity over different scales.

Mandelbrot and other mathematicians created several fractal objects applying the principle of self-similarity over different scales, like the Koch curve, which resembles a snowflake, and the famous "Mandelbrot set."[4]

They also demonstrated that fractal objects are not merely artificial creations; actually self-similar irregularities can be found in nature, from the shapes of the branches and leaves of most plants and trees to fractal landscapes like mountain ridges.

Is fractal geometry applicable to social phenomena as well? Batty (2007) applied it in his analyses of urban structures, which are physical structures that are products of planning and other forms of human behaviors and artifacts of human cultural beliefs and preferences. Batty observes "There are . . . spatial patterns in cities that are formed at different scales . . . from the same design principle being exercised by different agencies with differing levels of control over how the city develops" (p. 459). In these examples, the master plans laid out for larger areas are replicated at different levels. Batty gives the example of the spatial planning of the city of Savannah, Georgia, by James E. Oglethorpe, English colonist and the founder of Savannah. Oglethorpe designed the basic layout of the city as four identical squares. This square form was replicated as smaller squares within those squares and additional 20 squares adjacent to the original four ("Squares of Savannah"). Batty gives also several other examples of fractal urban structures and their evolutions (pp. 457–514). Most of his examples are mathematical and hypothetical abstractions, but he also demonstrates with examples from six cities in the northeastern region of the US that one can calculate their fractal dimensions from their densities.

Batty concedes that the fractal methods he used were only "caricatures" of the structural properties of real complex urban systems; they were "suggestive rather than definitive" (p. 514). Batty's illustrations and concession exemplify the limitations of the applications of fractal geometry in the social sciences.

METHODS OF STUDYING MACRO-LEVEL PROCESSES

Structural properties of systems change and evolve. There are methods that are designed to study the evolutions of structural properties of systems. These methods were designed to analyze time-series data on particular structural properties. In other words, these methods are not used to understand the system under study as a whole, but to measure and track a selected property of its structure. For example, they can be used to study the changes in the number of the members of a particular species in an ecosystem, but not the evolution of the interactions of the members of that species. The plots of time-series data presented in Figure 1.4 illustrate this methodological approach. These figures are reproduced in Figure 9.1, with some additions. The logistic equation was used to generate these figures. They illustrate the evolutionary patterns of a particular structural property under different initial conditions. These initial conditions are defined as the values of the k coefficient.

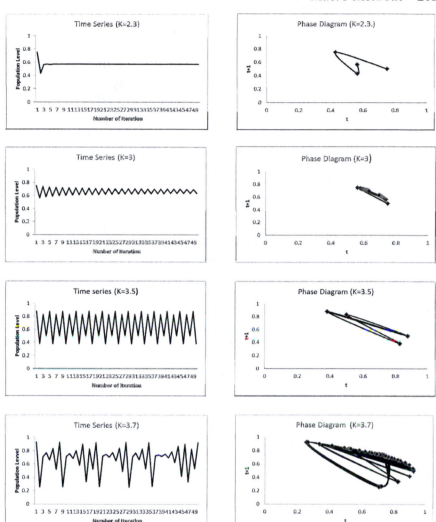

Figure 9.1 Solutions of the logistic equation and phase diagrams.

The reader will remember from Chapter 1 that ecologist Robert May demonstrated in his now classic 1976 *Nature* article that the growth of an insect colony follows the "logistic rule," as defined by the logistic equation ($Y_{t+1} = kY_t - k\ Y_t^2$) (Casti, 1994, pp. 93–94, cites May's work). In May's usage of the logistic equation, the k represents the birth rate (i.e., number of offspring each adult would produce), Y_t represents the population level at the beginning of a certain period of time (e.g., a generation), and Y_{t+1} represents the population level at the end of that period. If the equation is calculated iteratively, one can track the evolution of the population level over a long period of time.

The charts on the left in Figure 9.1 are time-series charts and the ones on the right are the *phase diagrams*. As the time series charts in illustrate, when the k is 2.3, the evolution is linear. When it is 3 or 3.5, one gets periodic fluctuations in time. When it is 3.7, it looks "chaotic"; there does not seem to be a particular pattern in it. The phase diagram for $k = 3.7$ reveals, however, that there actually is a pattern in the data. The phase diagrams for the k values of 2.3, 3.0, or 3.5 do not yield any new information. We could tell the patterns from the time-series charts. So they are important particularly for identifying patterns in seemingly chaotic time-series data sets.

Phase diagrams—also known as "return maps," "phase portraits," and "attractors"—are what Stroup (1997) characterizes as "methods of fingerprinting chaos" (pp. 137–138).[5] Phase diagrams are graphical displays of the patterns of change in a system's behavior. These patterns may be displayed on two or three dimensions. Two-dimensional displays are more common because they are easier to generate. The phase diagrams in Figure 9.1 are examples of two-dimensional phase diagrams. When generating these diagrams, the vertical axis was incremented versus the horizontal axis. For example, when the value at a particular time (t) is assigned to the X axis, the corresponding value in the Y axis will be the values in the lagged time periods of t+1, t+2, etc. In the examples in the figure, the t+1 values are plotted against the t values.

Figure 9.1 illustrates that when $k = 2.3$, the trajectory in the phase diagram swings around and settles into a value close to 0.6 (0.565217 to be precise). This pattern is known as "point attractor." The trajectory of the structural property (e.g., population level) is "attracted" to a particular point; it reaches that level and stay there. The phase diagram when $k = 3$ shows that the trajectory settles this time into an oscillating pattern, which is known as the "limit cycle attractor," and the range of this oscillation shrinks over time. The phase diagram of $k = 3.5$ shows that the trajectory shuttles between four distinct points in the chart. This pattern is known as the "period quadrupling attractor." The phase diagram of $k = 3.7$ reveals that actually there is a pattern in this seemingly random, "chaotic" data. Thus, phase diagrams allow us to make interpretations on geometrically represented data, and they can be useful particularly in revealing hidden patterns as in the case of $k = 3.7$.

Kiel and Elliot (1992) used phase diagrams to extract and interpret the patterns in long-term US federal budgetary outlays in the areas of defense, domestic discretionary, total mandatory, and unemployment compensation. Berry and Kim (1999) used them to demonstrate that the Federal Reserve policies helped reduce the fluctuations in the annual growth rates and the inflation rates in the US between 1866 and 1995. Their phase diagrams showed that the annual growth and inflation rates followed quite complex trajectories throughout this period, but the "attractors" of these rates covered smaller areas in the charts of the later periods, revealing that the fluctuations got smaller over time.

Priesmeyer and Baik's (1989) and Priesmeyer and Davis' (1991) applications of phase diagrams differ from these two studies in that Priesmeyer and his colleagues utilized this method in a deductive manner to test the fitness their data to ideal models. They first identified whether the trajectories of the profits and sales of a group of corporations are stable, oscillating, or chaotic. Then they compared their diagrams with the theoretically generated (mathematically calculated) pure models. Priesmeyer and Davis suggest that the "deviations" from the "pure" theoretical limit cycles are caused by "environmental factors (noise)." Left alone, the trajectories of the companies would be exactly like the pure ones, they argue. Priesmeyer and his colleagues point out that this method of comparing phase diagrams with theoretical models can be useful in prediction and control in management. They also argue that this approach works better than linear models and methods, like regression and traditional time-series analyses, in prediction, planning, and control.

Fourier power spectrum analyses, Lyapunov exponents, and spatial correlation analyses also are used to detect patterns in time-series data. I will not describe their details here. These methods are described and illustrated in other sources (e.g., Brown, 1995; Kaplan and Glass, 1995; Morçöl, 2002; Gros, 2008).

Fourier power spectrum analyses are used to detect well-defined cycles (periodic motions) in time-series data and plot them in charts called "periodograms" (Stroup, 1997, p. 137). A perfect periodic cycle—a cycle generated by mathematical sine function—is represented as a single spike in a periodogram. If there are multiple cycles (e.g., cycles within cycles, as in the case of cyclical seasonal data within larger business cycles), they will be represented by multiple, but recognizable, spikes. Chaos is represented by a broad band of spikes. If the data are random, then the spikes in the periodogram will not have a recognizable pattern. Fourier analyses do not yield precise results; the spikes in the periodograms may be interpreted differently.

Lyapunov exponents are preferred by those researchers who look for precision. Brown (1995) points out that Lyapunov exponents detect if there is a divergence in the observed/measured trajectory of a particular dynamical system from its projected trajectory. When there is a chaotic pattern generated by nonlinear relations in a system, the divergence from the projected trajectory is exponential (p. 22).

Spatial correlation analyses are used to distinguish chaotic patterns from randomness. A chaotic system has data points that are spatially correlated; random data are not spatially correlated (Stroup, 1997, pp. 137–138). If there are spatial correlations when they are plotted, the data points will be constrained in a discernible area on a phase diagram, as in the charts on the right-hand side in Figure 9.1. If the data points are random, not spatially correlated, then they will be dispersed on the diagram, not concentrated in a particular area. Stroup also notes that the fractal dimension of the data is calculated as part of a spatial correlation analysis. If the data are chaotic, this dimension will be between two and three (e.g., 2.78). If the calculated dimension is higher than three, this will indicate that the data are random, not chaotic.

Fourier analyses, Lypunov explonents, and spatial correlation analyses have been used only rarely in public policy studies. Dooley, Hamilton, Cherri, West, and Fisher's (1997) analyses of the time-series data of adolescent child bearing in Texas between 1964 and 1990 is one of those rare examples. They applied an array of methods, from return maps, to autocorrelations—a method similar to spatial correlation, as described by Stroup (1997)—power spectrum analyses, and Lyapunov exponents and calculated the fractal dimensions in their data. Their analyses showed that there were some cycles and "chaotic patterns" in the data. They made the observation that the policy changes in this area in Texas did make a difference. They recommend, based on their findings, that policy makers should make short-term predictions when making policies because of the large uncertainties in long-term predictions.

Systems Dynamic Modeling and Simulations

System dynamic modeling and simulations (SDMS), or *nonlinear dynamical models/analyses*, are used to study structural properties of systems. The difference between the methods like Fourier analysis, Lyapunov exponents, and spatial correlations, on the one hand, and the SDMS, on the other, is that whereas in the former the researcher tracks changes in one variable, in the latter he/she takes measurements on multiple variables and tracks structural changes on all of them simultaneously.

System dynamics models and simulations are the descendants of multivariate statistical methods. In the SDMS approach these methods are adapted to the systems thinking that systems are holistic and that systemic relations evolve. The multivarite methods evolved from the basic causal model: that dependent variable is caused by an independent variable. An illustration of the evolution of the models from the basic causal model to multivariate models and eventually the SDMS approach is presented in Figure 9.2. The evolution of the models can be traced from the top of the figure to the bottom.

Two major trends can be observed from top to bottom in Figure 9.2: (a) a movement from a single causal variable to multiple, and multi-level, causal variables and (b) a movement from unidirectional causal relations to multidirectional and/or circular causal relations. The first movement reflects the increasingly common understanding among social scientists that social events and phenomena cannot be explained with single and simple causes and therefore multiple casual variables should be used in models. The movement toward multidirectional or circular causal relations can be observed partially in structural equation models and more

Modeling Approach	Illustration	Equation(s)	Used in
The basic causal model	 X ⟶ Y	$Y = bX$	Experimental designs
Multivariate models	 X_1, X_2 ⟶ Y, X3	$Y = b_1X_1 + b_2X_2 + b_3X_3$	Multiple regression analyses
Multi-level multivariate models	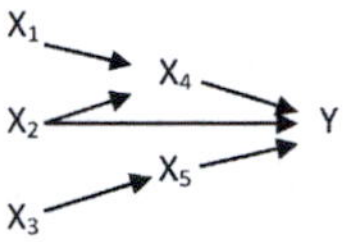 X_1, X_2, X_3, X_4, X_5 ⟶ Y	$X_4 = b_1X_1 + b_2X_2$ $X_5 = c_3X_3$ $Y = d_2X_2 + d_4X_4 + d_5X_5$	Path analysis, structural equation modeling and analysis
Multi-level multivariate models with non-recursive variables	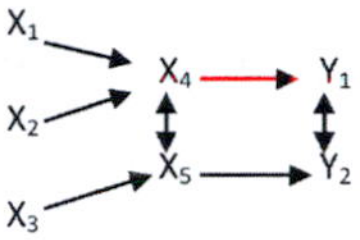 X_1, X_2, X_3, X_4, X_5, Y_1, Y_2		Structural equation modeling and analysis
Casual loop models	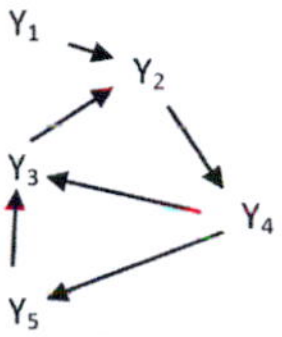 Y_1, Y_2, Y_3, Y_4, Y_5		Systems dynamics modeling and simulations

Figure 9.2   Evolution of models.

fully in system dynamics models. In structural equation models, there *can be*, but there does not have to be, non-recursive relations between variables (i.e., relations where causality can go both ways), but still structural equation researchers categorize dependent and independent variables separately.

The causal loop model in Figure 9.2 indicates that in the SDMS approach researchers do not make a differentiations between dependent and independent variables. Whereas in all the other modeling approaches, variables are grouped into dependent and independent variables (Ys and Xs, respectively), in the SDMS approach, there is no such differentiation (all variables are Ys). This reflects the system theoretical understanding that causal relations among the elements of a system are multidirectional, mutual, and sometimes distant.

However, in causal loop models some of the variables may still be interpreted as "dependent variables." Take the examples of the causal loop models in Figure 9.3. This is a model of the levels of CO_2 in the atmosphere under two policy options: adopting a carbon tax policy (a) and adopting an emission permits policy (b). In these two models, the level of CO_2 is obviously the variable of particular interest and analogous to the dependent variables in the basic causal model and multivariate models. Also the "carbon tax" "emission permits"—more specifically "permit quantity" and "permit price"—are like independent variables. Still the feedback loops in the models do not allow us to make a direct causal connection between the variables.

Forrester (1994) summarizes the view of causality in system dynamics modeling as follows:

> Most understandable experiences teach us that cause and effect are closely related in time and space. However, the idea that the cause of a symptom must lie nearby and must have occurred shortly before the symptom is true only in simple systems. In the more realistic complex systems, causes may be far removed in both timing and location from their observed effects. . . . In systems composed of many interacting feedback loops and long time delays, causes of an observed symptom may come from an entirely different part of the system and lie far back in time. (p. 14)

The SDMS approach is also dynamic. This is not apparent in Figures 9.2 or 9.3, because it is difficult to represent the dynamic aspects of the models on a two-dimensional paper. The plots of the iterative solutions of the logistic equation (Figure 9.1) illustrate this dynamism a little better. Once again, the logistic equation can be written in a form that represents an iterative process: $Y_{t+1} = kY_t - k\ Y_t^2$. In this iterative process, the

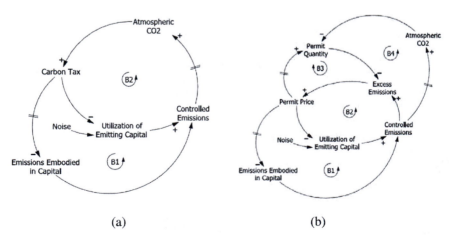

(a)   (b)

Figure 9.3   Causal loop models of CO_2 emissions with carbon tax and emission permits (Source: Fiddaman, 2007).

output of the first solution of the equation (value of Y_{t+1}) is entered into the equation as the value of Y_t in the next round, and so on. The values at each iteration are plotted to obtain the time-series charts on the left in Figure 9.1. System dynamic models are "solved" in a similar manner as the logistic equation is solved, but, of course, not one, but multiple values are generated at each stage and entered into the variables designated at the next stage.[6]

Jay Forrester, who pioneered the system dynamics modeling and analysis in the 1950s, was an engineer who applied his engineering knowledge to management and economic problems and developed dynamic computer simulation methods for the SDMS approach.[7] He first simulated management problems and the interactions in economic systems (Forrester, 1961). Later he applied the SDMS methodology in understanding urban systems (Forrester, 1969) and the global dynamics of the interactions between humans and the natural environment (Forrester, 1971).

The SDMS methodology has been used in a wide range of areas, like genetics, ecology, econometrics, and engineering.[8] Brown's (1994) simulations of the impacts of presidential policy changes in the US on environmental damage, public concern for environmental damage, and cost of cleanup is an example of how the SDMS approach can be used in policy analysis. Fiddaman's (2007) application of it on CO_2 levels with the two policy options of carbon tax and emission permits (Figure 9.3) is another example.

The SDMS methodology applies some of the basic notions of systems thinking: holism, mutual causality, and systemic evolution. The SDMS approach can be useful for complexity researchers. However, as I mentioned earlier, in the SDMS approach researchers conduct analyses at the macro level only. They do not include the relations between micro and macro levels in complex systems. There are other methodological approaches that are used to understand specifically micro–macro relations. I discuss them in the next chapter.

CHAPTER SUMMARY

I described the macro methods in this chapter. The first of these methods is regression analysis, which is not a specific method of complexity researchers, but a generic one. The methods of fractal geometry are used by complexity researchers to determine the fractal dimensionality of complex systems. Phase diagrams, Fourier spectrum analysis, Lyapunov exponents, and spatial correlation analysis are used to detect the changes at the system level and determine the patterns in them. System dynamics modeling and simulations are the most sophisticated version of the methods of detecting the patterns of macro-level changes. They are the products of the evolution of multivariate statistical models, but they also include some elements of systems thinking: holism, mutual causality, and systemic evolution.

10 Micro–Macro Methods

The methods covered in this chapter are used to investigate the micro–macro relations in complex systems. In Chapter 3, I noted that the "micro–macro problem" (or the "agent–structure problem") has been a central problem in sociology, economics, and political science for decades. I also noted that the roots of the problem can be traced farther back to the philosophies of Hobbes, Smith, Locke, Rousseau, and Mill in the 17th, 18th, and 19th centuries. In public policy, institutional rational choice theory and advocacy coalition framework, each its own way, conceptualize the relations between micro-level processes (i.e., individual and group behaviors) and macro-level (collective) policy processes and outcomes.

The micro–macro problem is obviously complex, and complexity theory can be useful in understanding it better. The three groups of methods I describe in this chapter—social network analyses, agent-based simulations, and qualitative case studies—are methodologies that can be used in studying the micro–macro processes in complex policy systems. These are not merely tools in a tool box, but each one is a methodology, with its own epistemological assumptions and congruent empirical tools.

SOCIAL NETWORK ANALYSES

Unlike system dynamics modeling and simulations, which are used to investigate structural properties of systems and their evolutions only, social network analyses (SNA) are used to address the micro–macro relations and transformations. In Knoke and Yang's (2008) words, in social network analyses

> The core issue is how large-scale systemic transformations emerge out of the combined preferences and purposive actions of individuals. Because network analysis simultaneously encompasses both structures and entities, it provides conceptual and methodological tools for linking changes in microlevel choices to macrolevel structural alterations. (p. 6)

Social structure is defined as patterned relationship among individuals and groups. Freeman (1992, pp. 12–17) traces the roots of this definition and the concern with social structures to the original publication of Herbert Spencer's *Principles of Sociology* in 1875 (p. 12). Spencer and his followers, according to Freeman, offered a large collection of "speculations, insights, and intuitions" about the emergence and workings of social structures. Later, between the 1930s and 1950s, Radcliffe-Brown recognized that the concern for structures implied a concern with the more general relations between parts and wholes of systems and pioneered the definition of social structures as patterned relationships among persons. In the 1950s and 1960s, the notion that *social structures are stable patterns* was questioned. Sociologists realized that different patterned relationships lasted for different periods of time; therefore, there were no universals in defining what constituted a structure. This led to the problem of how to represent patterned relationships in sociological theories and models. As Freeman puts it, there was a need not only to intuitively and creatively speculate about structures, but more importantly, to *formally* represent them in models and theories. The knowledge of social structures had to be codified not only conceptually, but also mathematically, according to Freeman.

Social network analysis, whose roots were in the invention of *sociometry* and *sociograms* in the 1930s by Moreno (Freeman, 1992, p. 17; Wasserman and Faust, 1994, p. 11), suited to the needs of sociologists who were looking for a methodology to represent and analyze patterned social relationships. Sociometry is the methodology of measuring interpersonal relations, and sociograms are the geometric models of those relations, or "visual displays of group structure" (Wasserman and Faust, p. 12). Freeman (1992) cites Levi-Strauss' "algebraic study of kinships" in the 1940s and Hägerstrand's computer simulation of "spatial ordering of adoption innovations" in the 1950s as improvements on Moreno's works and major steps toward the full development of the SNA methods. Wasserman and Faust cite the early applications of mathematical matrices to represent social network data in the 1950s and the later applications of statistical analyses, like multidimensional scaling, in analyzing such data in the 1970s as major steps in the evolution of SNA (p. 12). They note that the developments in graph theory, statistical probability theory, and algebraic models became the mathematical foundations of the SNA methodology.

As this brief historical note indicates, structural relations are analyzed with mathematical models in SNA. Social network analyses is heavily quantitative, but it differs from other quantitative methodologies like regression analysis and system dynamics modeling and simulations in two ways: (a) SNA researchers aim to find the connections between micro and macro levels, whereas regression analysis and system dynamics modeling and simulations stay at the macro level, and (b) at the micro level, the "units of observation" SNA uses are the *relations* between dyads or triads of actors, not the *attributes* of actors, such as age, gender, and political preference.[1] Wasserman and Faust (1994, p. 4) note that SNA is unique among all methodologies because it views actors as *interdependent* units and therefore takes their relations as units of observation. Note that this is a methodological expression of a systems theoretical assumption that elements of a system (e.g., actors) are interdependent. This interdependence assumption contrasts with the basic assumptions of most statistical analyses: that individual attributes are independent of each other. For example, the attributes of an individual (e.g., age) is not dependent on his/her relations with other individuals.[2] Actor attributes like age, gender, and race may be included in social network analyses but only in addition to the main analyses that use "relational ties" among actors as their observational and analytical units (p. 38).

SNA is concerned about relational ties of multiple types, such as friendship, business transactions, attending common social events, sending messages to each other, power/authority relations (Wasserman and Faust, p. 18). These relational ties are observed and quantified using a wide range of data collection methods: surveys, interviews, observations, using archival data, and others (pp. 45–54). Once the data are collected, they are analyzed mathematically to identify subgroups in a social network of individuals (clusters, cliques) and establish the structural properties of the social network and its subgroups. Structural properties of networks are characterized using measures like network *density* (to what extent the network is cohesive), network *centralization* (to what extent there are central actors in a network), and *clustering coefficient* (to what extent the actors in a network are clustered, as opposed to their relations being dispersed among network actors).

SNA researchers also use micro-level techniques to quantify the relationships of individual actors. For example, the *centrality* of an actor in a network can be identified quantitatively and compared to those of other actors. In SNA relational ties among actors can also be displayed visually in graphs. These graphs are interpreted to characterize the composition of a network and the relative positions (e.g., centrality) of particular actors. These graphs are useful visual tools that can help researchers interpret the overall structure of a social network, its composition, and the subgroupings in it. For the descriptions of and extensive discussions on quantitative and visual methods used in SNA, I refer the reader to Wasserman and Faust (1994) and Knoke and Yang (2008).

SNA offers a set of very valuable conceptual and observational/measurement tools. There are also problematic areas in SNA and areas in which conceptual clarification and improvements are needed. I discuss these tools and problematic issues in the following subsections.

Centralization and Power Relations

As I mentioned earlier, in SNA there are measures of how central a role a particular actor plays in a network (actor *centrality*) and how centralized the network is (network *centralization*). There are multiple centrality and centralization measures: degree centrality and centralization, closeness centrality and centralization, and betweenness centrality and centralization.[3] Researchers have used these methods in policy/governance network studies, but there is no clear agreement on what they mean in characterizing these networks. For instance, Provan and Kenis (2007) describe two kinds of governance networks, "highly brokered networks," which are networks with high centralization and "shared governance networks," which have low centralization. DeLeon and Varda (2009) point out low centralization as a "structural signature" of "collaborative networks" (pp. 67–68), which are similar to Provan and Kenis' shared governance networks. Neither study specifies what kind of a centralization measure—degree, betweenness, or closeness—should be used in identifying these types of networks, however. Provan, Fish, and Sydow (2007) address the issue of centralization and what it means for "interorganizational networks," but they do not offer a comprehensive conceptualization or typology of centralization in networks either.

The network centrality and centralization measures have implications for power relations in social networks. More central actors in networks are conceivably actors with more power, for example, but what power means in the context of network relations should be defined carefully. Does it mean that a "powerful actor" has formal power over other actors, as in the case of a hierarchical organization, where a "superior" is formally authorized to order other actors do things? Alternatively, does it mean that the actor has some "social capital," "political capital," "charisma," or "charm"? Or, maybe, he/she has the "trust of other actors," which enables him/her to influence others' behaviors. Which specific centralization measures should be used to investigate what kinds of power relations? These questions have not been fully addressed in the literature, but there are a few authors who did address some of them. Mika (2007), for example, points out that *degree centrality* should be as a measure of "social capital" in the sense that "an actor with a large number of links has wider and more efficient access to the network, less reliant on single partners and because of his many ties often participates in deals as a third-party broker" (p. 43). For SNA to be a more effective method in studying policy and governance networks, its core measures, like centralization, and their relations to the central concerns of social scientists, like power relations, should be established better.

Network Stability and Change

An important question for policy/governance network researchers is whether and to what extent a network's structure is stable. As I mentioned earlier, sociologists have known for quite some time that not all structures are equally stable or stable for equal periods of time. Complexity theorists know that complex systems are somewhat stable, but they also change. As I mentioned in Chapter 5, the models of system dynamics complexity theorists suggest that stable stability and change are actually not mutually exclusive in complex systems.

Network researchers also recognize that networks are both stable and dynamic. Policy and management network researchers all observe that relative stability is a primary characteristic of networks (Kickert, Klijn, and Koppenjan, 1997b, pp. 1–3, 6–7; O'Toole, 1997a, p. 45; Rhodes, 1997a, pp. 1–25; Agranoff, 2007, passim). De Bruijn and ten Heuvelhof (1997), O'Toole and Meier (1999), Marsh and Smith (2000), and Provan and Kenis (2007) recognize that policy/governance networks change over time. Provan, Fish, and Sydow (2007) recognize that network structures are both stable and flexible. They also note that determining *to what extent a network is stable* is important, because this has implications for the viability and effectiveness of policy/governance networks: Unstable networks cannot be effective in policymaking or governing.

Then the question is how can network stability and change be defined and measured in SNA? The structural measures like network density and centralization can be used and traced over time to determine the structural stability of a network. If these measures are stable over time, the network structure can be considered stable. The changes in these structural measures can be used to detect the evolutionary patterns in a network. Although SNA measures can be used to trace network evolution, SNA is essentially a static methodological approach. Its methods are geared toward studying stable structures, rather than changes in structures. This differs from agent-based simulations, which are specifically designed to study change in systemic relations (see the next section).

SNA researchers are aware of its essentially static nature, but some of them used it to study network evolution (e.g., Human and Provan, 2000; Provan, Huang, and Milward, 2009; Zaheer and Soda, 2009). These studies illustrate both the potentials and limitations of SNA in studying network evolution. Human and Provan studied the networks of wood-product manufacturing firms in the US in two distinct time periods. They used interviews, surveys, archival data, and observations to identify network relations. Provan, Huang, and Milward studied a network of community-based health and human service agencies in Arizona in two discrete time periods. They used surveys to collect their data. On the one hand, these studies highlight the usefulness of using SNA in studying network evolution. Both studies yielded useful information about how their respective networks changed between the time periods they studied. The researchers used this information to make inferences about the evolutions of these networks from their findings. On the other hand, the studies underscore the limitations of SNA in studying network evolution. In each of these studies, only two time periods were compared, partly because of the data collection methods the researchers used. Surveys and interviews, which are the most popular methods of social network researchers, have limitations in collecting longitudinal network data. That is because individuals' recollections of the relations that occurred in the past are usually sketchy and quite often inaccurate, as Freeman, Romney, and Freeman (2008, p. 41), and Knoke and Yang (2008, p. 35) point out.

An alternative data collection method for social network analyses is to use archival information to identify and track network relations that occurred in the past. This method has an advantage over surveys and interviews: The researcher does not rely on individuals' recollections. This is the methods Zaheer and Soda (2009) and my colleagues and I employed in our studies. Zaheer and Soda studied the evolution of the networks of TV production teams in Italy between 1988 and 1999 using the information they collected from the archives of the TV industry. In our study of the governance network of a downtown urban district, we used the newspaper articles on the governance network for a period of 20 years. Both Zaheer and Soda and my colleagues and I identified the network relations in each of the years we studied, and thus we could develop more detailed pictures of the evolutions of the networks. The downside of using archival methods in studying network evolution is that the researcher has to rely on what is available in the archives.

Emergent Structural Properties

Because it is used to analyze both the micro and macro levels of social networks, social network analyses can be useful in gaining insights into understanding *emergent structural properties* of networks. They can be used to identify emergent structural properties in a particular way. The reader will remember Holland's definition of emergence from the discussions in Chapter 3. He defines emergence as *persistence in the patterns of the structural properties of a network, a system,* particularly *when its constituents change* (1998, p. 7).

In the study my colleagues and I conducted on the governance network in a downtown area, we found that two structural properties of the governance network—centralization and density—were stable over the two decades we studied, although the compositions of the central actors in the network changed in this period. We interpreted this is as an indication that the network had emergent structural properties, applying Holland's (1998) definition of emergence: persistence in the patterns of the structural properties of a network, when its constituents change.

The two charts in Figure 10.1 illustrate the changes in central actors over time. These two charts are truncated images of the governance network in the downtown area in two years. I generated the images from the textual data my colleagues and I collected from the newspaper articles. I selected the years 1990 and 1999 to generate the network images in Figure 10.1, because our analyses showed that there were similarities in some of the structural characteristics of the networks in these years: The degree centralization scores were identical in 1990 and 1999, and the density scores were close. I simplified the charts by removing several actors from each year's network to make them less cluttered and more interpretable.[4] I also labeled only the five most central actors in each year not to clutter the images.[5]

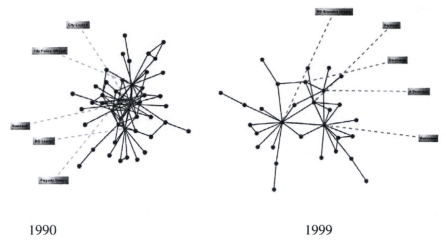

1990   1999

Figure 10.1   Network images of business improvement district in 1990 and 1999.

There was a consistently high degree of centralization in the network over the two decades.[6] This indicates that the network was quite stable for that period. We also found that the composition of actors changed quite significantly over the years we studied. The charts in Figure 10.1 are illustrative of the changes in the composition of the governance network. The top five most central actors in 1990 were the city council, property owners, the leader of the business improvement district management organization, residents, and city police officers. In 1999, the most important actors were the executive director of the business improvement district management management organization, developers, businesses, and residents. The 1999 chart also shows that neither the city council nor or any other representative of the city government, which were central actors in 1990, were a central actor in this year; instead businesses, their representatives, and the business improvement district management executive director became the most central actors.

Boundaries of Networks

In Chapter 2, I asked the question: Who defines a system's boundaries, its participants/actors or external observers? Then I cited Gerritts, Marks, and van Buuren's (2009) view that boundary definition is a social construction process and both actors and observers contribute to the definition of the boundaries. The next logical question was this: Is it at all possible for the observers of policy systems—policymakers, policy analysts, and social scientists—to define a system's boundaries *objectively*. Also, to what extent are these observers at the same time policy actors who contribute to the definition of a system they study? I followed up on the issue of defining the boundaries of a system in Chapter 6 and asked a set of broader epistemological questions: Is the knowledge of a system subject to episte-mological constrictions? Is the knowledge of a system (at least partly) in the eye of a beholder? Does, or to what extent, the knowledge of actors in a social system constitute the system itself?

All these questions are in the background of the discussions of bound-ary definitions in the social network analysis literature. Wasserman and Faust (1994) and Knoke and Yang (2008) discuss extensively the boundary specification problems and different approaches to it. In the SNA litera-ture the original conceptualization of boundary specification was offered by Laumann, Mardsen, and Prensky (1992).[7] Laumann and his colleagues define two approaches to boundary definition: the "realist" approach ("the investigator adopts the presumed vantage point of the actors themselves in defining the boundaries of social entities," p. 65) and the "nominalist" approach ("an analyst self-consciously imposes a conceptual framework constructed to serve his or her own analytic purposes," p. 66). In the real-ist approach "the network is treated as a social fact only in that it is con-sciously experienced as such by the actors composing it" (p. 65). Laumann and his colleagues (1992) cite Braithwaite, who calls this a "phenomeno-logical conception of facts" (p. 65). Researchers use a variety of data col-lection methods if they adopt this approach: surveys with specially worded questionnaires, snowball sampling (asking each actor who is in the network and asking the actors he/she identified the same question), etc.[8]

In the nominalist approach, although the researcher has the "upper hand" in defining the network's boundaries, his/her definition is not regarded as an expression of objective reality, according to Laumann and his colleagues (1992). In their own words, "Delineation of network boundaries is analytically relative to the purposes of the investigator, and thus network closure has no ontologically independent status. . . . [T]he perception of reality is assumed to be mediated by the conceptual apparatus of the analyst, be he or she an active participant in the social scene under study or an outside observer" (p. 66).

Laumann and his colleagues do not tell us which approach is ontologi-cally and epistemologically more sound. They leave that to the researcher to decide. Instead, they offer a framework for understanding the differ-ent "strategies" a researcher can use within each approach.[9] They define eight different strategies—four realist and four nominalist—based on their "definitional foci for delimitation" (p. 70). Both actors and researchers can define a network on the basis of the "attributes" of actors, their "relations," or "participations in events or activities." They can also use definitional strategies that use combinations of these foci.

In the study my colleagues and conducted on the governance network in a downtown that I described earlier, we took a nominalist approach in defining the boundaries of the network. We specified the network's bound-aries in two steps. First, we collected all the newspaper articles that per-tinent to our topic using an electronic database (NewsBank). Second, we selected a group of actors whom we thought were relevant to our research purposes. Therefore, initially newspaper reporters and editors specified the boundaries of our networks by selecting certain events and actors at the time of their reporting, based on their notions of what was important and relevant. Then we made our selections, based on our research purposes. Thus, ours was a two-step strategy: Both the perceptions/constructions of journalists and newspaper editors and our own perceptions/constructions played roles in the process of defining the governance network.

This strategy obviously did not yield a "complete and unbiased picture" of the network under study, but as Laumann and his colleagues' conceptualization and discussion show, there is no such thing as a complete and unbiased picture of a social network anyway. Their conceptualization of the approaches to and strategies of boundary definition highlight the fact that the boundaries of social networks are defined in social and/or individual construction processes, one way or the other, by the participants or observers. This does not make the studies of networks "objective" in the Newtonian/positivist sense, but by recognizing these construction processes, the researcher can make his/her study more rigorous and can understand its limitations.

Systemness

Social systems do not have definite and permanent boundaries. Actors go in and out of relationships and they are in multiple relationships at a given time. Thus an actor usually is an actor in multiple social systems: in his/her family, the organization he/she works for, community organization in which he/she is a member, and the interest group and/or policy network he/she is a member of. It is better to define a social system in degrees of systemness, as I argued in Chapter 2.

In that chapter, I adopted Giddens' (1984, p. 28) two concepts, *social integration* and *system integration* and said that these concepts operationalize the concept of systemness and enable researchers to discern the degree of reproduction of actors' activities in a given situation and thus help them define a system, a network. I argued in Chapter 2 that system integration is more important and meaningful in defining public policy systems: The face-to-face co-presence required in the definition of social integration is not typical or common for policy systems; the space-independent character system integration is more typical for policy systems/networks. Then I pointed out that to the extent that the activities of individual and collective actors are integrated (reciprocated and reproduced) across time and space, they constitute a policy system/network

Earlier in this chapter I pointed out that the SNA measures density, centrality, and clustering coefficient enable researchers to observe the degree of systemness in a given situation. Although these SNA measures are not direct operationalizations of Giddens' concepts, they are quite suitable for being used as such. These measures can be used to measure not only direct, face-to-face relations (measures of social integration) but also indirect relations in networks (potential measures of system integration). One should be careful in applying them, however. Social network analyses is essentially a static methodological approach. Therefore its density, centralization, and clustering coefficient measures do not measure whether the relations among actors are sustained over time or not. They are only snapshot measures of relations at a given time. But if these measures are taken from longitudinal network data, and if stable network structural properties are observed in those longitudinal data, then they can be useful in determining the degree and form of systemness in a given social situation.

Following Giddens' logic, the degree of systemness can be defined in terms of the degree of network density: The higher the density, the higher the systemness. This is because density is the measure of "group cohesion" or the degree of connectedness among the actors in a network (Wasserman and Faust, 1994, p. 181; Knoke and Yang, 2008, pp. 53–56). However, Wasserman and Faust note that density by itself is not always a good measure to characterize the network, and they recommend factoring in network size (number of connections among the actors in a network) and using measures of centralizations in conjunction with density (p. 182).

Following Wasserman and Fasut's advice, in the study my colleagues and I conducted on the governance network in a downtown area, we conducted both density and centralization calculations. As I mentioned earlier, we found that between 1990 and 2009 the density and centralization scores of the governance network remained stable: The density scores were low, and centralization scores were high. This can be interpreted that the network was not cohesive (it had low density), but it maintained its highly centralized structure. This was despite the fact that many actors that took parts in the network changed over time and the ones that remained in it moved from being more central to less central and vice versa. What we found in this study illustrates a low degree of cohesion, which can be interpreted as low degree of systemness, but the consistently centralized structure of the network over the years suggests that systemic relations can exist and persist over time, despite low cohesion in a network. This finding suggests that we can conceptualize different forms of systemness, as well as different degrees of systemness. The low density and high centralization we found may be characterized as a form of systemness among other forms (e.g., the high-density–high-centralization and high-density–low-centralization forms). More conceptual clarification and empirical research are needed on the degrees and forms of systemness and the applicability of SNA measures in measuring them.

Social (Downward) Causation

Not only sustained interdependency relations among actors, but also their reproduced *actions* constitute *social systems*, and these systems exhibit *structural properties*, as I discussed in Chapter 3. Structures are "recursively organized sets of rules and resources" (Giddens, 1984, p. 25), and they exist in the "instantiations in such practices and memory traces orienting the knowledge of human agents" (p. 17). Social systems are created and reproduced through social practices, but this is not a one-way relationship; it is a structuration process in which emergent structural properties of systems in turn enable or constrict the future behaviors of actors. How these structures enable and constrict the behaviors of actors is the problem of social (downward) causation, or social influence.

Does SNA offer any methods that can be used to study the entire structuration process or social causation? Because of its static nature, SNA is not very suitable for studying the entire structuration process. Agent-based simulations are better for that purpose. But it does offer some methodological solutions to the problem of social influence. Social influence is defined as unintentional, spontaneous contagion of an idea or behavioral pattern (Marsden and Friedkin, 1993, 1994). [10] Marsden and Friedkin identify two approaches to identifying social influence in SNA: Some do that in terms of the similarities between actors; others in terms of the connectivity among them.

Doreian (1992) cites the theoretical bases a particular model of social influence, the "network effects" model, which is commonly used in SNA, and explains its mathematical basis. In Doreian's model, the network effect is an addition to the causal linear model ($Y = bX$). The network effect can be expressed as the additional term (pWY) in the following equation:

$$Y = bX + pWY$$

In this equation Y is the influenced behavior of a particular actor (e.g., voting for a particular candidate or party). X represents an external influence (e.g., state of the economy, a war situation, etc.). WY represents the combined influence of other actors in the network (e.g., influence of the political preferences of the family, friends, and/or other acquaintances of the actor under study). [11] The coefficient p represents the intensity of that influence on the actor under study. For the details of how this equation is derived and how multiple network effects can be included in network effect models, I refer the reader to Doreian's chapter.

Limited Number of Abstract Relations

SNA offers a wide range of conceptual and analytical tools that can be useful in studying the structural properties of networks and the positions and compositions of actors. Like other quantitative/analytical methodologies, SNA has an important limitation as well: The researcher has to use abstractions and simplifications in his/her models. This is evident in the limits on the number of relations that can be included in social network analyses.

It is obvious that human actors engage in relations with others in multiple forms: kinship relations, friendship relations, official business relations, etc. In most of these relations, if not all, there is some form of interdependency among actors. In the policy networks literature it is often observed that interdependence is a key aspect of the relations among policy actors and that there are multiple forms of interdependence. Klijn (1997) notes that the interdependencies between policy actors may take on the forms of pooled, sequential, and mutual interdependencies (p. 31). These and other forms of interdependencies and relations can be modeled in SNA.[12] But, as Wasserman and Faust (1994) note, a social network analysis model can handle only one or few kinds of relations at a time. In "one-mode networks" the researcher can model only one type of relations among the actors, for example, friendship, transaction, or formal role (pp. 36–38). In "affiliation networks," affiliations of actors, events they are involved in, and their attributes can be modeled (pp. 40–41), which obviously expands analytical capabilities, but still does not capture the multidimensionality of human relations or their contexts.

The capabilities of SNA have been further expanded by some recent advances. The "dynamic meta-network assessment and analysis" software developed at Carnegie Melon University by Kathleen Carley, called "ORA," utilizes multiple matrices to analyze relations between individual, organizational, and collective actors, together with their locations, resources, and knowledge bases.[13] ORA also has the capability of analyzing network data longitudinally and simulating network relations over time. But as Carley, Diesner, Reminga, and Tsvetovat (2007) note, its capabilities have not been fully developed yet.

Even the most advanced software like ORA cannot model the subtleties in relations and their infinite complexity. Even the most advanced and sophisticated models use abstractions and simplify. The complexity of the "lived worlds" of the human actors cannot be modeled in quantitative/analytical approaches. To capture that, researchers will need qualitative methods, which I will discuss later in this chapter. There are also methods of studying the cognitive processes of individuals that combine quantitative and qualitative tools. I will discuss them in the next chapter.

AGENT-BASED SIMULATIONS

Researchers simulate the evolutions of relations among individual agents and the systemic patterns that emerge from them with *agent-based simulations* (ABS). Agent-based simulations are also known as *multi-agent simulations* and *individual-based models*. In these simulations initially agents are assigned certain values that represent their preferences, attributes, and sometimes geographical positions. Then the evolutions of their behavioral patterns are simulated. These patterns and their evolutions are observed, plotted, analyzed, and interpreted in ABS.

Epstein and Axtell (1996, pp. 2–3) trace the history of ABS back to John von Neumann's works on self-producing automata in the 1960s. His works were followed by the studies in cybernetics and connectionist cognitive science, distributed artificial intelligence, cellular automata, genetic algorithms, genetic programming, artificial life, and individual-based modeling in biology. Thomas Schelling's (1971) simulation of neighborhood segregation patterns are considered one of the earliest social science applications of ABS.[14] Robert Axelrod's (1997, 2006) simulations of cooperation in political communities and John Holland's (1995, 1998) conceptual and methodological works on ABS were the most significant advances in ABS in the 1980s and 1990s. Epstein and Axtell's (1996) own work is another important milestone in the evolution of ABS applications in the social sciences. In their simulation of the artificial society they called "Sugarscape," Epstein and Axtell's simple behavioral rules for agents can generate complex social patterns, social structures emerge through a self-organizing process of individual interactions, and these structures are sustained beyond the life span of the agents that generated them.

Agents or Actors

Before I proceed with a discussion of the concepts and principles of ABS, I want to touch upon a terminological issue briefly here. Is there a meaningful difference between the two terms used, respectively, in SNA and ABS: "actors" and "agents"? Gerrits, Marks, and van Buuren (2009) make a distinction between agents and actors and argue that the latter term should be preferred in complexity theory over the former, because

> Actors are *active* entities: they exhibit *adaptive* behavior and are able to adapt themselves to changing environments. Agents are *passive*; they exhibit *adoptive* behavior, because they process information but do not seek to fit within the system. [emphasis added] (p. 137)

Gerrits and his colleagues' reminder of the issue of passive versus active nature of agents and actors is important; to what extent actors agents are active or passive in constructing systemic relations should be of concern to complexity researchers. However, I do not think the distinction they make between the two terms is sustainable. The dictionary definitions of the two terms do not suggest that a meaningful distinction can be made between them on the basis of whether they are active or passive.

An *actor* may be someone who "represents a character"—a relatively passive stance—but also he/she may be "someone who acts" or someone who "takes part in any affair" (*Merriam Webster* online dictionary: http://www.merriam-webster.com/dictionary/actor; accessed on November 21, 2010). An *agent* is someone who is "authorized to act for" someone else—again a passive stance—but also someone who "acts or exerts power"—an active stance (*Merriam Webster* online dictionary: http://www.merriam-webster.com/dictionary/agent; accessed on November 21, 2010). To what extent an actor or an agent is passive or active in a given situation can be defined in the context of his/relations in a network. So, I do not think the categorical distinction Gerrits and his colleagues make is warranted. I think the two terms can be used interchangeably, without losing any meaning.

An Overview of Simulations Methods

ABS evolved and took on various forms over time. I will briefly summarize the characteristics of three types of agent-based simulations: cellular automata, neural networks, and genetic algorithms. These three illustrate the evolution of ABS from its simplest form, with most restrictive assumptions, to its most complex form, with least restrictive assumptions.

Cellular automata models are the most restrictive of all ABS models. In cellular automata simulations, each agent is placed in a particular position (a "cell") on a computer-generated lattice. Other agents are placed in the neighboring cells. Then the interactions among these agents are observed. This two-dimensional nature of the lattice is a constriction: Agents can have relations only with their neighbors. Another constriction is that all the agents operate under a small number of uniform behavioral rules, such as the rules of what to eat and how to procreate. These rules are deterministic in principle, but researchers may include probabilistic relations in their simulations as well. Once the initial, deterministic rules about the behaviors of agents and their environments are set, they are let to evolve. In cellular automata simulations collective forms emerge self-organizationally, as outcomes of the "local rules" individual actors and the evolution of their behaviors.[15] I will illustrate cellular automata simulations with an example later in this chapter.

Passerini and Bahr (1997) used cellular automata simulations "to examine the magnitude and frequency of the disaster necessary to influence a group with an established social structure and voting pattern" (p. 217). They simulated a community whose members were split between two positions: those who wanted to move the town to a less hazardous location and those who did not. They simulated the changes in the townspeople's opinions after major floods stroke the town successively. Passerini and Bahr tested different scenarios under the assumption of different magnitudes and frequencies of floods. They concluded that collective behaviors of the townspeople in their models were similar to the ones experts had observed empirically in similar disaster situations. They made the generalization that after each disaster, disaster preparation and mitigation levels increase rapidly and then they fade quickly. This pattern is repeated in a cyclical manner.

Neural network simulations are based on the connectionists theory and related models in cognitive science.[16] Some of the basic aspects of cellular automata simulations, such as that agents are placed in certain positions in a lattice and that they operate under deterministic behavioral rules for the most part, apply to neural network simulations as well. But unlike in cellular automata simulations, agents can have relations with others that are not their immediate neighbors. This is analogous to the workings of neurons in the brain: They can be connected to other neurons that are not their immediate neighbors. Also, each connection can be assigned a weight. Consequently, some cells may be more influential—they carry more weight—than others.[17] Duong and Reilly's (1995) neural networks simulation illustrates how the associative memories in the minds of individuals self-organize into dissipative structures, such as status symbols and racial, cultural, and economic class identities.

Genetic algorithms are the least restrictive form of agent-based simulations. Agents can have multiple rules, and each rule is assigned a "fitness" value. These values signify the degrees of fitness of the rules to their environmental conditions. In genetic algorithm simulations, rules compete with each other, and the winning rules guide the system's evolution. Genetic algorithms are used to find solutions to solutions to problems involving highly complex nonlinear dynamics (Anderson, 1999, pp. 226–227).

Emergence

One can observe the emergence of holistic structural properties in agent-based simulations. Agent-based simulation researchers have shown time and again that "local rules"—rules about agents' characteristics and their relations—can generate enduring collective forms and patterns through self-organizational processes (Casti, 1994, pp. 214–219). In this section I will summarize the advances ABS researchers made in modeling the emergence of social cooperation, macro (collective) agents, and cultural forms. I will also address the issues of structuration and downward causation.

Emergence of Cooperation

Political scientist Robert Axelrod developed the models and principles of simulating the emergence of cooperation, as well as those of the emergence of meta-agents and culture. His earliest contribution was in the area of simulating cooperation (Axelrod, 2006). In this early work, Axelrod aimed to answer the question: "Under what conditions will cooperation emerge in a world of egoists without central authority" (p. 3). In his simulations, Axelrod applied the principles of the "Prisoner's Dilemma" game under a variety of assumptions.[18] He concludes from the outcomes of his simulations that cooperation can emerge even from the interactions among egoists, who are not fully or comprehensively "rational." There are conditions for cooperation to emerge: Individuals must be able to recognize each other so that they can reciprocate in their relations, and they must have a good enough chance to meet each other in the future so that "defecting" (cheating) in their present encounter will not be profitable. Axelrod calls this latter condition the "shadow of the future."

Later, Axelrod and his colleagues developed more specific concepts and principles of cooperation. Riolo, Cohen, and Axelrod (2001) report that their simulations show that cooperation arise more easily between individuals who are "sufficiently similar" to each other and that individuals recognize similarity in each other based on observable traits. Cohen, Riolo, and Axelrod (2001) aimed to answer the question: How do "cooperative regimes" (stable patterns of cooperation) emerge and then influence the behaviors of individuals? Using Giddens' structuration theory, they define cooperative regimes as patterning of interactions or continuity of interactions. They show in their simulations that the "shadow of the future" (Axelrod) contributes to explaining how cooperation emerges, and the structural property of "context preservation" (continuity in the interaction of patterns among individual actors) helps explain how it is maintained.

Emergence of Meta-Agents

It is a fairly common assumption in political science, policy studies, and sociology that groups of individuals may act as collective actors/agents in way that is recognizable by the members of these groups and others outside the groups. A "government" may "choose" to act to solve an environmental pollution problem, for example. Whether governments and other collectives are truly collective entities, or perhaps deceptive fictions, is an unresolved issue, and it is relevant to ABS. The question is this: Is there sufficient commonality among the attributes and/or behaviors of a group of individuals so that we can call them a collective agent/actor?

Holland (1995) calls these collective agents "meta-agents." In his view, they emerge from "complex large-scale behaviors from the aggregate interactions of less complex agents" (p. 11). These meta-agents can also form "meta-meta-agents" (pp. 11–12). Holland gives the example of a human body, which is composed of atoms, molecules, and cells. Each molecule constitutes an entity (agent) in itself. It also becomes a part of an entity at the higher level: a cell. These meta-agents maintain their "identities"—they constitute wholes—but they also function as parts of meta-meta-agents. This multi-layered emergence is a major characteristic of complex adaptive systems, according to Holland.

Are there analogs of atoms, molecules, cells, and human bodies in the social world? And can ABS be used to identify them and/or illustrate their emergence? Axelrod (1997, pp. 124–144) describes a simulation in which collective political actors emerge endogenously from the interactions of local rules governing individual actors. Axelrod develops three criteria to identify the emergent properties in these collective actors.

1. They should have effective control over their subordinates. For example, a "federal government" exercises a unified "foreign policy" and does not allow its subordinates, "states," to develop their own policies.

2. There must be collective action. For example, once a foreign policy is set, all "states" should act in unison.
3. They should be recognized by others as actors. In other words, other collective and individual actors act in ways that indicate that they recognize this collective actor as a singular entity. (pp. 126–127)

Emergence of Culture

Both Epstein and Axtell (1996, pp. 71–82) and Axelrod (1997, pp. 148–177) demonstrate with simulations that cultural norms can emerge self-organizationally, through interactions among adaptive agents. Epstein and Axtell wanted to find out how certain values were "transmitted" among agents so that they would form groups with cohesive (similar) values. In their simulations, agents interacted over time and formed distinguishable clusters that could be identified as cultural groups and those groups remained relatively stable. Axelrod similarly defines culture as "dissemination" of values among individual agents. He asks the question: How come through this dissemination process all differences among agents do not disappear and different groups are maintained? He then defines culture not only in terms of similarities among agents, but also differences among them. Axelrod reaches the conclusion from his simulations that the number of features agents share among themselves will determine the emergence of a cultural group: If a group of agents share multiple features—one of them being geographic proximity—the chances of them to form a cultural group increases. Also, to the extent that this group of agents are dissimilar to other groups in multiple features, their chances of forming a cultural group increases.

Bednar and Page (2007) took a different approach when they simulated culture. They applied game theory principles in their ABS to demonstrate that, despite the beliefs to the contrary in the literature, game theory was a good framework to understand cultural behavior. They define culture as "individual and community level patterns that are context dependent and often suboptimal" (p. 65). Game theory assumes "isolated, context-free, strategic environments and optimal behavior within them," and as such it seems to be at odds with contextual and suboptimal cultural behavior. But when one considers that agents play not one, but multiple games in different venues, at a time in their lives, they may find cultural (context-dependent and suboptimal) behavior unavoidable. That is because making multiple optimal decisions simultaneously is costly.

Social (Downward) Causation

In Chapter 3 I noted that downward causation, or social causation, was a useful concept, but partly because of the lack of clarity in its definitions and partly because of the methodological challenges it poses, there are not many applications of it in the complexity theory literature. The primary challenge is to build models that would include representations of social structures, or social norms, in individuals. This can be done, according to Epstein (2006), through "feedback between macrostructures and micro-structures, as where newborn agents are conditioned by social norms or institutions that have taken shape endogenously through earlier agent inter-actions" (pp. 51–52).

Cohen, Riolo, and Axelrod's (2001) simulation of the emergence of cooperative regimes is an example of the potential and challenges of imple-menting the macro–micro feedbacks in simulations. As I mentioned earlier, they demonstrate how micro-level actions of actors can build and maintain cooperative regimes, which in turn stabilize micro actions and condition them. Cohen and his colleagues designed some of the structural constraints a priori. They entered and manipulated some social structures (initial con-ditions of interactions among actors, such as their locations and the rules of patterns of interactions) into their simulations themselves. This approach limits the fidelity of simulations to real-life social causation. On might argue, however, that in any simulation some initial conditions must be set and that inevitably will limit its fidelity to real-life processes.

An Illustration of ABS

Before discussing further the concepts of and issues in ABS, I want to illus-trate how agent-based simulations work. The following is a summary of Bin and Zhang's (2006) cellular automata simulations of how patterns of loyalty emerge in organizations. I present an example of cellular automata simulations, because, as I mentioned earlier, cellular automata models are the most restrictive, thus the simplest, ABS models. They are the easiest to illustrate on a few pages, without getting distracted by many technical details. The reader can find good explanations and elaborate examples of neural networks, genetic algorithms, and other advanced forms of ABS in the sources I cite in this chapter.

Bin and Zhang used the methods of *integrated qualitative simulation* and *cellular automata modeling*. They call their approach "cellular autom-ata based qualitative simulation."

Bin and Zhang make a series of simplifying assumptions, abstractions, which is typical of ABS models. They use particularly Blau's (1964) social exchange theory as the basis of their assumptions: that individuals are motivated by the exchange values of transactions with other individuals. Bin and Zhang's main hypothesis is that the loyalty of an individual to his/her organization is the product of his/her own characteristics and mana-gerial policies. They define two types of individuals for their simulations: "economic agents," who are motivated by material and monetary gains and "social agents," who are motivated by social status and respect of their colleagues. The members are also grouped into two: formal and informal members. Formal members are the core members of the organization; they

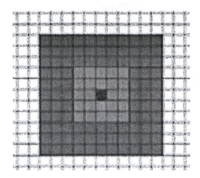

Figure 10.2   Degrees of loyalty in the lattice.

tend to adhere to group norms more and contribute to the evolution of the organization more directly. Informal members are peripheral; they may violate group norms and may have negative effects in the evolution of their organization. In Bin and Zhang's simulations, the managements of organizations use economic and social incentives.

The loyalty levels of individuals are represented as positions in lattices (see Figure 10.2 below). In the figure the cell in the center represent the highest degrees of loyalty; as one moves to the outer cells of the lattice the degree of loyalty decreases.

In the simulations, each actor is assigned to an initial cell in the lattice, as shown in Figure 10.3. In this figure the black circles represent the formal members of the organization, and the rings the informal members. In principle, formal members should be placed closer to the center and informal members farther from it, but the specific position of each formal and informal member is determined randomly.

Bin and Zhang conducted four series of simulations to find out "Which managerial policy would most effectively motivate group members to

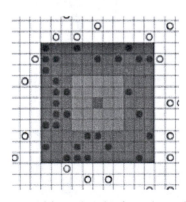

Figure 10.3   Initial positions of formal and informal members in the lattice.

behave more loyally?" For their simulations, they designed four managerial policy alternatives, based on different degrees of economic and social incentives the management provides

Alternative 1: absolute economic policy
Alternative 2: normal economic policy
Alternative 3: normal social policy
Alternative 4: absolute social policy

Under each alternative scenario, there are agents who are motived by economic and social incentives at varying degrees. The outcomes of the simulations under these four alternative policies are presented in Figure 10.4.

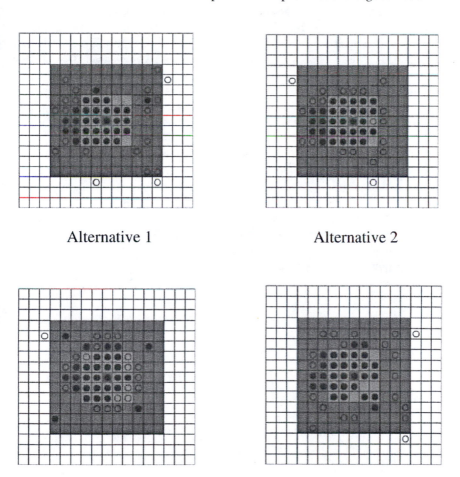

Alternative 1　　　　　　　　　　Alternative 2

Alternative 3　　　　　　　　　　Alternative 4

Figure 10.4　Outcomes of four alternative managerial policies.

Under all four alternative scenarios, agents moved to the center, but in different degrees and different specific configurations, as the figure illustrates. Bin and Zhang also made calculations to detect the emergent patterns in these simulations. Particularly, they measured the overall loyalty value of the organization, or what they call its "overall loyalty gravitation," under each managerial policy. In the measurement scale they used, if the loyalty gravitation is low, the loyalty value is high. (See the original paper for the way the researchers calculated these values.) Based on these overall gravitation scores, they found that Alternative 2 (normal economic policy) and Alternative 3 (normal social policy) were the most effective motivators. Then they compared these two alternatives. The evolutions of the overall loyalty gravitation scores of the two alternatives are shown in Figure 10.5. In the figure, the upper line represents Alternative 2, and the lower line represents Alternative 3.

The figure illustrates that the time stages required to reach equilibrium is shorter for Alternative 2 than for Alternative 3. Therefore, Bin and Zhang conclude, a normal economic managerial policy (Alternative 2) would be the most efficient scenario. However, if the goal of management is not efficiency, but to increase overall loyalty as much as possible, then Alternative 3 would be better, because the maximum loyalty value resulting from this alternative is the highest (the loyalty gravitation score is the lowest), as Figure 10.5 illustrates.

Bin and Zhang's simulations illustrate that agent-based simulations can be a powerful tools, even in their simplest form, cellular automata. They allow testing different scenarios under different assumptions. They are dynamic: One can see how the configurations of agents' positions change over time (in the above illustrations, I showed only the beginning and states of the simulations [Figures 10.3 and 10.4.]). They can also show how micro–macro transformations occur, and macro patterns emerge. Bin and Zhang's overall loyalty gravitations score is a measurement of the emergent patterns. Once can see also how this macro pattern evolves over time (Figure 10.5).

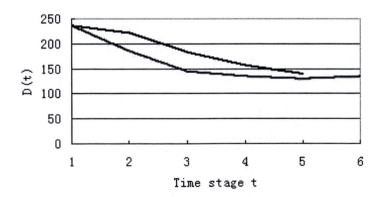

Figure 10.5   Overall loyalty gravitation scores of Alternatives 2 and 3.

Their simulations also illustrate a major limitation of agent-based simulations: They are based on abstract assumptions about agents' behaviors. Bin and Zhang adopted the abstractions of Blau's social exchange theory and elaborated on them by classifying the agents into formal and informal, and managerial policies into economic and social. These abstractions are based on social scientific findings, but they do not represent specific real human beings or specific managerial policies. Therefore, agent-based simulations are not empirically based.

I will address these strengths and limitations of agent-based simulations in more depth in the following section.

Issues in Agent-Based Simulations

Agent-Based Simulations and Social Network Analyses

Agent-base simulations take a different approach than social network analyses in three ways. First, unlike SNA, ABS is inherently dynamic. Earlier in this chapter I mentioned that social network analyses could be used in longitudinal studies. In such studies actually static snapshots of relations in networks are plotted and analyzed consecutively to gain a sense of how relations among actors and structural properties of a network change over time. Agent-based simulations is inherently dynamic in that actors' initial properties (beliefs, preferences, etc.) and their relations (geographic proximity, etc.) are entered into simulations and the development of these properties and relationships are tracked over time primarily at the macro and micro level (see the illustrations in the previous section). In these simulations dynamic images of the evolutions of systems may be "frozen" occasionally to take snapshots of the structural properties of the systems and the agents' positions.

Second, agent-based simulations are "artificial" in the sense that researchers use generalized assumptions about agents' preferences and behavioral tendencies as inputs in their simulations, not direct empirical observations on specific agents' preferences or behavioral tendencies, as I mentioned in the earlier section. "*Artificial* life simulations" is another name used for ABS for this reason.[19] SNA, on the other hand, takes an empirical approach: In SNA empirical relations among specific actors are investigated and entered into analyses. I will come back to the issue of the artificiality of ABS shortly.

The third area of difference between SNA and ABS is that the unit of observation and analysis shifts from the relations among actors in SNA to their attributes in ABS. The reader will remember from the previous section that in SNA in most cases the relations are the primary focus: Types and strengths of relational ties among actors are observed and analyzed to understand the structural properties networks, but actors' attributes may also be observed and entered into analyses additionally. In ABS, relations (like relative geographic locations) matter, but the primary inputs of simulations are agents' generalized attributes (preferences, behavioral tendencies, etc.). This third area of difference should not be overemphasized, however, because in many applications of SNA and ABS, both relations and attributes are used.

"Artificiality" of ABS

Agent-based simulations are "artificial," but this does not mean that the models ABS researchers use are devoid of any empirical basis. In ABS the issue of artificiality arises at both micro and macro levels. At the micro level the question is to what extent are the preferences and behaviors of agents reflective of real human beings? At the macro level the question is to what extent do the constructed model and the outputs it generates match real social mechanisms and processes?

Some ABS models are more empirically based and specific than others. In some simulations the assumptions about agents' preferences and behavioral tendencies and the rules governing their relations are more abstract, for example, the assumption that agents are "boundedly rational." In others, the attributes and relations of agents are modeled based on the scientific literature on human behaviors in behavioral, cognitive, and/or experimental psychology. In some simulations, the preferences and behavioral tendencies of agents are more modeled with the assumption that they are alike; in others, agents have more heterogeneous attributes.

Even when agents and their relations are modeled in more abstract terms and their behaviors are assumed to be more alike, agent-based simulations are still less abstract and more heterogeneous than the theoretical models of neoclassical economics. In neoclassical economics, all actors/agents are assumed to be uniformly "rational" economic agents whose common and sole motivation is to maximize their own utilities. The "boundedly rational" agents of ABS are more flexible than this characterization. As Miler and Page (2007) note, the attributes of agents in ABS are not uniform, nor are they independent of time or space. These agents are modeled with the assumptions that they are situated in space and time and they adapt their behaviors to their conditions and environments (pp. 78–89).

Still, the agents of ABS are not actual human beings. They are "agent-based objects": sets of attributes and rules of relationships that are coded using simulation software (Miller and Page, 2007, pp. 78–89). These agents do not represent particular real-life human beings. Agent-based simulation modelers use primarily four kinds of sources in constructing these objects: abstract assumptions about human behaviors, like "bounded rationality"; observations and generalizations about human behaviors made by anthropologists, sociologists, psychologists and other social scientists; social, psychological, and/or economic experiments they conduct with small groups of individuals; and surveys of key informants.

Usually the modelers use combinations of some of these sources, and some researchers make specific efforts to empirically ground their agent-based objects. In his simulation of a water incidence management organization, for example, Moss (1998) used two sources: information given by the emergency planning officer of the organization about the behaviors of intruders and the generalizations made by some cognitive scientists about human cognitive processes. In their simulations of the effects of geographic isolation and uneven communication technology on the functioning of virtual teams, Nan, Johnston, Olson, and Bos (2005) conducted a lab experiment to obtain behavioral patterns in such settings.

In some applications of ABS, either by necessity or by choice, modelers simulate generic situations based on some empirical, but generalized, information about human behaviors. The outputs of these applications can be used to gain insights into real-life situations, but the researchers do not aim to match the outputs of their simulations to correspond directly to those situations. Epstein (2006) and his colleagues' simulation of how civil violence emerges (pp. 247–270) and their simulation of epidemic dynamics (pp. 277–306) are examples of this kind of applications. So are Axelrod's simulations of emergence of cooperation and emergence of meta-agents, which I will discuss later in this chapter.

In other applications ABS researchers attempted to validate their models and/or the outputs of their simulations. Takadama, Kawai, and Koyama (2008) identified three forms of this "macro-level validation" in the literature: (a) *theoretical verification* (determining whether the model is an adequate conceptualization of the real world by asking situation experts), (b) *external validation* (determining whether the outputs of a simulation match the results from the real world), and (c) *cross-model validation* (determining "whether the results from one computational model map onto, and/or extend, the results of another model") (Introduction section, para.1).

An example of theoretical verification is Moss' (1998) simulation of a water incidence management organization, in which he verified aspects of his model with the emergency planning officer of the organization. Epstein and his colleagues' simulation of the evolution of the Kayenta Anasazi civilization is an example of external validation of simulation models (pp. 90–142). The Anasazi lived in northeastern Arizona between 1800 BC and AD 1300. In their study, Epstein and his colleagues simulated the "spatiotemporal history" of the Anasazi using actual and estimated data on the agricultural production and climactic conditions in the area. They found that the outcomes of their models matched the actual evolution of the Anasazi. After establishing the relevance of their simulations, Epstein and his colleagues derived conclusions about how important environmental conditions, such as hydrologic conditions, and the collective choices the Anasazi made, such as the choices they made in the levels and types of crop production, impacted the evolution of this civilization. An example cross-model validation is Axtell, Axelrod, Epstein, and Cohen's (1996) study. Axtell and his colleagues cross-validated the Axelrod's (1995) cultural transmission model with Epstein and Axtell's (1996) Sugarscape model.

Deductive Models vs. ABS

The problem of "artificiality" in ABS can be understood better in a broader epistemological and methodological context. That is why I turn to the issue of deductive versus "generative" approaches in inquiry now.

Part of the problem with the "macro-level validation" of models is that all sorts of models are simplifications, by definition. I discussed earlier the simplifying assumptions made by Bin and Zang in their cellular automata simulations. Even in more complex forms of ABS, researchers have to make simplifying assumptions and construct simplified models. Because it is not possible to describe all the details of complex systems, researchers use simplified models that capture their essential elements. If the models they use are robust with respect to modifications, then researchers can more confidently extrapolate their findings to real complex systems (Bak and Chen, 1991, p. 46).

Miller and Page (2007) point out that for a model to be successful, the world it describes has to be real and has to have enough structure to it. If there is enough structure, this will allow researchers to ignore some of the details of reality (p. 35). Then a certain degree of structural equivalence between the model and the world it describes (*homomorphism*) would be possible (p. 39). Miller and Page note: "the goal of theory is to make the world understandable by finding the right set of simplifications. Modeling proceeds by deciding what simplifications to impose on the underlying entities and then, based on those abstractions, uncovering its implications" (p. 65). In Cilliers' (1998) view, simulations must make a "generalized reference" to the world; they do not have to be in a direct one-to-one correspondence (p. 82); simulations should not attempt to represent essential aspects or units of something real, but to repeat the way reality works in general (p. 84).[20]

Like the causal models discussed in the previous chapter, ABS models simplify, but they do so less and for different purposes. In causal models only abstracted variables are used with the purpose of making abstracted generalizations. Agent-based simulation models, on the other hand, reflect the dynamic and contextual view of complexity theory, and their purpose is not to simplify. The ABS modeler aims to observe the complex and unique results generated for individual cases (Anderson, 1999).

Miller and Page (2007, p. 71) point out that ABS models are different from the deductive nomological of neoclassical economics in a very important sense. Neoclassical economists assume that static equilibria exist, or at least are achievable. In ABS, systems do not always settle into equilibria; sometimes they do, but more often they evolve from one state to another. Agent-based simulations generate both static equilibria and dynamic change. For example, Epstein and Axtell's (1996) simulations illustrate that, when left alone markets do not generate equilibrium conditions, but non-equilibrium conditions. Whether a simulated system will settle in an equilibrium state or not depends on the negative and positive feedbacks the system gets, according to Miller and Page. More negative feedback will lead to equilibria and more positive feedback will lead to non-equilibria (p. 75). This is why it is harder to reach generalizations from ABS.

Miller and Page contrast agent-based models and neoclassical models on their assumptions about individual actors. Whereas neoclassical models of economic systems use a top-down approach, in agent-based models bottom-up approaches are used (pp. 65–66). In the former, modelers assume that all individuals optimize their behaviors and all systems seek equilibrium. In the latter, systemic behavior emerges from the behaviors of agents. This bottom-up approach does not signify a bottom-up theory building (inductive approach), however. The aim of the simulations is not to find a "solution" to a given problem, or to build a theory by making generalizations, but to explore the collective patterns that emerge through nonlinear, self-organizational processes and track the coevolution of agents with their systems. The ABS researcher observes the evolutions of the simulated systems and interrupts the process to take "snap shots" at different points in time to identify the emergent collective properties at a given time. This is a contextual and interpretive approach to inquiry.

Epstein and Axtell argue that ABS offers a different approach altogether for the social sciences, a new and unified evolutionary social science, which they call "generative social science." This social science would not be deductive or inductive, but generative. In generative social science, evolutionary simulation models would replace nomothetic explanations. It would not be idiographic either, because its focus would not be on the behaviors of individual agents, but on the processes in which collective structures emerge out of individual interactions. In generative social science, the question would not be how to explain societies, but how to "grow" them, i.e., how to understand generative processes with simulations. We can draw our own conclusions about this from our knowledge of the societies we live in, Epstein and Axtell suggest.

Axelrod (2007) makes a similar point. In his view, the simulation methodology provides a "third way of doing science," different from, but also inclusive of, deduction and induction:

> Like deduction, it starts with a set of explicit assumptions. But unlike deduction, it does not prove theorems. Instead, a simulation generates data that can be analyzed inductively. Unlike typical induction, however, the simulated data comes from a rigorously specified set of rules rather than direct measurement of the real world. While induction can be used to find patterns in data, and deduction can be used to find consequences of assumptions, simulation modeling can be used as an aid intuition. (pp. 92–93)

The Nature of Agents in ABS

The nature of agents is a central problem in agent-based simulations. Miller and Page (2007) note that there are actually two problems regarding the nature of agents. The first problem is the "problem of generalized attributes of agent" (p. 238–239). The question is to what extent in a simulation the actors are modeled homogenously: to what extent they are alike in their beliefs, preferences, abilities to act, etc. As an example, in cellular automata simulations, agents are programmed more homogenously. Remember that in the illustration in the previous section, the agents were grouped into economically and socially motivated types. In other forms of simulation more heterogeneity is allowed.

The second problem is about the "level of sophistication" of agents. The question is to what extent agents should be programmed as rational, informed, and able to act in the way they desire to act (p. 239). I referred to this question in my discussion of rational actors in Chapter 3. The reader will remember Sawyer's (2005) dichotomous conceptualization: "reactive" ("behavioral") agents versus "cognitive" agents. Reactive agents do not have any "internal representations of the world." Cognitive agents do have internal representations of the world; they are intentional and deliberative and have views and beliefs about their environments, their actions, and their impacts (p. 148).

It is necessary to highlight the implications of this conceptual division between reactive and cognitive agents. I want to make three points. First, the assumptions about reactive agents versus cognitive agents create both technical and conceptual problems. When agents are assumed to be cognitive, the researcher faces more challenging technical problems in modeling. The issue is also conceptual, theoretical, and philosophical. The concepts of reactive agent and cognitive agent are abstractions that do not have direct, one-on-one referents in the real world. It is reasonable to assume that human beings are more cognitive than reactive, because they have internal representations of the world and they are intentional and deliberative. But not that human beings have different types of internal representations at different levels of sophistication.

Second, because human agents are more cognitive than reactive, the social systemic relations that emerge from their interactions have structural properties that are more complex than the properties of natural systems that emerge from the interactions of natural agents, such as molecules, physical objects, etc. This is where complexity theory meets the basic insights of hermeneutics, which I briefly discussed in Chapter 7. Hermeneutic philosophers argued that the social sciences had to be different from the natural sciences because of the fundamentally different natures of these two realms. Are they indeed fundamentally different or are the differences a matter of degree? This still is a big philosophical and empirical question. Complexity theory can help us understand conceptually the differences between the natural and social realms. The reactive and cognitive agent assumptions are simplifications, but they can be helpful in investigating the differences in the respective natures of the natural and social realms.

Third, we need to investigate conceptually and empirically whether, or to what extent, cognitive agents really have the knowledge of the structural properties of the systems that emerge from their interactions. Whether, or to what extent, agents have the knowledge of their systems is a profoundly important issue public policy. If public policy is not simply the act of a particular governmental unit, but a complex system, then the degree of the knowledge of the system held by its agents will have consequences for the system. If all the agents have the knowledge of the consequences of each agent's actions and the interactions among agents, then presumably they collectively should be able to take actions to remedy those consequences. For instance, if all human beings had the full knowledge of global warming, they could act collectively to solve the problem. Of course knowledge alone is not sufficient to take action and make difference at the system level; agents/actors should also have the intention and motivation to act.

Diamond's concise conceptualization of the "failures of group decision-making" in his book *Collapse: How Societies Choose to Fail or Succeed* (2005) illustrates this point succinctly. After describing in detail how various societies and civilizations failed over the human history (e.g., Easter Island, the Anasazi, the Maya, the Vikings, and others), Diamond identifies four groups of factors that contributed to these societal failures:

> First of all, a group may fail to anticipate a problem before the problem actually arrives. Second, when the problem does arrive, the group may fail to perceive it. Then after they perceive it, they may fail even to try to solve it. Finally, they may try to solve it but may not succeed. (p. 421)

So the knowledge of agents alone is not sufficient to solve systemic problems, like global warming. It matters *when* they know the problems: It may be too late by the time they know it. What is not clearly stated in Diamond's succinct summary of the four factors is that knowledge is not equally distributed in societies; some members of a society may have better knowledge of systemic problems than others. Atmospheric scientist and ecologists can have better knowledge of global warming, for example. Also not clearly stated by Diamond is that agents know the systemic problems they create through their own dynamic schema, which are socially and personally constructed and reconstructed. In other words, an agent's knowledge of a problem depends not only on available information but also on what specific cognitive frames he/she acquires from the culture and system of social relations in which he/she is embedded. Simply because the information about global warming and the role human played in it is available does not mean that agents will know it.

Just think of the state of the public opinion on global warming in the US in the first decade of the 21st century. Although there is clear evidence that the atmospheric temperatures have been rising steadily for the last 130 years, including the first decade of the 21st century and there is near consensus among scientists that this has been caused at least partly by human activities, primarily by carbon dioxide emissions (Houghton, 2004, pp. 216–225), the percentage of American people who think that "there is solid evidence that the earth is warming" and that "this is caused by human activity" declined drastically between 2006 and 2010.[21] In 2006 79% of American agreed that the earth was warming, and this declined to 59% in 2010. Likewise, 50% of Americans believed that the warming was due to human activities, and this declined to 34% in 2010. By comparison, larger percentages of the French, Germans, the British, Spaniards, and Italians thought that global warming was a threat and that governments should take actions to curb it.[22] The efforts to pass the climate legislation to curb the effects of global warming died a slow death in the US Congress in 2009 and 2010.

One can speculate that this clear discrepancy between the scientific knowledge, on the one hand, and people's beliefs and policymaking, on the other, was due to the economic problems of the period, particularly the Great Recession. Perhaps some people worried that the drastic actions that would be necessary to curb the warming (e.g., decreasing the use of fossil fuels and switching to renewable energy) would be too costly and changed their minds about the facticity of the information about the trend in atmospheric temperatures and human activities that contribute to it. The massive advertisement campaigns by the American Petroleum Institute, the trade association of the oil companies, probably helped shift the opinion on the issue. Whatever the reasons for this shift in opinions, it is clear in this example that the knowledge of individual agents is not reflective of the available information about the systemic problem.

This is why it is important to understand the cognitive process of specific agents in their own cultural contexts. It matters to understand to what extent agents are cognitive or reactive: to what extent they have the knowledge of the structural properties of the systems they create. It does matter to clarify what assumptions a researcher makes about agents in his/her simulations.

In most of the applications of ABS, agents are assumed to be and modeled as cognitive agents (e.g., Casterfranchi, 1998; Naveh and Sun, 2006; Ahmad, 2008) or "boundedly rational agents" (e.g., Holland, 1995; Axelrod, 1997; Cohen, Riolo and Axelrod, 2001; Epstein, 2006; Bednar and Page, 2007; Miller and Page, 2007). It is reasonable to assume that human agents have internal representations of the world and they are intentional and deliberate. This also is highly compatible with Giddens' structuration theory. The reader will remember from Chapter 3 Sawyer's (2005) critique of Giddens' structuration theory, particularly the latter's assumption that social systems are outcomes of "knowledgeable activities of situated actors" (p. 25). Giddens' actors are cognitive agents in this sense. Sawyer cites examples of agent-based simulations that demonstrate that actors do not have to be knowledgeable about their environments or systemic processes at all for structural properties to emerge (Steels, 1990; Deneubourg, Goss, Beckers, and Sandini, 1991). Epstein's (2006) concurs that "individual rationality is neither necessary nor sufficient for the attainment of macroscopic efficiency" (p. 144). This, according to Sawyer, refutes Giddens' claim that social structures cannot exist without the "practical consciousness" of individuals who participate in them.

Real human beings are cognitive agents in the sense that they have internal representations of their worlds and the systems in which they participate. They do have worldviews that help them make sense of their worlds. But the comprehensiveness and accuracy of their internal representations is debatable. And different agents may have different degrees of comprehensiveness and accuracy in their internal representations of the social systems they participate in. Therefore, the results of simulations with reactive agents may be interesting, but they do not tell us much about the mechanisms in real human societies. This dichotomous conceptualization of reactive agent versus cognitive agent can still be useful, however. The notion of reactive agent can be useful if a reactive agent is conceptualized as an agent who does not have an accurate and complete representation of the structural properties of the social system that he/she participates in. I think it would be more useful if these concepts are placed on a continuum, from those agents who have more comprehensive and accurate internal representations of their worlds to those who have less comprehensive and accurate representations.

This brings me to the conceptualization of boundedly rational agents. The reader will remember from Chapter 3 that the term bounded rationality was proposed by Herbert Simon in response to the utility-maximizing rational actor assumption of rational choice theory. Boundedly rational individuals do not have the full information about the world around them. Their information-processing capabilities are also bounded.

Miller and Page (2007) use this bounded rationality assumption in their simulations. In their models, agents receive information about the world, process it, and act on it. Miller and Page dispute the rational choice assumption that these agents know the world completely and in every detail and can optimize in their decisions. Because of the developments in behavioral economics, the neoclassical assumptions about information acquisition, processing, and acting must be relaxed (p. 30). In this relaxed version of the rational actor assumption, agents/actors selectively acquire information about the world through restricted channels of communication. These agents are adaptive, but their actions are "often limited and localized" (pp. 30–31).

Miller and Page (2007, pp. 65–67) draw a contrast between neoclassical modeling and agent-based modeling. Neoclassical modeling homogenizes agents. This approach is "abstraction based" in the sense that it makes generalizations about the behaviors of human agents (that they all are utility-maximizing individuals) and the economic system in which they operate (that it always seeks equilibrium). In this approach all the agents are "subsumed into a single object (a 'representative' agent)" (p. 65). This is a "top-down" approach to model building, because high-level rules, like utility maximization and systemic tendency toward equilibrium, are imposed on the model.

It is obviously problematic to homogenize agents, particularly given the fact that human agents have different personalities and cognitive construct systems. But homogenization may be justified with assumption that the actual heterogeneities of agents cancel out each other during simulations, and therefore researchers can ignore it. Under this assumption, researchers can safely homogenize agents by assigning "mean values" to their attributes. Miller and Page warn, however, that increased heterogeneity "may substantially alter the system's behavior" (p. 239), and therefore researchers should not dismiss its importance in simulations.

The ABS researchers make abstractions about human agents, but they relax the utility maximization assumption of neoclassical modeling. Thus agents are modeled more heterogeneously: "[C]ollections of these agent-based objects [are] 'solved' by allowing the objects to interact directly with one another using computation" (p. 65).[23] This is a "bottom-up" approach in the sense that abstractions are focused on lower-level entities (agents). In ABS behaviors of agents are not fixed; they are adaptive. They learn from their experiences and change their beliefs and behaviors (pp. 178–180).

The contrast Miller and Page draw between the neoclassical and agent-based modeling is quite telling. It underscores both the strengths and limitations of ABS in general and the bounded rationality assumption many complexity theorists apply in their simulations in particular. As in neoclassical modeling, in ABS researchers make simplifications about individual agents, but the "relaxation" of the utility-maximizing rational actor assumption (bounded rationality) injects some heterogeneity into these models and makes ABS much more realistic, of course. But the bounded rationality assumption still misses out on large parts of the immense complexity of human behaviors. Human beings are not merely information-processing computers; their cognitive processes involve complex interactions of emotional states, rational computations, influences of culture, etc.

Epstein (2006) is aware of this. He imagines that one day agent-based models would include "psychologically richer agents coevolving in and generating endogenous networks" (p. 346). He anticipates that such models would be challenging to analyze. More important than the challenges in analyzing such models are the challenges researchers would face in constructing them. It would be almost impossible to model all the complexities of cognitive and emotional processes. But it would be worth the effort, as Epstein recognizes.

I will come back to the issue of how to model agents more realistically by including as much of their complexities as possible in the next chapter.

I want to note briefly here that there are researchers who included their experimental findings in their models to make them more realistic. In their simulations of the effects of sharing the same space versus working from distant locations in organizations, Nan, Johnson, and Olson (2008) first conducted an experiment with a group of real actors and then used what they learned from this experiment in their subsequent simulations.

Koehler's Spatio-Temporal Agents

This discussion on the agents in ABS would be incomplete, if I did not briefly mention Koehler's (2004, 2008) insightful and challenging notion of "spatio-temporal agents." I mentioned Koehler's conceptualization of adaptive governance in Chapter 5. The basic idea was that as they coevolve, policy systems do not always do so in harmony, or synchrony, with natural systems or other policy systems. This is because each individual and each organizational structure, or a system, is situated in its own past, present, and future in a unique way. He calls the unique state of a system in a given place and at a given time its *temporal signature*. A temporal signature is an instance in the complex web of realities and the flow of time. As such, the relations among the individuals and organizations in a particular time ecology may be *synchronous* or *heterochronous*.

This innovative conceptualization has implications for ABS. As I mentioned earlier in this chapter, in a typical application of cellular automata simulations, agents are placed in particular positions, which signify how they "locally" relate to each other. In such simulations the agents have pre-given cognitions (preferences, information, etc.), which can evolve once the simulation is run and as each agent learns from others. In such simulations time and space are separated. In Koehler's conceptualization, agents, who are systems themselves, come into being in multiple and complex flows of time. Each agent has its own flow of time and his/her own memories of his/her past and images of the near and far futures. Koehler calls this "nootemporality," which is distinct from "eootemporality," general flow of time or physicist's time. In his conceptualization of nootemporality, Koehler cites Merleau-Ponty and his phenomenological understanding that the body exists in space and time. Each agent's nootemporality coevolves, but not synchronously, with others' and within the general eootemporality.

Koehler criticizes current simulations for "while recognizing the importance of networks, tend to downplay the fact that they are regulated by temporal variations between agents and across networks" and mistakenly locating all agents in the same temporal domain (i.e., eootemporality; 2004, pp. 12–13). In these simulations the researchers ignore the fact that agents are temporal beings. He offers an alternative conceptualization of time in simulations. He observes "Time is a topologically complex flow of relational events between and forming continuously structurating forms be they called 'agent' or 'landscape' or 'network,' instantiated in the complex system of a time-ecology. This is not existence within time; existence *is* time" (p. 14). In his alternative conceptualization human agents would be modeled within their nootemporality, which would be nested within the more general eootemporality. He then illustrates graphically the way agents should be viewed in his alternative conceptualization but stops there without giving specific example of how his ideas could be operationalized in agent-based simulations.

Koehler's insightful and innovative conceptualization stretches the boundaries of complexity thinking and makes a connection to phenomenology, at least Merleau-Ponty's phenomenology, which other complexity theorists like Prigogine cite as the epistemological direction for complexity science as well. This is an important opening for complexity theorists, but it would take further clarification and conceptual development by Koehler, or others, to make his vision directly applicable in ABS.

ABS and Policy Analysis

What would be the use of agent-based simulations in policy analysis? To understand this, we need to go back to the definition of public policy I proposed in Chapter 1: *Public policy is an emergent and self-organizational complex system. The relations among the elements (actors) of this complex system are nonlinear and its relations with its elements and with other systems are coevolutionary.* This definition suggests that we should revise the mainstream thinking about the causal relations between public policies (causes) and policy outcomes (effects). A governmental decision (law, ordinance, rule, etc.) and action can make a difference in the complex social systemic relations but not in a linear-causal manner: "Policy outcomes" are not necessarily direct results of such decisions or actions. As Salzano (2008) puts it, policy makers look for direct casual relations between their decisions and outcome, but this idea is "in direct contrast with the complexity concept" (p. 186). There are no direct correlations between policy inputs and outputs in complex systems.

An ABS researcher understands and simulates the complex relationships in social systems. The goal of an agent-based simulation is not to obtain optimal results but to understand how macro-level results emerge from the interactions of agents under different conditions and provide insights into where to find "policy leverages," according to Salzano. Likewise, Axelrod (1997) points out that ABS models can be used in policy analysis in such a way that they can "lead to insight into where there might be policy leverage in the real world" (p. 143).

Maroulis and his colleagues (2010) stress the role of agent-based simulations in helping bridge the "micro-macro gap" in educational policy and evaluation. They point out that the educational policy has progressed in two parallel tracks. In the first track researchers have studied the micro-level phenomena in schools: motivations and interactions of students, teachers, and administrators. In the second track, researchers have focused on the macro-level factors that contribute to the effectiveness of schools: teacher-pupil ratios, family background of students, and teacher quality. Maroulis and his colleagues argue, "a key challenge facing education research is to integrate insights about 'microlevel' processes with evidence about aggregate, 'macro-level' outcomes that emerge from those processes" (p. 38). Agent-based simulations would be effective in this integration.

How exactly should agent-bases simulations be used in policy analysis? The dynamic pictures that are generated by agent-based simulations can be used as heuristic tools in dynamic decision making processes. Richardson (2008) argues that ABS suggests a pluralist and pragmatic epistemology and a new modeling culture, what he calls "nonlinear modelling culture," for policy analysis.[24] This culture takes a "pragmatic stance," according to Richardson, and differs from the "linear modeling culture," in which the assumption is that certain "aspects of reality . . . are considered to be captured by the model," i.e., model is considered to be a static representation of reality. In the nonlinear modeling culture, the "modeling process is regarded as an ongoing dialectic between stakeholders (modelers, users, customers, decision makers, etc.)" (p. 50).

This dynamic and interpretive nature of agent-based simulations is suitable for a continual improvement approach, not one-shot solutions to social problems. Some years ago, Harold Lasswell, who formulated the vision of "policy sciences of democracy," described his vision in terms that is highly compatible with this dynamic and interpretive nature of agent-based simulations. Lasswell (1971) envisioned that policy sciences would use contextual maps of policy processes, what he called "developmental constructs," which would be constructed dynamically and improved continually to track policy development and pose new questions at each stage (pp. 72–79). The ABS approach provides tools of fulfilling this vision.

QUALITATIVE CASE STUDIES

Social network analyses and ABS are not sufficient to understand the contexts of complex systems. The knowledge of a complex social system must be contextual, as I stressed in Chapter 6. The observers of a complex social system should attempt to understand both the context of the system and the context of their own knowledge of the system.

The structural properties an observer identifies in a system are both unique and they have commonalities with other systems. Both social network analyses and ABS allow for limited generalizations about structural properties of systems. For instance the "size of a network" is a generalizable property. In the example I illustrated in Figure 10.1, the sizes of the governance systems in the downtown area of a US city can be compared numerically and a generalization can be made about the changes in the size of this network over time. But to understand what else changed in this network/system and why and how those changes happened specifically, we, the researchers needed to understand the specific context of the governance system. That requires qualitative descriptions of what city the network was located, the history of the city, etc.

Both SNA and ABS yield information about individual actors and their relations, as well the structural properties of systems/networks. But this information is quantitative, and quantification necessarily strips off some of the contextual information. For instance, in SNA the researcher can define and analyze different types of relations among actors. Thus SNA allows for some context entered into analyses. For example, we can understand that "friendship" is a different kind of relationship than "transactional business relationship." Even then the specific context of the friendship between two actors is lost in our analyses. All the subtleties of friendship relations are collapsed into one form. The subtleties can only be described qualitatively.

A researcher should also understand the context of his/her of knowledge process. Complexity theorists acknowledge that knowledge of complexity—or, reality in general—is constricted by our cognitive apparatuses and our situatedness or embeddedness in the world we observe (Chapter 6). Then the knowledge of a complex system must be reflexive (i.e., the researcher must be self-aware) as well. This is not quantifiable; it requires qualitative understanding.

The researchers in the Department of Public Administration at the Erasmus University, Rotterdam, the Netherlands, conducted a series of qualitative case studies in understanding complex systems and networks. These studies have been published in several books (e.g., Kickert, Klijn, and Koppenjan, 1997a; Koppenjan and Klijn, 2004) and articles (e.g., Teisman, 2008; Teisman and Klijn, 2008). The recent volume edited by Teisman, Van Buuren, and Gerritts (2009b) is a compendium of case studies that illustrate how qualitative methods can be used in understanding the macro structures and processes and micro–macro relations in complex governance systems. I will briefly introduce and discuss the case studies presented in this book to illustrate the strengths and shortcomings of qualitative case studies.

Buijs, Eshuis, and Byrne's (2009) chapter in the book is particularly important, because the authors make the case for case study research in complexity studies and propose a theoretical framework for doing so. Building on the conceptual framework developed earlier by Byrne (2005), they first make a distinction between two theoretical approaches in complex system studies: the "simplistic (general) complexity" approach and the "complex (situated) complexity" approach. In the former approach, the researchers make the assumption that the theories of complex systems are universal for all systems (physical, biological, and social) and that "a general set of rules from which emergent complexity flows." In the latter approach the assumption is that "reality is deeply complex and inherently contingent" and that social systems are different from physical and biological systems (p. 37).

Buijs and his colleagues favor this latter approach in studying socials systems. In Buijs and his colleagues' view, methods that are suitable for identifying idiosyncrasies as well as general patterns are required in the situated complexity approach. They argue that "in-depth case studies" and "qualitative comparative methods," as formulated by Charles Ragin (1987, 2000) should be the methods of investigating social systems.[25]

Buijs and his colleagues' conceptual framework seems to reflect the distinctions hermeneutic philosophers made (Chapter 8) between natural (physical, chemical) and social (cultural, human) systems. I agree with Buijs and his colleagues' argument that social systems are more complex than natural systems. They rightfully point to the reflexive nature of human agents as a major source of this higher-order complexity in social systems. Therefore, one can argue that researchers should use more specific and additional methods, particularly qualitative methods, in studying social systems. But one should not draw the conclusion that in-depth case studies and qualitative comparative methods are all that a researcher needs to understand social systems.

Case studies are idiographic. The goal is to understand a particular case in detail, not to make generalizations.[26] Ragin's comparative methods are "small-n" methods, which enable researchers to make limited generalizations. These methods can indeed be very useful in studying complex social systems, although there were not any examples of their applications in complexity research at the time of the writing of this book. The methodologies like SNA and ABS should not be dismissed, at the expense of in-depth case studies and qualitative comparative methods, however. As I showed in the previous sections, both SNA and ABS can be very useful in understanding stable and dynamic structural properties of social systems, as well as characteristics of individual agents/actors. The quantification used in both SNA and ABS removes the contexts in understanding social systems and thus causes loss of information. However, quantification is necessary to summarize large amounts of information. The complexity of social systems generates lots of information to be summarized. In order to understand complex social systems comprehensively—or at least to understand them better—complexity researchers need to use SNA, ABS, as well as in-depth case studies and comparative methods.

Buijs and his colleagues make an important contribution with their succinct summary of the "basic methodological guidelines" for complexity researchers. These guidelines are applicable not only to in-depth case studies and comparative methods but also to all methodological approaches employed in studying complex social systems. They posit that it is important to understand the context, that the knowledge of complex systems is always partial and provisional, and that a researcher must use multiple methods (pp. 49–51). They also propose that interactions should be the objects of research (p. 51). Social network analyses researchers do use relations as its units of observation and analysis, as I mentioned earlier.

Buijs and his colleagues also argue that complexity researchers must be reflexive and consider their own positions vis-à-vis the systems they observe and try to understand small details in these systems, which can have large consequences because of the nonlinear relations in systems (pp. 51–52). Researchers must be aware of the difficulties in defining the boundaries of social systems, as they are determined by actors/agents and researchers (pp. 52–53). Buijs and his colleagues also make specific recommendations for studying public policy/governance systems: First, complexity researchers should study seemingly insignificant actors, as well as seemingly central and powerful actors, because decision making is usually dispersed in these systems and the actions of seemingly insignificant actors may have large consequences. Second, they should also conduct continuous longitudinal research, rather than taking snapshots, in studying the coevolutions of systems. The methodological guidelines of Buijs and colleagues are useful for complexity researchers.

The case studies Teisman, van Buuren, and Gerrits (2009b) present illustrate the use of qualitative methods in investigating policy/governance systems. The topics of cases presented in the book cover a wide range. Teisman, Westerveldt, and Hertogh (2009) compare the importance of "change events"—seemingly trivial external events that turn out to be significant in the context of nonlinear relations and reactions—in the development projects of two rail system projects in the United Kingdom and the Netherlands. Van Gils, Gerrits, and Teisman (2009) compare two port projects in Germany and the Netherlands. Buijs, van der Bol, Teisman, and Byrne (2009) describe the self-organizational processes in the governance systems of the Randstad Holland region of the Netherlands. Pel (2009) describes the self-organizational processes in the traffic management system in Haren town in the same country. Gerrits, Marks, and van Buuren (2009) analyze the coevolutionary processes between natural systems and "policy action systems" in the cases of two estuaries in Germany and the Netherlands. Similarly, Van Buuren, Gerrits, and Marks (2009) describe the coevolutionary processes in managing water in a tract of low lands recovered from the sea in the southwest of the Netherlands.

All these case descriptions provide rich details of the attributes and relationships of the individual and collective policy actors in their respective systems. The authors of these studies apply selected complexity theory concepts to illustrate them specific cases and in doing so build bridges between generalized concepts and specific cases. Gerrits, Marks, and van Buuren's (2009) case study of the estuaries in Germany and the Netherlands, which is discussed more extensively by Gerrits (2008), illustrates the importance of the coevolution of social and natural systems. Gerrits and his colleagues describe the policy decisions made in Germany and the Netherlands to dredge the estuaries with the purpose of deepening them to allow larger ships to navigate more easily and the nonlinear processes these decisions unleashed. The authors make the observation that policy action systems and physical (natural) systems coevolve by making reciprocal selections and adaptations and reach the conclusion that policy makers cannot make natural systems obey their wishes and plans and that they have to understand the mutuality in the relations between policy and natural systems. This is a fundamental insight that can be carried over into understanding the relations between natural and social systems in other areas (e.g., climate change, biodiversity, and social and economic development).

Case studies offer rich details, but the generalizability of their results is always problematic. I have argued in this book that the generalizability of the information about complex systems is problematic as well; only limited generalizations can be made about their properties and behaviors. But still it is necessary to be able to make generalizations to the extent that systems have stable structural properties and there are similarities between systems. Without any generalization, no knowledge of complex systems could be generated and shared. A better methodological approach would be to combine case studies with SNA and ABS. The SNA methodology allows researchers to make some generalizations about the structural properties of systems/networks; it can be fruitfully combined with qualitative case studies. The ABS methodology can also be supplemented with case studies for more in-depth understandings of the micro–macro relations and transformations in the systems whose behaviors are simulated.

CHAPTER SUMMARY

In this chapter I discussed the methods of studying the micro–macro relations and processes in complex social systems. In particular, I described social network analyses, agent-based simulations, and qualitative case studies.

Researchers use social network analyses to investigate structural properties of systems and attributes, choices, and relations of individual actors. The roots of this methodology are in *sociometry* and *sociograms*, which were designed to represent and analyze patterned social relationships in the 1930s. In social network analyses researchers analyze structural relations quantitatively. Both the relations among actors and their attributes and the structural properties that emerge from their relations are analyzed. I discussed several issues in social network analyses: issues in analyzing centralization and power relations in networks, network stability and change, and emergent structural properties; constructing the boundaries of networks; and understanding structuration and social causation; and the limitations in the number of abstract relations that can be analyzed in social network analyses.

Researchers use ABS, also known as multi-agent simulations, to simulate the evolutions of systemic relations of individual agents. I described the three forms of ABS: cellular automata, neural and networks, and genetic algorithms. Agent-based simulation researchers simulated the emergence of cooperation in human societies, meta-agents (collective agents), and culture. After describing these works, I addressed the issue of social (downward) causation in ABS. Social causation is a crucial aspect of emergence, and some researchers attempted to model it in their ABS applications.

Then I discussed the epistemological and methodological issues in ABS. Agent-based simulations take a different approach than SNA in three ways: The former are inherently dynamic, not static; they are somewhat "artificial" in the sense that researchers usually use generalized assumptions about agents' preferences and behavioral tendencies as inputs in their simulations, not direct empirical observations on agents' preferences or behavioral tendencies; and whereas the unit of analysis is relations in SNA, it is attributes of agents in ABS. After elaborating on the "artificiality" of ABS, I discussed the issue of deductive versus generative approaches to knowledge generation. Agent-based simulations is an example of the latter. The nature of agents in ABS models is discussed to an extent in the literature. Both cognitive agents (those who have internal representations of their environments and are purposive) and reactive agents (those with no such representations of purposes) are used in ABS. I made the points that this dichotomous conceptualization may be useful, but it should be remembered that real human beings are more cognitive than reactive and that to what extent an agent has a good representations of his/her environment is an empirical question. Another issue regarding the nature of agents is whether they should be modeled homogenously or heterogeneously. The latter is more representative of real human societies. I discussed Gus Koehler's innovative conceptualization of "spatio-temporal agents" as an alternative conceptualization.

I noted that agent-based simulations are highly compatible with the definition of public policy I proposed in Chapter 1 and with Harold Lasswell's vision of policy sciences for democracy.

In the last section of this chapter, I discussed the qualitative case studies in studying complex policy systems. Qualitative studies are important and necessary to gain contextual understanding of complex systems, but they are not sufficient. They should be used together with quantitative methodologies, like SNA and ABS.

11 Micro Methods

THE PROBLEM OF ARTIFICIALITY IN ABS AND EXPERIMENTS

In the previous chapter I argued that there is an "artificiality" problem in ABS. Even when the agents are assumed to be cognitive, not reactive, only generalizations/abstractions about the attributes of cognitive agents are entered into simulations. The attributes (preferences and behavioral predispositions) of agents and the rules governing their interactions are abstracted from the literature on the empirical research findings in psychology, social psychology, economics, and sociology (Nan and Johnson, 2009). These generalizations do have some validity, of course, but they are only generalizations. To what extent these generalizations represent the attributes of the actual agents in a given situation—to what extent they are "realistic"—is an open question.

One way to deal with the problem of artificiality is to conduct experiments with real human beings and then enter the generalizations made from these experiments into simulations. Although this approach is empirically based, the values entered into simulations are still; they do not represent actual human beings directly.

Researchers of "common pool resources" use experimental results in simulations. Common pool resources are used by large numbers of individuals; they are not private properties, but individuals extract them for their own benefits. Deadman, Schlager, and Gimblett's (2000) simulations of "common pool resource institutions" is an example. Deadman and his colleagues used the generalizations made from the results of a series of experiments on common pool resources in their simulations. Deadman and his colleagues cite a series of experiments that were conducted on the dynamics of the "tragedy of the commons" (Hardin, 1968) in the 1980s and 1990s but focus particularly on Ostrom, Gardner, and Walker's (1994) experiments. Ostrom and her colleagues tested with experiments Hardin's prediction that individuals will over utilize common-pool resources: They will overgraze pastures when they are available. Deadman and his colleagues (2000) justify their selection of these experiments as follows:

> Thus, the common pool resource experiments provide particularly fertile ground for simulations because they capture real world dynamics,

they are widely recognized and accepted in the social sciences, and they have been replicated. These experiments were selected as the subject of these simulations because they are already themselves models of a real world system, and because they have been widely studied. These experiments have been simulated as a step towards the eventual development of simulations based on real world case studies. (Section 1.4)

Deadman and his colleagues' simulations are removed from direct empirical findings by a few steps, as they are based on generalizations from multiple earlier experiments. Janssen, Radtke, and Lee's (2009) study on the dynamics of common-pool resource situations is more directly connected to empirical results of experiments. They conducted their own laboratory experiments. Janssen and his colleagues are explicit about the methodological assumptions they made. They point out that agent-based models should be empirically grounded and should have enough "granularity" to capture the details of the behaviors of individual agents, but these simulations will be based on some generalizations inevitably. Then, they argue, these generalizations should be compatible with important features of the findings of empirical research.

In their experiments Janssen and his colleagues placed participants in a commons dilemma and conducted a series of experiments to study "how groups develop new institutional arrangements if they share common dynamic resources" (p. 510). They recruited the participants from undergraduate students at a state university and asked them to make decisions in a "real-time dynamic environment representing a virtual common resource" (p. 509). The researchers detected particular patterns in the actions of the participants (e.g., their speed and direction in decision making) and the inequalities that emerged among them in wealth accumulation. They used the generalizations they made from these patterns in their simulations.

Like Janssen and his colleagues, Nan, Johnson, Olson, and Bos (2005) conducted laboratory experiments first and used their generalized findings in a series of simulations later. In their studies Nan and his colleagues compared the performances of virtual teams (members at remote locations) and collocated teams (members in face-to-face relations) under different scenarios. They tested particularly the effects of use of communication technology and favoritism in team decision making.

In the first stage of their study, Nan and his colleagues conducted 13 laboratory experiments with virtual and collocated teams and extracted "behavioral patterns and benchmarks" for their later simulations from these experiments. They describe their "Shape Factory" lab experiments as follows:

> In Shape Factory, participants played the part of specialty producers of one of five different shapes. At the same time, each player had the task to collect different shapes from other players to fill "customer" orders. Players earned points by selling their specialty shapes and buying other

shapes to fill orders. We imposed production limits to players so that there was a scarcity of shapes relative to customer demand. Players had varied communication channels. To be successful in Shape Factory, players had to use the available channels to contact, negotiate and cooperate with others. (p. 1694)

The researchers made "simple abstractions" from their observations of these lab experiments to be used in their simulations. Then, Nan and his colleagues simulated virtual and collocated teams under a variety of scenarios in multiple steps. They found in their simulations that distance is an important factor in the functioning of virtual teams and that favoritism affects group performance negatively in both kinds of teams.

In all these examples, the researchers made efforts to make the inputs of their simulations as close to reality as possible. But in the end, the inputs stills are abstractions based on empirical findings.

METHODS OF COGNITIVE MAPPING

The artificiality problem in ABS could also be addressed by eliciting the cognitive constructions of particular agents and using them directly in simulations. I describe and discuss three such methods in this chapter: Q methodology, concept mapping, and repertory grids. Using these methods, researchers can elicit the cognitive constructions (or "concepts," "cognitive maps") of actual agents who are involved in the simulated situation. These methods are used to understand/measure the complexity of the minds of individual agents or the collective minds of groups participating in a policy-related situation. I call these methods together methods of cognitive mapping.

Cognitive scientists have known for a long time that when a human agent thinks, emotes, and acts, he/she does so not merely as a calculating and utility-maximizing ("rational") agent. There are multiple dimensions in a mind, and they interact in nonlinear ways. What one can observe as the behavior of an agent in a given moment is the composite outcome of the interactions of these dimensions. That is why it is important to understand the complexity of the mind.

Systematic conceptualizations of the multidimensionality and complexity of human minds can be traced back to the studies in psychology in the early 20th century. Gestalt psychologists developed a holistic understanding of the mind in the first decades of the 20th century. Kurt Lewin's (1938) theory of "life space"—a psychological space that consists of the memories of all the events in a person's past and his/her predispositions future actions—and his method of representing it geometrically can be considered one of the earliest attempts to conceptualize and quantify the multidimensionality of the mind. More developments took place in the 1950s. George Kelly's (1955) theory of "personal constructs" and Bieri's (1955) index of cognitive complexity can be cited among the most significant ones. There are some commonalities in Lewin, Kelly, and Bieri. The mind, or personality, is a multidimensional space ("life space" for Lewin, "personal construct space" for Kelly) whose dimensions are named "fields" (Lewin) or "constructs" (Kelly and Bieri).[1] Such dimensions can be elicited directly from individuals using specially designed methods and analyzed quantitatively, using specialized methods (as in Lewin's and Bieri's cases) or more general multivariate statistical methods, such as factor analysis, cluster analysis, and multidimensional scaling, as in Kelly's case. The relationships among the dimensions of the mind can be plotted as "cognitive maps" using the results of these quantitative analyses. The methods I describe in the following sections (Q methodology, concept mapping, and repertory grids) aim to do this by using different approaches.

Complexity theorists understand that cognitions of individual agents are complex systems as well. Gleick (1987, pp. 276–299) tells the stories of scientists working in disparate fields recognizing the complexity of human biology and mind, as early as in the late 1960s. In the studies on the rhythms of the heart, the biological clock, and schizophrenia, they observed that biological and cognitive patterns are nonlinear, chaotic, and complex. Torre (1995) applied chaos theory concepts in modeling the problem-solving processes in human cognition. His "dynamical problem-solving model" includes both the orderly and chaotic nature of the way human minds work when attempting to solve problems. In his model, the mind works utilizing both linear and cyclical ("rational") information-processing routines and emotional and nonlinear capabilities. Autopoiesis theory was formulated first as a theory of the self-referential and self-organizational processes of the human cognition.[2]

The reader will also remember from Chapter 7 that some complexity theorists cite phenomenology as the most suitable epistemology for complexity theory. They stress the "endophysical" nature of the knowledge of complexity (Rössler, 1986). Prigogine and Stengers (1984) propose a new epistemology that "presupposes an observer situated within the observed world" (p. 218). This view of knowledge is phenomenological in that it views human knowledge as situated and temporal. This phenomenological view calls for an understanding social systems from the perspective of their participants and an understanding of their "living worlds." So, at least some complexity theorists suggest that it is important to understand the living worlds (perspectives, values, preferences, etc.) of agents/actors in order to understand systems. This obviously is even more important when studying social systems.

Despite their recognition of the complexity human minds, complexity theorists have not developed the specific tools of measuring and interpreting the complexity of the minds of agents, nor have they utilized those measurements and interpretations in ABS. Q methodology, concept mapping, and repertory grids have the potential to be used in filling this gap.

There are methodological and conceptual problems that should be addressed, however. If researchers use the actual attributes of every agent, each agent would be unique and the valued entered into simulations would be extremely homogeneous. It certainly is not feasible to elicit all the details of the attributes of all agents in a system and enter them into simulations, and for practical reasons agents may have to be homogenized to a certain extent. However, the heterogeneity of real-life agents cannot dismissed. As Miller and Page (2007) remind us, because increased heterogeneity "may substantially alter the system's behavior" (p. 239), realistic simulations of the actual heterogeneity of agents should be taken into account.

Then the question is, to what extent can we elicit/extract the attributes of agents (values, preferences, ability to act, etc.)? A related question is this: Are there methods of eliciting those attributes? A third question is: Once they are elicited, can these attributes be entered into simulations?

My answer to the first question is that it is not possible to elicit/extract all the details of all the attributes of an agent and it would be sufficient, for practical purposes, to elicit only the attributes that are pertinent to the situation under study (e.g., a policy problem). Certainly, what is pertinent and what is not can be problematic. Also small details in an agent's attributes that are ignored in a particular simulation may have significant impacts on the way he/she acts and on the emergent outcomes. For instance, a deeply held subconscious ethnic prejudice an agent holds against another agent may affect the way the first agent votes in a policy situation, which may turn out to be the decisive vote that will impact the macro properties of a policy system. Because we cannot know all the attributes of all the agents, there will always be some level of uncertainty in predicting agents' behaviors, but it still is possible to elicit more details of agents' attributes.

The answer to the second question (Are there methods to elicit agent attributes?) is yes. The cognitive mapping methods I describe in this chapter are designed to elicit/extract the concepts/constructs of individual agents/actors and represent them in mathematically generated charts or maps. [3]

The third question (Can elicited agent attributes be entered into simulations?) is the most challenging one to answer. The methods I describe in this chapter were not designed to generate inputs for simulations; they developed independently of ABS and complexity theory. But I think the agent attributes elicited using the methods I will describe in this section could be used in simulations. The details of how that can be done and the conceptual and technical problems researchers would face in doing so are the problems to be solved in future studies.

Q METHODOLOGY

The roots of Q methodology were in the developments in cognitive psychology in the first half of the 20th century. The methodology was invented by

William Stephenson (1953), whose goal was to understand the subjectivities in human cognition. Like his contemporary George Kelly, who invented the repertory grid methodology, which I will discuss later in this chapter, Stephenson developed methods of eliciting concepts from individual minds and analyzing and mapping them using a combination of qualitative and quantitative methods. Q methodology has been applied in a variety of disciplines, including sociology, anthropology, medicine, and business management since then. Most notably, Steven Brown and his colleagues (S. Brown, 1980, 1993–1994, 2002, 2004; S. Brown, Durning, and Selden, 1999; S. Brown and Robyn, 2004; Durning and S. Brown, 2007) and Maureen Brown and her colleagues (M. Brown, Flowe, and Hamel, 2008) applied the methodology in political science and public policy. Detailed descriptions of the methodology can be found in these sources. I provide only a brief summary here.

A researcher can elicit thoughts, values, interests, or preferences of the participants of a decision-making group using Q methodology. The researcher may use interviews and/or surveys to elicit them or he/she may extract them from textual materials (official reports, newspaper articles, etc.). These thoughts, values, interests, and preferences are expressed in the form of statements, such as "X is a good policy." (Note that this will be different in the repertory grid methodology, with which a research elicits more basic "constructs.") Then the participants are asked to rate these statements using a Likert scale (e.g., a scale with categories from "strongly agree" to "strongly disagree") or similar one that would be more meaningful in the context of the specific study. These ratings are codified to generate mathematical matrices that can be analyzed using statistical methods, typically using a special kind of factor analysis. The factor analytical approach that Q methodology researchers use is called "Q factor analysis." This method differs from the regular "R factor analysis." In the latter approach variables (indicators) are grouped into factors based on their correlations. In Q factor analysis, the ratings of the participants are grouped to reveal the similarities and differences among different participants.

Durning and S. Brown (2007) note that Q methodology can contribute to the study of decision making by helping researchers understand " why and how decisions are made" and "providing information to decision makers about such things as the points of confluence and division among stakeholders" (p. 538). It can also be useful, according to the authors, in exploring "the complexity of thought leading to individual decisions such as whether to vote and for whom" (p. 538). Durning and S. Brown illustrate their points with the example of the board of trustees of a college making the decision to abolish a graduate degree program in Latin. One way to study how this decision is reached would be:

> . . . to understand what was going on in the minds of the trustees when they voted on the issue: What was the configuration of values, beliefs, interests, and information that influenced each vote (the person's decision) on whether the degree program should be eliminated? Such

research would be designed to understand the "decision structures" that led the individuals to decide how to vote on the issue. (p. 548)

Durning and Brown use the term "decision structures" to refer to the combinations of different judgments and considerations by individual decision makers (i.e., their complex, multidimensional cognitive structures).[4] They stress that Q methodology enables researchers to identify the subjective judgments of individual decision makers and their influences on the decisions they make, as well as identifying the differences among different decision makers.

CONCEPT MAPPING

The concept mapping methodology Trochim and his colleagues developed is similar to Q methodology in general but differs in some of its details (Trochim, 1989; Trichim and Cabrera, 2005; Kane and Trochim, 2007). The two are similar in the sense that in both researchers combine qualitative methods of eliciting the values and preferences of participants with quantitative methods of analyzing those values and preferences. Also in both researchers elicit values and preferences in the form of statements, unlike in repertory grids (next section). Concept mapping differs from Q methodology in that the former utilizes the multivariate methods of multidimensional scaling and cluster analysis, whereas the latter uses factor analysis. In concept mapping a researcher also generates visual illustrations of the relations among concepts ("concept maps"); Q methodology does not include a visual tool.

Concept mapping is a group method: Using this method one can generate the "group maps"—collective maps of participants in a group. Trochim and his colleagues developed the method for strategic planning and program evaluation. The details of the methods are described in all three sources I cited above; particularly elaborate descriptions and examples are provided in Kane and Trochim (2007). I provide only a brief description here.

Concept mapping is carried out in multiple steps. First, participants of a planning or evaluation process generate ideas about the policy situation they are facing, using brainstorming. Examples would be "Raise the awareness of the community about the problem" and "Raise necessary funds." Then, these ideas are sorted by each participant into piles and rated using a Likert scale (e.g., from "very important" to "not at all important"). The sorted ideas and their ratings are entered into a matrix to be analyzed in a series of analyses using multidimensional scaling and cluster analysis. After the analyses, a collective map of the participants is generated. In these maps, the statements are plotted typically in two-dimensional charts. (Three- or higher-dimensional charts pose technical challenges.) Then the collective map is shown to the participants in the decision group, and they are asked to interpret it. I should note here that Trochim and his colleagues' method can generate multiple types of charts and requires the expertise of a knowledgeable facilitator to help participants interpret them. The details of generating these different types of charts and illustrations and how they are interpreted are in Kane and Trochim (2007).

Trochim and Cabrera (2005) explain how the method of concept mapping is relevant to complex system studies. They suggest that their method can be used to generate input for ABS and as a simulation itself. It can be used to generate the "rules" that will be applied in an agent-based simulation. In ABS researchers define the "rules of the game" (i.e., interactions among agents, their priorities, etc.) for their simulations on the basis of some theoretical abstraction, such as the rules defined in game theory (e.g., "Prisoner's Dilemma"). The advantage of using concept mapping instead would be to allow the participants of a real system to define the rules as they see them. For instance, they can determine if "raising community awareness" or "raising fund" is more important and/or in what sequence these actions should be taken. Trochim and Cabrera put it thusly:

> [C]oncept mapping essentially turns the traditional modeling and simulation of CAS on its head. Whereas CAS simulations usually involve independent cellular automata that operate under simple rules and lead to adaptivity and emergent phenomena, in the internal case of concept mapping, the emergent property is a set of rules for the system. These rules were derived from a process based on what can be called "meta rules" of the concept mapping method. (p. 11)

Concept mapping can also be used as a simulation itself, according to Trochim and Cabrera. The process of constructing a collective concept map is an interactive group process. Trochim and Cabrera observe that in this process actors participate in a "complex adaptive system" and this systemic process a collective picture of the problematic situation (e.g., a policy satiation) emerges and evolves, just like the emergence and evolution of pictures in ABS. In their own words,

> Following simple rules of brainstorming, synthesis, sorting, rating, and cluster identification and naming, each map is an emergent property of the dynamics of the system. In this regard, concept mapping can be thought of as a "human simulation" that is analogous for complex social systems involving people and their ideas to similar computational simulations of more complex systems involving abstract agents and simple rules. (p. 11)

REPERTORY GRIDS

The repertory grid methodology differs from Q methodology and concept mapping in a fundamental way: The researcher elicits basic *cognitive constructs* from participants, not complete statements. I will explain what these constructs are shortly. It is similar to Q methodology and concept mapping in the sense that once the constructs are elicited, they are rated by participants and then analyzed using a multivariate statistical method. Each participant's constructs are placed in the rows of a grid—hence the name "repertory grids"—and then they are rated by the participant in a similar manner as statements are rated in concept mapping and Q methodology. These ratings are analyzed with multivariate analytical tools like factor analysis, cluster analysis, or multidimensional scaling, again in a manner similar to the analyses in concept mapping and Q methodology.

George Kelly (1955) not only invented the repertory grid methodology but also articulated an epistemological position and a theory of human psychology. He espoused a constructivist epistemology. He called it "constructive alternativism." The ontological assumption that underlies his epistemology is that the universe is a dynamic continuum (pp. 19–20). This assumption has obvious parallels with the dynamic picture of the universe complexity theorists depict. Again similar to Prigogine and others' "endophysical" view of the knowledge of the universe, Kelly thinks that this knowledge cannot be gained by an independent, external observer. He takes the argument one step further: that this knowledge is constructed by the knower, not by the incoming information. The "superodinating view of the knower"—a priori constructions or the gestalt of the mind—determines the nature of the knowledge, not the stimuli coming from external sources. This obviously is a strong constructivist epistemology, which brings Kelly's positions to those autopoiesis, which underscores that the mind is self-referential—it interprets external stimuli in its own way—and the post-structuralisms of Derrida and others, which consider the language a closed, self-referential system (see Chapter 7). As in these other epistemologies, in Kelly's reality is subject to many alternative constructions. However, he differs from them in the sense that he does not think that all constructions are equally valid. In Maher's (1969) interpretation of Kelly, among the "various ways in which the world is construed, some of them are undoubtedly better than others" (p. 15).

Kelly also articulated a psychological theory: "personal construct psychology." It is worth noting that Kelly considered his a theory of personality, not of cognition. He did not see cognition as a realm separate from other psychological and physiological processes (e.g., emotions are not separate from cognitive information processing in his view). Personality is a psychological and biological whole, according to Kelly. This view has obvious parallels with phenomenology, and Kelly was influenced by phenomenology.[5]

Even though half a century has passed since the time it was first articulated, Kelly's theory has a strong following even today. In their literature survey Woehr, Miller, and Lane (1997) found more than 1000 studies that had used Kelly's theory and methodology by the time of their study. In recent decades, also several computerized tools of eliciting and analyzing repertory grids have been developed (see their descriptions in Slater, 1977;

Shaw and Gaines, 1982; Woehr, Miller, and Lane, 1997; Eden and Ackerman, 1998; Hankison, 2004).

In Kelly's theory, humans use "constructs" and "elements" to construe reality (Kelly, 1955, pp. 8–9). Constructs are different from the statements used in Q methodology and concept mapping. A construct is a dichotomous dimension, a frame to "bracket" reality. Human minds hold some common constructs, such as "good versus bad" and "tall versus short." Constructs may also be specific to a person's own construct system. Elements are constructs too, but they are not dichotomous. They are the items, in a person's construct system (e.g., "ice cream cone," "my mother," or "Republican Party"). According to Kelly all the constructs and elements are related to each other at varying degrees in a person's construct system. He calls this the "personal construct space," which is a multidimensional hyperspace. The elements and constructs of a personal construct space can be analyzed mathematically and represented geometrically.[6]

The elements and constructs that are pertinent to a particular situation (e.g., a person's constructs of the environmental problems in his/her community) can be "elicited" (Kelly's own term) using a variety of methods.[7] Then, the person rates his/her elements, which are placed in the columns of a grid, on the constructs, which are placed in the rows of the grid. The matrix generated after these ratings are analyzed using multivariate analytical tools like factor analysis, cluster analysis, and multidimensional scaling. Cognitive maps can be generated using the factor loadings generated in factor analyses. The theory and applications of generating cognitive maps are explained by Slater (1977). Although each person's construct system is unique, the repertory grid methodology allows for comparisons between construct systems of different individuals.[8] They can be compared analytically (using the results of particularly factor analyses) and/or visually (comparing the cognitive maps of individual actors).

A researcher can also assess the cognitive complexity of an individual. Kelly did not define cognitive complexity directly, but his followers did that. His followers particularly used two of his key concepts: *differentiation* and *integration*. Remember that in his theory a person's construct space is a multidimensional hyperspace. The dimensions of this hyperspace (constructs) are not completely independent of each other. To the extent that the constructs are independent, the construct space is differentiated. To the extent that the constructs are grouped together (correlated among themselves), it is integrated.

A person's cognitive complexity is not simply a function of the number of constructs he/she has; we cannot say that the higher the number of constructs, the higher the complexity. (Remember the discussion in Chapter 1 of this book on the definitions of complexity in terms of large numbers.) Instead the "structural complexity" of a person's construct system is a function of the degree of differentiation (the number of constructs it has) and the level of integration among them (meaningful groupings among them) (Crockett, 1965). Fransella and Bannister (1977) point out that a high level of differentiation, without integration of constructs, is not an indication of complexity, but of schizophrenia. They stress that complex thinking requires a high degree of differentiation among constructs (e.g., the ability to hold multiple dimensions of a policy issue), but without some integration (i.e., finding relationships among constructs and grouping them into categories), the cognitive system cannot make sense of the external world in a coherent and consistent manner. The "complex normals," who have large numbers of integrated (organized) constructs, are different from both "dogmatic persons," who hold very few constructs in their minds and are fully integrated (all events are categorized into "good vs. bad "or "holy vs. sinful"), and "schizophrenics," who hold in their minds multitudes of constructs that are not consistently related to each other (Fransella and Bannister, pp. 61–62). Cognitive complexity matters, because a cognitively complex person is more capable of construing broader aspects of reality and thinking innovatively in solving problems (Bieri, Atkins, Briar, Leoman, Miller, and Tripodi, 1966; Adams-Webber, 1969).

The results of two studies in which I applied the repertory grid methodology show that it can be a powerful tool in two respects. First, it can be used as a simulation of a complex adaptive system, as Trochim and Cabrera (2005) used their concept mapping method. In my first study, I applied the repertory grid methdology to facilitate a strategic planning process in a graduate program at a research university (Morçöl and Asche, 1993). As in Trochim and Cabrera's, in this study a collective picture of the problematic situation emerged. But, as I mentioned earlier, repertory grids have the additional capability: With repertory grids a researcher can generate individual cognitive maps, as well as collective maps, and then compare the individual maps for differences and similarities.

In the second study, I elicited the constructs of a group of activists, bureaucrats, and students on environmental problems (Morçöl, 2002, pp. 227–241; 2007). In this case, I took a different approach and used factor analysis to generate the cognitive maps of participants to determine the degrees of cognitive complexity in these individuals. This application of repertory grids yielded valuable insights into the minds of agents/actors. In my application I found, for example, that the personal construct systems of the participants of the study had different degrees of complexity. I illustrated the difference between the cognitive map of a bureaucrat, which was differentiated but not integrated, and that of an activist, which was differentiated and integrated. Following the theoretical implications of Kelly's theory, I concluded that because of the higher complexity of his mind, the activist was more capable of thinking creatively and generating solutions to environmental problems.

Repertory grids offer more capabilities in mapping the cognitive systems of agents/actors of policy systems, compared to Q methodology and concept mapping. One reason for this is the coherent and comprehensive epistemology and theory behind repertory grids, which I summarized very briefly here. This coherence and comprehensiveness helped Kelly's followers to develop more refined concepts and advanced methods within the framework he developed. The other reason is that in repertory grids constructs (and elements, which are a form of constructs) are elicited in their most basic forms. This enables researcher to have access to the core dimensions in an individual's cognition by eliciting his/her constructions in his/her own words. In both Q methodology and concept mapping, statements are collected from cross-sectional surveys, interviews, and/or archival materials; these statements then are presented to participants for them to rate and interpret them. As such, the statements do not reflect directly a participant's thinking. There is also a practical problem in repertory grids. The construct elicitation process is long and cumbersome, compared to the processes in Q methodology and concept mapping. It can work only if participants are willing and patient enough to go through the process.

Like the concept mapping of Trochim and his colleagues, repertory grids have the potential to be used to simulate decision-making processes and to generate inputs for ABS. I mentioned my application of repertory grids in a simulation of decision making earlier. It is more challenging to use repertory grids to generate inputs for ABS. The repertory grid results of the values and preferences of real actors are better representations than the abstracted inputs of homogenous "average actors" that are commonly used in simulations. But there are no examples of the former in the literature yet. The conceptual and methodological challenges in linking repertory grids and ABS can be addressed in future studies.

CHAPTER SUMMARY

A major problem with ABS is that they use abstracted assumptions about agents' values, perceptions, and preferences and about the rules governing their relationships. When these attributes of agents are generalized—when they are "homogenized"—it decontextualizes the knowledge of a complex system. The problem is that when the differences among agents are ignored, the possible impact of those differences on systemic outcomes, through the nonlinear interactions among the agents, will be missed out. Then a simulation of the system's behavior may not be realistic.

One way to deal with the problem of artificiality in ABS is to conduct experiments with real human beings and then enter the generalizations made from these experiments into simulations, but the values entered into simulations are still generalizations/abstractions researchers make from experiments; they do not represent actual human beings directly. I cited three examples of using experimental results in simulations.

Then I discussed a different approach to the artificiality problem: cognitive mapping. By mapping the constructs (preferences, values, etc.) of real human beings, researcher cannot only gain insights into their minds but also potentially use them as inputs into simulations. I described the cognitive mapping methods: Q methodology, concept mapping, and repertory grids. These methodologies have not been used by researchers of complex social systems, but I suggest that they could be valuable in ABS.

The methodologies I described in this chapter emerged from the studies in cognitive psychology in the early 20th century and the developments in quantitative analytical methods, particularly multivariate statistical methods. Gestalt psychologists', Kurt Lewin's, and others works constituted the bases of understanding and measuring the complexities of human cognitive systems. The developments in factor analysis, cluster analysis, and multidimensional scaling were used and advanced by the inventors of Q methodology, concept mapping, and repertory grids.

In Q methodology, the values, perceptions, and preferences of participants of group decision-making processes are elicited using a variety of methods (surveys, interviews, and archival research), and they are sorted and rated by the participants. The results of the factor analyses of the ratings are then interpreted by the participants. Concept mapping uses similar methods in eliciting participants' values, perceptions, and preferences, but it also generates collective cognitive maps of participants.

Repertory grids are different in their approach to eliciting participants' values, perceptions, and preferences: The researcher elicits a person's *constructs* at the most basic level, unlike Q methodology and concept mapping, which elicit *statements* about issues at hand from a variety of sources, including, but not necessarily, participants themselves. This elicitation of constructs at the most basic level has the advantage of generating more authentic representations of cognitive systems, but repertory grids are also difficult to use. Repertory grids have also the capability of generating individual and collective cognitive maps and comparing the complexities of cognitive systems of individual participants.

All three methodologies have the potential to contribute to our understanding of complex social systems at the micro level, and their outputs can be used in micro–macro analyses, particularly in ABS. These potentials can be realized in future studies. Further advancements in cognitive mapping may come from the developments in *fuzzy sets*, or *fuzzy logic* (Kosko, 1993). Khan and Quaddus' (2004) application of this approach in generating "fuzzy cognitive maps" is particularly promising.[9]

Concluding Thoughts

The picture that emerges from the previous chapters is that complexity theory is a way of thinking, a metatheoretical language. It is not a theory of a substantive area of human experience, unlike theories of human psychology, sociology, economy, politics, policy, and the like. It is a set of abstract concepts that can guide our understanding of human experiences in these areas. I made the point in the introduction, and I want to stress it again here, that complexity theory is not a fully articulated theory, not yet. Complexity theory alone cannot help us understand policy processes or any other aspect of human experiences. Its concepts should be synthesized with those of some social theories. I proposed Giddens' and Luhmann's theories for this purpose, particularly in the context of understanding public policy processes.

In the previous chapters my goal was to demonstrate the richness and diversity of the conceptual and methodological tools of complexity theory in a broad framework. The downside of this approach was that I had to leave several "loose ends" in the discussions. I bring together and tighten up some of those loose ends in this chapter. I do not summarize here all the concepts and discussions that appeared in the previous chapters; the summaries at the ends of the chapters serve that purpose. Instead, I present a tighter, but still incomplete, framework for understanding policy processes. I hope this framework will constitute a basis for future theoretical refinements and empirical studies.

I begin with a discussion of what kind of a theory complexity theory is. Then I return to my conceptualization in Chapter 1 that policies are complex systems. I address the implications of the key concept of complexity theory—emergence, self-organization, and system dynamics—in the sections that follow this. These sections are followed by a discussion of governance systems from the perspective I propose in this book. I close the chapter with concluding thoughts.

WHAT KIND OF A THEORY IS COMPLEXITY THEORY?

As I mentioned in the introduction to this book, Christopher Pollitt (2009) challenges complexity theorists and asks what kind of a theory is complexity theory—ontologically, epistemologically, and methodologically? In Part II of this book, I made the point that the most important implications of the core concepts of complexity theory are epistemological. Because of the dynamic interrelatedness of the components of complex systems, their knowledge has to be contextual, generalizations about their properties and behaviors have to be limited, and there will be uncertainties in predicting their future behaviors. In Part III, I proposed a framework in which the methods of complexity theory can be applied.

I want to add here that the contextual and limited nature of the knowledge of complex systems denies the possibility of the ultimate goal of science: making universal generalizations about empirical observations. However, making generalizations is important in any kind of scientific inquiry. Without generalization, there is no theory. Furthermore, without generalization, there is no learning and no sharing of knowledge. We could not even talk about a "complexity *theory*" without making some generalizations. But complexity theory underscores the limitations of the generalizations we can make. Is there a contradiction in these statements?

Not necessarily. The epistemological implications of complexity theory do not prevent us from making generalizations, but they do contradict a specific scientific worldview, the Newtonian/positivist science, and the most prominent model of this worldview: the *deductive-nomological model* of science. The deductive-nomological model was formulated by Carl Hempel (1965) as part of the logical-positivist program of creating a universal methodology for science. This model is important because it encapsulates the universalist aspirations of the Newtonian science. The deductive-nomological model is important also because it was adopted and refined by even some mild critics of logical positivism (e.g., Karl Popper). The deductive-nomological model has penetrated the practice of social scientific research as well. Its applications can be observed in a number of social science research textbooks that are used in a variety of programs of study, from political science, to public policy, public administration, and others.

A researcher who uses the deductive-nomological model first formulates a theory about the phenomenon under study or borrows such a theory from others. This theory would not be a mere set of generalizations, but ideally a law, a set of universal principles from which the researcher extracts more specific hypotheses. The model is *nomological* because the underlying assumption is that law-like generalizations can be made about the phenomena under study. They have to be law-like generalizations about *causal relations* between events, and the hypotheses have to be expressions of causality in more specific forms. This is because science is about *explanation*, and explanation means establishing causal relations between variables. Once the hypotheses are extracted, they should be translated (operationalized) in such a way that the causalities they express can be tested empirically. The process of extracting hypotheses from universal laws and making them empirically testable is the *deductive* part of the model. If the empirical test verifies the *predictions* of the hypothesis, then the abstract universal law it was extracted from has been *verified*.[1] This prediction is a key issue in empirical testing of casual relationships. There must be a chronological order between the causes and effects: The occurrence of the independent variable (cause) in the hypothesis must precede the changes in the dependent variable (effect, outcome). In other words, the outcome should be predictable by the occurrence of the cause.

In the deductive-nomological model, the task is to keep testing hypotheses so that scientists can collectively verify the universal law that governs their field of study; in case it is not verified, their task will be to formulate an alternative universal law. In Hempel's view, although the deductive process—formulating universal laws first and then testing them—is the preferred model, scientists can work *inductively* as well. That is, a researcher may choose to accumulate empirical findings to *build up a theoretical generalization*—ideally and ultimately, a universal law. Regardless of whether this is done deductively or inductively, the ultimate goal of theory building remains the same: making universal, or near-universal, generalizations.

This notion of theory building is a strong undercurrent in the mainstream scientific thinking, particularly among the mainstream theorists of public policy processes. Even though most, if not all, theorists of policy processes acknowledge that it may not be possible to build a universal law of policy processes, theory building remains the driving force of the theoretical and empirical studies in the field. Pollitt's (2009) critique of complexity theory is also based in this theory-building approach. He critiques complexity theorists for not generating empirically testable universal generalizations about policy processes.

The epistemological implications of complexity theory are at odds with this theory-building approach and Hempel's deductive-nomological model. Although complexity theorists make generalizations about the properties and patterns of the dynamics of complex systems, as Pollitt (2009) correctly observes (p. 213), the concepts of complexity theory do not constitute a universal law from which specific hypotheses of causal relations could be extracted and tested. This does not mean, however, that complexity theory is "a bunch of descriptive concepts," as Pollitt (p. 222) suggests. Indeed, as he argues, the concepts of complexity theory have not been articulated into a tightly integrated whole. But they do have some abstract coherence, as I demonstrate in this book. Still these coherent concepts do not constitute a uniform and universal law, or set of laws. As I discussed in Chapter 7, there are differences among complexity theorists as to what specific epistemology complexity theory suggests, or which existing epistemology it should adopt, but no one argues that complexity theory should adopt the deductive-nomological model. Theory building in the sense of reaching universal generalizations about phenomena is not appropriate for complexity theory either.

To clarify my position that neither the deductive-nomological model nor theory building is appropriate for complexity theory, I want to bring in Flyvbjerg's (2001, chap. 3) argument to the discussion. He argues that theory is not possible in social sciences. He rejects the notion that theorization should be the goal of the social sciences, in the sense that it is in the natural sciences. He points out that since the 19th century, many social scientists tried to imitate the natural sciences in developing "context-independent theories" (i.e., universal laws) of the phenomena they studied. He cites specifically August Comte, Karl Marx, and Sigmund Freud, all of whom expressed their faith in developing one day an all-encompassing science of human affairs. They all believed that social scientific facts would cumulate to a point that one big explanation would cover the workings of all human affairs. Flyvbjerg correctly observes that despite all the Herculean efforts by many brilliant minds, the social sciences still do not have a universal theory. As Lichbach (2003) points out, rational choice theorists have tried to create a theory of all social science, with valiant efforts and tremendous amounts of intellectual power, but failed. There is nothing analogous to the Law of Gravity or the Relativity Theory in the social sciences. Nor are there near-universal theories that could be applied in the specific realms of social sciences, for example, "the theory of political science" or "the theory of psychology."

Flyvbjerg argues that this is because the ambition of the social scientists is misguided. This ambition met the problem of the "universality of hermeneutics," he argues. "Natural sciences are also historically conditioned and require hermeneutic interpretation" (p. 28). This, he argues, has been confirmed by chaos and complexity theorists, particularly Ilya Prigogine's views. Prigogine showed that because of the complexity natural phenomena, irreversibility of time, and evolution, theories in natural sciences are not as context independent and cumulative as Comte, Marx, and Freud thought they were. Flyvbjerg makes the point that natural science theories can still be more context independent and cumulative, because their objects are inanimate, whereas the objects of the social sciences are "self-reflecting humans," who "answer back" researchers, and this creates the situation called "double hermeneutic" (p. 32). While researchers are interpreting their "objects," the objects interpret them back. This is why the social scientific knowledge is contextual: "Relevant facts" are "determined by both the researchers' interpretations and by the interpretations of the people whom the researchers study" (p. 33). (I addressed this issue in the context of the discussions on "who defines a system" in Chapter 2.)

I agree with Flybjerg's criticism of the universalist aspirations in the social sciences, but I do not agree with his argument that generalizations are not at all possible in the social sciences. And that is not what complexity theory suggests. It suggests that one can make *context-dependent generalizations* about the properties of complex social systems and the patterns of their transformations but not context-independent theories, universal laws, as the deductive-nomological model would expect. As I noted in Chapter 6, nonlinear relations among a system's elements and between systems, self-organizational systemic processes, the process of emergence, and the coevolutions of systems are so complex that they together create a unique behavioral pattern for each system, which in turn does not allow making precise predictions about a system's behavior or universal generalizations about systems' behaviors. The behavioral patterns of social systems are even less predictable and generalizable and the knowledge of each system's behavioral pattern is more contextual, because they are constituted of the activities of and purposeful and reflective actors. These actors "answer back" researchers, and this creates the situation called "double hermeneutic," as Flyvbjerg puts it. The "context of the observer" plays a role in the process of knowing a complex social system as well, as I noted in Chapter 6.

Complexity theory is a way of thinking, a metatheoretical framework, which can help guide inquiries into the workings of complex social systems. A researcher can generate conceptual models and research questions using this framework, which can be empirically tested. The findings of these inquiries can be used to identify similarities among some systemic relations enhance and/or supplement our understanding of social phenomena but not to verify laws and law-like generalizations.

To help guide inquiries in studying policy processes, I proposed a definition of public policy as a complex system in Chapter 1: *Public policy is an emergent, self-organizational, and dynamic complex system. The relations among the actors of this complex system are nonlinear and its relations with its elements and with other systems are coevolutionary.* In the following sections, I address the components of this definition.

POLICIES AS SYSTEMS

Once public policies are conceptualized as complex systems, it becomes necessary to define or identify a system. I proposed that public policies should be conceptualized as systems that are constituted by the activities of self-conscious human agents and reproduced across time and space, following Giddens' (1984, p. 25) conceptualization of social systems. In his view, systems are not discrete entities, and systemic relationships are better conceptualized in terms of different degrees of systemness. The systemness of public policies can be determined by investigating the degrees of their integration. Giddens' concepts of *social integration* and *system integration* are particularly useful for conceptualizing an inquiry into the question "To what extent policy systems are systems, or to what extent is a particular policy system integrated?" (See Chapter 2 of this book.) The tools of social network analysis are particularly suited to answering this question, as I illustrated in Chapter10.

Even when we accept the guidance of Giddens' conceptualizations of systemness and system integration, however, serious epistemological and methodological problems remain. Many theorists made the point that systems' boundaries are socially constructed. Some complexity theorists brought this perspective into their conceptualizations of complex systems (e.g., Fuchs, 2002; Gerrits, 2008; Gerrits, Marks, and van Buuren, 2009). I discussed the implications of the understanding that systems' boundaries are socially constructed in Chapters 2 and 4. I want to reiterate briefly the issue at hand.

As I discussed in Chapter 4, self-organization is a core concept of complexity theory. Then a pertinent question is how can "self" be defined in a self-organizing complex policy system? Is self defined internally or externally? In other words, do the members/participants/actors of a system define their systems, or is the system defined by its "observers." As abstract as these questions sound, they have significant implications for studying complex policy systems. My general answer to the questions is that both actors and observers play roles in defining systems. Fuchs (2002), Gerrits (2008), and Gerrits, Marks, and van Buuren (2009) agree with this assertion.

Let's look at the actors' side of this multifaceted social construction process first. In Chapter 4, I cited Niklas Luhmann's (1995) theory of social systems, particularly his application of the concept of self-referentiality. I want to reiterate his arguments that social systems are self-referential and radically autonomous from other systems in their environments and that they determine the identities of their members. In other words, social systems not only socially construct their boundaries, but they can also determine how their members/actors define themselves. Luhmann's theory is obviously a very strong view of social construction. It is conceivable that religious cults can define themselves and the identities of their members self-referentially. The question is this: Are policy systems self-referential as well, or to what extent are they self-referential? More specifically, to what extent are they autonomous from their environments, and to what extent are they capable of determining the identities of their members?

The implications of Luhmann's theory are intriguing, but as I proposed in Chapter 4, they should be considered together with Giddens' notions of *systemness* and *degrees of system integration*. It is conceivable that what make some systems more integrated are their self-referential definitions of themselves and the identities of their members. But what also matters, particularly from the perspectives of the "observers" of social systems, is whether the patterned (systemic) activities of their members can be observed. Once again, in Giddens' view, systems are "constituted by the *activities of self-conscious human agents* and *reproduced across time and space*" [emphasis added] (1984, p. 25). To the extent that these patterned and reproduced activities can be observed, we can define particular social and policy systems.

By combining the conceptualizations of Luhmann and Giddens, we should be able to differentiate between strongly integrated, strongly self-referential, and strongly demarcated policy systems, on the one hand, and weakly integrated, weakly self-referential, and weakly demarcated systems. on the other. It is conceivable that policy systems are not as strongly integrated, self-referential, or demarcated, as religious cults. However, the conceptual gauge Luhmann and Giddens provide to use can be used to differentiate between different policy systems. In the context of understanding policy systems, we can ask two questions: To what degree the reciprocity between their actors is reproduced across time and space? To what degree the system is capable of differentiating the relations among its members from those with others? Understanding the ability of a policy system to self-referentially reproduce itself can help us understand its durability and effectiveness. These questions can be answered empirically by the "observers" of systems. The observers should be able to observe the cohesion of the self-images of the members of a policy system, which would require in-depth qualitative studies, and the differentiations in the interdependencies of its members within and outside the system, which can be done using social network analyses.

EMERGENCE: POLICIES AND OUTCOMES

If public policies are defined as emergent and self-organizational complex systems, then the direct and linear causal link between policy actions and outcomes will be broken. As Salzano (2008) puts it, the notion that there is a direct and linear casual relation between policymakers' decisions and their outcomes is "in direct contrast with the complexity concept" (p. 186). But, this does not mean that complexity theory is merely a negative theory; a justification for the belief that everything is so complex that there are no links between events, and therefore nothing could be understood. As I argued in the introductory chapter and demonstrated in the other chapters, it is a positive theory that can help us understand "*why* the output of governance processes often differs from initial expectations" [emphasis added] (Teisman, van Buuren, and Gerrits, 2009a, p. 5) and *how* specifically policy processes work. But complexity theory has multiple implications for epistemology and methodology, in general, and understanding policy processes, in particular, and it is important tease out these implications carefully.

An important epistemological implication of complexity theory is that uncertainties are inevitable in knowing the properties of and predicting future behaviors of complex systems. Policy analysts cannot know policy systems in their entirety, nor can they predict the future behaviors of the systems. This partly because of the multitude of actors involved in these systems and partly because of the nonlinear (uneven, disproportional) nature of the relations among them.

Because of the nonlinear relations among multiple actors who are involved in policy processes and the uncertainties in predicting future behaviors, complex policy systems cannot be controlled by policymakers or governmental authorities. The direction of a policy system and the way it functions do not necessarily follow the original intentions of governmental actors. It may go in an unintended direction, or even may dissipate, as it often happens to complex systems. If policy implementations are not "robust," if the link between policy intents and outcomes is broken, or nonlinear in shape, then is it meaningful at all to talk about "policy effectiveness."

Complexity theorists address the issue of "robustness" of policy systems and systems in general, but there are differences in their conceptualizations and the implications they draw. Bankes (2008), for example, argues that despite the complexity of policy situations and uncertainties in knowing policy actions and their consequences, policymakers can still design or find "robust" policy options ("options that will perform satisfactorily across the widest range of plausible assumptions," p. 123), rather than "optimal" options. Because of the uncertainties in policy processes, policy analysts should adopt a strategy of "adaptive planning," in which policy alternatives would be evaluated iteratively and constantly, he argues. Adaptation is an aspect of Innes and Booher's (2010) view of the "resilience of governance systems" as well (pp. 196–215). For them, however, the issue not how policymakers can design options, but how governmental and non-governmental actors can collaboratively create governance systems. These systems can be both resilient and adaptive, according to Innes and Booher: They can "withstand shocks and surprises, absorb extreme stresses, and maintain [their] core functions, through perhaps in . . . altered form[s]" (p. 205).

Resilience of a system against external shocks is not the only way to define robustness. According to Miller and Page (2007), the robustness of complex systems can be conceptualized in two ways: the "robustness of the entity to perturbations in the environment" and the "robustness of an entity relative to agent details" (pp. 236–237). In the latter conceptualization, the problem is whether and to what extent emergent system properties can remain robust when changes take place at a micro level.

This problem is actually part of a larger problem: the *agency–structure problem*, or the *micro–macro problem*: How do properties and actions of agents/actors affect structural properties and change and vice versa. Complexity theory's answer to the problem is "emergence." Because structural properties of policy systems are emergent, no direct causal linear link can exist between governmental policy actions and policy outcomes. I elaborated on this issue in Chapter 3 by addressing three related questions: (a) Do (and how) macro-level (structural) properties emerge from the interactions among actors? (b) Once emerged do they exist separately of the properties of individual actors (irreducibility)? (c) (How) do these emergent properties have causal effects on the behaviors of individuals (social causation)?

The second question suggests that because the properties of a whole is not reducible to those of its parts—persistent macro patterns do not follow micro processes—the outcomes of public policies ("macro patterns") do not necessarily match the policy goals of governmental actors or those of others. The persistent macro patterns cannot be understood as direct consequences of the intents or actions of policymakers. This brings some degree of humility to our understanding of the policy process: We cannot understand policy processes as direct causal links between governmental decisions and actions, on the one hand, and outcomes, on the other. Also, governmental actors and others should not expect that they will reach their goals exactly. If it is taken to an extreme, this may mean that what we call governmental rules and actions are actually exercises in futility. From the perspective of complexity theory, governmental rules and actions, on the one hand, and what actually happens—"outcomes" or "consequences"— on the other, *are* linked, but in a nonlinear fashion. Policy actions are not exercises in futility. The question of exactly how these nonlinear relationships work in a particular policy process can be answered only empirically. The conceptual and methodological tools I discussed in the previous chapters (Chapters 1 and 10) can be used to study the nonlinear relations between governmental decisions and outcomes.

The notion that public policies are complex systems with emergent properties suggests that governmental actors are among many whose actions influence "policy outcomes." Then we need to turn to the first question above: How do macro-level (structural) properties emerge from the interactions among actors? This is a central question for public policy research from the perspective of complexity theory. Complexity theory offers both conceptual tools—e.g., mechanisms of emergence, as described in Chapter 3—and methods of studying emergence processes—SNA, ABS, and case studies, as described in Chapter 10.

The third question of emergence (How do emergent properties have causal effects on the behaviors of individuals?) is about downward causation. This is an important issue, because we know intuitively, and many decades of sociological and anthropological studies have demonstrated, that social structures can influence/determine the beliefs, attitudes, and behaviors of individuals.

One of the main arguments I make in this book is that complexity theory by itself is not sufficient for us to understand social processes; complexity theorists need the help of some social theories into their conceptualizations. I proposed in Chapter 3 that the three questions of emergence can be brought together with the help of Anthony Giddens' (1984) structuration theory. Giddens states that reproduced *actions of intentional and knowledgeable actors* constitute *social systems*, which exhibit *structural properties*. Systems are created and reproduced through social practices, in a structuration process. In this process structural properties are both the media and outcomes of the practices they recursively organize. They both enable or constrain future behaviors of actors.

With the help of Giddens' conceptualization, complexity theorists can answer a set of questions. For instance, how specifically do the structural properties of complex policy systems emerge in particular cases? Social network analyses, ABS, and qualitative case studies can be used in answering this question. Another question is to what extent the emergent properties of particular complex policy systems are external to—independent of—those of individual actors? Alternatively, to what extent are they internalized by the actors?

Giddens' conceptualization of *span of time-space distanciation* underscores the importance of these questions and can be used to guide empirical studies. He posits that those structures that are more distant, in terms of time and geography, to a particular individual will be more external (constraining) to them and those that are closer to the individual will be more internalized. As I argued in Chapter 3, that this has implications for public policy in the sense that those governmental rules that were made in a distant past or in a distant location will be more external, and constraining, to individual actors. To what extent actors obey the constraints of those external structures is an empirical question. Giddens' concept of space-time distanciation also underscores the importance of participatory rule (policy) making. Conceivably those rules that are made in a more participatory manner are internalized more, and they can be implemented more effectively and robustly, without much revisions. Qualitative case studies would be needed to investigate the span of time-space distanciation in specific policy systems.

SELF-ORGANIZATION

The concept of self-organization has implications and connotations that are explored and discussed extensively in the complexity literature. In Chapter 4, I addressed such implications and connotations and asked questions for future studies on complex policy systems.

Complexity theorists make the observation that self-organization is natural, inherent, and inevitable. This means, in the context of policy systems, that organizational and policy actors self-organize, no matter what managers and governments do. Stewart and Ayres (2001) posit that policy interventions should not be viewed as linear processes that could be directed or controlled by a central authority, a government; instead they should be seen as self-organizational processes in which self-conscious policy actors play roles. Therefore, according to Stewart and Ayres, the aim of a governmental intervention should be to enhance the self-steering capacity of policy systems, not to reach predefined goals or follow predefined paths.

In some assessment of the self-organizational nature of policy systems, there is an implicitly positive normative view of self-organization. In this view, self-organization is closely associated with democracy, equality, participation, and the like. But, as I discussed in Chapter 3, self-organizational processes can generate inequalities and hierarchies as well. Epstein and Axtell (1996) demonstrated in their ABS that skewed wealth distributions can emerge from the activities of self-organizing agents. Barabási and Albert (1999) mathematically demonstrated that networks with power-law distributions—those with few central and more powerful actors and many peripheral and less powerful actors—can emerge self-organizationally. With the help of the findings of these prior works, complexity theorists can investigate empirically the outcomes of self-organizational policy processes: Do they (or under what conditions do they) generate democratic and participatory structures? And do they (or under what conditions do they) generate hierarchies and skewed distributions?

A related issue is that not all systems are equally self-organizational. Then the question is do some systems have more *self-organizational capacities?* If so, what are the characteristics of those systems with more self-organizational capacities? Ostrom's (2005) and Geyer and Rihani's (2010) conceptualizations provide some bases for future studies to answer these questions. Ostrom observes that individual actors are more likely to self-organize when the issue at hand is salient to individual actors, they have a common understanding of the issues, there is a good chance to improve the common resources, indicators to measure and assess improvements in conditions are available, outcomes are relatively predictable, there is not much external interference, and there is prior experience among the actors and local leadership (pp. 244–245). According to Geyer and Rihani, those nations with basic democratic and market structures and an appreciation of the value of social capital have more self-organizational capacities; these are the nations that develop economically more quickly (pp. 131–137).

Another important question is this: What is the role of the government, or governmental agencies, in self-organizing policy systems? Is the government one of many actors that has more or less equal capacity and power? Or does it play a special role, different from the roles other actors can play? Scholars of governance networks already asked these questions. Rhodes (1997a), Kettl (2002), Agranoff (2007), and Klijn and Snellen (2009) all agree that there are multiple governmental actors who play roles in larger governance processes, along with non-governmental actors. It is debated to what extent the roles of governmental actors are special in governance processes, such as steering non-governmental actors. Social network analyses and ABS can be used to answer these questions.

The observation that policy systems are self-organizational does not mean that they are isolated from their environments. There is an extensive discussion in the systems theory literature on whether, to what extent, and in what ways systems may be closed to their environments (see Chapters 2, 4, and 5). Even closed system theories, such as autopoiesis theory (Chapter 4), do not suggest that systems could be completely isolated from their environments, other systems. Systems self-organize in relationships with others. Then the question is how do systems relate to each other? For instance, what is the nature of the relationship between a policy system with other policy systems, other social systems, and natural systems? These questions can be answered better in the context of understanding system dynamics.

SYSTEM DYNAMICS

In Chapter 5, I discussed conceptualizations of system dynamics. The first and most general implication of complexity theory is that the natural tendency of a system is not toward stasis, or equilibrium, but away from it. This implication counters the foundational assumptions of neoclassical economics that economic systems tend toward equilibria. It also counters the notion that public policy problems can be "solved" in the sense that social actors would reach a state of equilibrium. Public policy processes are actually dynamic; new problems are created as others are "solved." Most policy theorists, if not all, would agree with this proposition. The real contributions of complexity theory are encapsulated in its more specific implications.

The second, and more specific, implication of complexity theory is that systemic change is endogenous. External events may trigger changes, but they are not the "causes" of systemic change. Complexity theorists differ in their views on whether systems are open or closed, but they all agree that systemic change has something to do with the internal dynamics of systems. In Luhmann's (1995) view social systems, which are self-referential and closed, may only be "perturbed" by external events, but they cannot be shaped by these events. These systems change in their own terms, based on their images of themselves. In Prigogine's open system view, systems exchange energy and information with their environments constantly, but still the source of system dynamics is within them (Prigogine and Stengers, 1984; Prigogine 1996). These open systems change naturally and endogenously. Their tendency is not toward equilibrium; they evolve toward far-from-equilibrium conditions, at which point dynamics of change are intensified.

The notion that systemic change is endogenous has implications for the relations between systems and the relations between a system and its actors. The environments of systems are other systems. Systems coevolve with these other systems. Gerrits and his colleagues' works put the issue of the coevolution of policy systems with other social systems and with natural systems on the agenda of policy studies (Gerrits, 2008, 2010; Gerrits, Marks, and van Buuren, 2009). I summarized their observations and discussed and their implications in Chapter 5. The most important implication is that policymakers should not view natural systems as malleable inanimate objects that could be exploited or pushed in the directions they desire but as self-organizing natural systems that "answer back" human interventions into them. In the long run social and natural systems coevolve. Understanding how these coevolutionary processes work should be part of policy analytical studies.

Although the changes at the micro and macro levels of systems are related, these changes are not proportional, synchronous, or parallel. A system's structural properties can remain stable, despite the changes in its elements. In fact, this is the definition of emergence, according to Holland (1998): Emergent macro properties persist despite continual turnover in their constituents (p. 7). Emergence of macro properties in policy systems can be investigated empirically, as I illustrated with an example in Chapter 9.

The coexistence of structural stability and change/turnover at the micro level is an important issue that is relevant to studying complex policy systems. To help conceptualize this coexistence, I brought Luhmann (1995) into the discussion again in Chapter 5. Luhmann suggests that stability and change are not mutually exclusive; in order for self-referential social systems to maintain their structures, they need to replace and/or renew their elements and the relations among them. In other words, stability at the macro level is ensured by changes at the micro level. Possible implications of Luhmann's view can be investigated empirically for policy systems. The question is this: Do, or to what extent, policy systems reproduce themselves by replacing their elements at the micro level?

Gerrits (2008) proposes a dichotomous conceptualization for understanding policy systems: "singular policy action systems," which are closed and self-referential, and "composite policy action systems," which are open and dissipative (p. 213). Gerrits' study indicates that singular policy systems try to maintain their structural stability by selecting the participants that "buy into" the pre-established self-image of the system, which is set by the leadership. They keep the members who support the pre-established views of the leadership and ignore and/or exclude those who have different views, whereas composite policy actions systems are open to differing views and dissent and they are more dynamic in the sense that they change their structures to adapt external events. In Gerrits' view composite policy systems are more effective compared to singular systems. The types of the relations between policy systems and their elements and their consequences in terms of effectiveness should be the topics of future conceptualizations and empirical studies.

MOVING FORWARD WITH COMPLEXITY THEORY

The view of complexity theory I presented in this book is partial, in both meanings of the word: incomplete and subjective. My goal was to articulate the concepts that are commonly associated with complexity theory into a framework, as comprehensively as possible, but also as cohesively as possible. And I did so in the context of understanding policy processes. Because the concepts of complexity theory have been conceived by different thinkers in different contexts, and because there are different, and sometimes conflicting, interpretations, it is not possible to articulate all of them in one big theory. I left some concepts that are popular among many complexity researchers, such as path dependency and fitness landscapes, out of my discussions. I interpreted the concepts I used in manners that others may disagree with. The reviewers of the earlier drafts of my manuscript did disagree with some of my interpretations and found omissions in them. Their critiques and suggestions were most valuable to me and I made several revisions in the text accordingly, but I did not follow all of their advice. So the resultant text remains my partial interpretation.

What I present in this book is also an incomplete picture of complexity theory. Complexity theory should remain incomplete because of its own logic. If reality is complex and dynamic and the future behaviors of complex systems are not precisely predictable, then there will always be unknowns. New concepts and conceptualizations will be required to grasp reality, but only partially. Having noted this, I hope, the conceptualizations and examples I presented in this book are useful for understanding policy processes better, and they offer some guidance for future conceptualizations and empirical studies.

I want to conclude with Joshua Epstein's words, which reflect my thinking exactly:

> No one who is still growing intellectually ever feels that he has said all he can in a book. I suppose, therefore, that I should take consolation in the sense of incompleteness I feel in arbitrarily closing the discussion at this point; it is a sign of life. (Epstein, 2006, p. 345)

Notes

NOTES TO THE PREFACE

1 For this, see Elinor Ostrom's tribute to Robert Axelrod (Ostrom, 2007a) and her Nobel Prize acceptance speech at http://www.nobelprize.org/media-player/index.php?id=1223&view=1.

NOTES TO THE INTRODUCTION

1. As of the writing of this book, there were still a significant number of US forces in Iraq, although they were not directly engaged in combat. President Obama set as his goal to pull all US forces out of Iraq by the end of 2011.
2. I borrow the concept of integration from Anthony Giddens (1984). I will draw on Giddens' understanding of systems and structuration heavily in Chapters 2 and 3.
3. See Giddens' notion of system integration in the next chapter.
4. One can find the best examples of the notion of inner causal mechanisms in Marxist theory, which was the primary inspiration for the initial formulations of critical realism, or theoretical realism. In Marxist political economy, it is theorized that different "modes of production" (e.g., feudal, capitalist, socialist modes of production) have different mechanisms, which may not be immediately visible when a researcher studies an economic system. The invisibility of these mechanisms does not diminish their fundamental importance, however. The task of a Marxist theorist is to formulate appropriate concepts that will enable him/her to penetrate the images on the surface of an economy and access these inner mechanisms.
5. Pollitt's critique is pertinent particularly to the contributors of *Managing Complex Governance Systems* (2009). Pollitt cites their claim that complexity theory is critical realist and argues that unless they describe the causal mechanisms of governance processes from the perspective of complexity theory, their claim will not be valid.

NOTES TO CHAPTER 1

1. In his theory of social systems, which I will discuss in the coming chapters, Luhmann (1995, pp. 24–28) takes the position that complexity is a function of the mismatch between observing (knowing) systems (individual brains or collective minds) and their environments. The environment is always more

complex than the image of it in the knowing system and that is why we perceive things as complex.

2. An extensive explanation of fractal dimensions is beyond the scope of my discussions in this book. The reader can find many good explanations and illustrations in other sources (e.g., Briggs, 1992; Peitgen, Jürgens, and Saupe, 2004; Batty, 2007). Briefly, an object with fractal dimensions (e.g., a coast line) is more complex than another object with Euclidian dimensions (e.g., a perfect sphere). That is because the Euclidian object can be described perfectly with a simple formula. For example, the volume of a sphere can be perfectly described with the formula , where π is the constant pi and r is the radius. But the volume of a fractal object is infinite and only approximate calculations can be made for a selected level of magnification of the view of the object. In Mitchell's (2009) words, "the fractal dimension quantifies the number of copies of a self-similar object at each level of magnification of that object. Equivalently, fractal dimension quantifies how the total size (or area or volume) of an object will change as the magnification level changes" (p. 108).

3. The other two definitions Mitchell cites are "complexity as size," which I discussed above, and "complexity as degree of hierarch." This latter definition is based on Herbert Simon's notion that those systems with multiple levels (subsystems nested within larger systems) are more complex than the ones without multiple levels.

4. For detailed discussions of different k values and other assumptions that go into iterative solutions of the logistic equation, see Casti, 1994, pp. 37–40, 93–97; or Morçöl, 2002, pp. 159–162.

5. Capra (1996, p. 44) notes that the Russian systems philosopher Alexander Bogdanov used the terms system and complex interchangeably in his classification of systems. He identified three kinds of systems: "organized complexes," "disorganized complexes," and "neutral complexes."

NOTES TO CHAPTER 2

1. In fairness to the author, I must also mention that he does discuss non-reductionist versions of systems understanding as well. For instance, he makes references to von Bertalanffy, but these references look more like appendages to the main body of the work in the book.

2. Note the singular use of the term "system" in von Bertalanffy and the plural "systems" in Capra. This difference does not connote a theoretical difference, but only a semantic one. Von Bertalanffy (1972) explains that he started out with the singular usage, and the plural usage was adopted by others later. He does not attribute a particular theoretical significance to his singular usage, nor does he suggest that it is different from the plural usages.

3. In his more detailed etymological discussion of the word *synhistanai*, Dieter (1994) notes that it is closely related to the Greek word *genesis*, which means coming into being (generation) of animals. *Synhistanai*, he says, refers to the beginning of the process of genesis. More generally, *synhistanai* can be interpreted as "the first step in the process of actualizing the potentiality of matter" (p. 234).

4. In von Bertalanffy's (1968) more technical explanation, "[s]*ummativity in the mathematical sense* means that the change in the total system obeys an equation of the same form as the equations for the parts" [emphasis in original] (p. 68).

5. For additional information on the long history of systems thinking, I recommend Flood's (1999) excellent account of the works of von Bertalanffy, Beer, Ackoff, Checkland, Churchman, and Senge.

6. For an elaboration on this point, see Koliba, Meek, and Zia (2011).
7. Koliba, Meek, and Zia (2011, chap. 7) demonstrate and illustrate with examples that governance networks have systems characteristics. They also note some of the differences between the systems and network conceptualizations in the literature. These minor differences are not pertinent to my discussions in this book.
8. For details of the assumptions and propositions of the Newtonian science, see Morçöl (2002, chap. 1).

NOTES TO CHAPTER 3

1. For summary descriptions of all these theories, see Sabatier (2007a).
2. For detailed accounts of the histories of the concepts of holism and emergence, I recommend von Bertalanffy's (1972), Capra's (1996, pp. 16–30), and Sawyer's (2005, pp. 27–99) narratives, particularly the last one. It is more detailed than the others. The following is summarized from these three sources unless specified otherwise.
3. I will come back to this issue of the reactions to reductionism in the 19th century in Chapter 7, when I discuss the rise of phenomenology.
4. Capra (1996) credits C. D. Broad, an emergentist philosopher, for coining the term "emergent properties" in the early 1920s. By this term Broad meant "those properties that emerge at a certain level of complexity but do not exist at lower levels," according to Capra (p. 29).
5. I highlighted the first sentence in this quote. I will come back to its potential implications. If one cannot "always trace the steps of the process," does this mean that there is a practical difficulty or an ontological boundary here that prohibits us from accessing the information about steps of the process?
6. Adam Smith's *Wealth of Nations* was originally published in 1776.
7. Thatcher said this in the context of arguing against individuals relying on government for solving their problems. The following is the full text of what she said:

   I think we've been through a period where too many people have been given to understand that if they have a problem, it's the government's job to cope with it. "I have a problem, I'll get a grant." "I'm homeless, the government must house me." They're casting their problem on society. And, you know, *there is no such thing as society. There are individual men and women, and there are families.* And no government can do anything except through people, and people must look to themselves first. It's our duty to look after ourselves and then, also to look after our neighbour. People have got the entitlements too much in mind, without the obligations. There's no such thing as entitlement, unless someone has first met an obligation. [emphasis added] (*Women's Own*, October 31, 1987) http://briandeer.com/social/thatcher-society.htm)

8. Differential persistence, a concept of evolutionary biology, has been applied in other areas that were influences by evolutionary theories in biology, most notably evolutionary archeology (e.g., Leonard, 2001; O'Brien and Lyman, 2002; Murrell, 2007).
9. The concept of scale-free networks emerged long before Barabási and Albert's (1999) work. In his study of the citations of scientific papers, de Solla Price (1965) showed that the number of citations these papers received could be represented with a power law distribution. He did not however use the term "scale-free network," which was coined later by Barabási and his coleagues. The first publication this term appeared seems to be Barabási and

Albert (1999). In a later paper, de Solla Price (1976) proposed a mechanism to explain the occurrence of power laws in citation networks, which he called "cumulative advantage," which is more commonly known as "preferential attachment" today.

10. It may seem that these assumptions are derived from a passage I quoted from Adam Smith' *Wealth of Nations* earlier in this chapter. However, Smith's views are more complex than that. Especially in his earlier book *The Theory of Moral Sentiments* (1759), he clearly makes the point that not all human behaviors are self-interested and independent of social or historical influences.

11. For these critiques and responses to them, see Edwards and Tversky (1967), Hogarth and Reder (1986), and Friedland and Roberston (1990).

12. Giddens captured the attentions of a few complexity and network theorists and researchers, like Cohen, Riolo, and Axelrod (2001), Klinj (2001), Fuchs (2002), and Zaheer and Soda (2009). They applied parts of his theory and in different ways.

NOTES TO CHAPTER 4

1. I should note here that Kauffman's usage of the terms like chaotic and complex do not match exactly the way I used them in the logistic equation example in Chapter 1. In his terminology, chaos is more like what some other chaos theorists would call randomness.

2. Autopoiesis is a pseudo-ancient Greek word, formed through the conjunction of two ancient Greek words, "auto" meaning "self" and "poiesis" meaning "creation" or "production" (Maturana, 1980, p. xvii).

3. I took the liberty to replace the word "machine" Maturana and Varela use with "system" in this quote. They use the term machine, because they conceptualize all systems as machines. But the following discussion in their book shows that their conceptualizations of machines are not different from the conceptualization of systems I use in this book. I chose to use the term system to prevent any confusion.

4. They use the term "closed domain of relations" (p. 88).

5. The reader will remember from Chapter 3 that there are strong parallels here with John Holland's (1998) definition of emergence: Emergent macro properties persist despite continual turnover in their constituents (p. 7).

6. This book was originally published in in 1961.

7. Ostrom (2005) defines common pool resources as follows: "A common pool resource, such as a lake, an ocean, an irrigation system, a fishing ground, a forest, the Internet, or the stratosphere, is a natural or man-made resource from which it is difficult to exclude or limit users once the resources is provided by nature or produced by humans" (p. 79).

NOTES TO CHAPTER 5

1. Note that unlike Bak and Chen, whose model of self-organized criticality suggests that the structural properties of a system, like the sand pile, do not change, Luhmann suggests that both stability and change are possibilities at the structural level.

2. His term "edge of chaos" is similar to Prigogine's "far from equilibrium." Both authors refer to the conditions that are not at equilibrium, those conditions in which systems are in dynamic states and inclined to change.

3. An interesting example of this singularity in policy actions was reported by Gillis (2010). He notes that in the US Congress, the representatives and senators who are inclined to downplay the connections between carbon dioxide emissions by human beings and global warming keep inviting to Congressional hearings the global warming skeptics, who are a small minority in the scientific community. These representatives and senators keep ignoring the majority of scientists who do think that global warming is real, it is caused by human beings' carbon dioxide emissions, and it will have dire consequences. This singular policy action system self-referentially reproduces itself and does not allow the federal government to make a major policy change in this area.

NOTES TO CHAPTER 6

1. Not all of these issues are epistemological. Whether the universe is deterministic or not is actually an ontological question: It is about the existence and nature of being, not about the nature of knowledge. I will not a make distinction between ontological and epistemological questions in this and following chapter. Although ontological assumptions are obviously very important, my main focus is on epistemology in this book, and I will address ontological questions only if they relate to epistemological questions.
2. Pierre Simon Laplace, a French mathematician who lived in the late 18th and early 19th centuries, expressed this best in his conjecture called "Laplace's demon." "He imagined a demon who would know all the details of the entities and events in the universe and who would be able to predict and retrodict all events with perfect precision. Laplace's demon would be able to do it, because it possessed the complete understanding of Newton's laws and had the knowledge of the current position and momentum of every particle in the universe" (Morçöl, 2002, pp. 61–62).
3. For details of these debates and findings in quantum mechanics on the nature of subatomic particles, see Morçöl (2002, chap. 5).
4. I discussed the relations between chaos and complexity theories at some length (Morçöl, 2002, chap. 6).
5. I elaborated on the philosophical and historical underpinnings of the Newtonian/positivist assumptions of objectivism, universalism, and methodological unity elsewhere (Morçöl, 2002).
6. The reader will remember from the logistic equation example in Chapter 1 that the small change in the value of k from 3.5 to 3.7 makes a big difference in the system's behavior and predictability (see Figures 1.4c and 1.4d).

NOTES TO CHAPTER 7

1. The contents of this section are summarized from Kerby (1993) and Radloff (1993), unless specified otherwise.
2. My descriptions of the theories here are extracted from an earlier work (Morçöl, 2002, chap. 7). The most authoritative and comprehensive account of the history of cognitive science I am familiar with is Gardner's (1985), which I cited extensively in my earlier work. Gardner points to 1956 as the date cognitive science was born (p. 28). He defines it as a combination of the insights from philosophy, linguistics, anthropology, neuroscience, artificial intelligence, and psychology (see particularly Chapter 3 in his book).

NOTES TO CHAPTER 8

1. For an example of the debates on King, Keohane, and Verba's book, see the symposium articles on this book in the June 1995 issue of the *American Review of Political Science* 89(2). For an example of broader debates on methodological issues, including King, Keohane, and Verba's position, see Schram and Caterino (2006) and Ragin (2008).
2. For descriptions of a wide variety of qualitative/interpretive methods, see Morgan (1983) and Yanow and Schwartz-Shea (2006).

NOTES TO CHAPTER 9

1. Note that my reference here is to one-stage regression analysis. Regression analysis is versatile and has multiple forms. Endogeneity can be modeled in multi-stage regression analyses, such as path analysis and in more advanced analyses like structural equation modeling.
2. For a more extensive discussion of the assumptions and applications of the experimental methods and regression analysis, see Morçöl (2002, pp. 37–54).
3. This process of iterations can be illustrated best with interactive software. Such an illustration can be found at http://classes.yale.edu/fractals/; accessed on November 3, 2010.
4. It is not easy to describe the Mandelbrot set with words. Its images that are generated iteratively can be found at http://classes.yale.edu/fractals/; accessed on November 3, 2010.
5. Different authors use different names for the same method of plotting "chaotic" data points. Stroup (1997) uses the term "return map" (pp. 136–137). Kaplan and Glass (1995) use the terms "return plot," Poincaré return map," and "phase plane" interchangeably (pp. 303–308). Gleick (1987) describes "phase space" diagrams (p. 50), "attractors" (p. 140), and "Poincaré maps" (pp. 142–143) somewhat differently from each other. Indeed there are some subtle differences in how "chaotic" patterns are plotted, but those differences and why different authors use different names are not of importance to my discussions here.
6. For interactive illustrations of how this dynamism works in system dynamic models, see, for example, the New Product Adoption Model ("System Dynamics" at Wikipedia, http://en.wikipedia.org/wiki/System_dynamics; accessed on November 8, 2010).
7. See his Web site at http://mitsloan.mit.edu/faculty/detail.php?in_spseqno=SP000041&co_list=F, accessed on February 18, 2012.
8. For descriptions of the modeling techniques in these areas and examples, see Ruth and Hannon (1997), Deaton and Winebrake (2000), and Hannon and Ruth (2001).

NOTES TO CHAPTER 10

1. Depending on their research objectives, researchers may use organizations and other collective entities (family, administrative unit, etc.) as their units of analyses. Then those collective entities are treated as "individuals" in analyses.
2. This assumption is fundamental for most statistical analyses. The independent-sample t-test and ordinary least-squares regression analysis are examples.

When the independence assumptions is violated, as in paired samples (e.g., before and after measurements) or time-series data (time-dependent measurements), different tests are employed, for example, paired-sample t-test or autocorrelation analyses.

3. *Degree centrality* measures the extent to which an actor connects to other actors and *degree centralization* is a measure of the distribution of degree centralities in a network (Knoke and Yang, 2008, pp. 63–64). *Closeness centrality* measures the extent to which each actor is close to the other actors in the network and *closeness centralization* is a measure of the dispersion of closeness centralities in a network (pp. 65–67). *Betweenness centrality* measures the degree to which each actor mediates relations among other actors, and *betweenness centralization* is a measure of the extent to which there are central actors by this definition in a network (pp. 67–69).

4. In our analyses we intentionally included individual, organizational, and collective actors. We identified 69 actors and 289 links among them in 1990, and 68 actors and 133 links among them in 1999. The numbers of actors and links in the charts in Figure 9.1 are far lower than these figures because of the truncations I made.

5. In our study we used the measure of "total degree centrality" to rank the actors. Only the top five actors are displayed in these charts. They are the ones with the highest total degree centrality scores.

6. We found that the total centralization score remained between 0.83 and 0.94 on a scale of 0 to 1, between the years 1990 and 2009.

7. Laumann and his colleagues' study was originally published in 1989. Wasserman and Faust and Knoke and Yang refer to this earlier edition.

8. For the details of these methods, see Laumann and his colleagues' study and Knoke and Yang (2008).

9. I will not discuss the details of these strategies here. They can be found in Laumann and his colleagues' chapter. A more updated version is in Knoke and Yang (2008, pp. 15–20).

10. Marsden and Friedkin's separation of social influence from intentional influence is important. Intentional application of influence is better defined as "power."

11. WY is a vector "whose elements are weighted combinations of values of Y," i.e., the values of other actors (Doreian, 1992, p. 302).

12. For the different kinds of relational ties that can be used in SNA, see Wasserman and Faust (1994, pp. 18, 37).

13. Brief information about ORA and associated software and detailed documents on the software can be found at the Web site of the Center for Computational Analysis of Social and Organizational Systems (CASOS) at Carnegie Mellon University (http://www.casos.cs.cmu.edu; accessed on November 17, 2010).

14. An extensive and updated discussion of his simulations and their theoretical implications can be found in Schelling (2006).

15. For more detailed descriptions of cellular automata, see Casti (1994, pp. 214–219) and Michaels (1995, p. 36).

16. See my discussion on connectionist theory/models in Chapter 7.

17. In this regard, neural network simulations are similar to social network analyses, where relational ties can be assigned different weights.

18. In this game two prisoners are locked up in two separate cells. "Each has two choices, namely cooperate and defect. Each must make the choice without knowing what the other will do. No matter what the other does, defection yields a higher payoff than cooperation. The dilemma is that if both defect, both do worse than if both had cooperated" (Axelrod, 2006, pp. 7–8).

19. See Epstein and Axtell (1996) as an example of this usage.
20. Note that the main focus of Ciller's discussion is the way the human mind works. He likens mental processes to Baudrillard's definition of simulations and asserts that the realism of simulations is not in their one-to-one representations of the units in reality but their generalized representation.
21. NASA's Goddard Institute for Space Studies, as reported at http://www.currentresults.com/Environment-Facts/changes-in-earth-temperature.php; accessed on April 26, 2011.
22. These results can be sees in a Harris poll conducted in 2009: http://wattsup-withthat.com/2009/10/22/harris-poll-europeans-tend-to-care-more-strongly-about-climate-change-than-americans/; accessed on April 26, 2011.
23. See also Epstein's (2006, chap.7) simulation of the retirement behavior of individuals (at what age they would retire under different conditions), where there were no "representative agents." Instead a mix of "fully informed optimizers" and less informed agents are included in the simulations, as well as the networks relations among these agents.
24. He develops his argument in the context of a discussion of linearity and non-linearity in modeling. He argues that the issue for complexity theorists is not whether or not to use linear models. They should not dismiss linear models at the expense of nonlinear models in their analyses. A linear model can be useful in understanding at least some parts of reality, and a well-developed linear model is better than a poorly constructed nonlinear model. The issue, according to Richardson, is the mindset ("culture") in which linearity and nonlinearity are used (pp. 44–46).
25. It is worth noting here that Ragin (1987, 2000, 2008) stresses that the distinction some make between quantitative and qualitative methods is quite artificial. His main goal is to synthesize the strengths of both.
26. Flybvjerg (2001) placed the issue of case studies and making generalizations with them at the center of the methodological debates in the social sciences. He makes two potentially conflicting arguments. On the one hand, he argues that making generalizations and thus formulating theoretical explanations should not be the primary purpose of the social sciences, because of the "hermeneutics blocks" that prevent researchers to make generalizations (such as the fact that human agents are reflective and highly complex; pp. 25–37). On the other hand, he posits, carefully chosen "critical cases" and "paradigmatic cases" are suitable for making generalizations (p. 73–81). Flybvjerg's book and the edited volume that continued the discussion on his ideas and positions (Schram and Caterino, 2006) made significant contributions to the literature by stirring up debates on the roles of generalization, theory, and explanation in the social sciences. The details of the arguments and counter arguments made in these debates are beyond the scope of my discussions here, but one can reach the conclusion that although some limited generalizations can be made from carefully crafted case studies, making generalizations still is not the primary purpose of case study research. Case study research is good primarily for understanding the context of individual cases.

NOTES TO CHAPTER 11

1. In the conceptualizations of the theorist I cite here, as well as in most other psychologists' conceptualizations, cognition (or the mind) is not an entity separate from personality or the body.

2. The title of Maturana and Varela's book is *Autopoiesis and Cognition: The Realization of the Living* (1980). The first half of the book is about the "biology of cognition." In the second part the authors extend the applications of their theory to the "organization of the living."

3. I use the terms "cognition" and "cognitive" in their broadest meanings, in the meanings Gardner (1985) uses them. In Gardner's definition "cognitive science" is a comprehensive approach in understanding how the human mind works. Cognition, in this cognitive science perspective, is not merely about how information is processed in the brain. It involves emotions, as well as rational information processing (Damasio, 1994, p. 199). Cognition is a complex system of interactions within the brain and between the brain and its biological and social environments. Understanding the mind requires bringing together the insights from philosophy, linguistics, anthropology, neuroscience, artificial intelligence, and psychology (Gardner, chap. 3).

4. Durning and Brown note that they borrowed the term "decision structure" from Harold Lasswell and that this concept is similar to Getalt psychologists' concept of schemata and others' "frames" and "narratives."

5. Butt (n.d.) notes, however, that his relationship with phenomenology was tenuous and that later in his life, after the publication of his magnum opus *The Psychology of Personal Constructs* (1955), he moved away from phenomenology.

6. Note that Kelly's conceptualization is similar to Lewin's "life space." He acknowledges this similarity (Kelly, 1955, p. 279)

7. These methods evolved over time, from using index card to note elements and constructs on them and rating them on paper "grids" to various computer applications that allow entering elements, constructs, and their ratings on the screen and analyzing the ratings instantaneously.

8. The basis of these comparisons is Kelly's (1955) view that "To the extent that one person employs a construction of experience which is similar to that employed by another, his psychological processes are similar to those of the other person" (p. 90).

9. In *fuzzy logic* categories are not discrete. This is contrast to the classical set theory in which categories are discrete and mutually exclusive. A swan may be either "black" or "white," for example. In fuzzy logic a swan may be "somewhat black" (black to a certain degree). Kosko and other proponents of fuzzy logic argue that their conceptualization is a better reflection of real entities and their relations.

NOTES TO THE CONCLUSION

1. In the Popperian "falsificationist" version of the model, universal laws (universal propositions, generalizations) cannot be verified; they can only be falsified. If a hypothesis is supported in an empirical test, then the researcher has only failed to falsify the universal law. The Popperian version of the model diverges from the verificationist version in important ways, but the principles of making universal generalizations and testing them in empirical studies remain the same.

References

Adam, S., and Kriesi, H. (2007). The network approach. In P. A. Sabatier (Ed.), *Theories of the policy process* (2nd ed.) (pp. 129–1540. Cambridge, MA: Westview Press.

Adams-Webber, J. R. (1969). Cognitive complexity and sociality. *British Journal of Social and Clinical Psychology, 8*, 211–216.

Adamson, J. (1993). Deconstruction. In I. R. Makaryk (ed.), *Encyclopedia of contemporary literary theory* (pp. 25–31), Toronto: The University of Toronto Press.

Agranoff, R. (2007). *Managing within networks: Adding value to public organizations.* Washington, D.C.: Georgetown University Press.

Agranoff, R., and McGuire, M. (1999). Managing in network settings. *Policy Studies Review, 16*, 18–38.

Ahmad, R. (2008). *A formal framework for engineering intelligent agents-based systems.* (Ph.D. dissertation), Southern Illinois University at Carbondale.

Allen, P. M. (1982). Evolution, modeling, and design in a complex world. *Environment and Planning B, 9*, 95–11.

Allen, P. M. (1997). *Cities and regions as self-organizing systems: Models of complexity.* Amsterdam: Gordon and Breach Science Publishers.

Anderson, P. (1972). More is different. *Science, 177*, 393–396.

Anderson, P. (1999). Complexity theory and organization science. *Organization Science, 10*, 216–232.

Argonne National Laboratory (n.d.). As a scientist: General science archive. Argonne National Laboratory, U.S. Department of Energy (*http://www.newton.dep.anl.gov/askasci/gen99/gen99810.htm*; accessed on December 15, 2010).

Axelrod, R. (1995). The convergence and stability of cultures: Local convergence and global polarization. Working paper, 95–03–028, Santa Fe Institute, New Mexico.

Axelrod, R. (1997). *The complexity of cooperation: Agent-based models of competition and collaboration.* Princeton: Princeton University Press.

Axelrod, R. (2006/1984). *The evolution of cooperation* (rev. ed.). Cambridge, MA: Basic Books.

Axelrod, R. (2007). Simulation in the social sciences. In J.-P. Rennard (Ed.), *Handbook of research on nature-inspired computing for economics and management* (pp. 90–99). Hershey, PA: Idea Group Reference.

Axelrod, R., and Cohen, M. D. (2000). *Harnessing complexity: Organizational implications of a scientific frontier.* New York: Basic Books.

Axtell, R., Axelrod, R., Epstein, J. M., and Cohen, M. D. (1996). Aligning simulation models: A case study and results. *Computational & Mathematical Organization Theory, 1*(2), 123–141.

Bak, P., and Chen, K. (1991, January). Self-organized criticality. *Scientific American*, 46–53.

Bankes, S. C. (2008). Robust policy analysis for complex open systems. In L. Dennard, K. A. Richardson, and G. Morçöl (Eds.), *Complexity and policy analysis: Tools and methods for designing robust policies in a complex world* (pp. 117–130). Goodyear, AZ: ISCE Publishing.

Barabási, A.-L. (2002). *Linked: The new science of networks*. Cambridge, MA: Perseus Publishing.

Barabási, A.-L., and Albert, R. (1999). Emergence of scaling in random networks. *Science, 286*, 509–512.

Batty, M. (2007). *Cities and complexity: Understanding cities with cellular automata, agent-based models, and fractals*. Cambridge: MIT Press.

Baumgartner, F. R., and Jones B. D. (2002). Positive and negative feedback in politics. In F. R. Baumgartner and B. D. Jones (Eds.), *Policy dynamics* (pp. 3–27). Chicago: University of Chicago Press.

Baumgartner, F. R., and Jones B. D. (2009). *Agendas and instability in American politics* (2nd ed.). Chicago: University of Chicago Press.

Bednar, J., and Page, S. (2007). The emergence of cultural behavior within multiple games. *Rationality and Society, 19*(1), 65–97.

Benton, T. (1977). *Philosophical foundations of the three sociologies*. London: Routledge & Kegan Paul.

Berg, B. L. (1998). *Qualitative research methods for the social sciences* (3rd ed.). Boston: Allyn and Bacon.

Berry, B. J. L., and Kim, H. (1999). Has the Fed reduced chaos? In E. Elliott and D. Kiel (Eds.), *Nonlinear dynamics, complexity and public policy* (pp. 47–56). Commack, NY: Nova Science Publishers.

Bianconi, G., and Barabási, A.-L. (2001). Competiton and multiscaling in evolving networks. *Europhysics Letters, 54*(4), 436–442.

Bieri, J. (1955). Cognitive complexity-simplicity and predictive behavior. *Journal of Abnormal and Social Psychology, 51*, 263–268.

Bieri, J., Atkins, A., Briar, S., Leoman, R. L., Miller, H., and Tripodi, T. (1966). *Cognitive structure and judgement*. New York: John Wiley & Sons.

Bin, H., and Zhang, D. (2006). Cellular-automata based qualitative simulation for nonprofit group behavior. *Journal of Artificial Societies and Social Simulation, 10*(1) (http://jasss.soc.surrey.ac.uk/10/1/1.html).

Blau, P. (1964). *Exchange and power in social life*. New Brunswick, NJ: Transaction Publishers.

Blomquist, W. (2007). The policy process and large-N comparative studies. In P. A. Sabatier, (Ed.), *Theories of the policy process* (2nd ed., pp. 261–298). Cambridge, MA: Westview Press.

Boris, E. T. (1999). Nonprofit organizations in a democracy: Varied roles and responsibilities. In E. T. Boris and E. Steuerle (Ed.), *Nonprofits and government: Collaboration and conflict* (pp. 3–30). Washington, D.C.: Urban Institute Press.

Brem, R. J. (2000). The Cassandra complex: Complexity and systems collapse. In G. Morçöl and L. F. Dennard (Eds.), *New sciences for public administration and policy* (pp. 125–150). Burke, VA: Chatelaine Press.

Bresser, H. T. A., and O'Toole, L. J. (1998). The selection of policy instruments: A network-based perspective. *Journal of Public Policy, 18*(3), 213–239.

Briggs, J. (1992). *Fractals: The patterns of chaos*. New York: Simon and Schuster.

Brown, C. (1994). Politics and the environment: Nonlinear instabilities dominate. *American Political Science Review, 88*, 292–303.

Brown, C. (1995). *Chaos and catastrophe theories*. Thousand Oaks, CA: Sage.

Brown, M. M., Flowe, R., and Hamel, S. (2008). Illuminating risk with Q methodology: The complexity of trans-disciplinary information system integration.

In L. Dennard, K. Richardson, and G. Morçöl (Eds.), *Complexity and policy analysis: Tools and methods for designing robust policies in a complex world* (pp. 305–319). Goodyear, AZ: ISCE Publishing.

Brown, S. R. (1980). *Political subjectivity: Applications of Q methodology in political science.* New Haven: Yale University Press.

Brown, S. R. (1993–1994). The structure and form of subjectivity in political theory and behavior. *Operant Subjectivity, 17,* 30–48.

Brown, S. R. (2002). Structural and functional information. *Policy Sciences, 35,* 285–304.

Brown, S. R. (2004). Q methodology. In M. S. Lewis-Beck, A. Bryman, and T. F. Liao (Eds.), *The SAGE encyclopedia of social science research methods* (vol. 3, pp. 887–888). Thousand Oaks, CA: Sage.

Brown, S. R., Durning, D. W., and Selden, S. (1999). Q methodology. In G. J. Miller and M. L. Whicker (Eds.), *Handbook of research methods in public administration* (pp. 599–637). New York: Marcel Dekker.

Brown, S. R., and Robyn, R. (2004). Reserving a key place for reality: Philosophical foundations of theoretical rotation. *Operant Subjectivity, 27,* 104–124.

Brown, T., Potoski, M., and Van Slyke, D. (2008). Simple and complex contracting. *PA Times 31*(7), 6.

Buijs, J.-M., Eshuis, J., and Byrne, D. (2009). Approaches to researching complexity in public management. In G. Teisman, A. van Buuren, and L. Gerrits (Eds.), *Managing complex governance systems: Dynamics, self-organization and coevolution in public investments* (pp. 37–55). London: Routledge.

Buijs, J.-M., van der Bol, N., Teisman, G. R., and Byrne, D. (2009). Metropolitan regions as self-organizing systems. In G. Teisman, A. van Buuren, and L. Gerrits (Eds.), *Managing complex governance systems: Dynamics, self-organization and coevolution in public investments* (pp. 97–115). London: Routledge.

Butt, T. (n.d.). Phenomenology. *The Internet Encyclopedia of Personal Construct Psychology* (http://www.pcp-net.org/encyclopaedia/pheno.html; accessed on December 5, 2010.

Byrne, D. (1998). *Complexity theory and the social sciences: An introduction.* London: Routledge.

Byrne, D. (2005). Complexity, configurations and cases. *Theory, Culture and Society, 22*(5), 95–111.

Capra, F. (1996). *The web of life: A new scientific understanding of living systems.* New York: Anchor Books.

Carley, K. M., Diesner, J., Reminga, J., and Tsvetovat, M. (2007). Toward an interoperable dynamic network analysis toolkit. *Decision Support Systems 43,* 1324–1347.

Castelfranchi, C. (1998). Simulating with cognitive agents: The importance of cognitive emergence. In J. S. Sichman, R. Conte, and N. Gilbert (Eds.), *Multi-agent systems and agent-based simulation. Proceedings of the First International Workshop, MABS 1998,* Paris, France, July 4–6, pp. 26–44. Berlin: Springer.

Casti, J. L. (1994), *Complexification: Explaining a paradoxical world through the science of surprise.* New York: Harper Perennial.

Chamberlain, D. (1993). Merleau-Ponty, Maurice. In I. R. Makaryk (Ed.), *Encyclopedia of literary theory: Approaches, scholars, terms* (pp. 423–425). Toronto: University of Toronto Press.

Cilliers, P. (1998), *Complexity and postmodernism: Understanding complex systems,* London: Routledge.

Cochran, C. L., and Malone, E. F. (1995). *Public policy: Perspectives and choices.* New York: McGraw-Hill.

Cohen, M. D., Riolo, R. L., and Axelrod, R. (2001). The role of social structure in the maintenance of cooperative regimes. *Rationality and Society, 13,* 5–32.

Cohn, J. (1999, October 25). Irrational exuberance: When did political science forget about politics? *New Republic*, 25–31.

Coleman, J. S. (1986). Social theory, social research, and a theory of action. *The American Journal of Sociology, 91*(6), 1309–1335.

Coleman, J. S. (1992). Introducing social structure into economic analysis. In M. Zey (Ed.), *Decision making: Alternatives to rational choice models* (pp. 265–272). Thousand Oaks, CA: Sage.

Comfort, L. K. (1999). Nonlinear dynamics in disaster response: The Northridge, California, earthquake, January 17, 1994. In E. Elliott and L. D. Kiel (Eds.), *Nonlinear dynamics, complexity and public policy* (pp. 139–152). Commack, NY: Nova Science Publishers.

Compston, H. (2009). *Policy networks and policy change*. New York: Palgrave Macmillan.

Crockett, W. H. (1965). Cognitive complexity and impression formation. In B. A. Maher (Ed.), *Progress in experimental personality research* (vol. 2, pp. 13–28). London: Academic Press.

Damasio, A. R. (1994). *Descartes' error: Emotion, reason, and the human brain*. New York: Avon Books.

Damasio, A. R. (1999). *The feeling of what happens: Body and emotion in the making of consciousness*. New York: Harcourt Brace & Company.

Deadman, P. J., Schlager, E., and Gimblett, R. (2000). Simulating common pool resource management experiments with adaptive agents employing alternate communication routines. *Journal of Artificial Societies and Social Simulation, 3*(2) (http://jasss.soc.surrey.ac.uk/3/2/2.html).

Deaton, M. L., and Winebrake, J. I. (2000). *Dynamic modelling of environmental systems*. New York: Springer-Verlag.

De Bruijn, J. A., and ten Heuvelhof, E. F. (1997). Instruments for network management. In J. M. Kickert, E.-H. Klijn, and J. F. Koppenjan (Eds.), *Managing complex networks: Strategies for the public sector* (pp. 119–136). Thousand Oaks, CA: Sage.

DeLeon, P., and Varda, D. M. (2009). Toward a theory of collaborative policy networks: Identifying structural tendencies. *The Policy Studies Journal, 37*(1), 59–74.

Deneubourg, J.-L., Goss, S., Beckers, R., and Sandini, G. (1991). Collectively self-solving problems. In A. Babloyantz (Ed.), *Self-organization, emergent properties and learning* (pp. 56–78). New York: Plenum.

De Solla Price, D. J. (1965, July). Networks of scientific papers. *Science, 149* (3683), 510–515.

De Solla Price, D. J. (1976). A general theory of bibliometric and other cumulative advantage processes. *Journal of the American Society for Information Science 27* (5–6), 292–306.

Diamond, J. (2005). *Collapse: How societies choose to fail or succeed*. New York: Penguin.

Dieter, O. A. L. (1994). Statis. In E. Schiappa (Ed.), *Landmark essays on classical Greek rhetoric* (pp. 211–242). Davis, CA: Hermagoras Press.

Dooley, K. J., and Van de Ven, A. H. (1999). Explaining complex organizational dynamics. *Organization Science, 10*, 358–372.

Dooley, K. J., Hamilton, P., Cherri, M., West, B., and Fisher, P. (1997). Chaotic behavior in society: Adolescent childbearing in Texas, 1964–1990. In R. A. Eve, S. Horsfall, and M. E. Lee (Eds.), *Chaos, complexity, and sociology: Myths, models, and theories* (pp. 243–268). Thousand Oaks, CA: Sage.

Doreian, P. (1992). Models of network effects on social actors. In L. C. Freeman, D. R. White, and A. K. Romney (Eds.), *Research methods in social network analysis* (pp. 295–317). New Brunswick, NJ: Transaction Publishers.

Dunn, W. N. (2008). *Public policy analysis: An introduction* (4th ed.). Upper Saddle River, NJ: Pearson/Prentice Hall.

Duong, D. V., and K. D. Reilly (1995). A system of IAC neural networks as the basis for self-organization in a sociological dynamical system simulation. *Behavioral Science, 40,* 275–303.

Durning, D. W., and Brown, S. R. (2007). Q methodology in decision making. In G. Morçöl (Ed.), *Handbook of decision making.* Boca Raton, FL: CRC Press.

Dye, T. R. (1992). *Understanding public policy* (7th ed.). New York: Prentice Hall.

Eden, C., and Ackermann, F. (1998). *Making strategy: The journey of strategic management.* Thousand Oaks, CA: Sage.

Edwards, W., and Tversky, A. (Eds.) (1967). *Decision making: Selected readings.* Middlesex, UK: Penguin Books.

Ehrlich, P. R., and Raven, P. H. (1964). Butterflies and plants: A study in coevolution. *Evolution, 18,* 586–608.

Elliott, E., and Kiel, L. D. (Eds.) (1999). *Nonlinear dynamics, complexity and public policy.* Commack, NY: Nova Science Publishers.

Engelen, G. (1988). The theory of self-organization and modeling complex urban systems. *European Journal of Operational Research, 37,* 42–57.

Epstein, J. M. (2006). *Generative social science: Studies in agent-based computational modeling.* Princeton: Princeton University Press.

Epstein, J. M., and Axtell, R. (1996). *Growing artificial societies: Social science from the bottom up.* Washington, D.C.: Brookings Institution Press.

Fayol, H. (1963). *General and industrial management* (Translated by Storrs, C.). London: Sir Isaac Pitman and Sons.

Fiddaman, T. (2007). Dynamics of climate policy. *System Dynamics Review, 23*(1), 21–34.

Fischer, F. (1990). *Technocracy and the politics of expertise.* Newbury Park, CA: Sage.

Fischer, F. (1995). *Evaluating public policy.* Chicago: Nelson-Hall Publishers.

Fischer, F. (2003). *Reframing public policy: Discursive politics and deliberative practices.* Oxford: Oxford University Press.

Fischer, F. (2009). *Democracy and expertise: Reorienting policy inquiry.* Oxford: Oxford University Press.

Flood, R. L. (1999). *Rethinking* The Fifth Discipline: *Learning within the unknowable.* London: Routledge.

Flyvbjerg, B. (2001). *Making social science matter: Why social inquiry fails and how it can succeed again.* Cambridge: Cambridge University Press.

Føllesdal, D. (1988). Husserl on evidence and justification. In R. Sokolowski (Ed.), *Edmund Husserl and the phenomenological tradition: Essays in phenomenology* (pp. 107–130). Washington, D.C.: Catholic University of America Press.

Forrester, J. W. (1961). *Industrial dynamics.* Waltham, MA: Pegasus Communications.

Forrester, J. W. (1969). *Urban dynamics.* Cambridge: MIT Press.

Forrester, J. W. (1971). *World dynamics.* Waltham, MA: Pegasus Communications.

Forrester, J. W. (1994). Learning through system dynamics as preparation for the 21st century. Keynote Address for *Systems Thinking and Dynamic Modeling Conference for K–12 Education,* Concord Academy, MA: Concord, June 27–29.

Fransella, F., and Bannister, D. (1977). *A manual for repertory grid technique.* London: Academic Press.

Frederickson, H. G., and Smith, K. B. (2003). *The public administration theory primer.* Boulder, CO: Westview.

Freeman, L. C. (1992). Social networks and the structure experiment. In L. C. Freeman, D. R. White, and A. K. Romney (Eds.), *Research methods in social network analysis* (pp. 11–40). New Brunswick, NJ: Transaction Publishers.

Freeman, L. C., Romney, A. K., and Freeman, S. C. (2008). Cognitive structure and informant accuracy. In L. C. Freeman (Ed.), *Social network analysis* (vol. 1, pp. 58–78). Los Angeles: Sage.

Friedland, R., and Robertson, A. F. (Eds.) (1990). *Beyond the marketplace: Rethinking economy and society*. New York: Aldine de Gruyter.

Fuchs, C. (2002). Some implications of Anthony Giddens' works for a theory of social self-organization. *Emergence: Complexity and Organization, 4*(3), 7–35.

Gardner, H. (1985). *The mind's new science: A history of the cognitive revolution*. New York: Basic Books.

Gell-Mann, M. (1995). What is complexity? *Complexity 1*(1), 16–19.

Gemmill, G., and Smith, C. (1985). A dissipative structure model of organization transformation. *Human Relations, 38*, 751–766.

Gerrits, L. (2008). *The gentle art of coevolution: A complexity theory perspective on decision making over estuaries in Germany, Belgium and the Netherlands* (Ph.D. dissertation), Erasmus University Rotterdam.

Gerrits, L. (2010). Public decision making as coevolution. *Emergence: Complexity & Organization, 12*(1), 19–28.

Gerrits, L. (2011). A coevolutionary revision of decision making processes: An analysis of port extensions in Germany, Belgium and the Netherlands. *Public Administration Quarterly, 35*, 315–332.

Gerrits, L., Marks, P., and van Buuren, A. (2009). Coevolution: A constant in nonlinearity. In G. Teisman, A. van Buuren, and L. Gerritts (Eds.), *Managing complex governance systems: Dynamics, self-organization and coevolution in public investments* (pp. 134–153). London: Routledge.

Geyer, R., and Rihani, S. (2010). *Complexity and public policy: A new approach to 21st century politics, policy and society*. London: Routledge.

Giddens, A. (1984). *The constitution of society*. Berkeley: University of California Press.

Giddens, A. (1995). *Politics, sociology and social theory: Encounters with classical and contemporary social thought*. Stanford: Stanford University Press.

Gleick, J. (1987). *Chaos: Making a new science*. New York: Penguin Books.

Goerner, S. (1995). Chaos, evolution, and deep ecology. In R. Robertson and A. Combs (Eds.), *Chaos theory in psychology and the life sciences* (pp. 17–38). Mahwah, NJ: Lawrence Erlbaum.

Goldstein, J. (1988). A far-from-equilibrium systems approach to resistance to change. *Organizational Dynamics, 17*, 16–26.

Goldstein, J. (1994). *The unshackled organization: Facing the challenge of unpredictability through spontaneous reorganization*. Portland, OR: Productivity Press.

Green, D. P., and Shapiro, I. (1994). *Pathologies of rational choice theory: A critique of applications in political science*. New Haven: Yale University Press.

Gros, C. (2008). *Complex adaptive dynamical systems: A primer*. Berlin: Springer-Verlag.

Guastello, S. J. (1995). *Chaos, catastrophe, and human affairs: Applications of nonlinear dynamics to work, organizations, and social evolution*. Mahwah, NJ: Lawrence Erlbaum.

Gulick, L., and Urwick, L. (Eds.) (1937). *Papers on the science of administration*. New York: Institute of Public Administration.

Hankison, G. (2004). Repertory grid analysis: An application to the measurement of destination images. *International Journal of Nonprofit and Voluntary Sector Marketing, 9*(2), 145–153.

Hannon, B., and Ruth, M. (2001). *Dynamic modeling* (2nd ed.). New York: Springer-Verlag.

Hardin, G. (1968). The tragedy of the commons. *Science, 162*, 1243–1248.

Harmon, M. M., and Mayer, R. T. (1986). *Organization theory for public administration*. Burke, VA: Chatelaine Press.

Heidegger, M. (1994a). Being-there as understanding. In K. Mueller-Vollmer (Ed.), *The hermeneutics reader* (pp. 215–221). New York: Continuum.

Heidegger, M. (1994b). Understanding and interpretation. In K. Mueller-Vollmer (Ed.), *The hermeneutics reader* (pp. 221–228). New York: Continuum.

Helbing, D., Kühnert, C., Lämmer, S., Johansson, A., Gelsen, B., Ammoser, H., and West, G. B. (2009). Power laws in urban supply networks, social systems, and dense pedestrian crowds. In D. Lane, S. van der Leeuw, D. Pumain, and G. West (Eds.), *Complexity perspectives in innovation and change* (pp. 433–450). New York: Springer.

Hempel, C. (1965). *Aspects of scientific explanation and other essays in the philosophy of science*. New York: Free Press.

Hogarth, R. M., and Reder, M. W. (Eds.) (1986). *Rational choice: The contrast between economics and psychology*. Chicago: University of Chicago Press.

Holland, J. H. (1995). *Hidden order: How adaptation builds complexity*. New York: Basic Books.

Holland, J. H. (1998). *Emergence: From chaos to order*. New York: Basic Books.

Honderich, T. (Ed.). (1995). *The Oxford companion to philosophy*. Oxford: Oxford University Press.

Houghton, J. (2004). *Global warming: The complete briefing* (3rd ed.). Cambridge: Cambridge University Press.

Hughes, J. A. (1990). *The philosophy of social research* (2nd ed.). London: Longman.

Human, S. E., and Provan, K. G. (2000). Legitimacy building in the evolution of small-firm networks: A comparative study of success and demise. *Administrative Science Quarterly, 45*, 327–365.

Hummel, R. P. (1994). *The bureaucratic experience* (4th ed.). New York: St. Martin's Press.

Innes, J. E., and Booher, D. E. (2010). *Planning with complexity: An introduction to collaborative rationality for public policy*. London: Routledge.

Jacobs, J. (1993). *The death and life of great American cities*. New York: The Modern Library.

Janssen, M. A., Radtke, N. P., and Lee, A. (2009). Pattern-oriented modeling of commons dilemma experiments. *Adaptive Behavior, 17*, 508–523.

Jantsch, E. (1980). *The self-organizing universeScientific and human implications of the emrging paradigm of evolution*. Oxford, UK: Pergamon Press.

Jantsch, E. (1981). Autopoiesis: A central aspect of dissipative organization. In M. Zeleny (ed.), *Autopoiesis: A theory of living organization* (65–88). New York: North Holland Publishers.

Jessop, B. (1990). *State theory: Putting the capitalist state in its place*. State College: Pennsylvania State University Press.

Jessop, B. (2001). Institutional re(turns) and the strategic-relational approach. *Environment and Planning A, 33*, 1213–1235.

Jessop, B. (2004). Critical semiotic analysis and cultural political economy. *Critical Discourse Studies, 1*(2), 159–174.

Jessop, B. (2008). *State power: A strategic-relational approach*. Cambridge, UK: Polity Press.

Jun, J. S. (1986). *Public administration: Design and problem solving*. Burke, VA: Chatelaine Press.

Kane, M., and Trochim, W. M. K. (2007). *Concept mapping for planning and evaluation*. Thousand Oaks, CA: Sage.

Kaplan, D., and Glass, L. (1995). *Understanding nonlinear dynamics*. New York: Springer.

Kauffman, S. (1993). *The origins of order: Self-organization and selection in evolution.* New York: Oxford University Press.

Kauffman, S. (1995). *At home in the universe: The search for laws of self-organization and complexity.* New York: Oxford University Press.

Khan, M. S., and Quaddus, M. (2004). Group decision support using fuzzy cognitive maps for causal reasoning. *Group Decision and Negotiation, 13,* 463–480.

Keat, R., and Urry, J. (1975), *Social theory as science.* London: Routledge & Kegan Paul.

Kellert, S. H. (1993). *In the wake of chaos: Unpredictable order in dynamical systems.* Chicago: University of Chicago Press.

Kelly, G. A. (1955). *The psychology of personal constructs.* New York: Norton.

Kenis, P., and Provan, K. G. (2006). The control of public networks. *International Public Management Journal, 9*(3), 227–247.

Kerby, A. (1993). Hermeneutics. In I. R. Makaryk (Ed.), *Encyclopaedia of contemporary literary theory* (pp. 90–94). Toronto: University of Toronto Press.

Kettl, D. F. (2002). *The transformation of governance: Public administration for twenty-first century America.* Baltimore: The Johns Hopkins University Press.

Kickert, W. J. M. (1993). Autopoiesis and the science of (public) administration: Essence, sense and nonsense. *Organization Studies, 14*(2), 261–278.

Kickert, W. J. M., Klijn, E.-H., and Koppenjan, J. F. (Eds.) (1997a). *Managing complex networks: Strategies for the public sector.* Thousand Oaks, CA: Sage.

Kickert, W. J. M., Klijn, E.-H., and Koppenjan, J. F. (1997b). Introduction: A management perspective on policy networks. In J. M. Kickert, E.-H. Klijn, and J. F. Koppenjan (Eds.), Managing complex networks: Strategies for the public sector (pp. 1–13). Thousand Oaks, CA: Sage.

Kiel, L. D. (1992). The nonlinear paradigm: Advancing paradigmatic process in the policy sciences. *Systems Research, 9*(2), 27–42.

Kiel, L. D. (1994). *Managing chaos and complexity in government: A new paradigm for managing change, innovation, and organizational renewal.* San Francisco: Jossey-Bass.

Kiel, L. D., and Elliot, E. (1992). Budgets as dynamic systems: Change, variation, time, and budgetary heuristics. *Journal of Public Administration Research and Theory, 2*(2), 139–156.

Kiel, L. D., and Elliot, E. (Eds.) (1997). *Chaos theory in the social sciences: Foundations and applications.* Ann Arbor: University of Michigan Press.

King, G., Keohane, R. O., and Verba, S. (1994). *Designing social inquiry: Scientific inference in qualitative research.* Princeton: Princeton University Press.

Klijn, E.-H. (1997). Policy networks: An overview. In J. M. Kickert, E.-H. Klijn, and J. F. Koppenjan (Eds.), *Managing complex networks: Strategies for the public sector* (pp. 14–34). Thousand Oaks, CA: Sage.

Klijn, E.-H. (2001). Rules as institutional context for decision making in networks: The approach to postwar housing districts in two cities. *Administration & Society, 33*(2), 133–164.

Klijn, E.-H., and Snellen, I. (2009). Complexity theory and public administration: A critical appraisal. In G. Teisman, A. van Buuren, and L. Gerrits (Eds.), *Managing complex governance systems: Dynamics, self-organization and coevolution in public investments* (pp. 17–36). London: Routledge.

Knodt, E. M. (1995). Foreword. In N. Luhmann, *Social systems.* Stanford: Stanford University Press.

Knoke, D., and Yang, S. (2008). *Social network analysis* (2nd ed.). Los Angeles, CA: Sage.

Koehler, G. (1999). The time compacted globe and the high-tech primitive at the millennium. In E. Elliott and L. D. Kiel (Eds.), *Nonlinear dynamics, complexity and public policy* (pp. 153–174). Commack, NY: Nova Science Publishers.

Koehler, G. (2003). Time, complex systems, and public policy: A theoretical foundation for adaptive policy making. *Nonlinear Dynamics, Psychology, and Life Sciences*, 7(1), 99–114.

Koehler, G. (2004). Sorting out the temporal confusion of computer simulations. Paper presented at the *International Society for the Study of Time Conference*, Cambridge, UK, July 25–31.

Koehler, G. (2008). Computer simulations as hidden time ecologies. In S. Vrobel, O. E. Rössler, and T. Marks-Tarlow (Eds.), *Simultaneity: Temporal structures and observer perspectives* (pp. 377–394). Hackensack, NJ: World Scientific Publishing.

Koliba, C., Meek, J. W., and Zia, A. (2011). *Governance networks in public administration and policy*. Boca Raton, FL: CRC Press.

Koppenjan, J., and Klijn, E.-H. (2004), *Managing uncertainties in networks: A network approach to problem solving and decision making*. London: Routledge.

Lakoff, G., and Johnson, M. (1980). *Metaphors we live by*. Chicago: University of Chicago Press.

Lakoff, G., and Johnson, M. (1999). *Philosophy in the flesh: The embodied mind and its challenge to Western thought*. New York: Basic Books.

Lane, D. (2006). Hierarchy, complexity and society. In D. Pumain (Ed.), *Hierarchy in natural and social sciences* (pp. 81–118). Dordrecht: Springer.

Lasswell, H. D. (1971). *A preview of policy sciences*. New York: American Elsevier.

Laumann, E. O., Mardsen, P. V., and Presnky, D. (1992). The boundary specification problem in network analysis. In L. C. Freeman, D. R. White, and A. K. Romney (eds.), *Research methods in social network analysis* (pp. 61–870. New Brunswick, NJ: Transaction publishers.

Leifer, R. (1989). Understanding organizational transformation using a dissipative structure model. *Human Relations*, 42, 899–916.

Leonard, R. D. (2001). Evolutionary archeology. In I. Hodder (Ed.), *Archeological theory today* (pp. 65–97). Cambridge, UK: Polity Press.

Levin, S. A. (2009). Games, groups, norms, and societies. In S. A. Levin (Ed.), *Games, groups, and the global good* (pp. 143–153). Berlin: Springer-Verlag.

Levine, R. A., Watts, H., Hollister, R., Williams, W., O'Connor, A., and Widerquist, K. (2005). A retrospective on the negative income tax experiments: Looking back at the most innovative field studies in social policy. In K. Wilderquist, M. Lewis, and S. Pressman (Eds.), *The ethics and economics of the basic income guarantee* (pp. 96–107). Burlington, VT: Ashgate.

Lewin, K. (1938). *The conceptual representation and the measurement of psychological forces*. Durham: Duke University Press.

Lichbach, M. A. (2003). *Is rational choice theory all of social science?* Ann Arbor: University of Michigan Press.

Little, J. H. (2000). Governing the government: Sociocybernetics of democratic administration. In G. Morçöl and L. F. Dennard (Eds.), *New sciences for public administration and policy: Connections and reflections* (pp. 151–175). Burke, VA: Chatelaine Press.

Lorenz, E. N. (1963a). Deterministic nonperiodic flow. *Journal of the Atmospheric Sciences*, 20, 130–141.

Lorenz, E. N. (1963b). The mechanics of vacillation. *Journal of the Atmospheric Sciences*, 20, 448–464.

Luhmann, N. (1995). *Social systems*. Stanford: Stanford University Press.

MacDonald, P. K. (2003). Useful fiction or miracle maker: The competing epistemological foundations of rational choice theory. *American Political Science Review*, 97(4), 551–565.

Madison, G. B. (1988). *The hermeneutics of postmodernity: Figures and themes*. Bloomington: Indiana University Press.

Maher, B. (1969). Introduction. In B. Maher (Ed.). *Clinical psychology and personality: The selected papers of George Kelly.* New York: John Wiley and Sons.

Mahurin, Matt. (2000, October). Twenty ideas that will rule research in the next twenty years. *Discover, 21,* 88–91.

Marczyk, G., DeMatteo, D., and Festinger, D. (2005). *Essentials of research design and methodology.* Hoboken, NJ: John Wiley & Sons.

Mardsen, P. V., and Friedkin, N. E. (1994). Network studies of social influence. In S. Wasserman and J. Galaskiewicz (Eds.), *Advances in social network analysis* (pp. 3–25). Thousand Oaks: Sage.

Maroulis, S., Guimerà, R., Petry, H., Stringer, M. J., Gomez, L. M., Amaral, L. A. N., and Wilensky, U. (2010). Complex systems view of educational policy research. *Science, 330,* 38–39.

Marsh, D., and Smith, M. (2000). Understanding policy networks: Toward a dialectical approach. *Political Studies, 48,* 4–21.

Maturana, H. R. (1980). Introduction. In H. R. Maturana and F. J.Varela (Eds.), *Autopoiesis and cognition: The realization of the living* (pp. xi-xix). Dordrecht: D. Reidel.

Maturana, H. R, and Varela, F. J. (1980). *Autopoiesis and cognition: The realization of the living.* Dordrecht: D. Reidel.

McKelvey, B. (1999). Avoiding complexity catastrophe in coevolutionary pockets: Strategies for rugges landscapes. *Organization Science, 10,* 294–321.

McMillan, E. (2004). *Complex organizations and change.* London: Routledge.

Meadows, D. H. (2008). *Thinking in systems: A primer.* Westchester Junction, VT: Chelsea Green Publishing.

Michaels, M. (1995). Seven fundamentals of complexity for social science research. In A. Albert (Ed.), *Chaos and society* (pp. 15–33). Amsterdam: IOS Press.

Mika, P. (2007). *Social networks and the semantic web.* New York: Springer.

Miller, H. (2002). *Postmodern public policy.* Albany: State University of New York Press.

Miller, H. T, and Fox, C. J. (2007). *Postmodern public administration* (rev. ed.). Armonk, NY: M. E. Sharpe.

Miller, J. H., and Page, S. E. (2007). *Complex adaptive systems: An introduction to computational models of social life.* Princeton: Princeton University Press.

Milward, H. B. (1996). Symposium on the hollow state: Capacity, control, and performance in interorganizational settings. *Journal of Public Administration Research and Theory* 6(2), 193–195.

Mingers, J. (1995). *Self-producing systems: Implications and applications of autopoiesis.* New York: Plenum Press.

Mirowski, P. (1990). From Mandelbrot to chaos in economic theory. *Southern Economic Journal, 57*(2), 289–307.

Mischen, P. A., and Jackson, S. K. (2008). Connecting the dots: Applying complexity theory, knowledge management and social network analysis to policy implementation. *Public Administration Quarterly, 32*(3), 314–339.

Mitchell, M. (2009). *Complexity: A guided tour.* Oxford: Oxford University Press.

Morçöl, G. (2002). *A new mind for policy analysis: Toward a post-Newtonian and postpositivist epistemology and methodology.* Westport, CT: Praeger.

Morçöl, G. (2005). A new systems thinking: Implications of the sciences of complexity for public policy and administration. *Public Administration Quarterly, 29*(3), 297–320.

Morçöl, G. (2008). A complexity theory for policy analysis: an outline and proposals. In L. F. Dennard, K. A. Richardson, and G. Morçöl (Eds.), Complexity and policy analysis: Tools and concepts for designing robust policies in a complex world (pp. 23–35). Goodyear, AZ: ISCE Publishing.

Morçöl, G. (2010). Reconceptualizing public policy from the perspective of complexity theory. *Emergence: A Journal of Complexity Issues in Organizations and Management, 12*(1), 52–60.

Morçöl, G., and Asche, M. (1993). The repertory grid in problem structuring: A case illustration. *The International Journal of Personal Construct Psychology, 6*, 371–390.

Moreno, J. L. (1953). *Who shall survive? Foundations of sociometry, group psychotherapy, and sociodrama* (2nd ed.). NY: Beacon House.

Moreno, A., and Ruiz-Mirazo, K. (2007). The maintenance and open-ended growth of complexity in nature: Information as a decoupling mechanism in the origins of life. In F. Capra, A. Juarrero, P. Sotolongo, and J. Van Uden (Eds.), *Reframing complexity: Perspectives from the North and South* (pp. 60–76). Mansfield, MA: ISCE Publications.

Morgan, G. (Ed.) (1983). *Beyond method: Strategies for social research.* Newbury Park, CA: Sage.

Morgan, G. (1997). *Images of organization* (2nd ed.). Thousand Oaks, CA: Sage.

Moss, S. (1998). Critical incident management: An empirically derived computational model. *Journal of Artificial Societies and Social Simulation, 1*(4) (http://jasss.soc.surrey.ac.uk/1/4/1.html).

Mueller-Vollmer, K. (Ed.). (1994). *The hermeneutics reader.* New York: Continuum.

Mumford, L. (1961). *The city in history: Its origins, its transformations, and its prospects.* San Diego, CA: Harcourt.

Murray, N. (1997). *An inner voice for public administration.* Westport, CT: Praeger.

Murrell, J. B. (2007). *Differential persistence of variation in prehistoric milling tools from the Middle Rio Puerco Valley, New Mexico.* Oxford, UK: Archaeopress.

Nan, N., and Johnson, E. W. (2009). Using multi-agent simulation to explore the contribution of facilitation to GSS transition. *Journal of the Association for Information Systems, 10*, 252–277.

Nan, N., Johnson, E. W., and Olson, J. S. (2008). Unintended consequences of collocation: Using agent-based modeling to untangle effects of communication delay and in-group favor. *Computational & Mathematical Organization Theory, 14*, 57–83.

Nan, N., Johnston, E. W., Olson, J. S., and Bos, N. (2005). Beyond being in the lab: Using multi-agent modeling to isolate competing hypotheses. *CHI 2005,* Portland, Oregon, April 2–7, 2005.

Naveh, I., and Sun, R. (2006). A cognitively based simulation of academic science. *Computational and Mathematical Organization Theory, 12*(4), 313–337.

Newell, W. H. (2001). A theory of interdisciplinary studies. *Issues in Integrative Studies, 19*, 1–25.

Newell, W. H., and Meek, J. W. (2000). What can public administration learn from complex systems theory? In G. Morçöl and L. F. Dennard (Eds.), *News sciences for public administration and policy: Connections and reflections* (pp. 81–106). Burke, VA: Chatelaine Press.

Newman, M., Barabási, A.-L., and Watts, D. J. (Eds.) (2006). *The structure and dynamics of networks.* Princeton: Princeton University Press.

Nicolis, G., and Prigogine, I. 1989. *Exploring complexity: An introduction.* New York: W. H. Freeman and Co.

OECD Global Science Forum (2009, September). Report on applications of complexity science for public policy: New tools for finding unanticipated consequences and unrealized opportunities (http://www.oecd.org/dataoecd/44/41/43891980.pdf; accessed on March 7, 2011).

O'Brien, M. J., and Lyman, R. L. (2002). *Applying evolutionary archeology: A systematic approach*. New York: Kluwer.

Olson, M. (1965). *The logic of collective action: Public goods and the theory of groups*. Cambridge: Harvard University Press.

Ornstein, R., and Ehrlich, P. (2000). *New world new mind: Moving toward conscious evolution*. Cambridge, MA: Malor Books.

Ostrom, E. (1990). *Governing the commons: The evolution of institutions for collective action*. Cambridge: Cambridge University Press.

Ostrom, E. (2005). *Understanding institutional diversity*. Princeton,: Princeton University Press.

Ostrom, E. (2007a). Biography of Robert Axelrod. *PS: Political Science & Politics, 40*(1), 171–174.

Ostrom, E. (2007b). Institutional rational choice: An assessment of the institutional analysis and development framework. In P. A. Sabatier (Ed.), *Theories of the policy process* (pp. 21–64), Cambridge, MA: Westview.

Ostrom, E., Gardner R., and Walker, J. (1994). *Rules, games, and common pool resources*. Ann Arbor: University of Michigan Press.

Ostrom, E., and Parks, R. B. (1999). Neither gargantuan nor the land of Lilliputs: Conjectures on mixed systems of metropolitan organization. In M. D. McGinnis (Ed.), *Polycentricity and local public economies: readings from the workshop in political theory and policy analysis*, (pp. 284–305). Ann Arbor: University of Michigan Press.

O'Toole, L. J (1997a). Implementing public innovations in network settings. *Administration & Society, 29*(2), 115–138.

O'Toole, L. J. (1997b). Treating networks seriously: Practical and research-based agendas in public administration. *Public Administration Review, 57*(1), 45–52.

O'Toole, L. J., and Meier, K. J. (1999). Modeling the impact of public management: Implications of structural context. *Journal of Public Administration Research and Theory, 9*(4), 505–526.

O'Toole L. J., and Meier, K. J. (2004). Desperately seeking Selznick: Cooptation and the dark side of public management in networks. *Public Administration Review, 64*(6), 681–693.

Passerini, E., and Bahr, D. (1997). Collective behavior following disasters: A cellular automaton model. In R. A. Eve, S. Horsfall, and M. E. Lee (Eds.), *Chaos, complexity, and sociology: Myths, models, and theories* (pp. 215–228). Thousand Oaks, CA: Sage.

Pel, B. (2009). The complexity of self-organization: Boundary judgments in traffic management. In G. Teisman, A. van Buuren, and L. Gerrits (Eds.), *Managing complex governance systems: Dynamics, self-organization and coevolution in public investments* (pp. 116–133). London: Routledge.

Peitgen, H.-O., Jürgens, H., and Saupe, D. (2004). *Chaos and fractals: New frontiers of science* (2nd ed.). New York: Springer-Verlag.

Pinker, S. (1997). *How the mind works*. New York: W. W. Norton & Company.

Pollitt, C. (2009). Complexity theory and evolutionary public administration: A skeptical afterword. In G. R. Teisman, A. van Buuren, and L. Gerrits (eds.), *Managing complex governance systems: Dynamics, self-organization and coevolution in public investments* (pp. 213–230). London: Routledge.

Portugali, J. (2000). *Self-organization and the city*. Berlin: Springer-Verlag.

Pressman, J. L., and Wildavsky, A. B. (1984). *Implementation: How great expectations in Washington are dashed in Oakland; or, why it's amazing that federal programs work at all* (3rd ed.). Berkeley: University of California Press.

Priesmeyer, H. R. (1995). Logistic regression: A method for describing, interpreting, and forecasting social phenomenon with nonlinear equations. In A. Albert (Ed.), *Chaos and society*. Amsterdam: IOS Press.

Priesmeyer, H. R., and Baik, K. (1989). Discovering the patterns of chaos. *Planning Review, 17*(6), 14–21.

Priesmeyer, H. R., and Davis, J. (1991). Chaos theory: A tool for predicting the unpredictable. *The Journal of Business Forecasting, 10*(3): 22–28.

Prigogine, I. (1996). *The end of certainty: Time, chaos, and the new laws of nature.* New York: The Free Press.

Prigogine, I., and Stengers, I. (1984). *Order out of chaos: Man's new dialogue with nature.* New York: Bantam Books.

Provan, K. G., Fish, A., and Sydow, J. (2007). Interorganizational networks at the network level: A review of the empirical literature on whole networks. *Journal of Management, 33*(3), 479–516.

Provan, K. G., Huang, K., and Milward, B. (2009). The evolution of structural embeddedness and organizational social outcomes in a centrally governed health and human services network. *Journal of Public Administration Research and Theory, 19*(4), 873–893.

Provan, K. G., and Kenis, P. (2007). Modes of network governance: Structure, management, and effectiveness. *Journal of Public Administration Research and Theory, 18*(2), 229–252.

Publication manual of the American Psychological Association. (2010). Washington, DC: American Psychological Association.

Quade, E. S. (1989). *Analysis for public decisions* (3rd ed.). New York: North Holland.

Radloff, B. (1993). Hermeneutic circle. In I. R. Makaryk (Ed.), *Encyclopaedia of contemporary literary theory* (pp. 550–551). Toronto: University of Toronto Press.

Radder, H. (1996). *In and about the world: Philosophical studies of science and technology.* Albany: State University of New York Press.

Ragin, C. C. (1987). *The comparative method: Moving beyond qualitative and quantitative strategies.* Berkeley: University of California Press.

Ragin, C. C. (2000). *Fuzzy-set social science.* Chicago: University of Chicago Press.

Ragin, C. C. (2008). *Redesigning social inquiry: Fuzzy sets and beyond.* Chicago: University of Chicago Press.

Rescher, N. (1998). *Complexity: A philosophical overview.* New Brunswick, NJ: Transaction Publishers.

Rhodes, M. L., Murphy, J., Muir, J., and Murray, J. A. (2011). *Public management and complexity theory: Richer decision-making in public services.* London: Routledge.

Rhodes, R. A. W. (1997a). *Understanding governance: Policy networks, governance, reflexivity and accountability.* Maidenhead, UK: Open University Pres.

Rhodes, R.A.W. (1997b). Foreword. In W. J. M. Kickert, E.-H. Klijn, and J. F. M. Koppenjan (Eds.), *Managing complex networks: Strategies for the public sector* (pp. xi–xv). Thousand Oaks, CA: Sage.

Richards, D. (2000). Nonlinear modeling: All things suffer change. In D. Richards (Ed.), *Political complexity: Nonlinear models of politics* (pp. 1–20). Ann Arbor: University of Michigan Press.

Richardson, K. A. (2007). Complex systems thinking and its implications for policy analysis. In G. Morçöl, (Ed.), *Handbook of decision making* (pp. 189–222). Boca Raton, FL: CRC Press.

Richardson, K. A. (2008). On the limits of bottom-up computer simulation: Toward a nonlinear modeling culture. In L. F. Dennard, K. A. Richardson, and G. Morçöl (Eds.), *Complexity and policy analysis: Tools and methods for designing robust policies in a complex world* (pp. 37–54). Goodyear, AZ: ISCE Publishing.

Richardson, K. A. (2010). *Thinking about complexity: Grasping the continuum through criticism and pluralism*. Litchfield Park, AZ: Emergent Publications.

Riolo, R. K. L., Cohen, M. D., and Axelrod, R. (2001). Evolution of cooperation without reciprocity. *Nature, 414*, 441–443.

Roe, E. (1994). *Narrative policy analysis*. Durham: Duke University Press.

Roe, E. (1998). *Taking complexity seriously: Policy analysis, triangulation, and sustainable development*. Boston: Kluwer Academic Publishers.

Roe, E. (2007). Narrative policy analysis for decision making. G. Morçöl (Ed.), *Handbook of decision making*. Boca Raton, FL: CRCPress.

Rosenau, P. M. (1992), *Post-modernism and the social sciences: Insights, inroads, and intrusions*. Princeton: Princeton University Press.

Rosenkopf, L., and Padula, G. Investigating the microstructure of network evolution: Alliance formation in the mobile communications industry . *OrganizationScience, 19*, 669–687.

Rössler, O. E. (1986), How chaotic is the universe? In A. V. Holden (Ed.), *Chaos* (pp. 315–320). Princeton: Princeton University Press.

Ruth, M., and Hannon, B. M. (1997). *Modeling dynamic economic systems*. New York: Springer-Verlag.

Sabatier, P. A. (Ed.) (2007a). *Theories of the policy process* (2nd ed.). Cambridge, MA: Westview Press.

Sabatier, P. A. (2007b). Fostering the development of policy theory. In P. A. Sabatier (Ed.), *Theories of the policy process* (pp. 261–275). Cambridge, MA: Westview Press.

Sabatier, P. A., and Jenkins-Smith, H. (1993). Policy change and learning: An advocacy coalition approach. Boulder, CO: Westview Press.

Salzano, M. (2008). Economic policy hints from heterogeneous agent-based simulations. In K. Richardson, L. Dennard, and G. Morçöl (Eds.), *Complexity and policy analysis: Tools and methods for designing robust policies in a complex world* (pp. 167–196). Goodyear, AZ: ISCE Publishing.

Sarup, M. (1989). *An introductory guide to post-structuralism and postmodernism*. Athens: University of Georgia Press.

Sawyer, R. K. (2005). *Social emergence: Societies as complex systems*. Cambridge: Cambridge University Press.

Schaap, L, and van Twist, M. J. W. (1997). The dynamics of closedness in networks. In W. J. M. Kickert, E.-H. Klijn, and J. F. M. Koppenjan (Eds.), *Managing complex networks: Strategies for the public sector* (pp. 62–78). Thousand Oaks, CA: Sage.

Schelling, T. C. (1971). Dynamic models of segregation. *Journal of Mathematical Sociology, 1*, 143–186.

Schelling, T. C. (2006). *Micromotives and macrobehavior*. New York: W. W. Norton & Company.

Schneider, A. L., and Ingram, H. (1997). *Policy design for democracy*. Lawrence: University Press of Kansas.

Schram, S. F. (1993), Postmodern policy analysis: Discourse and identity in welfare policy. *Policy Sciences, 26*, 249–270.

Schram, S. F. (1995). *Words of welfare: The poverty of social science and the socisl science of poverty*. Minneapolis, MN: The University of Minnesota Press.

Schram, S., and Cateriono, B. (Eds.). (2006). *Making political science matter: Debating knowledge, research, and method*. New York: New York University Press.

Sharkansky, I. (2002). *Politics and policymaking: In search of simplicity*. London: Lynne Rienner Publishers.

Shaw, M. L. G., and Gaines, B. R. (1982). Tracking the creativity cycle with a microcomputer. *International Journal of Man-Machine Studies, 17*, 75–85.

Simon, C. A. (2007). *Public policy: Preferences and outcomes.* New York: Pearson/ Longman.

Simon, H. A. (1979). Rational decision making and business organizations. *The American Economic Review, 69*(4), 493–513.

Simon, H. A. (1986). Rationality in psychology and economics. In R. M. Hogarth, and M. W. Reder (Eds.), *Rational choice: The contrast between economics and psychology,* (pp. 25–40). Chicago: University of Chicago Press.

Slater, P. (1977). *The measurement of intrapersonal space by grid technique.* London: Wiley.

Smith, A. (1902). *The wealth of nations.* Princeton: Princeton University Press.

Smith, J., and Jenks, C. (2006). *Qualitative complexity: Ecology, cognitive processes and the re-emergence of structures in post-humanist social theory.* London: Routledge.

Squares of Savannah, Georgia, http://en.wikipedia.org/wiki/Squares_of_Savannah, accessed on November 3, 2010.

Stacey, R. D., Griffin, D., and Shaw, P. . (2000). *Complexity and management: Fad or radical challenge to systems thinking?* London: Routledge.

Steels, L. (1990). Cooperation between distributed agents through self-organization. In Y. Demazeau and J.-P. Müller (Eds.), *Decentralized AI. Proceedings of the First European Workshop on Modelling Autonomous Agents in a Multi-Agent World,* pp. 175–196. Amsterdam: Elsevier.

Stephenson, W. (1953). *The study of behavior: Q-technique and its methodology.* Chicago: University of Chicago Press.

Stewart, J., and Ayres, R. (2001). Systems theory and policy practice: An exploration. *Policy Sciences, 34*(1), 79–94.

Stockey, E., and Zeckhauser, R. (1978). *A primer for policy analysis.* New York: W. W. Norton & Company.

Stone, D. (2002). *Policy paradox: The art of political decision making* (rev. ed.). New York: W.W. Norton & Company.

Strauch, R. E. (1976). A critical look at quantitative methodology. *Policy Analysis, 2*(1), 121–144.

Strogatz, S. (2003). *Sync: The emerging science of spontaneous order.* New York: Hyperion.

Stroup, W. F. (1997). Web of chaos: Implications of research design. In R. A. Eve, S. Horsfall, and M. E. Lee (eds.), *Chaos, complexity, and sociology: Myths, models, and theories* (pp. 125–140). Thousand Oaks, CA: Sage.

Suen, H. K., and Ary, D. (1989). *Analyzing quantitative behavioral observation data.* Hillsdale, NJ: Lawrence Erlbaum.

Szathmáry, E., Jordán, F., and Pál, C. (2001). Molecular biology and evolution: Can genes explain biological complexity? *Science, 292*(5520), 1315–1316.

Takadama, K., Kawai, T., and Koyama, Y. (2008). Micro- and macro-level validation in agent-based simulation: Reproduction of human-like behaviors and thinking in a sequential bargaining game. *Journal of Artificial Societies and Social Simulation, 1*(2–9) (http://jasss.soc.surrey.ac.uk/11/2/9.html).

Taylor, F. W. (1947). *Scientific management.* New York: Harper & Row.

Taylor, M. C. (2001). *The moment of complexity: Emerging network culture.* Chicago: University of Chicago Press.

Teisman, G. R. (2008). Complexity and management improvement programs: An evolutionary approach. *Public Management Review, 10*(3), 341–359.

Teisman, G. R., and Klijn, E.-H. (2008). Complexity theory and public management: An introduction. *Public Management Review, 10*(3), 287–297.

Teisman, G. R., van Buuren, A., and Gerrits, L. (2009a). An introduction to understanding and managing complex process systems. In G. R. Teisman, A. van Buuren, and L. Gerrits (Eds.), *Managing complex governance systems:*

Dynamics, self-organization and coevolution in public investments (pp. 1–16). London: Routledge.

Teisman, G. R., van Buuren, A., and Gerrits, L. (Eds.). (2009b). *Managing complex governance systems: Dynamics, self-organization and coevolution in public investments.* London: Routledge.

Teisman, G. R., Westerveld, R., and Hertogh, M. (2009). Appearances and sources of process dynamics. In G. R. Teisman, A. van Buuren, and L. Gerrits (Eds.), *Managing complex governance systems: Dynamics, self-organization and coevolution in public investments* (pp. 56–75). London: Routledge.

Torre, C. A. (1995). Chaos, creativity, and innovation: Toward a dynamical model of problem solving. In R. Robertson and A. Combs (Eds.), *Chaos theory in psychology and the life sciences* (pp. 179–198). Mahwah, NJ: Lawrence Erlbaum.

Trochim, W. M. K. (1989). An introduction to concept mapping for planning and evaluation. *Evaluation and Program Planning, 12*(1), 1–16.

Trochim, W. M. K., and Cabrera, D. (2005). The complexity of concept mapping for policy analysis. *Emergence: Complexity and Organization, 7*(1), 2–10.

True, J. L., Jones, B. D., and Baumgartner, F. R. (2007). Punctuated equilibrium theory: Explaining stability ad change in public policymaking. In P. A. Sabatier (Ed.), *Theories of the policy process* (2nd ed., pp. 155–188). Cambridge, MA: Westview Press.

Tullock, G. (1979). Public choice in practice. In C. S. Russell (Ed.), *Collective decision making: Applications from public choice theory,* (pp. 27–45). Baltimore: Johns Hopkins University Press.

University of Illinois (n.d.). Ask the Van. University of Illinois, Physics Department (http://van.physics.illinois.edu/qa/listing.php?id=1462; accessed on December 15, 2010).

Valdes, M. J. (1993). Hang-Georg Gadamer. In I. R. Makaryk (Ed.), *Encyclopedia of contemporary literary theory* (pp. 326–329). Toronto; The University of Toronto Press.

Van Buuren, A., Gerrits, L., and Marks, P. (2009). Public policy-making and the management of coevolution. In G. R. Teisman, A. van Buuren, and L. Gerrits (Eds.), *Managing complex governance systems: Dynamics, self-organization and coevolution in public investments* (pp. 154–171). London: Routledge.

Van De Pitte, M. (1993). Husserl, Edmund. In I. R. Makaryk (Ed.), *Encyclopedia of contemporary literary theory: Approaches, scholars, terms* (pp. 363–365). Toronto: University of Toronto Press.

Van Gigch, J. P. (1978). *Applied general systems theory* (2nd ed.). New York: Harper & Row.

Van Gils, M., Gerrits, L., and Teisman, G. R. (2009). Non-linear dynamics in port systems: Change events at work. In G. R. Teisman, A. van Buuren, and L. Gerrits (Eds.), *Managing complex governance systems: Dynamics, self-organization and coevolution in public investments* (pp. 76–96). London: Routledge.

Von Bertalanffy, L. (1968). *General system theory: Foundations, development, applications.* New York: George Braziller.

Von Bertalanffy, L. (1972). The history and status of general system theory. *Academy of Management Journal, 15*(2), 407–426.

Von Bertalanffy, L. (2008). An outline of general system theory. In A. Juarrero and C. A. Rubio (Eds.), *Emergence, complexity, and self-organization* (pp. 219–236). Goodyear, AZ: ISCE Publishing.

Von Foerster, H. (1974). *Cybernetics of cybernetics.* Urbana: University of Illinois Press.

Wade, N. (2010, June 12). A decade later, genetic map yields few new cures. *New York Times* (http://www.nytimes.com/2010/06/13/health/research/13genome.html?th&emc=th, accessed on November 23, 2011).

Waldrop, M. (1992). *Complexity: The emerging science at the edge of chaos.* New York: Touchstone.

Wasserman, S., and Faust, K. (1994). *Social network analysis: Methods and applications.* Cambridge: Cambridge University Press.

Wilderquist, K.(2005). A failure to communicate: What (if anything) we can learn from the negative income tax experiments? *Journal of Socio-Economics, 34*(1), 49–81.

Woehr, D. J., Miller, M. J., and Lane, J. A. S. (1998). The development and evaluation of computer-administered measure of cognitive complexity. *Personality and Individual Differences, 25,* 1037–1049).

Women's Own Magazine (1987, October 31). Epitaph for the eighties? "There is no such thing as society." (http://briandeer.com/social/thatcher-society.htm; accessed on December 16, 2010).

Yanow, D., and Schwartz-Shea, P. (Eds.) (2006). *Interpretation and method: Empirical research methods and the interpretive turn.* Armonk, NY: M. E. Sharpe.

Young, T. R. (1991a). Chaos and social change: Metaphysics of the postmodern. *The Social Science Journal, 28,* 289–305.

Young, T. R. (1991b). Chaos theory and symbolic interaction theory: Poetics for the postmodern sociologist. *Symbolic Interaction, 14,* 321–334.

Zaheer, A., and Soda, G. (2009). Network evolution: The origins of structural holes. *Administrative Science Quarterly, 54,* 1–31.

Zaitchik, A. (2010, Fall). "Patriot" paranoia: A look at the top ten conspiracy theories. *Intelligence Report,* Southern Poverty Law Center, (139) (http://www.splcenter.org/get-informed/intelligence-report/browse-all-issues/2010/fall/patriot-paranoia?ondntsrc=MBC100870NWS&newsletter=newsgen-20100819; accessed on March 12, 2011).

Index